London 2012 and the Post-Olympics City

Phil Cohen • Paul Watt
Editors

London 2012 and the Post-Olympics City

A Hollow Legacy?

Editors
Phil Cohen
Centre for East London Studies
University of East London
London, E 16 United Kingdom

Paul Watt
Geography, Environment and Development
Birkbeck, University of London
London, United Kingdom

ISBN 978-1-137-48946-3
DOI 10.1057/978-1-137-48947-0

ISBN 978-1-137-48947-0 (eBook)

Library of Congress Control Number: 2017947827

Cover illustration: Snapparazzi / Alamy Stock Photo

Printed on acid-free paper

This Palgrave Macmillan imprint is published by Springer Nature
The registered company is Macmillan Publishers Ltd.
The registered company address is: The Campus, 4 Crinan Street, London, N1 9XW, United Kingdom

Acknowledgements

We would like to thank our contributors for the quality of their engagement with the project and their patience in answering our editorial queries. At Palgrave Macmillan, Dominic Walker commissioned the book and Stephanie Carey saw it through to publication. Thanks to Joana Barros (Department of GEDS, Birkbeck) for providing Fig. 1.2, and to the Building Exploratory for providing Fig. II.1. Thanks to John Wallett for preparing the images in Chapter 5 for publication and to Bernadette O'Shea of Triathlon Homes for allowing us to reproduce the tenure map of East Village (Fig. 5.3). We are very grateful to the World Cup and Olympics Popular Committee of Rio de Janeiro for allowing us to reproduce an extract from their brilliant report in Chapter 14.

Contents

List of Abbreviations

ABI   Area Based Initiative
BAME   Black and Minority Ethnic
BTL   Buy-to-Let
DCLG   Department for Communities and Local Government
DCMS   Department for Culture, Media and Sport
GLA   Greater London Authority
GLL   Get Living London
IOC   International Olympic Committee
IPC   International Paralympic Committee
JSC   Japan Sports Council
LBH   London Borough of Hackney
LBN   London Borough of Newham
LBTH   London Borough of Tower Hamlets
LBWF   London Borough of Waltham Forest
LDA   London Development Agency
LDDC   London Docklands Development Corporation
LHA   Local Housing Allowance
LLDC   London Legacy Development Corporation
LOCOG   London Organising Committee of the Olympic and Paralympic
          Games
NEET   Not in Education, Employment, or Training
ODA   Olympic Delivery Authority
ONS   Office for National Statistics
OPLC   Olympic Park Legacy Company

QDD	Qatari Diar and Delancey
QEOP	Queen Elizabeth Olympic Park
PRS	Private rented sector
SRH	Social rental housing
TMG	Tokyo Metropolitan Government
UEL	University of East London
UKTI	United Kingdom Trade and Investment
WHU	West Ham United

List of Figures

List of Tables

1

Introduction: A Hollow Crown – Understanding the Olympics in Prospect and Retrospect

Phil Cohen and Paul Watt

Our title is a reference to a public artwork installed at Queen Elizabeth Olympic Park, as seen in Fig. 1.1. Ackroyd and Harvey's 'History Trees' and consists of a series of large tree installations planted to mark the entrances to the Olympic Park. Each tree has a brass 'memory ring,' weighing half a ton placed in its crown, engraved on its interior face with words and phrases reflecting the area's history. The official handout tells us that 'over time, the tree branches and ring will slowly fuse together, becoming a living memory of the Olympic Park' (www.ackroydandharvey.com). Each year, the handout continues the two will momentarily align to commemorate a significant event during the Games. How this is to be

P. Cohen (✉)
University of East London, London, United Kingdom
e-mail: pcohen763@hotmail.co.uk

P. Watt
Department of Geography, Birkbeck, University of London, London, United Kingdom
e-mail: p.watt@bbk.ac.uk

© The Author(s) 2017
P. Cohen, P. Watt (eds.), *London 2012 and the Post-Olympics City*,
DOI 10.1057/978-1-137-48947-0_1

1

Fig. 1.1 A hollow crown?

Source: Phil Cohen

achieved remains quite a mystery. The words on the rings are, of course, deliberately unreadable, except by someone bold enough to actually climb the tree. Anyone who does so will discover a series of enigmatic and evocative phrases with a variety of local resonances: It's all about water – Cockles from Leigh – a cormorant, symbol of marsh, etc. Otherwise, the story they have to tell is strictly for the birds. Eventually the rings will also be invisible, at least in summer, as they form each tree's 'hollow crown'.

An artwork that is designed to celebrate the living legacy of the Olympics, inscribed with signifiers of a landscape which the construction of the Olympic site has largely effaced, will thus serve as an elaborate metaphor of occlusion and forgetfulness, in which cultural memory and local history are overgrown by the hand of nature and the march of time. Plato would have loved the idea of the arbitrary coincidence of two shadows, one permanently inscribed and the other ephemeral. Socrates would have grumbled about the expense to the public purse, not to mention the inconvenience of having to hang

the fact that Britain could put on a successful show as an independent nation, open to the world, and united in the spirit of enterprise that had once upon a time (i.e. before our accession to the EU) made us great. Post-imperial nostalgia, only evoked in passing during the actual 2012 ceremonies, thus made a comeback bid in a retrospective claim that the Games prefigured a collective desire to reinvent the island story. But what if the economic outcome of Britain leaving the EU were to finally dash the hopes of those who believed that the legacy of the Games would bring about an economic transformation of East London for the immediate benefit of its existing communities?

From Olympics Mega-Events to Post-Olympic Studies

This spectacularised, schizoid vision of the Olympics is often carried over into the way it is constructed as an object of academic research. The Games are often described as a 'mega-event' in a way that assumes the host city is a tabula rasa with no other existence outside, before or beyond the contexts imposed by the Games themselves. If nothing else, the long build up and even longer aftermath of an Olympiad suggests a different kind of analytic approach than that provided by narrow 'impact studies' or traditional kinds of evaluation, one which recognises that the outcomes are embedded within and refracted by deeply-sedimented urban histories and socio-cultural geographies.

Our aim in bringing together this collection of recent research on the 2012 legacy is to begin to define a distinctive field of 'Post-Olympic Studies'. Most of the research that is conducted on the Olympics concentrates on the run up to the Games, Games time itself and its immediate impact, and for the simple reason that it is within this restricted time frame that public interest and research funding is concentrated. Recent academic books have been almost exclusively based on research carried out before, during and immediately after 2012, with some speculative projections into the future (see *inter alia* Cohen, 2013; Bernstock, 2014; Boykoff, 2014; Lindsay, 2014; Kennelly, 2016).

around in the cold, while Clio, in alliance with Mother Nature, gets her act together. Philosophically, the project is a no-brainer and its aesthetic rationale – a kind of anti-ruinology – is at best a rather glib double take on Anselm Kiefer's explorations of traumatic memoryscape: representing the unrepresentable, by rendering it into an undecipherable code. Is this what it means to 'live the Olympic Dream', to remain permanently poised between an utopian project, demanding the impossible and repressing the hopes and desires for a better world that it evokes?

The installation can thus be read as a meta-statement about the central issue which this book addresses. How is it possible to create a 'Post Olympics', which is neither a simple material trace of a historical event (the 2012 Games), a sentimental retrieve of a liminal moment of national triumphalism (as celebrated in the Ceremonies and Team UK's crock of golds), nor a re-iteration of an original compact with the host city struck in the heat of the bid, but which has long since lost any rhetorical purchase it once had on its citizens? It is characteristic of any post-Olympic city that it remains haunted by extravagant promises of regeneration, and by the disappointment that come with the discovery that it is indeed impossible to live the dream. The form of this haunting is unique to each Olympiad and bears on the specifics of the deal struck with local communities and their political representatives. But it also derives from a generic disjuncture between pre- and post-Olympic time, the first flooded with high anxiety and anticipation, the second by an interminable fading of horizons of possibility – will the 2012 Games be finally over in 2020, or 2050, or whenever some legacy body decides to call a halt to the evaluation of its 'catalytic effects'? If Olympic cities are imagined looking forwards to a more or less utopian future in which the hopeful vision of the bid will have materialized on the ground, they are remembered looking back in regret at what was a once-upon-a-time ideal. This split temporality also has its spatial analogue in the imagineering that conjures up an area of urban dereliction in desperate need of large-scale regeneration, only to project onto it a futuristic scenario of its magical transformation.

More recently in the context of Britain's EU referendum campaign (2016), we have seen the London 2012 dream reanimated yet again, mainly on the side of the so-called Brexiteers, who used it as 'proof' of

This analytical tendency of looking at the Olympics through a relatively short time frame is even more pronounced in the official Games' evaluations (MacRury and Poynter, 2009; AMION Consulting, 2015). Comparisons that are made between Olympiads tend to be confined to superficial impacts produced by and registered within the narrow scope provided by the mechanisms of Olympic delivery. By generating standardised performance indicators for evaluating the impact of each Olympiad, the International Olympic Committee (IOC) creates a platform of statistical comparison which the academic and consultancy research industries may supplement with more specialised case studies, but without challenging the principle of comparison itself. This in turn creates a 'league table' in which the reputational status of each Games is logged and is subject to continual revision and debate (Smith, 2008; MacRury and Poynter, 2009). Moreover, as AMION Consulting (2015: 92) note, official assessments of previous Games 'should be treated with a degree of caution, because the studies are primarily concerned changes in conditions rather than attribution of effects, and as such, the counterfactual (if present) is unlikely to be measured consistently'. In other words, the careful separation of 'Games effects' from the myriad of 'other effects' is rarely pursued, such that almost everything that happens in a post-Games city is all too often treated as a de facto *result* of the Games.

This issue, and the more general limited provenance of official evaluations, are illustrated by the Economic and Social Science Research Council funded *Olympic Games Impact Study – London 2012 Post-Games Report* written by a team of academics from the University of East London (UEL, 2015). This study takes the form of an analysis of quantitative secondary data largely gathered from government departments and the Olympic Delivery Authorities. The aim was to test this data against the original legacy claims. For this purpose, 67 indicators (15 environmental, 27 socio-cultural, 25 economic) were studied in detail, some of these being further designated as relating to 'context' or to 'events'. The study scrupulously follows the methodology stipulated by the IOC, which pre-empts the use of qualitative data, including ethnographic material, as lacking in 'scientific value'. As might be expected, such an approach works best when dealing with quantifiable measurable issues regarding physical geography, economic activity and environmental change – the so-called hard legacy. When it comes to the 'soft legacy', the 27 socio-cultural indicators are a mix of crude behavioral or participation measures, which in only one case (disability) deals with the crucial intervening variable of social perception. In order to introduce a more 'subjective' dimension into the analysis, the report includes a number of short essays ('reflective vignettes') by 'experts in their respective fields [. . .] who have been actively involved in the planning, delivery and legacy of the London 2012 Games' (UEL, 2015: 13). Although some of these vignettes do include critical points most, perhaps unsurprisingly, tend towards portraying Games and legacy 'successes'.

The UEL report includes the bold statement that 'Poverty and social exclusion [PSE] rates have reduced in the six Host Boroughs, in part due to the legacy effect' (UEL, 2015: 15). This heartening conclusion is reached on the basis of comparing the 2010 Index of Multiple Deprivation (IMD) with the 2015 IMD. As an area-based measure, the IMD provides a, 'description of areas; but this description does not apply to every person living in those areas' (DCLG, 2015: 21). In other words, there is only a tangential relationship between spatial and individual measures of deprivation, as Shiels et al. (2013) argue; area-based PSE measures are not equivalent to people-based measures (Powell et al., 2001).

Leaving this point to one side, the official guidance on using the 2015 Indices of Deprivation makes it clear that there are significant technical problems in using the IMD to make comparisons over time. Not only should the versions of the indices '*not* be construed as a time series' (DCLG, 2015: 28; our emphasis), but the various changes made to the indices 'make it difficult to determine real changes in deprivation from the Indices rankings and scores, such as those arising from social, economic or demographic trends and *the impact of specific policies or interventions*' (DCLG, 2015: 29–30; our emphasis). Therefore not only do changes to the IMD scores and rankings not necessarily reflect real-world changes in PSE, but one cannot readily attribute any IMD changes to specific programmes – such as the 2012 Olympic Games. Such technical caveats are notably absent from the UEL report.

Furthermore, the UEL report provides no indication as to what causal mechanisms might potentially link changes in IMD scores and ranks to the 'legacy effect' – even 'in part'. Instead the attribution of a legacy effect is simply an inference with no underpinning intellectual justification. This absence, and the related thorny question of causality, can be gauged by placing the IMD 2010–15 changes within a London-wide context. As the DCLG (2015: 53) note, Hackney and Newham, two of the Host Boroughs, experienced 'a decrease in relative deprivation of at least five rank places since the 2010 Index'. However, so did two other London boroughs – Haringey and Islington – and yet these were not Host Boroughs! How can one therefore infer causality on the basis of a putative 'Games effect' if non-Games boroughs experienced a similar change? Our own comparison between the local authority 2010 and 2015 IMD scores reveals that while five of the six Host Boroughs (except Barking and Dagenham) witnessed a reduction in their rank of average scores, so did another 19 London boroughs – these include several south and north London boroughs, such as Brent, Haringey, Lambeth and Lewisham, which are long-term deprived areas but lying well *outside* the hallowed Host Boroughs' arena.

Such broad metropolitan-wide changes might lead one to consider the existence of a potential 'London effect' – or rather a 'London gentrification effect'. Recent research on the after-effects of an England-wide regeneration programme, the New Deal for Communities (NDC), has found that several London NDC areas have been among those which have become less deprived indicating that a 'broader gentrification process is at work' (Taylor, 2016: 14).[1] As is well known from the urban studies' literature, many formerly deprived East London areas such as Hackney (Wessendorf, 2014; Butcher and Dickens, 2016) and Stratford (Watt, 2013; Bernstock, 2014), plus equivalent south London areas such as Brixton (Mavrommatis, 2010) and the Elephant and Castle (Lees and Ferreri, 2016), are experiencing rapid gentrification – or

---

[1] The NDC is an area-based initiative (ABI) which lasted from 2000 to 2010 and was aimed at regenerating 39 of the most deprived areas in England including 10 in London (Beatty and Cole, 2009; Watt, 2009a).

'gentrification on steroids' as one of us has recently suggested (Watt, cited in Watt and Minton, 2016: 218). It is salutatory that despite the well-known, long-running academic debates over the extent, causes and consequences of contemporary gentrification in London (see *inter alia* Butler, 2007; Davidson and Wyly, 2012; Hamnett and Butler, 2013; Watt, 2013), there is not a single mention of the term 'gentrification' in the whole 187-page UEL (2015) report – a depressingly model example of the 'Olympics effects' cul-de-sac. If gentrification is a prominent absence, the main body of the UEL report makes scant reference to processes of what Raco (2014) calls 'state-led privatisation' in relation to urban politics and the Games, or even to government-imposed austerity. However, as Mooney et al. (2015: 911) have argued in their examination of the Glasgow Commonwealth Games 2014 aftermath, the impacts of mega-events need to be embedded within in an understanding of how these are implicated in 'wider government policies in disadvantaged areas delivered in a post-crash, "post-welfare" era of austerity'. Without such understanding, upbeat blanket statements regarding reductions in PSE in East London are wilfully ignorant and misleading, as the analysis of housing in Chapter 4 indicates and as already available in-depth, qualitative research on low-income Newham residents demonstrates:

> Life in general, and rising costs in particular, make survival increasingly difficult for the people we interviewed. Rent, energy bills, the cost of childcare and food reduce even the best 'managers' to a sense of power-lessness. Many people we interviewed have recently experienced a decline in job security, income and prospects. They feel worse off and are generally worried and insecure. (LSE Housing and Communities, 2014)

The UEL report is dogged by the problem of how to identify and extrapolate a specific 'Olympic effect' from the vast array of local, regional, national and global variables being studied, and since it entirely lacks any conceptual framework, such as actor-network theory, which would have enabled the scoping and scaling of effects to be precisely embedded in the relays between diverse agencies, infrastructures and events, the problem remains insoluble. Like all orthodox impact studies, it also denies effective agency and voice to the host communities – they are merely the passive recipients being impacted upon – and instead conducts an internal audit of how well the various delivery agencies have performed in meeting their operational targets. Inevitably, after demonstrating its 'scienticity' through hundreds of diagrams, graphs and flow charts, the report ends by falling back on a soap opera formula and concludes lamely:

> That London 2012 has been a catalyst for positive change is not in doubt, but when and where the process ends and what will be the full magnitude of the effect is not yet known. The story of London 2012 will continue to unfold for a long time to come. (UEL, 2015: 5)

A moment's thought about the process of 'Olympification' would register the fact that it makes host cities more not less like themselves, ergo more not less different from each other. However superficially similar its impact on the urban fabric, for example via brandscaping and venue design, the Games distinctive significance can only be established through an in-depth analysis of the political economy, social history, cultural geography and physical fabric of each host city. The irony is that while these dimensions of understanding are sometimes added retrospectively (although not often together), they are rarely present to inform the actual bid, a myopia which is again duplicated in mega-event studies. The justification for this intellectual laziness is that the Olympics represent the globalisation of sport and globalisation involves the homogenising of urban cultures, whereas the evidence is that the impact is actually the reverse: globalisation produces cultural hyper-diversity, creates and valorises (i.e. commodifies) local 'ethnoscapes' (Appadurai, 1996), and generally sponsors elite forms of cosmopolitanism as well as popular multiculturalism.

Against the main trend in Olympic Studies, this book focuses on emergent evidence of the longer term impact and key features of the post-Olympic environment in East London. For this purpose we have commissioned contributions from an array of academics, several of whom have been undertaking research on East London for many years. Before we summarise the chapters, we will firstly analyse the twin notions of 'Legacy' and 'Convergence', the main post-2012 Olympic framing concepts.

Converging on Legacy

The London 2012 Games are widely seen as a success story – a moment in which the nation came together to surmount its internal divisions and triumphantly showed its best face to the world. Even if the moment did not last long as the recession blues struck home and austerity kicked in, there is still official optimism that 2012 will provide lasting benefits to the communities of East London. In terms of regeneration, the London 2012 Olympics promised to trigger a mega-regeneration project that was different. This time the mistakes of other large-scale projects like the Docklands, The Dome and Canary Wharf would be put right: top-down planning would be replaced by civic participation, communication and 'the local' (Bernstock, 2009). Rather than being imposed on the East End, Olympic-led regeneration was supposed to focus on building connections with neighbouring areas, extending the reach of global capital into even the most deprived and neglected areas. 'Legacy' was the umbrella concept that symbolised this new regeneration and planning approach and 'Convergence' has become its watchword.

The 2012 Olympic Games were originally sited in the five East London Host Boroughs (now Growth Boroughs) of Greenwich, Hackney, Newham, Tower Hamlets and Waltham Forest, with the borough of Barking and Dagenham added in 2011; see Fig. 1.2. The official over-arching aims of the Games in relation to East London, were nothing if not ambitious. As encapsulated in the London's Olympic Bid to the IOC, 'The most enduring legacy of the Olympics will be the regeneration of an entire community for the direct benefit of *everyone who lives there*' (LOCOG, 2005: 19; our emphasis). This legacy commitment is to be assessed via the goal of 'Convergence' whereby, 'within 20 years the communities who host the 2012 Games will have the same social and economic chances as their neighbours across London' (Growth Boroughs Unit, 2014: 3). In other words, each and every

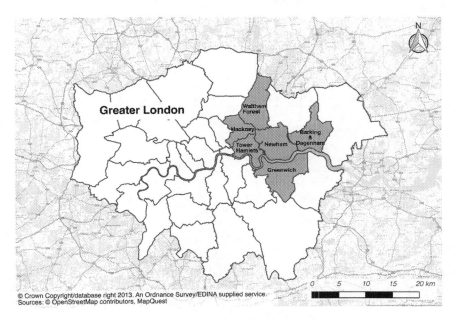

Fig. 1.2 Map of 2012 London Olympics Host Boroughs

East Londoner will directly benefit from the Games, and within 20 years they will also have equivalent life chances to those living in the rest of London, so over-turning centuries-long class-based inequalities (Marriott, 2011).

As several chapters in the book highlight, such grandiose-sounding aims as regenerating an 'entire community' and 'convergence' are at considerable variance to East London residents' lived reality as they find themselves struggling in a bleak post-crash landscape characterised by 'austerity urbanism' (Peck, 2012), as existing reports on the Host Boroughs duly acknowledge (Shelter, 2013; LSE Housing and Communities, 2014).

Available data on income levels in the post-Games period shows that median annual household income estimates for 2012–13 for all six Host Boroughs were considerably below the London average of £39,110 and well below the average £55,620 for the most affluent borough of Kensington and Chelsea, as in Table 1.1 above. By going back to 2005–06, the year the Games was announced, Table 1.1 also shows that the Host Boroughs had

Table 1.1 Total median annual household income estimates for Host Boroughs, Kensington and Chelsea, London and UK, 2005–06 – 2012–13

Host boroughs	2005–06	2012–13	£ increase 2005–06 – 2012–13	% increase 2005–06 – 2012–13	Reverse rank in London Boroughs, 2012–13
Host Boroughs					
Barking and Dagenham	£22,390	£29,420	£7,030	31.4	2
Greenwich	£26,180	£35,350	£9,170	35.0	10
Hackney	£25,450	£35,140	£9,690	38.1	8
Newham	£20,740	£28,780	£8,040	38.8	1
Tower Hamlets	£26,090	£34,930	£8,840	33.9	7
Waltham Forest	£25,490	£33,080	£7,590	29.8	5
Kensington and Chelsea	£42,040	£55,620	£13,580	32.3	32
London	£30,140	£39,110	£8,970	29.8	
UK	£24,330	£30,600	£6,270	25.8	

Source: GLA (2015)

average or above London average increases up until 2012–13. Despite this, all the Host Boroughs were among the bottom 10 London boroughs on median income levels, with Newham the lowest and Barking and Dagenham the second lowest. In fact these two boroughs even had income levels *below* the national UK level of £30,600 in 2012–13. As Chapter 4 argues, these ongoing low income levels are at considerable variance with rising house prices and private sector rents which are making parts of East London unliveable for many long-term East Enders, some of whom are even being displaced from the area. It is exactly this kind of incongruity in the post-Olympic urban landscape which many of the chapters in the book highlight.

Structure of the Book

The chapters are based on new research, most of which has been carried out since 2012, which considers how far the London legacy has been delivered and how far it has been a hollow promise. In making their arguments, many of the authors, as East London specialists, have been able to locate their recent findings within a deep understanding and appreciation of how this area of the city has changed over several decades – and as such their contributions are able to illuminate the long duree of East London's development in a far longer time-span than the Games themselves.

The book is organised into four sections. Part I provides an overview of two contrasting dimensions of post-Olympic London which tie into globalisation processes: the financialisation of public assets and the securitisation of public amenity. Gavin Poynter, the author of the first chapter, is a major academic figure in the analysis of how the 2012 Games has affected East London (MacRury and Poynter, 2009; Poynter and MacRury, 2009), notably in economic terms (Poynter, 2009). In Chapter 2, Poynter identifies what might be called the 'London Model', but cautions how the official legacy narrative is achieving the opposite of its declared intentions. The period since the 2012 Games has revealed tensions arising from the roles given to public agencies and private investors in relation to inward investment, as exemplified in new commercial and residential developments within the Queen Elizabeth Olympic Park and along the corridor of the Lower Lea Valley between Stratford and Canary Wharf. The chapter concludes by suggesting that this corridor is characteristic of the splintered form of urbanism arising in the post-Olympic East End.

Pete Fussey and Jon Coaffee, the authors of Chapter 3, have examined the security and policing aspects of the 2012 Games in several publications (see *inter alia* Fussey et al., 2011, 2012). In their chapter, Fussey and Coafee examine the form, impact and 'legacy' of security practices put in place for the Games. They look at the creation of 'regenerated' spaces that are hardened and insulated against the urban milieu in which they are situated and the tension between formal and informal processes of securitisation. Such processes illuminate the multiple ways the post-Olympic legacy becomes embedded in the urban landscape.

In Part II the perspective is reversed as we turn to consider how the Olympic legacy is sociologically working out on the ground in East London. In Chapter 4, Paul Watt and Penny Bernstock examine housing in East London, a key component of the infrastructural and social legacy. Paul Watt has undertaken extensive research on social housing, regeneration, gentrification and homelessness in East London (Watt, 2009a, 2009b, 2013, 2016). This includes collaborating with Jacqueline Kennelly on a longitudinal study of how the 2012 Olympics affected young homeless people living in Newham (Kennelly and Watt, 2011, 2012, 2013; Watt, 2013; Kennelly, 2016). Penny Bernstock has published a major study of housing and the 2012 Games (Bernstock, 2014). Watt and Bernstock's chapter updates their previous research by drawing upon post-2012 ethnographic, statistical and documentary data, and questions how far an inclusive Olympics' housing legacy has resulted for East Londoners. The chapter examines post-Games housing costs in terms of rents and prices. New housing developments in E15 'old Stratford' and E20 'new Stratford' are then analysed, notably in relation to issues of affordability. The chapter moves onto consider affordable and social rental housing output more broadly in the Host Boroughs. This is followed by an analysis of overcrowding and homelessness, which leads onto an update of previous published research on young homeless people living in Newham. The controversial issue of the displacement of homeless people from East London is then examined, while the final section examines how such processes of 'social cleansing' are being contested by housing campaigners.

Phil Cohen, the author of Chapter 5, has written extensively about East London over the past 30 years focussing on the impact of structural and demographic change on issues of class, race and gender, especially as these affect young people (Cohen, 1996, Rathzel, Cohen, et al., 2008) In his chapter, Cohen draws on an ongoing study which started in 2007 using a rich mix of ethnographic research to track the impact of Olympic-led regeneration on the lifestyles, livelihoods and life stories of the people of East London. He looks at how the Olympic Legacy narrative is being enacted through the development plans for the Olympic Park and at how residents moving into the East Village (the converted Athletes Village) are making sense of this new piece of city. A close grained reading of incomers' narratives and mental maps reveals very different strategies of inhabitation on the part of well-to-do, middle-class 'residents' and disadvantaged social 'tenants' and a striking split perception of new and old East London.

The chapter goes on to look at various attempts to micro manage the resulting tensions and promote a shared sense of belonging to an 'urban village' and 'living the Olympic Dream'. This strategy is analysed in relation to the notion of 'hysterical materialism', and the tension between moral and market economies of worth in the delivery and evaluation of the 2012 regeneration legacy.

This chapter is followed by a photo essay by Debbie Humphry drawn from the same East Village Study. The essay mixes photographic portraits of residents with text to provide an in-depth visual exploration of place, identity and belonging. Humphry considers what kind of place is this 'best new place to live'? How do residents view this new neighbourhood and 'community'? What kind of 'mixed community' might be evolving in this mixed-tenure development? And what is the relationship between the material infrastructure – of flats, pavements, shops and health facilities – and the overly-signified post-Olympic landscape?

The next two chapters focus on Hackney Wick, an area of East London which is now closely associated with artists and also one that is experiencing considerable change in the Post-Olympic period. Isaac Marrero-Guillamón, the author of Chapter 7, is also co-editor of *The Art of Dissent: Adventures in London's Olympic State* (Powell and Marrero-Guillamón, 2012), a densely layered, multidisciplinary collection of written and photographic essays which collectively offer one of the richest accounts of what was never recognised in the official Olympic regeneration rationale – that this area of London had a unique, untamed character and topography – 'one of the few remaining informal spaces in London' (Edensor et al., 2008: 285) – which is now largely lost. In Chapter 7, Marrero-Guillamón draws on his involvement in community politics in the Olympic fringe area of Hackney Wick and Fish Island to examine urban planning, governance and local democracy. The chapter focuses on a situation where non-elected officials from the London Legacy Development Corporation enter in a dialogue with self-appointed local groups, raising the issue of a radical transformation of established notions of democracy. Are these prototypes of a new form of governance which match the so-called post-political city? Do they represent a radical re-imagination of the ways in which the local community participates in politics? Or do they produce a deactivation of dissent?

In addressing these questions the author draws on direct participation and observation of the processes involves, as well as interviews with key local actors.

One of the contributors to *The Art of Dissent* is Fran Weber-Newth who in our Chapter 8 considers how the notion of 'community' has been deployed within planners' conceptualisations of the 2012 legacy. Her findings are taken from her doctoral research which examines regeneration 'winners' and 'losers' via a comparative analysis of two neighbourhoods – Hackney Wick Fish Island and Rudolfkiez – that are adjacent to the large-scale regeneration schemes London 2012 and Mediaspree in Berlin (Weber-Newth, 2015). In her chapter, Weber-Newth argues that rather than presenting a new planning paradigm of inclusion, the priority has been on attracting *new* community rather than 'nourishing what is there'. Hackney Wick is again the case study with a focus on its 'artists-in-residence'. What does the emphasis on artists mean for residents who are *not* artists and which culture and which communities are presented as the future of the area? The chapter looks at a number of contested sites in which different visions of the post-Olympic city are coming into conflict, whether based on commercial activity and consumerism, or a more visceral and socially embedded notion of urban vitality.

In Chapter 9, Jack Fawbert shifts the focus away from the New East London centred on creative industries to a long-term fixture of the traditional East End sporting landscape – football. Fawbert has been a closet 'auto-ethnographer' of West Ham United (WHU) fans – in other words a fan himself – for many decades. As a sociologist, Jack has been especially interested in mapping the class, ethnic and spatial composition of the WHU fan-base, the most geographically dispersed in the football league. As he has written elsewhere (Fawbert, 2005, 2011), this fan base is very largely composed of white ex-East Enders who are now part of the 'Cockney Diaspora' living in suburban Essex (Watt et al., 2014); this fan base is also very different from the black and Asian communities who are now demographically and culturally prominent in twenty-first century East London. In his chapter, Fawbert traces the history of WHU's move from the Boleyn ground to the Olympic stadium and focuses on the shifting attitudes of Hammers' fans to the move and what it represents.

Using a Gramscian framework, he argues that in this 'war of position', bourgeois rationality was forced to compromise with traditional fandom for 'consented coercion' to be realised. However, Fawbert also suggests that the issue was more complex than a straightforward Gramscian analysis would suggest. Whilst economic imperatives are important, sporting success can trump profit maximisation for both supporters and directors of football clubs, especially where there are deep-rooted lifetime ties with the club.

As noted above, twenty-first century East London is a multi-ethnic place and has even been characterised as 'super-diverse' (Wessendorf, 2014). Anthony Gunter, the author of Chapter 10, has undertaken long-running ethnographic research on disadvantaged BAME youth living in East London social housing estates and has made a major contribution to understanding how youth transitions are experienced in the context of de-industrialised – now post-industrial – East London (Gunter, 2010, 2017). In his chapter, Gunter looks at various regeneration initiatives, not least the London 2012 Olympic project, tasked with tackling youth exclusion in East London. The chapter reviews the impact of the post-Olympic austerity climate with stringent cuts to public sector expenditure and presents a case study outlining how these cuts have impacted upon young people. The study includes empirical data from a five-year ethnographic study of two East London neighbourhoods and includes semi-structured interviews with key community stakeholders and practitioners as well as biographical interviews with young adults.

Part III shifts focus to examine the Games' wider social legacy. In Chapter 11, Mike Weed looks at the so-called health dividend of 2012, one of the key features in the official legacy with its injunction to 'inspire a generation'. The chapter asks three questions: firstly, what evidence exists that it is possible to improve physical activity, health and sport participation through an Olympic and Paralympic Games? Secondly, what evidence exists that London 2012 had any impact on physical activity, health and sport participation in London and across the UK? Thirdly, was London 2012s strategy and approach to improving physical activity, health and sport participation through the Olympic and Paralympic Games effective, or could more have been done? In addressing these questions, the chapter draws on work commissioned from the Department of Health, Sport England and the Greater London Authority and Mayor's Office.

In Chapter 12, P. David Howe and Shane Kerr present ongoing research into the legacy of the 2012 Paralympic Games, specifically in relation to disability and disability sport. Using discourse analysis of bidding and planning documentation and interviews with key actors from the corporate (including media), government, disability and disability sport fields, this chapter illuminates the ambiguity surrounding the concept of legacy and calls for a reappraisal of its importance.

In the following chapter, Ian Brittain and Leonardo Mataruna present findings from a comparative research project which is using evidence about the social legacy of London 2012 to create a framework of evaluation for the Rio 2016 Games. Their conclusions from the London case study – in particular the need for long-term job opportunities rather than temporary short-term jobs, and the inclusion of the local culture in the preparations for the event itself and the legacy programmes – have considerable relevance for Rio and its legacy.

This discussion leads us onto the final section of the book which explicitly looks forward from 2012 to the Rio 2016 and Tokyo 2020 Games. Is there such a thing as a 'London model' and if so, is it one that Rio or Tokyo could possibly emulate? Chapter 14 presents an excerpt from the dossier on 'Mega-Events and Human Rights Violations in Rio de Janeiro' produced by the World Cup and Olympics Popular Committee of Rio de Janeiro (2015), a group of academics and activists concerned to articulate the concerns of the favela communities which have been the prime target of the Olympic regeneration process. The chapter documents the numerous human rights violations that have been inflicted on the favelistas by the police, the city authorities, the construction companies and the State. It goes on to present a manifesto of legacy demands in relation to housing, the environment, transport, public services and cultural amenity which, taken together, represent a plan of action for creating a post-Olympic city based on principles of social justice.

In the final chapter, Grace Gonzalez Basurto draws on in-depth interviews with key stakeholders in London and Tokyo and official documents to read 2020 against 2012. She examines the stakes which

Japanese politicians have invested in the 2020 Games as a policy tool to boost the country's economic growth and renovate the national brand after the 3/11 earthquake disaster and suggests the limits and conditions of applying the so-called London legacy model to the Tokyo Games.

The book's conclusion draws some of these many threads together to argue for a paradigm shift in post-Olympic urban studies. We argue firstly that it is time to move on from so called mega–event analysis and towards the comparative analysis of micro-histories – and geographies of transition. Legacy should no longer regarded mechanistically as a 'catalytic effect', but as a re-negotiation of the original Olympic compact, constituting a discrete site of contestation between the rival claims of host communities and corporate business interests, variously mediated by civic authorities. Secondly, if the story of each Olympiad is pre-eminently that of its host city, we can only understand its meaning for its citizens if we place their experiences of its costs and benefits at the centre of the account, *and* interpret this locally situated information within a deeper analysis of the urban regeneration process as it unfolds over the *long duree*. London 2012 makes little sense unless it is placed in the context of the social transformation of East London since the closure of the Docks in the 1960s. Equally, Rio 2016 has to be understood in relation to the collapse of the Brazilian economic miracle of the 1970s presided over by the military junta. Finally, in place of the empirical myopia of the official evaluations and the endless deferral of 'final judgements', we propose a principle of analytic parsimony and narrative closure.

References

AMION Consulting. (2015) *London 2012 Olympics: Regeneration Legacy Evaluation Framework*. London: DCLG.

Appadurai, A. (1996) *Modernity at Large: Cultural Dimensions of Globalization*. Minneapolis: University of Minnesota Press.

Beatty, C. and Cole, I. (2009) 'Stability, residential satisfaction and the dynamics of change: evidence from the New Deal for Communities programme in England', *Journal of Urban Regeneration and Renewal* 3(2): 141–153.

Bernstock P. (2009) 'The regeneration game', in G. Poynter and I. MacRury (eds.), *Olympic Cities: 2012 and the Remaking of London*. Aldershot: Ashgate.

Bernstock P (2014) *Olympic Housing: A Critical Review of London 2012's Legacy*. Farnham: Ashgate.

Boykoff, J. (2014) *Activism and the Olympics: Dissent at the Games in Vancouver and London*. New Brunswick: Rutgers University Press.

Butcher, M. and Dickens, L. (2016) 'Spatial dislocation and affective displacement: youth perspectives on gentrification in London', *International Journal of Urban and Regional Research*, 40(4): 800–816.

Butler, T. (2007) 'Re-urbanizing London Docklands: gentrification, suburbanization or new urbanism?' *International Journal of Urban and Regional Research* 31(4): 759–781.

Cohen, P. (1996) '"All White on the Night": narratives of nativism on the Isle of Dogs', in M. Rustin and T. Butler (eds.), *Rising in the East: The Regeneration of East London*. London: Lawrence & Wishart.

Cohen, P. (2013) *On the Wrong Side of the Track: East London and the Post Olympics*. London: Lawrence and Wishart.

Davidson, M. and Wyly, E. (2012) 'Class-ifying London: questioning social division and space claims in the Post-industrial Metropolis', *City* 16(4): 395–421.

DCLG. (2015) *The English Indices of Deprivation 2015: Research Report*. London: Department for Communities and Local Government.

Edensor, T., Christie, C. and Lloyd, B. (2008) 'Obliterating informal space – the London Olympics and the Lea Valley: a photo essay', *Space and Culture* 11(3): 285–293.

Fawbert, J. (2005) 'Football fandom, West Ham United and the "cockney diaspora": from working-class community to youth post-tribe?', in P. Bramham and J. Caudwell (eds.), *Sport, Active Leisure and Youth Cultures*. Eastbourne: Leisure Studies Association.

Fawbert, J. (2011a) '"Wot, no Asians?" West Ham United fandom, the cockney diaspora and the "new" East Enders', in D. Burdsey (ed.), *Race, Ethnicity and Football: Persisting Debates and Emergent Issues*. London: Routledge.

Fussey, P., Coaffee, J., Armstrong, G. and Hobbs, R. (2011) *Securing and Sustaining the Olympic City: Reconfiguring London for 2012 and Beyond*. Aldershot: Ashgate.

Fussey, P., Coaffee, J., Armstrong, G. and Hobbs, D. (2012) 'The Regeneration Games: purity and security in the Olympic City', *British Journal of Sociology* 63(2): 260–284.

GLA (2015) GLA Household Income Estimates 2001/02 to 2012/13. London: Greater London Authority. http://data.london.gov.uk/dataset/household-income-estimates-small-areas

Growth Boroughs Unit. (2014) *Convergence: Annual Report, 2013–2014*. London: Growth Boroughs Unit.

Gunter, A. (2010) *Growing Up Bad: Black Youth, Road Culture and Badness in an East London Neighbourhood*. London: The Tufnell Press.

Gunter, A. (2017) *Race, Gangs and Youth Violence: Policy, Prevention and Policing*. Bristol: Policy Press.

Hamnett, C. and Butler, T. (2013) 'Re-classifying London: a growing middle class and increasing inequality', *City* 17(2): 197–208.

Kennelly, J. (2016). *Olympic Exclusions: Youth, Poverty and Social Legacies*. London and New York: Routledge.

Kennelly, J. and Watt, P. (2011) 'Sanitizing public space in Olympic host cities: the spatial experiences of marginalized youth in 2010 Vancouver and 2012 London', *Sociology* 45(5): 765–781.

Kennelly, J. and Watt, P. (2012) 'Seeing Olympic effects through the eyes of marginally housed youth: changing places and the gentrification of east London', *Visual Studies* 27(2): 151–160.

Kennelly, J. and Watt, P. (2013) 'Restricting the public in public space: the London 2012 Olympic Games, hyper-securitization and marginalized youth', *Sociological Research Online* 18(2), http://www.socresonline.org.uk/18/2/19.html

Lees, L. and Ferrari, M. (2016) 'Resisting gentrification on its final frontiers: Learning from the Heygate Estate in London (1974–2013)', *Cities*, 57: 14–24.

Lindsay, I. (2014) *Living with London's Olympics: An Ethnography*. Basingstoke: Palgrave Macmillan.

LOCOG [London Organising Committee of the Olympic and Paralympic Games]. (2005) *2012 London Olympic Bid Candidate File*. London: LOCOG.

LSE Housing and Communities. (2014) *Facing Debt: Economic Resilience in Newham*.CASE Report 83. London: Centre for Analysis of Social Exclusion, London School of Economics.

MacRury, I. and Poynter, G. (2009) *London's Olympic Legacy*. London: London East Research Institute, University of East London, www.uel.ac.uk/londoneast/.../20101008-CLG-OECD-2012.pdf

Marriott, J. (2011) *Beyond the Tower: A History of East London*. Yale: Yale University Press.

Mavrommatis, G. (2010) 'Stories from Brixton: gentrification and different differences', *Sociological Research Online*, 16(2), http://www.socresonline. org.uk/16/2/12.html.

Mooney, G., McCall, V. and Paton, K. (2015) 'Exploring the use of large sporting events in the post-crash, post-welfare city: a "legacy" of increasing insecurity?', *Local Economy* 30(8): 910–924.

Peck, J. (2012) 'Austerity urbanism', *City*16(6): 626–655.

Powell, H. and Marrero-Guillamón, I. (2012) *The Art of Dissent: Adventures in London's Olympic State*. London: Marshgate Press.

Powell, M., Boyne, G. and Ashworth, R. (2001) 'Towards a geography of people poverty and place poverty', *Policy & Politics* 29(3): 243–258.

Poynter, G. (2009) 'The 2012 Olympic games and the reshaping of East London', in R. Imrie, L. Lees and M. Raco (eds.), *Regenerating London*. London: Routledge.

Poynter, G. and MacRury, I. (2009) *Olympic Cities: 2012 and the Remaking of London*. Aldershot: Ashgate.

Raco, M.(2014) 'Delivering flagship projects in an era of regulatory capitalism: state-led privatization and the London Olympics 2012', *International Journal of Urban and Regional Research* 38(1): 176–197.

Rathzel, N., Cohen, P., Back, L., Keith, M. and Hieronymous, A. (2008) *Finding the Way Home: Young People's Stories of Gender, Ethnicity, Class and Places in Hamburg and London*. Gottingen: V&R unipress.

Shelter. (2013) *When the Golden Dust Settles: Housing in Hackney, Newham and Tower Hamlets after the Olympic Games*. London: Shelter.

Shiels, C., Baker, D. and Barrow, S. (2013) 'How accurately does regeneration target local need? Targeting deprived communities in the UK', *International Journal of Public Sector Management* 26(3): 203–215.

Smith, M. (2008) *When the Games Come to Town: Host Cities and the Local Impacts of the Olympics* (LERI Working Papers). London: London East Research Institute, University of East London.

Taylor, M. (2016) 'Postcode poverty', *Inside Housing*, 8 June.

UEL [University of East London]. (2015) *Olympic Games Impact Study – London 2012 Post-Games Report*. London: University of East London.

Watt, P. (2009a) 'Housing stock transfers, regeneration and state-led gentrification in London', *Urban Policy and Research* 27(3): 229–242.

Watt, P. (2009b) 'Social housing and regeneration in London', in: R. Imrie, L. Lees and M. Raco (eds.), *Regenerating London*. London: Routledge.

Watt, P. (2013) '"It's not for us": Regeneration, the 2012 Olympics and the gentrification of East London', *City* 17(1): 99–118.

Watt, P. (2016) 'A nomadic war machine in the metropolis: en/countering London's 21st century housing crisis with Focus E15', *City* 20(2): 297–320.

Watt, P., Millington, G. and Huq, R. (2014) 'East London mobilities: the Cockney Diaspora and the remaking of the Essex ethnoscape', in P. Watt and P. Smets (eds.), *Mobilities and Neighbourhood Belonging in Cities and Suburbs*. Basingstoke: Palgrave Macmillan.

Watt, P. and Minton, A. (2016) 'London's housing crisis and its activisms', *City* 20(2): 204–221.

Weber-Newth, F. (2015) *The Game of Urban Regeneration: Culture and Community in London 2012 and Berlin's Mediaspree*. Unpublished PhD thesis, University of Aberdeen.

Wessendorf, S. (2014) *Commonplace Diversity: Social Relations in a Super-Diverse context*. Basingstoke: Palgrave Macmillan.

World Cup and Olympics Popular Committee of Rio de Janeiro. (2015) *Rio 2016 Olympics: The Exclusion Games*. Rio de Janeiro: World Cup and Olympics Popular Committee of Rio de Janeiro.

Phil Cohen is Professor Emeritus at the University of East London, and a Research Fellow at the Young Foundation. He is the founder/research director of the LivingMaps Network and the editor-in-chief of its online journal *LivingMaps Review*. His ethnographic fieldwork over the last 30 years has been based in East London and has dealt with issues of racism and multi-culturalism, public safety and danger, the role of the cultural economy in urban regeneration, and popular participation in planning. His research with young people has developed new methods of visual ethnography, social mapping and dialogic engagement with informants. Most recently he directed a multi-project initiative examining the Post Olympic Legacy in East 20. He is the author of *On the Wrong Side of the Track? East London and the Post Olympics* (Lawrence and Wishart, 2013). Other books include *Knuckle Sandwich: Growing up in the Working Class City* (with Dave Robins, 1978), *Rethinking the Youth Question* (1997), *New Ethnicities, Old Racisms* (2001), *London's Turning: the Making of Thames Gateway* (edited with Mike Rustin, 2008). He has also published a memoir *Reading Room Only: Memoir of a Radical Bibliophile* (Five Leaves, 2013) and a book of poetry and prose, *Graphologies* (Mica Press, 2014). A collection of his new research, *Material Dreams: Maps and Territories and the Un/making of Modernity* is forthcoming from Palgrave Macmillan. www.philcohenworks.com

Paul Watt is Reader in Urban Studies at Birkbeck, University of London. He has published widely on topics including the London housing crisis, social rental housing, urban regeneration, suburbanization, and the 2012 Olympic Games. He is the co-author (with Tim Butler) of *Understanding Social Inequality* (Sage, 2007), co-editor (with Peer Smets) of *Mobilities and Neighbourhood Belonging in Cities and Suburbs* (Palgrave Macmillan, 2014) and co-editor (with Peer Smets) of *Social Housing and Urban Renewal: A Cross-National Perspective* (Emerald, 2017). He sits on the Editorial Board of City (Taylor & Francis) and is Board Member of the Research Committee on Sociology of Urban and Regional Development (RC21), International Sociological Association.

Part I

London 2012: The Mega-Event in Context

2

East London's Post-Olympic Economy

Gavin Poynter

Introduction

For more than a century, East London has been the location of successive rounds of urban intervention by the city's professional and business
elite and a political class for whom the residents of the east end were
often the subject of their fears and philanthropy (Stedman-Jones, 1984;
Marriott, 2011). As the location of the city's docks and the industries
that accompanied it, East London was the other side, the site of migrant
and casual labour and the likely location, at various times, of social
unrest, riots and industrial disputes. The phases of urban renewal have
arisen from the perceived necessity to achieve social stability and urban
improvements through slum clearance in the early twentieth century to
implementing the post-1945 reconstruction arising from the extensive
war damage, to the social reforms recommended in the Beveridge Report
and, in the mid to late twentieth century, to respond to the devastating

G. Poynter (✉)
University of East London, London, England
e-mail: g.poynter@uel.ac.uk

© The Author(s) 2017
P. Cohen, P. Watt (eds.), *London 2012 and the Post-Olympics City*,
DOI 10.1057/978-1-137-48947-0_2

social consequences of the closure of the docks themselves (Risebero, 1996). These attempts at urban renewal have initiated social and structural changes, prompted by different forms of state intervention.

The most recent Olympic inspired development represents a significant new phase in the remaking of East London. This latest phase institutionalised the concept of mega-event legacy; appropriated its imputation of the 'public good' and harnessed it to a programme of urban renewal led by the State and delivered by private enterprise. London's attention to legacy has been characterised as providing a 'model' of a city achieving significant long term benefits from hosting a global sports event. It is argued here, however, that East London's post-2012 legacy is being shaped far less by the promises made by successive governments and far more by a city economy that has been dominated over recent decades by London's 'financial turn'.

London's Financial Turn

In post-Olympic East London the social and economic conditions following London's 'financial turn' have melded with the stimuli provided by significant and sustained public investment, at first in Docklands and, subsequently, in the Olympic Park and its borders, to create a very different kind of economy to that historically based upon the production and processing industries that arose from their proximity to London's docks. The 'financial turn', has several characteristics that require some explanation before its implications for East London in the post-2012 legacy phase is discussed. As David Kynaston's excellent study of the City of London reminds us, London has long been a centre of finance, trade and insurance; a role firmly established in the late eighteenth century when it serviced three major segments of British commerce – American and Asian consumer goods, raw materials sourced from northern Europe and the markets for British manufactures in the American colonies and Africa (Kynaston, 2012: 9).

The 'financial turn' here, however, has more recent origins and refers to the period since the late 1960s during which London has reinvented itself as a hub for international financial intermediation. Over this period, London has assumed many of the features of the global city identified by Saskia Sassen (1991). It has become in her words, a 'free trade zone for finance' (1991: 18), a territory which is simultaneously detached from its national economy and yet is dependent upon a complex relationship to its own nation state which facilitates the institutional and legal forms needed for the 'material and place bound' resources that enable the city to perform its global role. For London, the material resources are symbolized by the emergence of Canary Wharf on the city's east side[1] and its global role arises from the myriad of what Sassen (1991: 19) calls the 'hypermobile and de-materialised financial instruments', that the City's activities have given rise to. According to TheCityUK (2014: 6), by 2014 London and the wider UK had:

> the leading share of trading in many international financial markets such as foreign exchange trading (41% of the global total), OTC derivatives trading (49%), cross-border bank lending (19%) and international insurance (22%). The UK is also the leading European centre for investment and private banking, hedge funds, private equity, exchange traded derivatives and sovereign wealth funds.

London's reinvention is exemplified, as TheCityUK report suggests, by its significance to the markets for derivatives. Derivatives trading arises from contracts between buyers and sellers over the future price of an asset (a share, currency, commodity or index). On the date of the contract's expiry, if the value of the asset has risen the seller pays the buyer; if it has fallen the buyer pays the seller. Derivatives began life in the mid-1970s in the USA (as stock options, foreign exchange futures, interest futures and stock index futures) and in Europe through the swap contracts that arose from the Eurodollar market. The 1980s witnessed a

---

[1] In 2013, the Office for National Statistics reported that employment in Canary Wharf had vastly expanded in the preceding decade, rising nearly fourfold from to 27,000 to 100,000 (ONS, 2013). And in her commentary on the ONS report, the *Financial Times'* Kate Allen reported that 'Last year, the number of bankers employed in Canary Wharf officially overtook the number employed in the City of London, making it the biggest employer of bankers in Europe. FT research shows that the 16 biggest banks in the UK employ 44,500 in Canary Wharf, compared with 43,300 in the Square Mile' (Allen, 2013).

huge expansion in the global market for derivatives with London becoming a major player in the markets for Over the Counter (OTC) derivatives and exchange-traded derivatives. OTC derivatives are those exchanged by dealers, exchange-traded derivatives operate via an institution or exchange (such as the London Stock Exchange Derivatives Market). According to the Bank for International Settlements' *Triennial Central Bank Survey 2013*, London:

> . . . consolidated its role as the main financial centre trading OTC interest rate derivatives. UK-based turnover rose by 9% to $1,348 billion, or just under one half of the global total . . . Turnover in the United States slipped 2% to $628 billion, or 23% of the total, which is in line with the lower share of contracts on US dollar interest rates'. (Bank for International Settlements, 2013: 6)

Whilst it is extremely difficult to estimate the size of the various derivatives markets from data relating to the notional or market value of contracts (Lapavitsas, 2013: 7), it is possible to conclude that the major financial institutions residing in London have taken a leading role in establishing the organizational and technical infrastructures required for the creation and growth of these forms of financial product – products that symbolize the importance of financial markets in the contemporary international economy.[2]

The finance sector's contemporary significance to the city and global economy, not only in derivatives but other major financial markets, has been attributed to a number of factors including London's historic role in the provision of a wide range of financial service products and services, its concentration or clustering of expertise, the time zone advantage of a location halfway between western (New York) and eastern (Tokyo, Hong Kong, Shanghai) financial centres, and the skilled

---

[2] For example, a report produced by the United Nations Conference on Trade and Development (UNCTAD, 2012) in autumn 2012 on the volatility of oil and commodity prices argued that 'with the volumes of exchange-traded derivatives on commodity markets now being 20 to 30 times larger than physical production, the influence of financial markets has systematically transformed these real markets into financial markets'.

workforce that has been drawn to the metropolis from across the globe. This list merely describes but does not explain the origins of these comparative advantages. They have arisen from what might be called a confluence of conditions – emerging from domestic policy decisions made by successive governments in response to the underlying structural problems that have persisted in the UK economy since de-industrialisation began in the late 1960s and 1970s and from major changes in the sources of dynamism in the international economy.

Reinvention has not been a smooth ride or a product of long term strategic thinking from within the finance sector or by the State. Domestically, successive UK governments, since the early 1970s, have grappled with the decline in the relative importance of production industries to the nation's economy. The decline has arisen from the underlying tendency of capitalist economies, particularly evident in the UK even in the late 1950s, for profit-making from production slowing considerably or reaching limits a consequence of which is that capital (especially non-financial corporations) has increasingly sought to boost profits elsewhere, often in the world of finance, in ways that at best support but often replaces the 'real' production-based economy (Clarke, 1988).[3] In their attempts to stimulate the domestic economy, successive British governments have loosened restrictions on credit for businesses and households with the former becoming increasingly dependent upon the financial economy as a source of profit and the latter increasingly dependent upon monetizing their assets (particularly property) or upon private debt to sustain living standards. The result of these trends is that industrial and financial capital have tended to merge or meld together (Ben-Ami, 2012). In an increasingly credit driven economy such as the UK, this merging has given rise to the expansion of what Krippner (2011) has called a 'new finance industry'.

This process has been supported by the State in various ways whether by the liberalization of financial markets in the late 1980s (the Big

---

[3] It is beyond the scope of this chapter to discuss this process in detail. For insights into the structural problems in the UK economy that provided the conditions for the financialisation of the UK economy see, for example Turner (2009). For a conceptual analysis of financialisation arising from the melding of industrial and finance capital, see Epstein (2005) and Lapavitsas (2013).

Bang), through credit-induced booms (late 1980s, early 2000s) or by changes in the structural role and policies of the central bank (the Bank of England) – from managing the reduction of inflation in the early 1980s to its recent role in maintaining historically low interest rates.[4] London, in particular, has fared well from these forms of State intervention. The Big Bang, designed to safeguard London's financial sector in the face of growing international competition, was timely in providing the City with opportunities to renew its physical infrastructure and, more significantly, take advantage of a major change in international financial markets, especially the rapidly rising offshore (Euro) financial transactions (Kynaston, 2012: 567). The 'new finance industry' and the professions and services it has spawned in turn created the conditions for the eventual expansion of the industry into East London's former docklands at Canary Wharf.

By 2013, London's contribution to the UK's total Gross Value Added[5] was 22.2 per cent, up from 18.9 per cent in 1997 and over two thirds of the city's total GVA was created in Inner (West) London (GLA Economics, 2015: 6). The finance and insurance industry made a significant contribution to the London's GVA performance:

> In 2010 over a fifth of London's output was generated by the financial and insurance industry (£57.7 billion) . . . The value of this industry has grown by 172 per cent since 1997, more than any other industry in London and it accounts for 7 per cent of the UK's total output growth since 1997. In 2010, nearly half (47 per cent) of the UK's output in the financial and insurance industry was generated in London (up from 41 per cent in 1997). . . . Indeed, London's financial and insurance industry made up 4.5 per cent of the UK's total output in 2010. (GLA Economics, 2015: 10)

---

[4] In such an economy, the central bank's role becomes increasingly important, with financial markets being highly sensitive to any pronouncements on or changes in the direction of monetary policy.

[5] GVA is an estimate of the value created by a unit of production. It may be measured in different ways – production, income, expenditure; see: http://www.ons.gov.uk/ons/guide-method/method-quality/specific/economy/national-accounts/gva/relationship-gva-and-gdp/gross-value-added-and-gross-domestic-product.html

Whilst Inner London (West) has made the greatest contribution, London (East) has emerged over the period from 1997 to 2013 as a relatively important location of GVA creation. Over this period its contribution to the finance and insurance sector's GVA rose from 19 to 26 per cent (GLA Economics, 2015).

At the international level, the inward flows of capital into London over recent years have arisen from the global imbalances in productive dynamism between east and west. The large current account surpluses achieved by emerging economies, particularly China, enabled them to lend to nations such as the USA, so the latter could sustain significant current account deficits. Since the 2007–8 financial crisis, China and other emerging economies (and not least their Sovereign Wealth Funds and wealthy private individuals) have sought to diversify their investment portfolios moving from the purchase of mainly US government bonds into, for example, commercial and residential property in secure, tax friendly and open economies. In the post-Olympic period, London and its east-side, have become favoured sites for this form of investment (Poynter, 2016).

In summary, the 'financial turn' has systemic features particularly evident in the USA and Britain (Lapavitsas, 2013; Poynter, 2013) – the crisis of profitability in the productive sectors in the late 1960s and early 1970s, the response of non-financial firms in shifting capital into financial markets with a resultant inflation of financial assets, the inexorable rise in credit and the emergence of a variety of new financial instruments designed to manage risk have given rise to a new finance industry – all trends from which London's economy has benefitted (not least in achieving a significant share of the global business in the financial instruments, such as derivatives, spawned by financialisation). Coupled with the search by institutional investors for profitable investment in global city hotspots, parts of East London such as the Olympic Village, The International Quarter and even the relatively remote Royal Docks have or seem set to benefit from this inflow of capital.

Over the past decade East London has provided a stable environment for inward investors seeking to profit from residential and commercial property developments whose emergence has benefitted considerably from the State's investment in the improvements made to the

(Olympics-inspired) transport infrastructure. Qatari Holdings, established by the Qatari Investment Authority, a Sovereign Wealth Fund, owns half of the Olympic Village; Westfield, an Australian company along with two pension funds APG, a pension fund asset manager for the Dutch education, government and construction sectors, and the Canadian Pension Plan Investment Board (CPPIB) own the Westfield Shopping Mall located at Stratford; ExCel London, the exhibition centre, is owned by the Abu Dhabi Exhibition Company and Inter Ikea Group (Sweden) is developing a mixed housing/commercial area called Strand East in the lower Lea Valley corridor located between Stratford and Canary Wharf. In the Silvertown and Royal Docks areas, Siemens has created the Crystal, a centre that showcases sustainable construction and ABP, a Chinese company, is set to build an Asian business centre by 2018, an investment costing, it is estimated over £1 billion on its completion.[6]

In a city which by the early 1980s had experienced years of population decline, had an outdated transport infrastructure and areas of deep social deprivation, not least in East London, the rapid expansion of financial and business services and the open economy these require to operate has, it seems, facilitated an upturn in economic fortunes – an expanding retail sector serving private consumption, a hot property market and an attractive location for foreign direct investment (FDI). These trends are reflected in East London's emerging post-Olympic economy. As the following discussion about recent developments in the Olympic Park and The International Quarter reveal, they also have significant social and economic implications for the existing and new communities being created in East London.

The Queen Elizabeth Olympic Park

In an article about the China Summit Forum on the International Sports Industry held in Beijing in August 2013, *China Daily* acknowledged that 'A successful bid for the 2022 Winter Olympics could give a

---

[6] For a detailed discussion of these developments see Poynter (2016).

second life to the major venues built for the 2008 Summer Games in Beijing. But creating a profitable business model remains a difficult puzzle for healthy venue operations' (Xiaochen, 2013). This muted criticism related to the failure of Beijing, five years after the Games, to establish the viable use of several of the venues. Even the famous Birds Nest, the Olympic Stadium, with its dependence on tourism and occasional events, was struggling to meet its maintenance costs. The problems incurred by Beijing appear to affirm the negative experiences of other nations like Athens (2004), in integrating the permanent facilities built for the Games into the fabric of the post-Olympic city.

Three years on from the 2012 Olympics, London seems to have avoided this trend. In establishing its legacy planning for the Olympic Park well before the Games took place, London has developed an area that has made progress in integrating into the city via new and improved transport networks, securing uses for the permanent venues constructed for the Games and implementing a long term plan covering the 560 acres of the renamed Queen Elizabeth Olympic Park. The Park even contains its own iconic tower, the AcelorMittal Orbit, designed by the Indian sculptor, Sir Anish Kapoor and architect Cecil Belmond and named after it sponsor, Lakshmi Mittal, owner of the world's foremost steel company. It is the UK's largest piece of public art and is, perhaps, a fitting symbol for the Park – a testimony to branding (of its sponsor), a location promoted as a site for private functions and weddings as well as being a viewing space open to the public; a confusing mix of public and private purpose not unlike the Park that is emerging post-2012.

The London Legacy Development Corporation (LLDC), under the guidance of the Mayor of London and Greater London Authority, was given the task of developing the Park in the period following the closure of the Games. The local plan was drafted by summer 2014 with implementation taking place over the period 2015–2031 (LLDC, 2013a, 2014a, 2015). The plan incorporates proposals for the creation of 'clusters' of employment, five new neighbourhoods in which approximately 1,400 houses per annum will be built over the lifetime of the plan, two town centres (Stratford and Hackney Wick), new parkland and waterway leisure spaces, and a social infrastructure that will include what has been called 'Olympicoplis' – an area designated for universities, museums and other cultural institutions such as Sadlers Wells (LLDC, 2015).

The LDDC plan has modified and adapted earlier legacy plans, with the most recent version increasingly focused on employment and the attraction of cultural and business activity rather than primarily housing and residential development. The Olympicopolis proposal, for example, reduces the number of housing units planned for construction within the Park by about 1,000, though it is anticipated that the cultural and educational institutions that locate to the park will, in turn, encourage, new housing developments to come forward on the Park's borders. Two housing developments, Sweetwater and East Wick (1,600 homes), are planned for development by 2023 rather than 2029. But the focus on employment clusters has arisen from, for example, the development of the International Quarter by Lend Lease and London Continental Railways (LCR) and the transformation of the Olympic Press and Broadcasting Centre into 'Hear East', a digital technologies centre which by early 2015 had 40 per cent occupancy with tenants including BT Sport, Loughborough University and Hackney Community College.

The modifications to the plan for the Olympic Park and the border areas for which the LDDC has assumed responsibility are a result of the public/private contractual relations being struck to enable development to take place. The public agency uses land disposal (via sales and leasing) to promote developments with corporate partners. The former seeks to leverage public gain (public amenities, social infrastructure) while the latter is primarily concerned with 'scheme viability', the potential profits to be attained from the investment made. In East London, the precondition for such negotiations has been a long term commitment by successive governments to invest in the creation of the Olympic Park and the infrastructure to support it. In turn, investors are attracted by the reduction of the financial risks of development projects arising from the shelter provided by long term public investment, the capacity to phase the project over time and the access to favourable terms for the navigation of local planning rules and regulations arising from the partnership with the public agency (Karadimitriou et al., 2013; Poynter, 2016). Paradoxically, public agencies have designed ambitious plans but rely on private enterprise to enact them whilst private enterprise can only pursue their narrower interests by relying upon state agencies to rene-gotiate or modify the plans they have produced. By early 2015, public investment in the Park was estimated at some £12.5 billion, including £5.6 billion on transport and approximately half a billion pounds on the repurposing of the Park post-Games. This 'negotiated order' behind the implementation of the plans for East London's post-Olympic develop-ment may be illustrated by the International Quarter and Olympicopolis.

The International Quarter

The International Quarter divides into two locations and a number of plots within 'Stratford City' the high density development area close to Stratford International Station and the Westfield Shopping Mall. The land is owned by London and Continental Railways (LCR), which, in turn, is wholly owned by the Department of Transport. LCR leased the land on which the International Quarter is being constructed to the Olympic Delivery Authority (ODA) until the end of the 2012 Games. A joint venture company was established between LCR and Lend Lease for the development of the area post-Games with a large office development preceding a planned residential development. LCR has ownership of two major regeneration sites in London at Kings Cross and Stratford:

> where values will mature over time, as the schemes develop; the market recognises the full potential of location; and infrastructure investment is completed. LCR has worked with long-term development partners to manage the key assets at King's Cross Central and Stratford City. The aim has been to share in the equity growth that comes with participation in development joint venture companies. LCR has been able to use the land as equity to match capital contributions from the development partners. Working closely with our partners LCR has fully participated in setting the strategic direction on the joint venture businesses. (Department of Transport, 2011)

An important impetus for the major office development was the announce-ment that the Financial Conduct Authority (FCA) will be moving its 3,000 staff to the International Quarter by 2017, taking up about 10 per cent of the available office space and this announcement was followed by Transport for London (TfL) stating it would move a similar number of staff to the same location by 2018. The FCA argued that the move made economic sense since office space in the City cost an annual average of £65 per square foot, Canary Wharf £45 and Stratford an estimated £30 (Allen and Shafer, 2014) and TfL indicated its reason for relocation to Stratford as arising from its consolidation of staff in fewer locations in London.

The first residential development, Glasshouse Gardens, was launched in January 2014. The residential site consists of 330 homes which include 1, 2 and 3 bedroom apartments. The developers, Lend Lease claimed considerable success in launching the site with purchases taking place 'off plan' as a result of UK and overseas sales initiatives:

> Kristy Lansdown, Project Director for The International Quarter, said: 'We are delighted with the response to Glasshouse Gardens at the UK, Singapore and Hong Kong launch events, and hope to mirror the success in the upcoming Shanghai exhibition taking place on 22–23 February'. (Lend Lease/LCR, 2014)

The International Quarter's mixed development trajectory was also affirmed in 2014 when a real estate investment company, Union Hannover, acquired Starboard Hotel's share in the construction of a hotel on the site. Starboard Hotel's plan was to construct an 'Urban Villa' (an extended stay, internationally branded hotel) but on its take-over, the new owners decided to construct a £70 million hotel, The Penny Brook, as a 'destination boutique' hotel. The thinking behind the new scheme was described by Eric Jafari, the Managing Director of Union Hanover:

> 'We believe that we can create a New York-inspired boutique hotel that will inject a real buzz into Stratford, which has unrivalled access to the City, West End and Canary Wharf', he said. 'We are in talks with a number of high-end restaurant operators and have a number of creative initiatives which will ensure this will offer a unique hospitality experience'. (Harmer, 2014)

The rest of the site will consist of 137 apartments developed by Union Hanover and Equity Bridge Asset Management. It will be called Adagio London Stratford, aimed at 'long-stay visitors and will provide fully-furnished studios and one and two-bedroom apartments, complete with kitchens and bathrooms, to provide high quality self-catering accommodation' (Harmer, 2014). This high density development of the sites located by Stratford City will be complemented by the emergence of Olympicopolis.

Olympicopolis

The museum quarter (sometimes referred to as Albertopolis in recognition of the role of Prince Albert in its creation) founded in mid-Victorian West London, provides, it is claimed, the inspiration behind the Olympicopolis project to be developed in the Olympic Park in East London. It seems likely that the contemporary project will meet with fewer obstacles, at least in its early stages of development, to those experienced by its predecessor. Albertopolis arose from the work of the Commissioners of London's Great Exhibition of 1851. The Commissioners in partnership with government and the Science and Art Department established its South Kensington Museum, in 1856. The partnership was not, however, an unproblematic affair. The Commission's proposals to relocate many of London's institutions promoting the arts and sciences within the South Kensington estate met with opposition not least from inside parliament and the National Gallery Royal Commission (which rejected the proposal to relocate the National Gallery to the site in 1857). Uncertain of continued government support, the Commissioners sought in the 1860s to develop the site through raising funds by a combination of loans and the construction of houses for lease and sale. It took over two decades, including a period of considerable indebtedness in the 1880s before Albertopolis' future was secured when the Imperial Institute (now Imperial College, London) was constructed between 1887 and 1893.

By contrast, Olympicopolis' initial phase of development appears secure - the land is assembled, central government has allocated

£141 million to support construction and several cultural and higher education institutions are committed to moving to the site including the Victoria and Albert Museum, University College London, Sadler's Wells, the University of the Arts and the Smithsonian Institute. An international competition for the design of the site had realised, by early, 2015, a shortlist of five consortia, one of which will be chosen to plan and develop the site on behalf of the institutions seeking to move into it. Prince Albert's initial proposals for the Kensington site drew upon the inspiration of the Great Exhibition of 1851 'where, by the constant interchange of ideas, experience, and its results, each nation may gain and contribute something' (Sheppard, 1975: 50) but subsequent reports produced by the Commissioners reflected an appreciation of the growing insularity and anxiety within the nation's elite about Britain's place in the world and fears of foreign competition to its manufacturing industries: 'The Second and Third Reports (the latter of April 1856) showed a great awareness of industrial education abroad but the effect of this raised the fear of foreign rivalry' (Sheppard, 1975: 5).

By contrast, to date, Olympicopolis has provoked little public debate about the cultural and educational content provided by the institutions likely to locate to the site in East London. Unlike in mid-Victorian London, there is no concern for the 'national self-protection' of Britain's productive industries. Today, in fact, the *opposite* is the case. The UK, and London's economy in particular, has relatively few domestically owned production plants and is open to rather than seeking protection from international enterprise. Olympicopolis is conceived in this light as a cultural attraction that has the potential to affirm the Park's integration into the global city, its desirability as a visitor attraction and a showcase, not for British industry, but for foreign direct investment to be attracted to the area. The historic parallels drawn with South Kensington (which typically ignore Albertopolis' politically and financially troubled origins) serve now largely to assist in the re-imagining of East London, and specifically the Olympic Park, as London's Mayor Boris Johnson put it, as a 'pole of attraction' for East London, a cultural palace 'of a kind to knock the Pompidou Centre ... into a cocked hat' (cited in

Pickford, 2015). The Mayor's undoubted enthusiasm for the post-Olympic development of the Park and its borders reflects the depth of the political commitment to, and public investment involved in, creating a viable legacy for East London. Three years into its creation, it seems likely to succeed, not least in extending the designation of 'inner' London eastwards.

A Viable Legacy?

But what is a viable legacy of London 2012 and for whom? Reconnecting the east involves reproducing characteristics of inner London's economy and society in areas such as Stratford City and along the corridor of the Lower Lea Valley that runs between Stratford and Canary Wharf. The International Quarter and development plans for Olympicopolis are but two illustrations of the direction of East London's economy post-2012. They do, however, provide insights into the ways in which London's 'financial turn' has combined with the stimuli provided by Olympics-inspired investment to reconnect areas of East London with the city in ways that are tending to reinforce social divisions rather than redress them. Several dimensions of the emerging legacy of London 2012 illustrate this trend.

An Emergent Metropolitan Centre: In 2003, the GLA noted that East London, unlike many other parts of the city, did not have a leisure economy, there were no chains like 'All Bar One', employment in pubs and bars was falling and visitor attractions were scarce (GLA Economics, 2003). By May 2014, a review of retail and leisure facilities undertaken for the LLDC reported that Stratford in particular was emerging as a 'Metropolitan centre – a focus for major retail and leisure' (LLDC, 2014b). The ability of local residents, however, to access this emergent retail and leisure economy is at best varied. The *Newham Household Panel Survey* (LBN, 2014: 37) reported that, 'A significant proportion of households struggle to afford goods and services'. A major influence upon this limited capacity to participate in the new leisure economy arises from the prevalence in the borough of low incomes after housing costs are accounted for.

The higher housing costs associated with living in London push net income after housing costs below the threshold for relative low income. Once housing costs are accounted for, the median net equivalised household income in Newham falls to £12,172 (mean £15,916). This means that the median weekly income after housing costs in Newham is £234, which is 64% of the national median income of £367. Income levels fall relative to the national median, despite the fact an increased proportion of Newham residents are now in receipt of housing benefit. (LBN, 2014: 95)

It seems that living in an emergent 'metropolitan centre' is one thing but being able to afford to access its new amenities located in the new Stratford city for a significant proportion of the borough's local residents is another.

The emerging leisure sector may be attractive to the higher skilled professionals and administrators moving east into Stratford but is less accessible for a significant proportion of existing residents. The International Quarter is illustrative of this trend. The Financial Conduct Authority and Transport for London (TfL) each plan to relocate around 3,000 staff to the area over the next few years and both employ staff who may benefit from local amenities but neither seem likely to provide significant jobs opportunities for local residents, replicating (or perhaps, more accurately, reinforcing), in Newham the income and employment trends evident in Tower Hamlets over the period of the emergence of Canary Wharf. The high income levels for those employed on the Isle of Dogs, for example, contrast starkly with the low wages of the residents of adjacent wards in Tower Hamlets. The 'Time to Act' Evidence Pack produced by the Tower Hamlets Fairness Commission in 2013, documented the average salary (£78,000 per annum) of those who *work* in the borough (boosted by the salaries of those working in the wards located within Canary Wharf) with the distribution of the household income levels of those who *live in* the borough revealing the considerable divide between the income rich and the income poor (Table 2.1):

Employment. The new economy emerging in East London is tending to enhance rather than reduce social divisions via the new jobs being created or relocated into the area and through the new housing schemes

Table 2.1 Distribution of household income levels for Tower Hamlets and London, 2013 (%)

	Under £15,000	Under £30,000	Under £45,000	Under £60,000	Over £60,000	Over £100,000
Tower Hamlets	20.7	50.8	71.6	84.5	15.5	3.5
London	17.3	47.4	69.9	83.8	16.2	3.4

Source: (2013) Time to Act, Tower Hamlets Fairness Commission, LB Tower Hamlets: Mayor of Tower Hamlets/Toynbee Hall.

under construction. The recent pattern of Olympic-led and foreign direct investment has witnessed job relocation and job creation that in turn has accelerated a process of change in the structure of employment. In Newham, for example, the public sector remains the most important employer. By 2014, however, the retail sector was the largest private sector employer of the borough's residents (not least because of the presence of Westfield's shopping mall in Stratford) with wholesale, distribution and transport also providing a significant proportion of private sector jobs (LBN, 2014). But employment trends are also subject to other significant influences such as the high level of population movement in and out of boroughs such as Newham and Tower Hamlets and the different employment/unemployment rates within and between ethnic groups.

The Olympic, now Growth, boroughs adopted the policy of 'Convergence' in 2011. The policy is designed to ensure that its residents achieve within two decades the same social and economic chances as those achieved across London as a whole (see Introduction). Since its inception, a range of indicators have been used to monitor progress. By 2015, despite considerable Olympics-led investment, employment rates in the Growth Boroughs had risen, but not at the same speed as the average employment rate for London as a whole. The Growth Boroughs agreed that the Action Plan adopted for the period 2015–18 should focus, in particular, on increasing employment rates and improving average income levels. Employment rates remained particularly low in Hackney, Newham and Tower Hamlets and especially low for women, as seen in Table 2.2.

The growth in employment in East London arising from the development of the Olympic Park and other locations, such as the Royal Docks and Canary Wharf, is publicly presented as an example of the area's

Table 2.2 Employment rates for Growth Boroughs, London and England (12 months to December 2013)

Area	Age 16–64 (%)		
	Total	Male	Female
Barking and Dagenham	64.5	73.6	55.8
Greenwich	64.4	73.1	56.0
Hackney	62.8	69.6	56.4
Newham	62.6	72.5	52.0
Tower Hamlets	63.4	73.5	52.5
Waltham Forest	71.2	81.5	60.4
Growth Boroughs	**64.8**	**74.0**	**55.4**
London	70.1	73.3	62.9
England	71.7	77.0	66.4

Source: Author, adapted from ONS Annual Labour Force Survey (2013).

positive future but they rely heavily upon forms of inward investment and cultural/educational and enterprise relocations that, at the time of writing in autumn 2015, had done little to improve employment rates in boroughs such as Newham and Hackney and are likely into the future to accentuate the polarity between high and low income occupations with the latter service-oriented jobs filled by local residents, often on wages considerably lower than the national median level. In short, East London's workforce, from a broad historical perspective, is being re-shaped primarily as a service class to the professional and managerial occupations that have continued to rise as a result of London's financial turn.

Housing (see also Chapter 4). In post-2012 East London, three trends are also reshaping the housing market. First, the 'Olympic-effect' on property prices has been uneven but the underlying trend is upwards with East London boroughs such as Tower Hamlets, Hackney and Newham experiencing price rises that have outstripped those in the higher value West London boroughs, such as Chelsea and Kensington (Savills, 2014); see Table 2.3. Such price rises, including in the expanding private rented sector, coupled with the implementation of the government's housing benefit reforms is making the area unaffordable for low income families.

Second, East London is set to account for a third of new homes to be constructed over the next five years, many of which will be high

Table 2.3 House price growth 2005–2014, selected Host Boroughs (%)

Borough	Price growth since June 2005	Annual price growth	Transactions increase vs pre-peak average	Transactions increase past 12 months (May 2013–May 2014)
Hackney	102	22	96	11
Newham	19	13	56	48
Tower Hamlets	57	18	100	29

Source: Savills (based on Land Registry data, May 2014).

rise, but this growth in provision reflects in large measure the aspirations of institutional and corporate investors and developers, such as those involved with The International Quarter, to attract overseas buyers and young professionals into the area and is unlikely to assist in meeting the demand for affordable (social) or affordable private rented housing for existing residents. The International Quarter may follow the pattern of ownership emerging in locations such as Wapping and Canary Wharf where international buyers constitute a significant proportion of the market. In Canary Wharf, for example, overseas buyers were responsible for over 70 per cent of sales in 2012, 41 per cent in 2013 and around two thirds of sales in 2014 (Savills, 2014). Stratford Plaza, located in Stratford City illustrates this trend. It was completed in 2015. It consists of 198 units all of which were sold off plan and three quarters to overseas buyers.

Finally, the issue of determining in whose interests scheme viability will be defined is being played out within the Queen Elizabeth Olympic Park itself, with affordable housing for new homes falling far short of that required (Bernstock, 2014: 191–202), as the LLDC (2014c: 24) candidly recognised in August 2014:

The SHMA Review, 2013 sets out that 100 per cent of the housing requirement would need to be affordable to meet overall needs; However this is not considered practical or viable. The 35 per cent target has been used to set the affordable housing target which was in turn determined by the evidence between the Affordable Housing Viability Testing, 2013 and Combined Policies Viability Study, 2014.

Housing provides a further illustration of how London's 'financial turn' (particularly in its implications for the property market), government social policies and the impetus to urban development arising from hosting the Olympics, are impacting upon East London. The impacts produce divergent social trends. First, new developments located between Stratford and Canary Wharf have become increasingly attractive to overseas and corporate buyers, a market facilitated by the operations of London's major real estate firms whose activities are increasingly globalised.[7] And, secondly, domestically, within the communities of East London, some home-owners may be 'beneficiaries', of the upward trend in house prices by being able to compensate, if necessary for the prolonged stagnation of wages levels over recent years by securing credit on the back of owning bricks and mortar. Those, however, without such assets are forced to rely on low wages and social benefits to make ends meet. When this combination can no longer keep up with the cost of social housing (typically 80 per cent of the market rate) or the cost of private rented accommodation, low income households are forced to move especially from those areas close to or within the locations of major urban renewal. The political legitimation for significant public, particularly Olympics-related, investment, rested upon improving the housing conditions of the most socially disadvantaged communities in East London. The process of urban renewal taking place is, however, largely being shaped by the economic forces arising from London's financial turn, the consequence is that the public investment is set to achieve the

---

[7] Trobor Capital a UK located investment company, published a report on 'London Real Estate' in September 2014 (Trobor Capital, 2014). The report provides insights into the property investment operations of international companies and their significant interest in London's prime and mainstream residential property markets. The report noted the significant level of new builds being purchased by overseas buyers: 'Currently about 51% of the real estate purchasers in prime central London are from the United Kingdom. Of the 49% of international buyers, 16.5% of them are from other European countries. The next largest percentage of international buyers is Russia and the Commonwealth of Independent States at about 9.1%. After that is the Middle East with approximately 7.5% of the international residential real estate purchases in London. However, not all of these purchases indicate residence. The actual amount of foreigners who reside in London is about 28% of the total residents. Research done by the Knight Frank Residential Research has shown that about 69% of the purchases of newly-built homes in London are international in nature, leaving just 31% for natives of the United Kingdom'. (Trobor Capital, 2014)

opposite of its declared intention – an inflow of cash rich international investors and an outflow or displacement of low-income households (see Chapter 4).

Conclusion

London's housing market is symbolic of and integral to the city's highly financialised economy; major developments not only in areas of the West but also in pockets of East London, are increasingly taking the form of speculative investments. Employment patterns in the city are also being redesigned taking the form an hourglass – secure, higher paid occupations at the top, low paid and insecure employment at the bottom and a relatively small proportion of jobs in between.

The urban legacy of London's hosting the 2012 Games is being shaped by the underlying trends evident within the wider city economy. Quasi-state agencies, such as the LDDC, along with local and city-wide authorities, are tasked with obtaining benefits for East London's socially disadvantaged communities in a context that is, to say the very least, unfavourable. It is likely that for the foreseeable future, a viable legacy for East London will be largely defined by the developer, the inward investor, cultural and educational 'showcase' institutions and the professional, managerial and administrative occupations attached to those sectors that have been and continue to be the beneficiaries of London's most recent financial turn.

The recent history of the city's east-side is testimony to the pivotal role of public agencies in economic and urban policy in enabling a pattern of top-down urban renewal that binds together in partnership the State and capital. Significant state infrastructure spending, planning and tax exemptions provided the foundations for the emergence of a new financial district at Canary Wharf and, most recently, Olympic-inspired State investment has facilitated the transformation of Stratford and the border areas of the Queen Elizabeth Olympic Park. The State has provided the conditions to attract inward investment for property and commercial development while successive governments have promised a socially beneficial legacy as an important legitimation for the investment of public money into the city's east side. The achievement of the former rests uneasily with the aspirations expressed in the latter.

The partnership between state and capital that is re-shaping significant areas of East London is, in turn, reliant upon 'a confluence of conditions' in the international economy that currently favour London as an international hub for the finance and related industries, a location for inward flows of capital and a site for the location of a hot property market. London has moved eastwards as it has also consolidated its role as a global centre for financial intermediation and as a site for the myriad of professional and managerial services that complement and support it. The renewal of the east side of the city has been accelerated by Olympic-led investment but the pattern of urban renewal has been set less by the promised social legacies so prominent in the Olympic narrative and far more by the underlying logic of a highly financialised form of urban capitalism.

Such conditions of renewal are, however, fragile. The policies of successive UK governments have since the late 1980s supported the economy's openness but this, in the longer term, also means that the city's economic fortunes are largely outside the former's control (Allen, 2014). As Sassen's 'free trade centre' for finance, London relies upon its capacity to continue to exploit the imbalances arising between the stalling economies of the west and the more dynamic economies of the east, acting often as their go-between. In short, London adeptly recovered from the last global financial crisis but there will always be a next one. In the meantime, London's 'financial turn' that helped create Canary Wharf has now melded with the public investment inspired by the hosting the 2012 Games to attract the income rich into an area that was for most of the twentieth century the province of the city's working classes.

References

Allen, K. (2013) 'Canary Wharf workforce quadruples in a decade', *Financial Times*, 18 August 2013.

Allen, K. (2014) 'London's property tipping points', *Financial Times*, 29 September 2014.

Allen, K. and Shafer, D. (2014) 'FCA confirms it will move HQ to Olympic Park', *FT.com*, 2 April 2014, http://www.ft.com/cms/s/0/e5649848-ba71-11e3-aeb0-00144feabdc0.html#axzz3T8Ne6sg3http://www.ft.com/cms/s/0/b06a7f6e-0440-11e3-8aab-00144feab7de.html#axzz3p6o6FhnU.

Bank for International Settlements. (2013) *Triennial Central Bank Survey 2013*, http://www.bis.org/publ/rpfx13ir.pdf.

Ben-Ami, D. (2012) 'London's financial services after the Credit Crunch', in G. Poynter, I. MacRury and A. Calcutt (eds.) London after Recession. Farnham: Ashgate.

Bernstock P (2014) *Olympic Housing: A Critical Review of the 2012 Legacy*. Farnham: Ashgate.

Clarke, S. (1988) *Keynesianism, Monetarism and the Crisis of the State*. Aldershot: Edward Elgar.

Department of Transport. (2011) *Department of Transport Land Strategy Annex C, 2011*, https://www.gov.uk/government/uploads/system/uploads/attachment_data/file/3738/land-strategy.pdf.

Epstein, G. (2005) *Financialisation and the World Economy*. Cheltenham: Edward Elgar.

GLA Economics. (2003) *Spending Time: London's Leisure Economy*. London: Greater London Authority.

GLA Economics. (2015) *Regional, sub-regional and local gross value added estimates for London, 1997–2013*. London: GLA.

Harmer, J. (2014) 'Union Hanover reveals plan for boutique hotel in Stratford City', *The Caterer*, 1 July 2014.

Karadimitriou, N, Magalhães, C, de and Verhage, R. (2013) *Planning, Risk and Property Development: Urban Regeneration in England, France and the Netherlands*. London: Routledge.

Krippner, G. (2011) *Capitalising on Crisis*. Cambridge, MA: Harvard University Press.

Kynaston, D. (2012) *City of London: The History*. London: Vintage.

Lapavitsas, C. (2013) *Profiting Without Producing*. London: Verso.

Lend Lease/LCR. (2014) 'Glasshouse Gardens Sales Launch Success', 23 January 2014, http://ghgstratford.com/news-events.

LBN. (2014) *Understanding Newham: Newham Household Panel Survey, Wave 7 Survey Findings*. London: London Borough of Newham/Ipsos MORI.

LLDC. (2013a) *Local Plan: Draft Version*. London: LLDC.

LLDC. (2014a) *Local Plan: Publication Version*. London: LLDC.

LLDC. (2014b) *Retail and Leisure Review, Final Report, May 2014*. London: LLDC.

LLDC. (2014c) *LLDC Local Plan Background Paper: Housing, August 2014*. London: LLDC.

LLDC. (2015) *Local Plan: 2015–2031*. London: LLDC. http://queeneliza betholympicpark.co.uk/~/media/lldc/local%20plan/adoption%20july% 202015/lldc_localplan_2015_interactive100dpi%20(4).pdf.

Marriott, J. (2011) *Beyond the Tower: A History of East London*. Yale: Yale University Press.

ONS. (2013) *Small and Large Firms in London, 2001 to 2012*, http://www.ons. gov.uk/ons/rel/regional-trends/london-analysis/small-and-large-firms-in-lon don–2001-to-2012/index.html.

Pickford J. (2015) 'London Mayor's vision for Olympicopolis gathers steam', *Financial Times*, 30 January 2015.

Poynter, G. (2013) 'The Olympics: East London's renewal and legacy', in H. Lenskyj and S. Wagg (eds.), *The Palgrave Handbook of Olympic Studies*. Basingstoke: Palgrave MacMillan.

Poynter G. (2016) 'Olympics inspired inward investment – transforming East London?', in G. Poynter, V. Viehoff and Y. Li (eds.), *The London Olympics and Urban Development*. London: Routledge.

Risebero, B. (1996) 'Architecture in East London', in T. Butler and M. Rustin (eds.), *Rising in the East*. London: Lawrence and Wishart.

Sassen S. (1991) *The Global City*. Princeton: Princeton University Press.

Savills. (2014) *London Development: Building opportunities East of City*. London: Savills World Research, Autumn 2014, http://pdf.euro.savills.co. uk/uk/residential-other/east-of-city.pdf.

Sheppard, F. H. W. (1975) 'The estate of the commissioners for the exhibition of 1851', in F. H. W. Sheppard (ed.), *Survey of London: Volume 38, South Kensington Museums Area*, http://www.british-history.ac.uk/survey-london/ vol38/pp49-73, accessed 2 March 2015.

Stedman Jones, G. (1984) *Outcast London*. London: Penguin.

TheCityUK. (2014) *Driving Economic Growth, Creating Sustainable Jobs: How Financial and Related Professional Services Serve the UK*. London: TheCityUK, http://www.thecityuk.com/research/our-work/reports-list/driv ing-economic-growth-creating-sustainable-jobs-how-financial-and-related- professional-services-serve-the-uk/.

Tower Hamlets Fairness Commission. (2013) *Time to Act*. London: Tower Hamlets Council and Toynbee Hall.

Trobor Capital. (2014) 'London real estate', 1 September 2014, http://trobor capital.com/wp-content/uploads/TBC_EN1.pdf.

Turner, G. (2009) *No Way to Run an Economy*. London: Pluto Press.

UNCTAD [United Nations Conference on Trade and Development]. (2012) Don't Blame the Physical Markets: Financialisation is the root cause of oil and commodity price volatility, Policy Brief No 25. September 2012. New York: UNCTAD.

Xiaochen S. (2013) 'Olympic Venues seek a sustainable business model', *China Daily USA*, http://usa.chinadaily.com.cn/epaper/2013-11/14/content_17104891.htm, accessed 20 January 2015.

Gavin Poynter is Professor (Emeritus) in the School of Social Sciences, University of East London. His recent publications include Valerie Viehoff and Gavin Poynter (eds.) *Mega-Event Cities: Urban Legacies of Global Sports Events* (Ashgate, 2016), and Gavin Poynter, Yang Li and Valerie Viehoff (eds.) *The London Olympics and Urban Development* (Routledge, 2016).

3

Hollow Sovereignty and the Hollow Crown? Contested Governance and the Olympic Security Edifice

Pete Fussey and Jon Coaffee

Introduction

Hosting the Olympics is increasingly seen by urban managers as a once-in-a-lifetime opportunity for large-scale redevelopment and rebranding of a city and to advertise particular urban geographies to an international audience (Burbank et al., 2001). A focus upon transformational urban regeneration has now become a key rationale for cities to be awarded the Games by the International Olympic Committee (IOC). Although much has been made of London 2012's commitment to 'the regeneration games' and 'legacy' benefits, previous host cities have consistently used the Games as a lever for urban change

P. Fussey (✉)
University of Essex, Colchester, UK
e-mail: pfussey@essex.ac.uk

J. Coaffee
University of Warwick, Coventry, England
e-mail: J.Coaffee@warwick.ac.uk

© The Author(s) 2017
P. Cohen, P. Watt (eds.), *London 2012 and the Post-Olympics City*,
DOI 10.1057/978-1-137-48947-0_3

(Chalkley and Essex, 1999)[1] and, more generally, with conventional approaches to reconfiguring and revalorising urban spaces.

Olympic-led urban valorisation is, of course, not without its critics. Following Harvey's (1970) analysis of the contested nature of urban planning, regeneration attempts have often overly focused on spatial form at the expense of social processes (Gold and Gold, 2005). Grand Olympic projects often fail to fulfil their very public promises to regenerate communities or improve the environment once international attention has shifted. Here, less visible localised community-oriented benefits are consistently forfeited in order to secure the more spectacular and globally-focused features of the spectacle (Coaffee, 2010).

In this context, and with reference to the Olympic-related regeneration of East London, we identify and argue that one of the key – and often underplayed – transformations amid this regeneration process has been increased concerns for *safety and security* in the Olympic neighbourhood. This chapter draws on key debates within urban sociology and empirical data from safety and security strategies deployed at the 2012 London Olympic and Paralympic Games. In doing so, we argue that, via a number of processes, the Games have shepherded in a more intensive securitisation of East London. At the same time, idealised visions of the area are constructed, defined and protected, which strongly resonate with urban sociological notions of 'cleansing' space.

This chapter analyses the Olympic-related securitisation of East London and situates the city's Olympic experience within broader processes of mega event-driven urban securitisation and transformation. In doing so, the discussion is organised around two core themes of analysis: direct and overt forms of securitisation, such as visible the military presence and the fortress aesthetics of Stratford's various enclosed padded bunkers, and indirect forms of securitisation, ushered in by broader process of urban transformation replete with demographic shifts, repurposing of space and ushering in of new regimes of regulation.

---

[1] The key moment for thinking about the regenerative impacts of hosting Summer Olympics was undoubtedly Barcelona 1992. Indeed, it is now the 'Barcelona Model' of regenerating through the Olympics that provides the blueprint for other cities bidding for Summer Games (Garcia-Ramon and Albert, 2000).

Olympic security asserts physical, spatial and organisational imprints and is also situated within dual processes of globalised mega-event security practices and the traditions and path dependencies of domestic security approaches. To address such breadth of practice, this chapter is divided into three main areas of analysis. First, the key relevant yet generalised processes accompanying the reconfiguration of Olympic cities are examined. Rather than relaying a narrative list of temporal shifts, this discussion focuses on core thematic elements accompanying the creation of Olympic-related synthetic urbanism. The second area of discussion focuses more explicitly on the relationship between these processes and security and securitisation processes more explicitly. Here we argue that such contrived place-making is underpinned by multiple regimes of regulation and control. After a brief methodological discussion the paper then shifts to consider more explicit London-specific processes in Part III of the paper. Drawing on empirical analysis of the 2012 Games, this discussion examines how the capital's experience is situated against these broader trends and processes. Of particular importance here are the Olympic-specific modes of ordering the urban realm in the lead up to the Games. Overlayering these practices is a range of complex governance arrangements. Whilst notions of cohesive assemblages of control and of 'lockdown London' are common on the literature, and are acknowledged here, we argue that a series of contrasting, antagonistic and institutionally framed approaches to security reveal a more complex and negotiated Olympic security milieu.

Reconfiguring Olympic Cities

We have argued elsewhere (Fussey et al., 2012) that Olympic redevelopments reflect Sorkin's (1992a, 1992b) critique of the commercialised urban realm as a *variation on the theme park*. Here, Sorkin argued that despatialised urban hierarchies reshape the urban realm comprising three salient characteristics: the dissolution of the connection between spatial and cultural geographies, an obsession with security and new modes of segregation and the creation of a 'city of simulations' built upon a contrived and spuriously appropriated vision of the past (1992a: xiv).

Sorkin critiques the proliferation of commercially-oriented Disneyland-inspired fabricated geographies, drawing particular attention to the role of early globalised major events as a foundry in which these processes were forged, citing the Crystal Palace World's Fair of 1851 as the 'first great utopia of global capital' (1992b: 209).[2]

Whilst characterising such developments as an Olympic theme park provides a useful conceptual tool, there are a number of important variations that apply to the specific context of London. Here, urban governance arrangements are further complicated in this setting. Whilst the social, political and commercial cultures of global cities are shaped by the fluid circuits of globalisation (Zukin, 1995), the Olympic City is also subjected to governance by international sporting committees (in this case the IOC), which assert an array of demands imposed upon and mediated at multiple scales of urban governance. This brings an additional set of agendas that both influence local geography, but also embed additional visions and functions into the regeneration and branding of these spaces.

Many prior Olympic urban transformations have occurred on the fringes of extant urban settings or have shifted incumbent populations in order to accommodate the spectacle and its attendant theme park. The former Olympic cities of Beijing, Athens and Sydney all catalysed the creation of an extra-urban or suburban Olympic theme park. Olympic-related developments have also been viewed as attempts to 'cleanse' an area, and build it anew with corporate interests creating spaces reflecting their own image (Fussey et al., 2012). Commonly, this search for 'clean' tabula rasa space to safely enact the Games has resulted in the eviction or removal of 'offending' groups or unwanted businesses that do not suit the legacy criteria for the regenerated neighbourhood, or who are simply deemed 'in the way' of planned change. For example, over a million inconveniently-sited people were forcibly evicted from their homes ahead of the 1988 Seoul Olympics (Lenskyj, 2002) and up

---

[2] Indeed, Roche (2000: 135) has referred to what he termed the 'Olympic city theme park', relating to standardised requirements that must be delivery by Olympic city managers although he did not make mention of security as a key characteristic.

to 1.5 million residents were forcibly relocated as part of the *'New Beijing, Great Olympics'* spectacle of 2008 (Reuters, 2007). Yet, whilst grand-scale Hausmannisation has been an option for extra-urban settings and/or one-party states, for London 2012, however, the concentration of Olympic infrastructure on a brownfield site in the heart of an existing urban milieu raises additional considerations for its development. In particular, and notwithstanding the evictions of businesses (Raco and Tunney, 2010) and residents of social housing (Fussey et al., 2012), more subtle, and less visible, forms of regulation and 'civilising' processes can be observed exerting themselves upon London's Olympic geographies.

Siting the Games in the heart of an existing urban milieu renders impossible the adoption of 'blank-slate' approaches to cleansing apparent in the development of other Olympic theme parks. As such, more subtle approaches have been taken towards the reconfiguration of space and the cultivation of the Olympic brandscape. At the heart of this process are multiple expressions of security. In one arena, security has been a constant feature of Olympic planning since the terrorist attacks at Munich (1972) and, particularly, since 9/11 (see Fussey et al., 2011). But this chapter argues, in line with a strong theme now evident within urban sociology, that security does not operate according to straightforward logic of providing protection against a range of (real and perceived) malicious threats to athletes, spectators and the inhabitants of the Olympic theme park. Instead, attempts are made to contrive spatial dynamics that promote and protect the symbolic economies of the entrepreneurial city and 'manage-out' those deemed to challenge its prospects of commercial success. Such attempts and processes are discussed next.

Securitising the Olympic City

Running in tandem have been a series of elaborate security programmes that have served to draw a range of explicit and overt mechanisms of control into Olympic spaces. Whilst many commentators have sought to describe these in terms, often evoking Agamben's (2005) short monograph, of exceptionalism (e.g. Fussey et al., 2011; Marrero, 2011), such measures overflow from their contained Olympic landscapes and inundate the surrounding urban milieu.

The contemporary era of elaborate Olympic security can be traced to the mid-1970s with organisers of the 1976 Montreal Games determined not to host a repeat of the spectacles of barbarism played out in Munich. Munich's utopian low security experiment was thus followed by an unequal and opposite reaction of elaborate and intensive security measures, since woven into the fabric of Olympic planning, culminating in the dystopian symbols of electrified fences, military hardware and pervasive surveillance that accompany current celebrations of sporting excellence. Drawing heavy criticism at the time, the 1976 summer Olympics saw the first major deployment of public surveillance cameras alongside a significant and visible military presence and the isolation of Olympic-related transportation from the everyday movements of the city. Further mergers between the martial and metropolitan were cemented in Moscow four years later with infantry covering the city's streets bringing blanket zero-tolerance style measures to smother variously imagined infractions. In counterpoint, the rival and antagonistic cold-war creeds were showcased in Los Angeles during 1984, which allowed security planning to mirror the free market principles that governed the overall management of the Games. Olympic security thus extended beyond the mundane protection of competitors and spectators and adopted the requirements of supporting the needs of private capital and protecting sponsor's privileged access to the Olympic marketplace; a role that remained a focal point for anti-Olympic activists in London decades later; see Fig. 3.1. Rather than militarised Soviet assertions of sovereign monopolies of violence standing in counterpoint to capitalistic reliance on private security, both approaches became merged into Seoul's edifice of Olympic security four years later. This merger of military and private forms of security serves to challenge the notion of Olympic security as a manifestation of neo-liberal forms of control and remain a central axis of such programmes today. The uneasy co-existence and continual negotiations of these approaches – with G4S contractors initially training military personnel and the military eventually supplying soldiers to cover G4S's 'spectacular failure' (their words) to fulfil the basic terms of their Olympic contract – was played out publicly in

Fig. 3.1 Activism and the corporate image of Olympic security. Photo: Pete Fussey

London during the 2012 Games. These elements of military, surveillance, zero-tolerance policing, private security, and fortified architectures of enmity have since become consistent motifs of Olympic security programmes (see Fussey and Coaffee, 2012). Since the 1980s, these themes have found form in myriad ways including tanks on Barcelona's streets less than 15 years after Franco's death, sandbagged barricades scoring Atlanta's cityscape, alongside prohibitions on public assembly and marching for indigenous rights in 'Share the Spirit' Sydney.

The post 9/11 era ushered in a period of mega-sporting spectacles, often seen akin to cities under siege as terrorist risk, has seen security professionals attempt to deliver events in maximum safety and with minimum schedule disruption (Samatas, 2007; Boyle and Haggerty, 2009; Boyle, 2011; Fussey et al., 2011). Particularly notable among many examples, and extremely poignant when juxtaposed with its current fiscal plight, is the exorbitant (and in many senses inept) security plans delivered in Athens for the first post-9/11 summer Games. Termed 'superpanoptic' by some critics (Samatas, 2007), Athens spent well over five times' the security budget of Sydney 2000, deploying over 70,000 specially trained police and soldiers at Olympic venues whilst another 35,000 military personnel patrolled the streets. The military hardware utilised included 13,000 surveillance cameras, mobile surveillance vans, chemical detectors, Patriot anti-aircraft missile sites, NATO troops specialising in weapons of mass destruction, AWACS early warning surveillance planes, police helicopters, fighter jets, minesweepers and monitoring airships (Samatas, 2007).

Despite the apparent standardisation of these Olympic security motifs, the territory-blind 'security guarantee' demanded of host cities by the IOC, and the repeated presence of the same transnational security contractors across time and place it would be an error to consider such operations as completely alien to the environments that host them. As the following discussion relates, for all the simulated urbanism, imported security and orientation of domestic spaces toward external (media and tourist) audiences, Olympic security programmes are not reducible to simple colonial impositions of externally defined practice. Nor, despite initial appearances, do they comfortably sit in simple neo-liberal political-economic models of governance or, conversely, linear neo-Marxist conceptions of power. Deeper analysis reveals transnational governance to be just one of many scales of action exerting agency, institutional practice and operational orthodoxy, upon mega-event security practice. Particularly important here are the governance and security practices operating at local and regional levels that serve to accommodate, filter and shape these broader transnational processes. Local flavours remain. Global networks and processes intersect with, and become filtered through, the local. Due to this, analysis beyond taxonomies of Olympic security measures is necessary to understand how such strategies are executed in practice and to assess their diverse impacts upon the subjects and landscapes to which they are applied.

In doing so, this analysis of London's Olympic security strategy argues for the importance of accounting for three core locally situated processes when understanding its form and impact. These are: the traditions, organisational cultures and path dependencies of extant approaches towards urban security; the ways these intersect with the construction of specific threats; and the varied forms of nationally- and locally-situated security governance. Drawing on empirical analysis of related security practices in London before, during and after the Olympics, and following a brief methodological description, this chapter now addresses these three themes in turn.

Research began in 2005 utilising an array of qualitative techniques principally focussing on qualitative interviewing, focus groups and ethnographic methods amid key actors and agencies involved in developing and operationalising safety and security agendas in London, and specifically those areas of London hosting the 2012 Summer Olympics. Many of these participants operate in networks that have a restricted membership and access. As such, snowball-sampling techniques were extensively employed to identify, access, and engage key actors in these fields. Participants included (principally senior) strategic managers and decision-makers involved in devising and delivering national security policy, pan-London and, also, Olympic-specific security strategies. These interviews were complemented by two ethnographic projects. The first involved accompanying police and security professionals on patrol during the London Olympics and the second involved data drawn from more than a decade of engagement within the Olympic neighbourhood. Fussey had lived within two kilometres of the Olympic stadium for 14 years and between 2003 and 2010, worked less than 200 metres from the Olympic site and was in or passed through Stratford every day of the Games and for most of the preceding decade.

London's Security Traditions and Orthodoxies

London has a considerable track record in generating fortified enclaves in response to a range of perceived security challenges. Among the many candidates, the large scale 'ring of steel' and 'iron collar' developments aimed at demarcate large swathes of respectively, the City of London and Canary Wharf through physical and technological borders (Fussey et al., 2011) serve as particularly prominent examples. Here previous techniques focused on 'designing out' threats have commonly led to the use of ever-advancing surveillance technologies and the construction of fixed territorial borders, security cordons and 'rings of steel' to protect 'at risk' or vulnerable locations (Coaffee, 2004). Moreover, such techniques have often been supported by an array of legislative powers and regulatory guidance which targets the control of particular activities deemed unacceptable or inappropriate and repurposed toward more common yet less destructive acts.

Yet the Olympic park does not stand as a sterile promontory amid an otherwise dangerously imagined landscape. Instead, wider Olympic-inspired urban valorisation in progress both before and since the Games ushered multiple new formal and informal security measures across East London's splintered geographies. In doing so, a range of international, national and regional processes and demands have filtered through the local area. These in turn have been shaped and directed by London's extant traditions of ordering and 'purifying' the public realm.

'Cleansing' and 'purifying' strategies have a long history in the domain of urban management and were in particular evidence in London in the lead up to the Games. Sibley (1995: 72), for example, argued that the organisation of (urban) social space is often related to processes of 'spatial purification' where the scared spaces of the city – today the commercial zones rather than places of worship – are sanctified, with guardianship increasingly given over to security guards, not priests. In developing his analysis, Sibley (1995) drew on the classic work of Michel de Certeau who highlighted that the search for utopian urban organisation was often characterised by the need to create 'clean space' through the construction of exclusionary boundaries, 'strong feelings of abjection, a heightened consciousness of difference and, thus, a fear of mixing or the disintegration of boundaries' (Sibley, 1995: 78).

More recently, attempts to regenerate the urban realm has entailed multiple processes of control, including the criminalisation of those characterised as obstructing these developments as well as attempts to embed of security features into the built environment. For example, a number of writers have identified purified elements of the suburban living experience (Sennett, 1970), the socially 'cleansed' fortress city where the rich decant to hermetically sealed and spatially separate zones (Davis, 1998), or the myriad of attempts by urban authorities to systematically exclude the less powerful and less economically viable citizens though revanchist-style approaches (Smith, 1996).

This engineering of safe and secure public space has received particular attention in connection to the development of centres of urban consumption, particularly as part of a process to counteract the development of extra-urban shopping malls (Atkinson and Helms, 2007). In such accounts, urban centres regularly pursue conditions conducive to consumption via the improvement of security and the removal of visible signs of disorder. Here, new forms of controlled, neo-liberal and (conterminously) security-conscious urbanism has been seen to impact, most heavily, on minority groups such as buskers, street entertainers, leafleters, beggars, skateboarders and the homeless (Belina and Helms, 2003). Such marginalisation is targeted against social pollutants' (Urry, 1995: 188) or 'flawed consumers' (Bauman, 2005), flawed in their ability to consume the commercial and leisure industries championed and generated by the Olympics.

Urban regeneration associated with major sporting events has similarly focused on de-stigmatising low-demand neighbourhoods. As Ward (2001) noted in relation to the regeneration of East Manchester, UK, ahead of the 2002 Commonwealth Games, attempts to 'civilise' the city became an active strategy to reassure potential new residents that the area was safe, as the linkages between civil renewal and criminal justice system were made explicit:

> Heavy, time-intensive and intrusive in-your-face policing strategies would form the basis of a wider and sustained effort to perform a civilising of the area...it was made clear that...so called 'inappropriate behaviour' would not be tolerated. (Ward, 2001: 122)

A similar story has been articulated by Grey and Mooney (2011) in relation to the regeneration of Glasgow's East End in preparation for the 2014 Commonwealth Games. They point out how 'a concerted effort by the local state in conjunction with a range of central state and other agencies to "civilise" the population of Glasgow East' (Grey and Mooney, 2011: 9). Under the banner of 'community regeneration', a range of market-led and punitive polices in the fields of welfare, housing and environment are being deployed in an attempt to alter the perception and reality of such stigmatised areas.

Techniques of Ordering

In reality, de-stigmatisation is attempted through a range of strategies. Perhaps most visible are the Potemkin façades concealing the area's down-at-heel high streets and post-Blitz experiments with modernist architecture, such as Stratford's egregious 'Shoal' (Fig. 3.2), lest the area's socio-economic identity, built on decades of underinvestment, become visible to outsiders. In such circumstances, a splash of pastel colour becomes synecdoche for regeneration and deemed sufficient to bleach long histories of socio-economic injustice and cumulative disadvantage. Such is the power of these specious interventions, *The Guardian*

Fig. 3.2 The 'Shoal': public sculpture designed to conceal Stratford's municipal architecture. Photo: Pete Fussey

(2012a) unctuously announced to the nation that Leyton 'was like a village again' after one of its journalists witnessed a row of shop fronts shop fronts in immediate view of the Underground station (and extending no further) that had received a coat of paint as part of the area's Olympic Fringe investment (Fig. 3.3).

In London, such outward-facing urban beautification initiatives have been accompanied with a range of physical, technological and behavioural forms of regulation, many of which have remained in place after the Games. Key has been the design and manipulation of the physical environment to generate specific forms of social order. Here, a number of commentators have drawn attention to a raft of features designed to repel 'undesirable' populations. These include the design of street furniture to deny the homeless a place to sleep

Fig. 3.3   Potemkin Façades in Leyton: pastel colours as a signifier of regeneration. Photo: Pete Fussey

(Davis, 1990) and other architectures of enmity such as the 'anti-homelessness spikes' that proliferated across London's sheltered door-ways during 2014 (*The Guardian*, 2014). New urban developments are thus saturated with situational crime prevention measures draw-ing on Oscar Newman's (1972) classic concept of 'defensible space', which sought to establish ownership over 'dead spaces' or, at least, prevent their desecration. For example, UK planning legislation requires housing developments to conform to the Association of Chief Police Officers' (ACPO) standards of secure-by-design. In a further extension of these principles, the ACPO funded National Counter Terrorism Security Office (NaCTSO) expends considerable resources campaigning for additional situational security features to protect against urban terrorism. The former Olympic Athletes village, now East Village, has been embedded with the most stringent ACPO secure-by-design standards yet conceived which, as part of London's Olympic security legacy, have become a template for new housing developments in the area (interview with Olympic security planner 2012).

Other interventions include the increasing deployment of increasingly potent and pervasive expansive surveillance technologies (at a time when many other public spaces, reshaped by recession, are scaling back their CCTV coverage, see Fussey, 2012). Whilst many strategies, such as Automatic Number Plate Recognition (ANPR) cameras were originally commissioned for military use, they are being increasingly redeployed to regulate domestic spaces. In the process, strategies of digital surveillance are increasingly central to narratives of urban renaissance (Coleman, 2004; Fussey, 2004). The Olympics stimulated substantial expansion of ANPR capability in Newham both in terms of hardware and the tech-nological means to gather and analyse large volumes of data. As the Metropolitan Police Service (MPS) publically stated, a radically strength-ened approach to ANPR was introduced where,

During the Olympics new ANPR tactics were developed, enabling crime to be solved and risk to be mitigated in new ways. This exposed the chronic shortcomings of [existing approaches to managing ANPR data] and made it clear that significant risk would be reintroduced if the National CT ANPR System was switched off. (Metropolitan Police Service, n.d.)

New data handling methods developed for the Olympics thus formed a range of material security legacies via retention of computational and surveillance hardware and, crucially, the development of techniques that informed wider and more enduring practices. These new 'technologies of control' (Foucault, 1977) have since become a foundational principle for current approaches to ANPR data handling at the national level (Metropolitan Police Service, n.d.).

Asserting territorial control and the redistribution of risks through a hardened environment is only one social control practice among many. Rose (2000) argues that the application of risk management may generate contradictory results, with outcomes that may both include *and* exclude different subjects of control. Nor are spatial articulations of control reducible to binaries of inclusion and exclusion. As the rise and widespread Olympic deployment of technologies such as ANPR attests, the surveillance and monitoring of mobilities has become increasingly prominent. This monitoring is also not always direct, formal, and coercive. As Adey (2008) identifies in his analysis of attempts to engineer feeling and emotion through architecture, a number of affective and suggestive forms of control – modes of seduction *and* coercion – are increasingly incorporated into the fabric of the physical environment. Indeed, since the IOC's creation of the 'Olympic identity' – and its associated imagery – in 1968, mega-event management planning has placed a premium on creating conspicuous and contrived atmospheres of festivity (see Pavoni, 2012). In London this translated into the language of 'Look and Feel', a mantra that animated police work as much as any area of Olympic planning.

As such, these physical and technological means are complemented by a range of behavioural regulations, policing strategies and neighbour-hood management techniques embedded within regimes of urban regeneration. For example, in the UK since 1998, attempts by many local governments and police authorities to manage out 'anti-social' activities through punitive orders and curfews have escalated with rapidity. In the search for secure and purified urban space, urban regeneration is thus far from a neutral, benevolent and egalitarian process with specific visions of order, variously constructed around utilitarian terms of 'respect' and 'civility' (Bannister et al., 2006). Hence, as Raco (2003) notes, new discourses and meanings of place accompany their physical transformation. For the Olympics, such behavioural management tools included bespoke Olympic Anti-Social Behaviour Orders (ASBOs), pre-charge bail conditions (see Fussey, 2015), and the creation of 'dispersal zones' to limit assembly of groups of individuals (see Kennelly and Watt, 2013, for analysis of how the latter measures are experienced by marginalised youth in the area).

Whilst the proliferation of security and regulation are pivoted towards specific versions of order and citizenship, as well as the management of specific security threats, the varied approaches do not necessarily cohere around an integrated assemblage of, or unified aspiration for, authority. Although the winners and losers are easily identified in such securitised and purified settings, it is important not to overlook the contestations involved in the governance of reconfigured spaces. Notwithstanding the fact that national policies can and are reflected locally (Smith, 1996), the UK over the past 15 years has seen the devolution of many functions of urban governance to the local level. This particularly applies to issues of crime and security, which, as Raco (2003) argued also formed the main site of contention between different agencies and actors involved in regenerating the urban realm. These relationships become further complicated in the Olympic city, where global sponsors and international regulatory bodies place demands on, and seek to influence policies of, the local state. These different voices do not necessarily harmonise. An added complexity is the multiplicity of space. Spaces simultaneously hold different functions that also shift over the course of time (Zukin, 1995). In such settings, singular visions of order will inevitably generate conflict given the range of claims to particular spaces. Such contestations impact on regimes of control. Here, drawing Foucault's (2007) lesser commented-upon lectures at the Collège de France, Fussey (2013) has identified how different institutions may simultaneously apply different aims and values to subjects as they traverse their differing spheres of influence hosted within the same space. In such circumstances, souls are neither trained nor moulded. Nor is there an overarching goal, or a finished (reformed) subject, as more traditional interpretations of discipline and panopticism would have it.

Pluralities of Security Governance

Part of the explanation for this plurality is the sheer scale and range of activities considered threatening to an event governed by planners exerting a very low threshold of acceptable risk. Formal security measures were as the then director general of MI5 stated at the time, geared toward an increased emphasis on 'home grown' terrorism and on the internationalisation of domestic grievances. Such was the emphasis during this period that the government was compelled towards an unprecedented doubling of the agency's budget (Manningham-Buller, 2011). Indeed, the threat of terrorism at the Olympics was deemed so significant that the Games occupied a central theme of the UK's national counter-terrorism (CONTEST) strategy when revised in 2011 (HM Government, 2011a). Here, among talk of the overall strategic responses to terrorism the document noted that that the UK had guaranteed to the IOC to 'take all financial, planning and operational measures necessary to guarantee the safety and the peaceful celebration of the Games' (p. 105). Specifically, it highlighted a set of issues related to the threat and response to heightened anticipation of terrorist attack:

> Terrorism poses the greatest security threat to the Games . . . London 2012 will take place in an unprecedentedly high threat environment. Threat levels can change rapidly but by planning against a threat level of Severe we have maximised our flexibility to respond to a *range of threats* (HM Government, 2011a: 106; emphasis added).

At the same time the UK threat level[3] for the Games was classified at an elevated 'severe' rating rather than the less precarious 'substantial' grading that had applied for much of the period preceding and succeeding the Games.

The urban rioting that engulfed London (and elsewhere in England) – including the Host Boroughs of Hackney and Waltham Forest – during 2011 coincided with an IOC delegation visit to check on logistics ahead of

---

[3] The government's Joint Intelligence Analysis Centre (JTAC) and Mi5 grade the level of threat to the UK's critical national infrastructure. There are five categories of threat, in order: low, moderate, substantial, severe and critical.

the 2012 Games and a series of 'test events' in some Olympic venues. Whilst the IOC publically expressed confidence in the local security operations, others were more critical. Perhaps most notable were concerns voiced by the Chinese government that, 'The image of London has been severely damaged, leaving people sceptical and worried about the public security situation during the London Olympics' (*The Daily Telegraph, The Daily Telegraph*, 2011). Although officially denied at the time the rioting exerted an important influence on Olympic planning. Following the cancellation of a number of high profile sporting fixtures at the time on police advice, the rioting also occurred just prior to a review of Olympic policing numbers that concluded with a recommendation to dramatically increase the provision of private security guards, a commitment that G4S failed to uphold.

A number of key issues are raised here. First is the breadth of such objectives and how, on reflection, they are a combination of aims, strategy and operational outcomes. Related and important are the number of different organisations and agencies responsibilised to address the range of conceived risks and threats to the Games. Many of these issues were addressed during the period of intensive security testing in the year leading up to the Olympics.

Five formal testing events took place with the aim of incrementally increasing the stress on the various security systems. Yet these events were not self-contained. Olympic search and screening processes were tested at English Premier League football matches during January 2012 (Johnson, 2012), the military undertook additional exercises in London in late 2011 and May 2012 (Parker, 2012) and numerous affiliated events aimed at binding hitherto unconnected organisations also took place and identifying the range of risks and threats to the Games.

Given such dynamism and diversity of threats, and the plurality of actors and agencies involved, security aims were defined broadly, and possible Olympic-related infractions defined broader still. Regarding the latter, traditional judicial definitional precision was subverted by the Metropolitan Police Service's ambiguous and extensive definition of Olympic-related offences as, 'any crime that has or may have an impact upon the effective delivery *or image* of the Games' (The London Criminal Courts Solicitors' Association, 2012; emphasis added). These infractions therefore incorporated challenges to the external presentation of the Games and, also, threats, however minor, to the commercial monopolies of Olympic sponsors. Such curated representations also extended to security agencies themselves. In addition to the importance of expressing the symbolism of security measures (Boyle and Haggarty, 2012), the police were particularly sensitised to their representation in the media. For example, during the course of ethnographic observations of the Games, Fussey was continually asked if he was a journalist and offered meetings with press officers. Among many examples, was on 12 July 2012, whilst observing the deployment of surface-to-air missiles on a residential block a few hundred metres from his home of 10 years, a member of the Metropolitan Police asked if he was a journalist before reeling off some of the benefits Olympic security would bring the local neighbourhood. He was an apparent member of the Metropolitan Police Territorial Support Group, specialising in violent public order confrontations and likely first-time visitor to the neighbourhood.

Olympic security aims were defined widely. In early 2012, these core aims were defined as:

1. Borders;
2. Transport;
3. VIP protection;
4. Venue security;
5. Mitigating disruptive elements;
6. Intelligence of threats;
7. Disrupting those who pose a threat to the games;
8. Deploying resources and personnel effectively;
9. Maintaining effective command and control and coordination;
10. Ensuring parallel events are safe and secure;
11. Reassuring the public;
12. Obtaining effective support from informational partners. (Raine, 2012)

Under such arrangements, it is clear that specific state agencies do not have the capacity or capability to deliver on all 12 of the stated Olympic security objectives. To a large extent, diverse agencies remain heterogeneous within larger coalitions of security practice. As Foucault (2008: 42) recognised in his later work on biopolitical power, strategies do 'not stress resolution in a unity. The function of strategic logic is to establish the possible connections between disparate terms which remain disparate . . . the logic of connections between the heterogeneous'. It is therefore important to acknowledge that, whilst homogenising tendencies and attempts to co-ordinate activities exist, security ensembles are necessarily diverse. Moreover, within such a breadth of aims, security providers, with differing institutional agendas, found different elements to prioritise, some of which existed in competition with other stakeholders. As such, a premium was placed on enhanced co-ordination between the various security actors, something that had proved a critical point of failure at other Olympic Games including Munich, Atlanta and Athens. Organizational infrastructure and processes were thus developed to foster co-ordination and communication.[4] A brief examination of the way in which London's Olympic security strategy was mobilized, thus underlines the heterogeneity of actors, alongside the scale and novelty of the task. In doing so, it challenges the view that control is exerted cohesively and in concert. Much of the command and control was exercised locally but these arrangements were organised under the National Olympic Security Co-ordination (NOSC) strategy, which served as a single point of coordination and a means of embedding the National Olympic Safety Security plan (NOSSP) into local activities. As well as its hierarchical layering, such arrangements are nodal in terms of geography and organisation. The NOSC cleaved London into three distinct areas of influence (each attributed a bronze commander): 'Central', 'River' (incorporating large non-Park venues such as the ExCel centre) and 'Park' (Stratford). Organizationally, NOSC is also configured over four 'hubs' rendered visible by the NOSC 'paw print' diagram. The four metacarpal hubs were: COBR (an acronym of Cabinet Briefing Rooms, a central government crisis response committee normally convened at times of threat or crisis), The London Operations Centre (focused towards the governance structures of London such as

---

[4] This premium on sharing information within the Olympic authorities contrasted sharply with way information was shaped and impressions managed across the boundary to non-Olympic agencies via LOCOG's stringent communications strategy.

the Greater London Authority), The Main Operations Centre (focusing on Olympic venues and 'partner' agencies), The Transport Co-ordination Centre (police and transport operators), and The National Olympic Co-ordination Centre (NOCC). Each of these hubs then linked to further sub-organisations within their respective domains.

Security policies and practices inhabited all four hubs but were most heavily concentrated in the National Co-ordination Centre. Here connectivity between the central government and gold commanders was prioritized and enacted, situation and intelligence reports collated and disseminated and plans developed for operations covering the days that then lay ahead. Despite the plurality of actors and public articulations of multi-agency operations, the police were unequivocally the lead partners and to underline the point, the core NOCC team was based in Scotland Yard under the management of the Metropolitan Police. Such congregations were significant and ahead of the games it was anticipated that the NOCC would involve as many as 60 decision-makers in a single room (Morris, 2012). The extent to which effective co-ordination and unified action resulted is, of course, an empirical question. For some senior practitioners, the co-ordination effort evoked a high degree of uncertainty. Indeed, one of the Metropolitan Police heads of operational planning for Games' security felt that because, 'many elements and organisations [of the Paw print model] are new, it cannot be anticipated how they will work together' (Broadhurst, 2012). Other senior practitioners present in the NOCC during the Games expressed a different view:

> . . . integrated decision-making during the Olympics was one of the real success stories of the Games. Now the Games are over and people have drifted off into different roles we're looking to implement similar decision-making models across a range of infrastructure settings.[5]

Under such arrangements, security legacies adopt abstract and procedural forms rather than the more familiar manifestations of hardware and personnel.

---

[5] Government Olympic Executive representative, interviewed January 2013.

Yet the delivery of such procedures and processes was far from seamless and, in many cases, exposed tensions between varied operational aims pursued by different Olympic security actors. As Fussey (2015) notes, particular tensions existed between Metropolitan Police Service responses to suspicious activity to generate a sterile crime scene compared to the British Transport Police that are incentivised to keep people and transport infrastructure moving. In other respects, the primacy given to maximising crowd flow meant fewer restrictions and coercive mechanisms than those existing during non-Games' time. As one senior manager at Network Rail interviewed during the Games expressed, under normal circumstances a heavy emphasis falls on fare dodging. During the Olympic period, ticket barriers were left open and priorities shifted toward the free movement of people and preventing crushing. Here, the maintenance of flow and movement attained primacy over rail operators' revenue raising, and thus nuances totalising conceptions of 'lockdown London'. Indeed, as the Games progressed it became clear from multiple interviews with crowd managers and public order police officers alongside observations in surveillance camera control rooms that, in the absence of a major terrorist incident, much of the Olympic security architecture became repurposed towards crown management. Flow became the principle focus.

Other areas of formal social control were also characterised by tension. In the years leading up to the Games, and in a climate of financial austerity many 'Host Borough' municipalities in the suspended plans to expand their public surveillance camera networks, believing this would be funded as part of the broader Olympic security strategy (CCTV manager, interviewed March 2012). However, Olympic security planners, affronted by such opportunistic instrumentality, threatened local community safety managers with the deployment of mobile systems that could be redeployed elsewhere after the Games (interview with Olympic surveillance camera strategist, March 2012).

Other strategically placed areas were left without ownership as late as five weeks before the opening ceremony. Meridian Square, the area outside of Stratford station's south (and, before the Games, only) exit, in front of the transport hub feeding 80 per cent of the Olympic Park, was eventually afforded to Transport for London (TfL) whilst other stakeholders (including the Metropolitan Police and Newham Council) were reluctant to take control of such a high-profile, high-risk (and presumably resource hungry) site. Moreover, further counterbalancing public expressions of integrated operations, preparedness and 'business as usual', some of the event planning was not finalised with only two days remaining before the Opening Ceremony.[6] Such events demonstrate how territorial control may be less about avaricious and insatiable desires for coercion in the service of particular interests – as volumes of dystopian conspiratorial accounts envisage – but, rather, is conditioned by issues of realpolitik and aversion to reputational risk.

As the aforementioned discussion has detailed, much is made of the connectivity of different security organisations and, conceptually, the magnetism of varied Olympic security stakeholders towards each other implies upscaled and highly potent coalitions of coercive agents. Whilst such accounts have much to offer, the fragmentation, incoherencies and contradictions of security governance also reveal much about the intensity and coercive scope of Olympic security operations. As the failure of G4S at the Games, and the streams of senior police officers, themselves threated by post-Games austerity cuts, queuing up to ensure this ineptitude was afforded maximum exposure in the national media attests, these partnerships are far from harmonious. Moreover, other tensions existed within the same type of organisation. For example, one initial ambition was to have 'mutual aid' (i.e. police from outside of London) patrol within the less challenging, more sanctified and pre-screened Olympic Park whilst local officers would operate in the more complex and challenging urban milieu that encircled it. According to one public order specialist interviewed during the Games, almost all of the public order incidents and crimes identified in the opening days of the Games were reported by mutual aid police brought in from outside of London. This indicates differing frames of risk management, diverse readings of the urban environment and varied acceptability of ambient levels of low-level disorder across different public police forces.

---

[6] Interview with TfL Olympic crowd manager 22 August 2012.

Further still, some expressions of security were excessive in terms of pedantry and lapses in common-sense and served to both undermine the public relations strategy of the Olympic security programme and, also, irritate many of those charged with delivering it. Moreover, such excesses demonstrate both the reach and embeddedness of corporate branding of the Games and, crucially, the ways in which policing and securitisation practices are implicated in upholding this connection. Of the many possible candidates, particularly notable examples include: the questioning of a man photographing a fish tank on suspicion of conducting hostile reconnaissance for a terrorist attack (*Amateur Photographer*, 2012); excessive questioning of those wearing clothes with prominent displays of competing (non-Olympic) brands ('Brand Police on Patrol to Enforce Sponsors' Exclusive Rights', *International Business Times*, 2012); pre-emptive arrest of a graffiti artists, 'Ser' (Darren Cullen) who had previously been approached by Team GB to adorn part of the Olympic Village with its self-professed 'edgy' and 'urban' (and now 'iconic') aesthetics; in Surrey, a man with Parkinson's disease and attendant facial muscle rigidity was arrested for 'not smiling' during the men's cycling road race (Police claimed they were concerned about his demeanour, proximity to protestors and that he was 'not visibly enjoying the event') (*The Guardian*, 2012b); and a Breton man watching his daughter compete in the Women's football was threatened with ejection from Hamden Park and possible arrest for waving the non IOC endorsed Gwenn-ha-du, the flag of Brittany, to celebrate her regional affiliation (*le Parisien*, 2012). Moreover, the police themselves became subjected to such zealous forms of image management, with those monitoring the rowing events at Eton Dorney being forced to empty their snacks into clear bags to avoid inadvertently advertising non-sponsors' lines in junk food (*The Daily Telegraph, The Daily Telegraph*, 2012).

Conclusion

Many analyses of Olympic security correctly focus on the dizzying array of military hardware and the range of intensive measures designed to restrict behaviour and mobility. However, the existence of such initiatives tells only part of the story. Often missing are examinations of their operation in practice, the tensions and inconsistencies that accompany their deployment and, also, the more indirect forms of regulation that become yoked with programmes of professed regeneration or urban valorisation. A spectrum of controlling mechanisms are shepherded into urban spaces during processes of regeneration and renewal. Much of the urban sociological literature has pointed to the ways in which these mechanisms have been used to assert particular commercially-oriented values at the expense of marginalised population. However, drawing on empirical analysis of London's Olympic area this chapter argues that numerous tensions within this process, including contested governance arrangements and the plurality of social control requirements, are particularly important. In the Olympic city, these processes gain further complexity and exceptionality via the incursion of international sponsors and regulatory bodies (and their values) into the local realm as well as the importance placed upon ensuring the games will pass off without serious security breaches. Hosting urban mega-events draws a multitude of local, national and international agencies into the governance of associated security practices (see *inter alia* Boyle, 2011; Fussey et al., 2011). As a corollary, although Olympic security operations place a premium on co-ordination it may be argued that multiple ambitions, aims and organisational logics, and thus different ambitions for control, may be seen to operate simultaneously.

Many attempts also exist to try to make sense of these enormous incursions of security techniques and technologies into the civil sphere of the Olympic neighbourhood. Particularly prominent are notions of 'lockdown London' where, to misappropriate Thomas Carlyle, the velvet glove of 'celebration capitalism' (Boykoff, 2013) is delivered with an iron fist of militarised security. Variously, the State is conceived as sovereign in coercive intent and presence or, conversely, replaced by commercial security as part of a wider project of neoliberalisation of security. With Olympic security programmes attaining such scale and exceptionality, both explanations can be accommodated. Ethnographic analysis of the form, delivery and impact of the London Olympic security operation reveals a more complex, contested and negotiated set or arrangements. Under such circumstances the State is neither omnipresent nor washed away by currently of neoliberalism or governmentality. In such circumstances Eick's (2011) evocation of Jessop's (1994) notion of the 'hollow state' – in the sense that numerous social and welfare-focused state responsibilities become absented yet the 'harder' coercive functions persist – may hold particular utility. Yet, as we have argued throughout this chapter, it is not just the presence of these power relations, interests and coercive mechanisms that are important, but their modes of application and delivery.

In this sense, security legacies become complex and multi-faceted and do not solely attend to the retention or otherwise of visible hardware. Much does remain in place, however. Legacy was always an important feature of key component of the overall London 2012 security plan and was at the forefront of policing strategies. As one Metropolitan Police chief articulated in 2006 during the early days of Olympic security planning,

> we want the security legacy to be us leaving a safe and secure environment for the communities of East London after the Games, on issues such as safer neighbourhoods, lighting and crime prevention. We want a Games legacy that will reduce crime and the fear of crime. (cited in Boyle and Haggerty, 2009: 267)

Yet many of the more visible, and particularly militarised, features of the Olympic security project were removed after the Games. Missiles were dismantled and troops redeployed. Comprehensive Spending Reviews, austerity measures and radical restructuring of many policing infrastructures after the Games meant that London's Olympic security arrangements could not continue unaltered and in situ. Leave was cancelled for many policing and military personnel during the Games, finite security resources were transferred to London from other parts of the country to London and Olympic planning progressed in a fiscal bubble unmoored from the global financial realities of the time. All of these processes point to the unsustainability of maintaining things as they were. A range of material and political realities thus prevented the exceptional becoming the norm and perhaps provide some relief to the many dystopian nightmares and other Orwellian-inspired imaginaries offered at the time.

Olympic security legacies are complex entities and persevere in a range of both direct and indirect ways across multiple temporal and spatial frames. Despite the emphasis on deploying tried and tested techniques, a degree of security experimentation is common at Olympics and other urban mega-events. For example, a progenitor of the NSA's programme of colossal data harvesting, mining and matching, was carried out at Salt Lake City where the FBI and NSA employed US telecommunications carrier Qwest Communications International to intercept and monitor all email and SMS traffic around the time of the 2002 Winter Games (*Wall Street Journal*, 2013). Urban mega-events such as the Olympics host and catalyse the development and transfer of security knowledge and practice and, in this sense, regularly contribute to security legacies.

In terms of material security architecture, much was left behind after the London Olympics. One such example has been the retention of large numbers of mobile ANPR camera units in Newham, one of the five Olympic host boroughs (NPCC, n.d.). As noted before, more sophisticated forms of handling and processing data from automated smarty CCTV systems such as these are a direct result of London's Olympic security operation. In other respects, the armed British Transport Police officers that regularly patrol London's major train stations are another legacy of the Games (interview with senior police security planner 2012). Dispersal orders, outlined earlier, remain in place in many Host Boroughs years after the well-protected Olympic flame was extinguished. Most significantly, it is the security infrastructure embedded within transformative urban regeneration programmes, and promoted as central to long term community safety, yet also implicated in redrawing lines of inclusion and disqualification, that are the most significant and lasting material security legacy of the Games. The story of securitising the 2012 Games did not start on 6 July 2005, but evolved over many decades into protection of the Olympic spectacle. Nor did it end once the Games concluded. The security legacy in London is one in which urban regeneration *and* security are most closely integrated in modern Olympic history. In London *permanent* design and architectural features have been embedded within the material landscape.

In other respects, a significant repository of knowledge and expertise has been retained in London-based networks regarding civil contingency planning for an array of disruptive challenges, and securitising urban areas at home and abroad. For example, in Glasgow preparations for the 2014 Commonwealth Games, aimed at mitigating risks from international terrorism, drew heavily on London's experiences and similarly built on of perimeter security, technological surveillance, Crime Prevention through Environmental Design (CPTED) principles and intensified policing strategies. This knowledge is mobile and becomes transported via the commercial marketplace for security knowledge, in addition to other means, and is transferred across the globe for when mega-events arrive elsewhere. Following Massey's (2007) analysis of London, and her arguments of how the city is not just the recipient of global processes, but also its producer, London is not just a centre for producing and reproducing global circuits in the financial realm, but also occupies a similar role in relation to security practice. Clear lines of security transfer exist between London and Rio, for example. Indeed recent visits to Brazil by the UK Foreign and Commonwealth Office, intended to allow the UK security industry 'to pursue commercial opportunities and become the partner of choice for sport security' has reported that: 'Brazil sees a step change in the security situation in Rio as a legacy of the Olympic Games in 2016 in particular and is making progress on sustainable "pacification" of favelas' (FCO, 2011).

Notably, elements of Rio's Olympic-linked favela 'pacification' programme, extend beyond locally-specific militarise forms of policing to embrace a range of technological security practices also deployed in London. As a result of the 2016 Games local policing units responsible are better able to purchase more advanced surveillance equipment with some local claims that *Rocinha*, the largest *favela* in Rio has the most expansive public camera surveillance in the world, with more cameras per resident than London (BBC, 2013).

Also overseas, core elements of the London experience was replicated at the 2014 Winter Olympics in Sochi, where a hyper-carceral security plan was executed. Whilst risk was framed differently in Sochi where the concern was the ethno-national conflict in the Northern Caucasus amidst threats by Islamic separatists to attack the Games, clear replication of security themes took place. Here, the security deployed included familiar features such as: air missile defence systems; restricted airspace;

tighter national border controls; the nearby stationing of warships and high-speed patrol boats; checkpoints in perimeter fencing with an array of scanning devices for explosives and radioactive material and controlled zones for searching people and their belongings; a plethora of surveillance camera systems with an estimated 5,500 cameras deployed as part of the 'safe Sochi' initiative; a bespoke Olympic CCTV control centre; passenger profiling at Sochi international airport; drones hovering overhead; robotic vehicles for bomb detection; and surface to air missile installations (see, for example, *Moscow Times*, 2013). Alongside this standardised security operation sat unprecedented monitoring efforts to track telephone and online communications.

The increasing trend towards siting the Olympic theme park and its ordering mechanisms within such congested urban settings, piloted in Barcelona and finessed in London, generates the likelihood of hosting ever-more elaborate security programmes in increasingly complex and heterogeneous urban environments. Here, security will always become negotiated and uneven in its application. It will also inevitably exert a legacy imprint on the spaces to which it is applied. Moreover, as we have argued elsewhere (Fussey et al., 2012) it will always encounter ambiguities that are likely to become exaggerated. In such circumstances, the anthropological insights of Mary Douglas (1966), offered 50 years ago, gain particular prescience. With diversity, ambiguity and the uncategorisable being perpetually encountered in the global city, and thus readily characterised as threatening and disorderly, threats become perennial and demands for security to address them become insatiable.

References

Adey, P. (2008) 'Airports, mobility, and the calculative architecture of affective control', *Geoforum* 1: 438–451.

Agamben, G. (2005) *State of Exception*. Chicago, IL: University of Chicago Press.

Amateur Photographer. (2012) 'Fish photographer caught in Olympics terror alert', 23 May 2012.

Atkinson, R. and Helms, G. (2007) *Securing the Urban Renaissance*. Bristol: Policy Press.

Bannister, J., Fyfe, N. and Kearns, A. (2006) 'Respectable or respectful? (In)civility and the city', *Urban Studies* 43(5/6): 919–937.

Bauman, Z. (2005) *Work, Consumerism and the New Poor.* Maidenhead: Open University Press.

BBC News. (2013) 'Rio favela has more CCTV cameras than London', 11 January 2013, http://www.bbc.co.uk/news/world-latin-america-20992062

Belina, B. and Helms, G. (2003) 'Zero tolerance for the industrial past and other threats: policing and urban entrepreneurialism in Britain and Germany', *Urban Studies* 40(9): 1845–67.

Boykoff, J. (2013) *Celebration Capitalism and the Olympic Games.* London: Routledge.

Boyle, P. (2011) 'Knowledge networks: mega-events and security expertise', in C. Bennett and K. Haggerty (eds.), *Security Games: Surveillance and Control at Mega-Events.* London: Taylor and Francis.

Boyle, P. and Haggerty, K. (2009) 'Spectacular security: mega-events and the security complex', *International Political Sociology* 3(3): 257–74.

Boyle, P. and Haggerty, K. (2012) 'Planning for the worst: risk, uncertainty and the Olympic Games', *British Journal of Sociology*, 63(2): 241–259.

Broadhurst, R. (2012) 'Policing the Games', Paper presented at the Olympic and Paralympic Security Conference, Royal United Services Institute, Whitehall, 25 January.

Burbank, M. J., Andranovich, G. D. and Heying, C. H. (2001) *Olympic Dreams: The Impact of Mega-Events on Local Politics.* London: Lynne Reiner.

Chalkley, B. and Essex, S. (1999) 'Urban development through hosting international events: a history of the Olympic Games', *Planning Perspectives* 14: 369–94.

Coaffee, J. (2004) 'Rings of steel, rings of concrete and rings of confidence: designing out terrorism in central London pre and post 9/11', *International Journal of Urban and Regional Research* 28(1): 201–211.

Coaffee, J. (2010) 'Urban regeneration and renewal at the Olympics', in J. Gold and M. Gold (eds.), *Olympic Cities: Urban Planning, City Agendas and the World's Games, 1896 to the Present.* London: Routledge.

Coleman, R. (2004) *Reclaiming the Streets: Surveillance, Social Control and the City.* Cullompton: Willan.

Daily Telegraph. (2011) 'Robertson rejects Chinese criticism of 2012 security', 10 August 2011.

Daily Telegraph. (2012) 'London 2012: police told to empty crisps into plastic bags to avoid advertising rival brands in Olympics', 17 July 2012.

Davis, M. (1990) *City Of Quartz*. London: Verso.

Davis, M. (1998) *Ecology of Fear: Los Angeles and the Imagination of Disaster*. New York: Metropolitan Books.

Douglas, M. (1966) *Purity and Danger*. London: Routledge.

Eick, V. (2011) 'Secure our profits!: the FIFA in Germany 2006', in C. Bennet and K. Haggerty (eds.), *Security Games: Surveillance and Control at Mega-Events*. London: Routledge.

FCO [Foreign and Commonwealth Office]. (2011) *Rio 2016 Olympics: Sport Security*, Rio de Janeiro: British Consulate General Rio de Janeiro, 2011.

Foucault, M. (1977) *Discipline and Punish: The Birth of the Prison*. London: Penguin

Foucault, M. (2007) *Security, Territory, Population: Lectures at the Collège de France 1977–1978*. Basingstoke: Palgrave Macmillan.

Foucault, M. (2008) *The Birth of Biopolitics: Lectures at the Collège de France 1978–1979*. Basingstoke: Palgrave Macmillan.

Fussey, P. (2004) 'New Labour and new surveillance: theoretical and political ramifications of CCTV implementation in the UK', *Surveillance & Society* 2(2/3): 251–269.

Fussey, P. (2012) 'Eastern promise: East London transformations and the state of surveillance', *Information Polity* 17(1): 21–34.

Fussey, P. (2013) 'Contested topologies of UK counter-terrorist surveillance: the rise and fall of Project Champion', *Critical Studies on Terrorism* 6(3): 351–370.

Fussey, P. (2015) 'Command, control and contestation: negotiating security at the London 2012 Olympics', *The Geographical Journal* 181(3): 212–223.

Fussey, P. and Coaffee, J. (2012) 'Balancing local and global security leitmotifs: counter-terrorism and the spectacle of sporting mega-events', *International Review of the Sociology of Sport* 47(3): 268–285.

Fussey, P., Coaffee, J., Armstrong, G. and Hobbs, R. (2011) *Securing and Sustaining the Olympic City: Reconfiguring London for 2012 and Beyond*. Aldershot: Ashgate.

Fussey, P., Coaffee, J., Armstrong, G. and Hobbs, D. (2012) 'The Regeneration Games: purity and security in the Olympic City', *British Journal of Sociology* 63(2): 260–284.

Garcia-Ramon, M. and Albert, A. (2000) 'Pre-Olympic and post-Olympic Barcelona, a model for urban regeneration today?' *Environment and Planning A* 32(8): 1331–34.

Gold, J. and Gold. M. (2005) *Cities of Culture: Staging International Festivals and the Urban Agenda, 1951–2000*. Aldershot: Ashgate.

Gray, N. and Mooney, G. (2011) 'Glasgow's new urban frontier: "Civilising" the population of Glasgow East', *City* 15(1): 4–24.

Guardian. (2012) 'London Olympics 2012: Leyton "like a village again" after council makeover', *The Guardian*, 22 June 2012.

Guardian. (2014) 'Anti-homeless spikes are just the latest in "defensive urban architecture"', *The Guardian*, 12 June 2014.

Harvey, D. (1970) 'Social processes and spatial form: an analysis of the conceptual problems of urban planning', *Papers in Regional Science* 25(1): 47–69.

HM Government. (2011a) *CONTEST: The United Kingdom's Strategy for Countering Terrorism*. London: The Stationery Office.

International Business Times (2012) 'London Olympics 2012: Brand Police on Patrol to Enforce Sponsors' Exclusive Rights', accessed 1 May 2017, http://www.ibtimes.co.uk/london-2012-olympics-banned-words-advertising-gold-363429.

Jessop, B. (1994) 'The transition to post-Fordism and the Schumpeterian Workfare State', in R. Burrows, and B. Loader (eds.), *Towards a Post-Fordist Welfare State*, London: Routledge.

Johnson, I. (2012) 'Managing the security challenge', Presented at the Olympic and Paralympic Security Conference, Royal United Services Institute, Whitehall, 25 January.

Le Parisien. (2012) 'Prière de ranger ce drapeau breton!', 30 July 2012, http://www.leparisien.fr/sports/JO/jeux-olympiques-londres-2012/jo-priere-de-ranger-ce-drapeau-breton-30-07-2012-2107593.php.

Lenskyj, H. (2002) *Best Olympics Ever? The Social Impacts of Sydney 2000*. New York: State University of New York Press.

Manningham-Buller, E. (2011) 'Terror', *BBC Radio 4 Reith Lectures Securing Freedom Series*, 10 September 2011.

Marrero, I. (2011) 'London 2012: espacio de excepción', *URBE (Brazilian Journal of Urban Management)* 3(2): 34–54.

Massey, D. (2007) *World City*. Cambridge: Polity.

Metropolitan Police Service. (n.d.) *ANPR: The Olympic Data Feed and Retention of Data Beyond Two Years*, http://content.met.police.uk/Article/ANPR-Olympic-Data-Feed-and-retention-of-data-beyond-two-years/1400035664946/1400035664946, accessed 10 May 2015.

Morris, R. (2012) 'Managing the security challenge', Paper presented at the Olympic and Paralympic Security Conference, Royal United Services Institute, Whitehall, 25 January.

Moscow Times. (2013) 'Russia boosts security for Sochi Olympics with Pantsir-S Systems', *Moscow Times*, 23 September 2013.

Newman, O. (1972) *Defensible Space: Crime Prevention Through Urban Design*. New York: Macmillan.

NPCC. (n.d.) *ANPR: The Olympic Data Feed*, 1 May 2017, http://www.npcc. police.uk/documents/ANPR%20Olympic%20Data%20Feed.pdf.

Parker, N. (2012) 'The army perspective: managing the security challenge', Paper presented at the Olympic and Paralympic Security Conference, Royal United Services Institute, Whitehall, 25 January.

Pavoni, A. (2012) 'Tuning the city: Johannesburg and the 2010 World Cup/ Ajustando a cidade: Joanesburgo e a Copa do Mundo 2010', *Urbe: Revista Brasileira de Gestão Urbana (Brazilian Journal of Urban Management)*, 3(2): 191–209.

Raco, M. (2003) 'Remaking place and securitising space: urban regeneration and the strategies, tactics and practices of policing in the UK', *Urban Studies* 40(9): 1869–1887.

Raco, M and Tunney, E. (2010) 'Visibilities and invisibilities in urban development: small business communities and the London Olympics 2012', *Urban Studies* 47(10): 2069–2091.

Raine R. (2012) 'Managing the security challenge', Paper presented at the Olympic and Paralympic Security Conference, Royal United Services Institute, Whitehall, 25 January.

Reuters. (2007) 'Beijing to evict 1.5 million for Olympics: group', 5 June 2007, http://www.reuters.com/article/2007/06/05/us-olympics-beijing-housing-idUSPEK12263220070605.

Roche, M. (2000) *Mega-Events and Modernity: Olympics and Expos in the Growth of Global Culture*. London: Routledge.

Rose, N. (2000) 'Government and control', *British Journal of Criminology* 40(2): 321–339.

Samatas, M. (2007) 'Security and surveillance in the Athens 2004 Olympics: some lessons from a troubled story', *International Criminal Justice Review* 17(3): 220–238.

Sennett, R. (1970) *The Uses of Disorder: Personal Identity and City Life*. New York: Alfred A. Knopf.

Sibley, D. (1995) *Geographies of Exclusion*. London: Routledge.

Smith, N. (1996) *The New Urban Frontier: Gentrification and the Revanchist City*, London: Routledge.

Sorkin, M. (1992a) 'Variations on a theme park', in M. Sorkin (ed.), *Variations on a Theme Park: The New American City and the End of Public Space*. New York: Hill and Wang.

Sorkin, M. (1992b) 'See You in Disneyland', in M. Sorkin (ed.), *Variations on a Theme Park: The New American City and the End of Public Space*. New York: Hill and Wang.

The London Criminal Courts Solicitors' Association. (2012) *The Definition of an Olympic Offence*, http://www.lccsa.org.uk/index.asp?mid=100&mid2=50, accessed 10 May 2015.

Urry, J. (1995) *Consuming Places*. London: Routledge.

Wall Street Journal. (2013) 'New details show broader NSA surveillance reach', 20 August 2013, http://online.wsj.com/article/SB10001424127887324108204579022874091732470.html.

Ward, K. (2001) 'Entrepreneurial urbanism, state restructuring and civilising New East Manchester', *Area* 35(2): 116–127.

Watt, P. (2013) '"It's not for us": Regeneration, the 2012 Olympics and the gentrification of East London', *City* 17(1): 99–118.

Zukin, S. (1995) *The Culture of Cities*. Oxford: Blackwell.

Pete Fussey is Professor of Sociology at the University of Essex. He has published widely in a number of areas including terrorism and counterterrorism, critical studies of resilience, major-event security, surveillance and society, organized crime and urban sociology. He currently serves as a Director of the Surveillance Studies Network, a global network of over 300 surveillance studies scholars and is currently working on a 5-year ESRC project analysing the Human Rights implications of 'big data' practices. Professor Fussey is co-author of *Securing and Sustaining the Olympic City* (Ashgate, 2011), and co-editor of *Terrorism and the Olympics* (Routledge, 2010).

Jon Coaffee is Professor in Urban Geography based in the School of Politics and International Studies at the University of Warwick. At Warwick Jon has established the Resilient Cities Laboratory, and directs the Warwick Institute for the Science of Cities. His research focuses upon the interplay of physical and socio-political aspects of urban resilience and he has also published widely, especially on the impact of terrorism and other security concerns on the functioning of urban areas and in the security surrounding mega-events. During this research he has worked closely with a range of private and governmental stakeholders to ensure his research has real world impact. This work has been published in multiple disciplinary areas such as political science, geography, town planning, sociology and civil engineering. Most notably he published *Terrorism Risk and the City* (2003), *The Everyday Resilience of the City* (2008), *Terrorism Risk and the Global City: Towards Urban Resilience* (2009), *Sustaining and Securing the Olympic City* (2011) and *Urban Resilience: Planning for Risk, Crisis and Uncertainty* (2016). His work has been supported by a significant number of EU and UK Research Council grants and he is also an Exchange Professor at New York University's Center for Urban Science and Progress (CUSP).

Part II

The 2012 Legacy Story: Views from East London

4

Legacy for Whom? Housing in Post-Olympic East London

Paul Watt and Penny Bernstock

Introduction

Looking around Stratford visually in my head, I think it [2012 Olympic Games] has provided housing, but like I say not so much for the poor but people who are willing to pay rent for...I dunno £2,000 a month or something like that, there's no way I can afford that right now. There are skyscrapers being built, I mean not skyscrapers as such, but tower blocks being built for...I believe for private renting. So in a way it did [provide more housing], but not in a way people expected it, if that makes sense? (Leroy, aged 20, Black British – living in the 'Hostel' temporary accommodation, Newham, December 2014).[1]

---

[1] See section on young people and note 3.

P. Watt (✉)
Department of Geography, Birkbeck, University of London, London, England
e-mail: p.watt@bbk.ac.uk

P. Bernstock
University of East London, London, England
e-mail: P.Bernstock@uel.ac.uk

© The Author(s) 2017
P. Cohen, P. Watt (eds.), *London 2012 and the Post-Olympics City*,
DOI 10.1057/978-1-137-48947-0_4

This chapter examines the 2012 Olympic Games' legacy in relation to housing in the six East London Host Boroughs (now Growth Boroughs). It does so bearing in mind the official aims of the Games in relation to Legacy and Convergence, as discussed in the Introduction. With regards to housing, providing 'homes for all' was one of seven proposed outcomes in order to tackle deprivation and meet the convergence objectives (Host Boroughs Unit, 2009: 18). As this chapter argues, whatever 'successes' might be claimed for the overall 2012 legacy in the official evaluation report (UEL, 2015), the housing-related legacy has fallen well short of the Games' grandiose-sounding aims.

This chapter builds upon the authors' previous publications on the 2012 Games housing legacy (Bernstock, 2014; Kennelly and Watt, 2012; Watt, 2013). These existing works are based on research undertaken in the period leading up, during and immediately after 2012. By contrast, this chapter focuses on the post-Games 2012–15 period based on secondary analysis of official statistics, analysis of policy documents and websites, plus three ethnographic research studies (interviews and participant observation) undertaken by Paul Watt with those experiencing various forms of homelessness. Of the latter, two studies were based at the same temporary supported housing unit (the 'Hostel') for young people in Newham; one study was carried out in April 2013,[2] and the second was from August–December 2014.[3] The third ongoing study (2014–17) examines the experiences of homeless adults and youth in East London, including

---

[2] Paul Watt and Jacqueline Kennelly conducted three focus group and 12 semi-structured interviews with young people living at the Hostel in April 2013. These formed the final post-Games stage of a 2010–13 research project funded by a Standard Research Grant from the Social Sciences and Humanities Research Council of Canada examining disadvantaged youth experiences of the 2010 Vancouver and 2012 London Olympics Games; Jacqueline Kennelly was Principal Investigator (Kennelly and Watt, 2011, 2012, Kennelly, 2016).

[3] Paul Watt returned to the Hostel several times during 2014; this included interviewing a worker in September and five young people from August to December. The combined 2013–14 youth interviewees at the Hostel were aged 18–25 years, of mixed gender, and included a large proportion from BAME backgrounds as reflects Newham's demographic profile.

those who have been relocated either elsewhere in London or outside the city.[4]

The chapter first of all discusses the already-existing evaluations of the 2012 Games housing legacy. It then outlines recent house price and rent increases in the Host Boroughs (see Chapter 2). The third section examines new housing developments in 'new' and 'old' Stratford, including the East Village (see Chapters 5 and 6). The chapter moves onto consider affordable and social rental housing (SRH) output in the Host Boroughs as a whole; SRH is provided by local authorities or housing associations at substantially below market rents, while 'affordable housing' covers a bewildering plethora of sub-market tenures including SRH. This section is followed by an analysis of overcrowding and homelessness, which leads onto a discussion of the research findings from the Hostel. The next section examines the increasing displacement of the homeless from East London, while the final section examines how such processes of 'social cleansing' are being contested by housing campaigners.

Evaluating the 2012 Games' Housing Legacy

The potential impact of the 2012 Games on housing and regeneration in East London has been the focus of several dedicated studies (Shelter, 2013; Watt, 2013; Bernstock, 2014; Thompson et al., 2017), and has also appeared in broader legacy analyses (see *inter alia* Minton, 2012; DCMS, 2013; Growth Boroughs Unit, 2014, 2015; UEL, 2015; Kennelly, 2016). In the chapter, we highlight the often narrow parameters within which the official evaluations have operated. One example is the Department of Culture, Media and Sport (DCMS, 2013) report which forms part of the official London 2012 meta-evaluation. Annex A of this report devotes 12 pages to

---

[4] Since summer 2014, Paul Watt has undertaken ethnographic research on both homelessness and housing activism in East London (Watt, 2016, 2017). This includes formal and informal interviews with homeless youth and adults who have been relocated away from their boroughs of origin to temporary accommodation outside of London with a focus on Welwyn Garden City and Basildon.

'Property Value Growth' including nine figures on house prices (DCMS, 2013). However the same report contains no charts on housing needs' measures such as homelessness, waiting lists or overcrowding, while the terms 'social housing' and 'affordable housing' only appear twice and five times respectively in its 116 pages. This analytical bias gives an indication of the narrow economic rather than social priorities of the report's commissioners and producers.

The housing and homelessness charity Shelter (2013) has provided a more socially insightful analysis of the post-Games housing legacy in their report on Hackney, Newham and Tower Hamlets. This report considers whether displacement effects (rising rents and house prices, and local populations being pushed out of Games' neighbourhoods) could be identified, but concludes that 'these concerns about the potential impact of the London 2012 Olympic Games were not realised' (Shelter, 2013: 1). At the same time, the report also highlights 'much deeper, systemic problems with the housing situation in east London' (Shelter, 2013: 1), notably the expense and insecurity of the private rented sector (PRS), the lack of affordable homes and the negative impact of the Coalition Government's welfare reforms, all points we concur with.

The Shelter report illustrates an important dilemma when assessing the Olympics' housing and regeneration legacy – the difficulty of separating out those trends which are the direct result of the Games from those which have occurred as a result of broader policy shifts, notably national housing and welfare policies under the 2010–15 Coalition Government including the 2011 Localism Act (Hodkinson and Robbins, 2013; Somerville, 2016). This wider policy context, especially the introduction of the 'affordable rent' model in 2010 – which means rents can be up to 80 per cent of market rents – has undoubtedly made it more difficult to deliver affordable housing in high-value areas and in particular larger family housing that is urgently needed in East London. The East Thames Group (2011) explored the implications of the introduction of the affordable rent model in Newham and concluded that 44 per cent of households could not reasonably afford a two-bedroom property and 65 per cent could not afford a three- or four-bedroom property.

Another confounding factor in assessing the post-Games housing legacy is that London, as a whole, is currently facing a deep housing crisis. This crisis manifests itself by galloping house prices and private rents, coupled with increasing homelessness, overcrowding, insecurity and displacement, while one of the major long-term causal factors is the dearth of social homes to rent (Watt and Minton, 2016). In this chapter, we acknowledge the significance of London's housing crisis, but we are also wary of saying that *all* of East London's housing problems are simply the result of this wider crisis given that the Host Boroughs have pursued *different* housing and planning strategies with *differential* results, as we discuss below.

The authors' previous published research on the period leading up to and during the 2012 Games generally takes a more sceptical view on the Games' housing legacy than the Shelter (2013) report. The current research findings, which we present in this chapter, do not lead us to alter our earlier judgement (see also Thompson et al., 2017).

House Prices and Rents

In the period leading up to London hosting the Games, substantial house price increases were identified in boroughs such as Hackney and Tower Hamlets, but these had not been as marked in the borough of Newham (Bernstock, 2014). Indeed in March 2013 the *Financial Times* (2013) reported that 'the much vaunted "Olympic bounce" has failed to materialise' with Newham's prices 'trailing the rest of London'. However the 'bounce' arrived two years later since Newham recorded a 22 per cent price rise by year-end 2015, the largest annual increase of any local authority area in the country (Halifax Press Team, 2015). Within Newham, Stratford, the Royal Docks and Canning Town are substantially more expensive than other areas (Savills, 2014).

The increase in demand is not primarily fuelled by families and individuals wanting to buy housing to live in, but rather by buy-to-let [BTL] and overseas investors seeking speculative opportunities. If London is the dominant region in the nation-wide BTL market (Council of Mortgage Lenders, 2015), then Newham is 'the capital's top BTL

Fig. 4.1 New and Old Stratford – Stratford Plaza tower and Dennison Point, Carpenters' Estate, August 2014

Source: Paul Watt

hotspot' with rental yields of 5.2 per cent (The Telegraph, 2015). Bernstock (2014) discusses the importance of Stratford in relation to BTL investors. While Stratford does not as yet have the appeal of central London for foreign investors, it has nevertheless attracted considerable interest; for example the 198 units at the 25-storey Stratford Plaza tower (see Fig. 4.1) were sold off-plan, three quarters to overseas buyers (*Financial Times*, 2013; also Savills, 2014).

Table 4.1 shows mean rents in the PRS over the three and half years' period from Q1 2012 (just before the Games) to Q3 2015. Rents have increased at well above the London average of 27.7 per cent in the two Host Boroughs of Hackney (40.8 per cent) and Newham (35.1), and to a lesser extent in Waltham Forest (29.5 per cent), but at a below London average in the remaining three Host Boroughs. Such rental increases are

Table 4.1 Mean private rents (all properties, 12 month rolling average), £ per month, Host Boroughs and London, 2012–15

	2012 Q1	2015 Q3	£ increase 2012–15	Percent increase 2012–15
Host Boroughs				
Barking and Dagenham	835	1,006	171	20.5
Greenwich	1,004	1,257	253	25.2
Hackney	1,249	1,759	510	40.8
Newham	914	1,235	321	35.1
Tower Hamlets	1,369	1,660	291	21.3
Waltham Forest	925	1,198	273	29.5
London	1,312	1,676	364	27.7

Source: Valuations Office Agency Private Rental Market Statistics (accessed from Shelter Housing Databank, http://england.shelter.org.uk/professional_resources/housing_databank, May 2016).

of course associated with the rapid gentrification which is occurring in Hackney (Wessendorf, 2014; Butcher and Dickens, 2016), and parts of Newham especially Stratford (Bernstock, 2014).

We can further see how rents have increased in the post-Games period with reference to the PRS properties at East Village, the converted Athletes Village in 'new Stratford', London E20. These are managed by Get Living London (GLL), which is in turn owned by QDD, a joint venture between Qatari Diar Real Estate Company and Delancey. In October 2015, weekly rents for a one-bedroom apartment flat *started* at £405 (Delancey, 2015). As Table 4.2 shows, there have been massive rental increases for four-bedroom town houses (52 per cent) and one-bedroom apartments (31 per cent) over the two year period from September 2013 to October 2015, and somewhat lower increases for three-bedroom (20 per cent) and two-bedroom (14 per cent) apartments. With the exception of the latter, these increases are well above the mean private rent increase for London as a whole at 14 per cent for the equivalent period Q3 2013 – Q3 2015 (Shelter Housing Databank, accessed 16 May 2016). Although the GLL flats are all owned by QDD and are therefore not BTL properties (Bernstock, 2014: 127), their rent increases reflect the increasingly investment-driven nature of the PRS market in Stratford, which was facilitated by the substantial public investment leading to an uplift in land values.

Table 4.2 Weekly rents for Get Living London properties at East Village, 2013–15

	September 2013	October 2015	£ increase 2013–15	Percent increase 2013–15
1 bedroom apartment	£310	£405	£95	31
2 bedroom apartment	£370	£420	£50	14
3 bedroom apartment	£474	£570	£96	20
4 bedroom town house	£515	£785	£270	52

Sources: September 2013 – Inside Housing (2013); October 2015 – Delancey (2015).

The increase in house prices and rents are taking private sector housing costs well above affordability levels for the majority of East London residents, especially in Newham, a borough where many households are struggling with low incomes and austerity cuts (Shelter, 2013; LSE Housing and Communities, 2014). Newham has the dubious honour of record house price increases and an average price of nearly £320,000 – £90,000 *more* than the UK average (Halifax Press Team, 2015) – while its median income levels are *below* the UK average (see Introduction).

New Housing in 'Old Stratford' and 'New Stratford'

The substantial investment in Stratford has resulted in a considerable interest from private developers in developing schemes in the area. According to a London Legacy Development Corporation report (LLDC, 2014a), there were over 20,000 units in full or outline proposal within the LLDC boundary. This includes 6,382 units in what was originally referred to as 'Stratford City' and includes the East Village; over 6,000 on the Queen Elizabeth Olympic Park; 1,036 units at Chobham Farm; 1,200 units at Sugar House Lane and a number of other smaller schemes such as those described later. However, each of these major schemes highlights the tensions and contradictions in London's allegedly inclusive housing strategy. In its report on the affordable rent model, the East Thames Group (2011) identified three Newham sub-areas – Stratford and New Town, Canning Town South and the Royal Docks – that would be least affordable and would have the most significant challenges; ironically these are also where much of the new housing development is taking place (Savills, 2014). This section examines new housing provision in both E15 'old Stratford' and E20 'new Stratford'.

We firstly look at the East Village in E20 which forms the first tranche of the new homes which will be built in and around the Queen Elizabeth Olympic Park [QEOP]. As Tessa Jowell (2015), the Labour Olympics Minister 2005–10, says, 'Here is the legacy – East Village, the best place in London to live – 3,000 homes there and more coming'. This 'jewel in the crown' of the Olympics' housing legacy, is increasingly held up as an example of good practice since the homes are of good quality, meet environmental standards, include a large proportion of homes for disabled people, and comprise 49 per cent affordable housing; although the latter is less the result of good planning and more the outcome of a set of compromises in the interests of private business (Bernstock, 2014).

The 2,818 new homes at the East Village are split between two sets of owners – QDD and Triathlon Homes – and five housing tenures. QDD were awarded the contract for the long-term management and purchase of 1,439 private homes for rent which are managed by GLL. QDD also acquired six further development plots with planning permission for 2,000–2,500 units. QDD paid £557 million for these units and additional plots of land. The latter were those that were to have been utilised for the Athletes Village had it comprised 4,200 units, as initially specified. Since planning obligations with regard to affordable housing had already been met at East Village, there will be no requirement for affordable housing on these other plots. Indeed the Olympic Development Authority submitted a planning application under the trading name 'Stratford Village Property Holdings 2 Limited' arguing that 'no affordable housing is proposed [. . .] ostensibly to dilute the concentration of affordable housing across Stratford City' (cited in Bernstock, 2014: 133).

The 'affordable' element of the housing at East Village is managed by Triathlon Homes, a joint venture between two housing associations – East Thames and Southern Housing Group – and First Base, a private development company. Triathlon Homes manages four affordable housing tenures totalling 1,379 units, the largest of which comprises 675 social rental units (49 per cent). Because this scheme was agreed as part of an earlier planning agreement, SRH was delivered at 'target' as compared to 'affordable' rents. This new SRH provision is a significant development for those East London residents in housing need and is of a high standard. However, it needs to be offset against the social housing supply that was *lost* as a result of hosting the 2012 Games. The Clays Lane co-operative for single persons was demolished to make way for the QEOP resulting in the loss of 450 social rental tenancies and the displacement of 425 residents (see Chapter 8). The latter were rehoused in 327 housing association and council properties, largely in East London (Bernstock, 2014: 42). Hence there has been a gross reduction of 777 social tenancies and a net decrease of around 100 such tenancies even when factoring in the new provision at the East Village.

A complex allocations process was put in place for the social rental units. The London Borough of Newham has allocation rights for half (348), and the boroughs of Barking and Dagenham, Hackney, Havering, Waltham Forest and Redbridge had allocation rights to 100 units each, while Triathlon Homes and the GLA had allocation rights to 150 and 70 units respectively. Following a shift in housing allocations policy, Newham Council began to prioritise applicants in paid work and from military backgrounds (Inside Housing, 2012, LBN, 2012b). Triathlon's own data shows that 58 per cent of East Village social renters are in paid work (Burns, 2014). The access criteria therefore favour 'hard-working', 'respectable' families in paid work, alongside the 'deserving poor' such as those with disabilities and ex-armed forces members. By comparison, the 'rougher' elements of the local working classes are effectively excluded since they form part of the 'undeserving poor'. The interviewees living in temporary accommodation were aware of the 'exclusive' and 'exclusionary' nature of the East Village, as we discuss below.

The remaining affordable housing at the East Village comprises 376 intermediate rented flats (i.e. 'affordable rents'), 269 shared ownership flats and 79 shared equity flats. Affordable rents are set at 20 per cent below market levels and intermediate rent is aimed at those on lower incomes not eligible for SRH. One well-known problem in London, which official Games' evaluations routinely ignore (e.g. UEL, 2015), is that in reality – once one factors income into the equation – so-called affordable housing *is anything but affordable* (London Tenants Federation, 2012). This is especially the case in East London where incomes are generally lower than the rest of London (see Introduction). It is hardly surprising that the non-SRH 'affordable' element of the East Village properties excludes not only those on low incomes, but even those on median incomes:

> ... the intermediate rents on one bedroom flats in the East Village, set at 80 per cent of market rent, would demand 52 per cent, 46per cent and 41per cent of median wages in Hackney, Newham and Tower Hamlets respectively. [...] 80% of market rent is beyond the reach of most east Londoners. (Shelter, 2013: 7)

Intermediate rental (IMR) units at East Village are subject to a complex set of arrangements resulting in varying costs and tenancy agreements. Some are let at 70 per cent of market rent and others at 80 per cent. Moreover, while some IMR units are let on a rolling tenancy with annual increases of RPI plus 0.5 per cent, others are let on a fixed-term one year tenancy and revalued at the end of each year. In March 2014, monthly rents for the IMR homes *started* at £1,244 for two-bedrooms and £1,668 for three-bedrooms (Triathlon Homes, 2014). Annual rents for two and three-bedroom homes were thus around £14,928 and £20,016 respectively, i.e. 52 per cent and 70 per cent of Newham's median household income of £28,780 (for 2012–13; see Table 1.1, Introduction). By 2015, a blogger and Triathlon tenant suggested that his intermediate neighbours were facing 'rent rises of up to £300 per month' (Generation Rent, 2015). This figure is replicated in a letter from one Triathlon intermediate tenant who had been living there since May 2014 and which showed the monthly rent for her two-bedroom apartment would increase from £1,251.47 to £1,542.67 from May 2015, i.e. £291 or 23 per cent. While our direct evidence for such rent rises is limited, the way that some intermediate rent increases track market rents (Table 4.2) suggests that some IMR homes in the East Village are becoming *even less* genuinely affordable for East Londoners in the short space of time since they have been made available.

In terms of the other main tenure of the East Village 'affordable' development – shared ownership – a similar story can be told. An East Village shared ownership property was advertised on the *Rightmove* website in August 2015. This was a 25 per cent share on a resale three-bedroom apartment at £130,000 based on a full price of £520,000. Estimated monthly outgoings were £1,794 which included £658 for the mortgage, £866 rent and £271 service charges (Rightmove, 2015), in other words £21,528 per annum or three-quarters of the Newham median income (2012/13). In addition, the mortgage requires a deposit of £13,000 and minimum earnings of £65,661. The phrase 'affordable housing' is increasingly Orwellian, as many Londoners recognize, and this seems to be especially true of East Village.

In addition to East Village, the QEOP will have more than 6,000 new properties by 2030 in the new Stratford E20 postcode divided into five neighbourhoods: Chobham Manor, East Wick, Sweetwater, Marshgate Wharf and Pudding Mill. The level of affordable housing included on the Park has declined overtime. For example, the first Olympic Park Legacy Company (OPLC) plan indicated that there would be between 35 and 40 per cent affordable housing on the Park. However, this was revised downwards in the Legacy Communities Scheme published in 2012 that stipulated that there would be a maximum of 35 per cent and a minimum of 20 per cent, and was revised downward again to a maximum of 31 per cent following plans to expedite housing development at Sweetwater and Eastwick (OPLC, 2011, 2012; LLDC, 2014a, 2014b).

Chobham Manor is the first of these five neighbourhoods scheduled for completion (see Fig. 4.2), and new residents began moving in during 2015. Chobham Manor is described on its website as 'Destined to be one of London's most sought after addresses' (Chobham Manor E20, 2016). The first phase of market properties has already been sold off-plan. One-bedroom flats were on sale in the first phase at £370,000 and two-bedroom properties in excess of £600,000. In mid-2015, one-bedroom apartments were being sold 'from' £375,000, two-bed apartments started at £495,000 while two-bed mews houses were from £675,000. With no hint of irony, an 'Easier Property' (2014) website headline was 'Raft of measures mean Chobham Manor homes are accessible for all', and reported that Simon Baxter, spokesperson for Chobham Manor LLP, said, 'A key aim of Chobham Manor is to become a neighbourhood that is suitable for a wide range of people – if it wasn't, it simply wouldn't be a neighbourhood'. According to the QEOP website, 'around a third' of

Fig. 4.2 New homes advertisement, Queen Elizabeth Olympic Park, August 2014

Source: Paul Watt

the 828 new homes at Chobham Manor will be affordable; in reality this is 28 per cent and the lower level was rationalised by higher levels at the East Village.

The acceleration of development plans at East Wick and Sweetwater have resulted in cuts to the numbers of affordable housing units; this highlights the contradictions between the LLDC's role as a landowner and its wider commitment to ensuring a lasting legacy. In April 2014, a committee paper was submitted by the LLDC Planning Committee setting out the rationale for the plans. It was noted that accelerated delivery will result in loss of income as they will lose six years of house price inflation. Therefore, the reductions in affordable housing are presented as an inevitable price to pay for the loss of income. The market housing has also been amended to include a proportion for private rent as well as sale. There are two key drivers for this; it will limit the impact of the loss of uplift, and more importantly:

> The introduction of PRS also seeks to address the potential impact of delivering a large number of private sale units onto the market within a short period of time which might otherwise potentially produce an over-supply which would impact on land value by putting sales values at risk. (LLDC, 2014b, para 7.19)

This highlights a tension between a quasi-governmental agency briefed to pursue public good through legacy, whilst maximising profit through the sale of land, and it appears intervening in the market in a way that will ensure ongoing increase in house prices despite a rhetoric that pays lip service to the need for affordable housing. These ongoing increases will have a direct impact on those in housing need through the setting of rents that link to market prices, and through the inability of Registered Social Landlords to develop housing in high value areas.

One of us (Penny Bernstock) has analysed five planning schemes in Stratford with scheduled completions from now until 2017: Stratford Central, Stratford Plaza, Stratosphere, Glasshouse Gardens and the Manhattan Loft Garden Company. They are all located in close proximity to Stratford Train Station and the QEOP and are clearly capitalising on the substantial public investment in the area. Average house prices in these new developments are substantially higher than the near £320,000 average for Newham as a whole (Halifax Press Team, 2015); apartments in Stratford Plaza range from £499–625,000 for example. This means that any affordable rent products that are linked to market values will be higher than in other parts of Newham. It is also hard to imagine that the development of these apartments will create the envisaged 'inclusive neighbourhoods'.

The high cost of market housing could be offset by the inclusion of affordable housing, as Bernstock (2014) discusses. However, recent research by Brownill et al. (2015) demonstrates that there has been a nation-wide decline in the proportion of affordable housing delivered through planning gain and that there are increasing challenges to levering affordable housing in this way, with issues of so-called 'financial viability' increasingly raised by developers, as has happened at several major developments in south London where affordable housing is around 5 per cent (Flynn, 2016). Perhaps unsurprisingly therefore, the most striking feature of these five 2017 Stratford schemes is the absence of SRH. Four of the five schemes include some on-site affordable housing, although this is intermediate and unlikely to be affordable to most Newham residents.

New Affordable and Social Rental Housing

This section examines the technically complex and ideologically contentious issue of new affordable and SRH. Delivering 50,000 new homes including 12,000 affordable homes by 2015 were included under the hyperbolic outcome of providing 'homes for all' (Host Boroughs Unit, 2009). The *Convergence Annual Report 2014–2015* suggests that both the original overall and affordable homes targets have been 'exceeded' such that between 2009 and 2014 over 24,000 completions are 'projected' alongside a 'confirmed delivery of over 18,000 affordable homes' (Growth Boroughs Unit, 2015: 21). These figures beg two questions which many ordinary Londoners ask: 'what does affordable housing mean' and 'who is it affordable for'? As mentioned earlier, 'affordable housing' covers a complex and proliferating range of tenure types, including SRH. The East Thames Group (2011: 5) notes that 'affordability is a particularly acute issue in Newham, with incomes near or at the bottom of the London scale yet housing costs ranking at the lower end of the middle third of all London boroughs'.

Table 4.3 shows the additional affordable and social rent dwellings for the Host Boroughs and London for the longer six-years' period 2009–15, i.e. three years before and after the Games.[5] In relation to 2010–14, the same period as the Convergence report refers, 15,840 affordable and 9,390 social rented dwellings were completed. Although doubts remain over the dates, this is nevertheless a general confirmation

---

[5] This table is an update of an earlier table (Bernstock, 2014: 81).

Table 4.3 Additional affordable and social rent dwellings provided by local authority area, Host Boroughs and London, 2009–15

LA numbers of affordable housing and social rent	2009–10	2010–11	2011–12	2012–13	2013–14	2014–15	Pre-Games Total 2009–10 – 2011–12	Post-Games Total 2012–13 – 2014–15	Total
Barking & Dagenham AH	180	270	370	90	500	1,190	820	1,780	2,600
Barking & Dagenham SR	60	110	250	50	120	380	420	550	970
Barking & Dagenham SR % of AH	33	41	68	56	24	32	51	31	37
Greenwich AH	390	1,340	490	270	640	930	2,220	1,840	4,060
Greenwich SR	240	810	240	160	370	250	1,290	780	2,070
Greenwich SR % of AH	62	60	49	59	58	27	58	42	51
Hackney AH	1,260	690	1,020	590	550	890	2,970	2,030	5,000
Hackney SR	610	370	610	460	360	240	1,590	1,060	2,650
Hackney SR % of AH	48	54	60	78	65	27	54	52	53
Newham AH	700	580	810	280	1,350	480	2,090	2,110	4,200
Newham SR	260	310	510	150	700	60	1,080	910	1,990
Newham SR % of AH	37	53	63	54	52	13	52	43	47
Tower Hamlets AH	1,990	1,260	1,800	440	900	1,220	5,050	2,560	7,610

Tower Hamlets SR	1,260	820	1,430	240	450	290	3,510	980	4,490
Tower Hamlets SR % of AH	63	65	79	55	50	24	70	38	59
Waltham Forest AH	250	460	630	320	190	1,010	1,340	1,520	2,860
Waltham Forest SR	150	280	440	150	-	30	870	180	1,050
Waltham Forest SR % of AH	60	61	70	47	0	3	65	12	37
Total Host Boroughs AH	4,770	4,600	5,120	1,990	4,130	5,720	14,490	11,840	26,330
Total Host Boroughs SR	2,580	2,700	3,480	1,210	2,000	1,250	8,760	4,460	13,220
Total Host Boroughs SR % of AH	54	59	68	61	48	22	60	38	50
Total London AH	13,560	14,010	17,220	8,710	9,230	18,270	44,790	36,210	81,000
Total London SR	7,060	8,890	11,370	5,060	3,590	3,180	27,320	11,830	39,150
Total London SR % of AH	52	63	66	58	39	17	61	33	48

Source: Tables 1006 and 1008, DCLG Live Tables on affordable housing supply, https://www.gov.uk/government/statistical-data-sets/live-tables-on-affordable-housing-supply.

Notes: AH = Affordable Housing

SR = Social Rental housing

of the *Convergence Annual Report 2014–2015* delivery numbers as exceeding the original 12,000 additional affordable homes.

Nevertheless Table 4.3 highlights several issues. Most obviously is that the original target of 12,000 additional affordable homes was based on five boroughs, and therefore the later inclusion of Barking and Dagenham perforce increased the absolute numbers. At a deeper level, the mere provision of additional affordable homes is hardly in itself a major achievement given that *all* London boroughs have to build increased numbers of such dwellings as part of London planning requirements. These requirements, notably around SRH, were stepped up in the 2004 London Plan and were then subsequently watered down under the Johnson Mayoralty (Bowie, 2010; Bernstock, 2014).

It is therefore important to consider two sets of proportional figures in assessing the Host Boroughs' production of new homes. The first is the percentage of SRH among affordable housing. As Table 4.3 shows, over the entire 2009–15 period, this was 50 per cent for the Host Boroughs, i.e. only marginally above the 48 per cent London total. Indeed the Boroughs' 60 per cent was slightly below the London average (61 per cent) in the pre-Games period, whilst the gap only reversed in the post-Games period: 38 per cent and 33 per cent respectively.

We can also examine the *proportions* of London's affordable and social rental homes provided in the Host Boroughs for the entire 2009–15 period which are 33 per cent and 34 per cent respectively, considerably above the six boroughs' population of 18.4 per cent of London's total. Furthermore, the Host Boroughs affordable housing output was an impressive 45 per cent of the London total in 2013–14, as the Convergence Report for that year highlights. However, as Fig. 4.3 shows, this year was quite exceptional and probably reflects the completion of the East Village. In marked contrast, the trend during the preceding 2009–13 period was firmly *downwards* to 23 per cent of affordable and 24 per cent of social renting in 2012–13 (Fig. 4.3). Following the blip 2013–14 year, the numbers were again down to 31 per cent and 21 per cent respectively in 2014–15; the latter is only slightly above the Boroughs' population percentage. With the sole exception of 2013–14, these yearly figures for affordable and especially social housing output hardly demonstrate that the Host Boroughs are punching greatly above their weight.

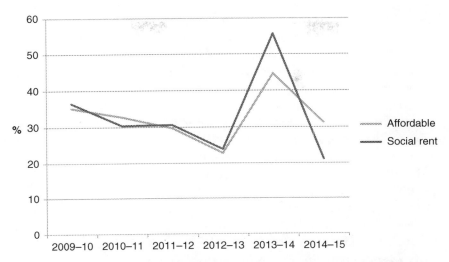

Fig. 4.3 Percentage of additional affordable and social rent dwellings in London provided by Host Boroughs, 2009–15

Source: DCLG Live Tables, Tables 1006 and 1008 (authors' calculations); https://www.gov.uk/government/statistical-data-sets/live-tables-on-affordable-housing-supply

The previous figures demonstrate that, despite exceeding their original targets, the Host Boroughs have only marginally out-performed the London average for proportional affordable and SRH production. This is hardly a major achievement given their acknowledged massive pre-Games housing needs. For example, in April 2011 there were nearly 104,000 households on local authority housing waiting lists across all six Host Boroughs, with Newham and Tower Hamlets alone accounting for 55,000, that is over half of this staggering total (Watt, 2013; Bernstock, 2014).

Like many official reports (e.g. Growth Boroughs Unit, 2014, 2015; UEL, 2015), Fig. 4.3 aggregates the Host Boroughs into a single score regarding affordable or SRH completions However this aggregation can hide distinctive patterns *within* the Host Boroughs. Table 4.3 disaggregates the data and demonstrates how far the borough of Tower Hamlets has disproportionately contributed to the provision of affordable and SRH from 2009 to 2015 and especially during the pre-Games' period. In total Tower Hamlets accounted for 7,610 affordable units and 4,490 social rental units, i.e. 29 per cent and 34 per cent of the Host Boroughs' output respectively over the six years. These proportions are also well above this borough's one-sixth of the Host Boroughs' total population. Furthermore Tower Hamlets achieved the highest proportion of SRH at 59 per cent, significantly above the 50 per cent Host Borough average.

A relevant and salutary comparison can be drawn with Newham, the largest of the Host Boroughs with nearly 308,000 residents (2011 Census). Newham had 32,045 households on its waiting list in 2011, the largest number in the country, while Tower Hamlets had 23,128 (Bernstock, 2014: 80). Despite this, Newham provided far lower numbers of affordable (4,200) and social rental (1,990) units than Tower Hamlets from 2009 to 2015, as seen in Table 4.3. Over this period, social renting was 47 per cent of the total, i.e. below the Host Borough average of 50 per cent, and well below Tower Hamlets' 59 per cent. Newham's figures are even lower in terms of social rental provision than Greenwich both in absolute (2,070) and percentage (51 per cent) terms. The latter is especially significant given that Greenwich had by far the smallest waiting list in 2011, i.e. nearly 7,000. Going further back to the mid-2000s, whilst Tower Hamlets consistently provided over one thousand new affordable units every year from 2005 to 2012 (9,990 total) and 6,360 social rental dwellings, Newham managed respective figures of 5,190 and 3,030, i.e. approximately half Tower Hamlets' (DCLG Live Tables). Thus despite having the largest need for affordable and especially social renting among the Host Boroughs, Newham's performance is at best inadequate and far worse than that of Tower Hamlets, the borough with the next greatest housing needs.

To frame this issue in counter-factual terms, had Tower Hamlets achieved the *same level* of housing output as Newham, there would have been 3,410 fewer affordable units and 2,500 fewer social rental units across the Host Boroughs from 2009 to 2015. Or to put it another way, had Tower Hamlets *not* been one of the Host Boroughs, the latter's share of the capital's additional affordable and social rent dwellings from 2009 to 2015 would have slumped to 23 per cent and 22 per cent respectively while the Boroughs' total population would have gone down to 15.3 per cent of the city's. In other words, the over-representation of new affordable and social rent housing in the Host Boroughs is largely, albeit not solely, a result of a Tower Hamlets' exceptional performance in this regard (Building construction design, 2015).

This performance stretches back to 2005–06 when, for the first time in a decade a single London borough provided over 1,000 affordable units (DCLG, Live Tables). In fact, Tower Hamlets has done this in eight of the 10 years from 2005 to 2015 and has been the highest London producer in six years. Similarly Tower Hamlets has been the largest social rental producer in six out of these 10 years, and even produced over 1,000 such homes in two years (Table 4.3).

Why is this any of this significant? It allows us to examine *causality* which is, or at least should be, at the forefront of any examination of Games' housing legacy. If one aggregates housing production data to the six Host Boroughs level, as most official analyses do (Growth Boroughs Unit, 2014; UEL, 2015), the simplistic conclusion is that the overall increases in affordable housing *must* be the result of the 2012 Games. However this approach is flawed if it does not take into account divergences *between the boroughs*, both in relation to their housing needs and their outputs, differences which cannot be attributed solely to a singular 'Olympics effect' given that these were *all* Host Boroughs.

Our suggestion is that these divergences, notably between the two boroughs with the largest waiting lists – Newham and Tower Hamlets – reflect different political and ideological priorities regarding affordable and SRH provision. All London borough councils have faced deteriorating financial capacity as a result of social housing grant cuts. However their political commitment to new social housing provision has varied throughout the last 15 years. Tower Hamlets Council has promoted the importance of new SRH as a way of meeting its manifest housing needs: 'The amount of affordable housing, particularly social housing in Tower Hamlets needs to be maximised' (LBTH, 2010: 3). This can be seen in its exceptional record of building new council homes for rent whereby it directly provided 420 of these from 2010 to 2015, i.e. a massive 84 per cent of the Host Boroughs' total (500) and 29 per cent of the London total (1,470) (Shelter Databank, accessed 16 May 2016).

Newham Council, on the other hand, has had a long-standing antipathy towards social housing estates – and their residents – blaming them for creating 'ghettos of worklessness' (LBN, 2012a: 1) and high levels of 'benefit dependency', a stigmatising discourse which gels with neoliberal ideology as espoused by right-wing think-tanks and politicians (Slater, 2014). Indeed

Newham's Unitary Development Plan from 2001 to 2012 had a vision for the Stratford area 'that involved rebalancing the housing mix as it was perceived that there was an *over-supply of social housing*' (Bernstock, 2014: 145; our emphasis). Newham planners did not therefore need to accede to Newham-wide targets for affordable and social renting in new schemes in Stratford, but could allow lower levels. 'Rebalancing' has subsequently occurred with a plethora of new private developments in and around Stratford which have done next to nothing to alleviate the dire housing circumstances of many Newham residents.

We conclude this section by arguing that a large part of the supply of new affordable and social dwellings in the Host Boroughs was not an Olympic legacy effect so much as a result of the commitment by one Host Borough local authority – Tower Hamlets – to meet its extensive housing needs. This is not to say that Tower Hamlets has somehow magically escaped London's housing crisis – it hasn't. Nevertheless, had Tower Hamlets Council adopted Newham Council's approach to social housing, its waiting list would be even longer than it is now and its use of temporary accommodation for its homeless population would have undoubtedly been greater.

Housing Needs and Insecurities: Overcrowding, Waiting Lists, Homelessness and Evictions

Overcrowding in England and Wales is unsurprisingly higher in London at 11.3 per cent of households, as 2011 Census data shows (ONS, 2014a). The *Convergence Annual Report 2014–15* states that reducing overcrowding is one of its two key targets in its Convergence aims for housing, the other being building additional units (Growth Boroughs Unit, 2015: 21). If providing new affordable housing has consistently received a green for progress in the Convergence Reports from 2011 to 2015, reducing overcrowding received a red assessment since the 'overcrowding gap' – between the Host Boroughs and London as a whole – widened during the 2001–11 inter-Censal period.

Within London, five out of the six Host Boroughs (except Greenwich) appear in the ten most overcrowded local authorities in the country with Newham and Tower Hamlets as 1st (25.2 per cent) and 3rd (16.4 per cent) respectively (ONS, 2014a, 2014b). If this picture is indicative of dire housing needs, it is important to note that it contains a strong ethnic/racial inequality element given that, in each of the 10 London local authorities with the largest percentage of overcrowded households, the *majority* of overcrowded households had a Household Reference Person (HRP) from a minority ethnic group (i.e. other than White British) (ONS, 2014b). Among the top five local authorities, including Newham and Tower Hamlets, this figure was at least four out of five overcrowded households. In other words, overcrowding is not only higher in the Host Boroughs, but also disproportionately impacts upon BAME groups.

The *Convergence Annual Report 2013–14* admits that there is a risk that the overcrowding gap may even increase further partly as a result of welfare reforms such as benefit caps (Growth Boroughs Unit, 2014: 34). Despite this, the same report admits that, 'currently we do not have a strategy to address this worsening trajectory'. A later report makes no mention as to how this gap maybe tackled and notes that 'annual data on overcrowding is no longer available' (Growth Boroughs Unit, 2015: 21), a data paucity that stands in stark contrast to the many pages of house price data in other official reports (e.g. DCMS, 2013). It is also note-worthy that ethnic/racial inequalities issues in relation to Host Boroughs' overcrowding do not appear in any official reports as far as the authors can identify.

As we saw before, the numbers on social housing waiting lists in the Host Boroughs are high and the latest Growth Boroughs Unit (2015) report acknowledges that they worsened since 2011. However recent changes to national housing policy have dramatically shrunk these lists both on the Host Boroughs and London generally (Inside Housing, 2014a; Watt and Minton, 2016). The 2011 Localism Act removed nationally prescribed rules on who has access to social housing in favour of local authorities setting their own rules, albeit that the Coalition Government encouraged local authorities to prioritise certain groups notably those in paid employment and those who make a 'contribution to the community'. According to Inside Housing (2014a), the Host Boroughs of Waltham Forest and Newham used the Localism Act 2011 powers to cut nearly 12,000 and 5,000 applicants off their waiting lists, the largest and eighth largest reductions in England respectively. Newham Council enthusiastically embraced these reforms and was one of the first councils in England to change its policies in October 2012 (LBN, 2012b). Thus ex-armed forces members and those in paid work moved to the top of Newham's social housing queue, while other applicants, notably female lone parents such as the Focus E15 mothers, were pushed to the back (*The Guardian*, 2013; Watt, 2016). In addition to such gendered effects, the shift in allocations' policy has also had racialised effects in that a declining proportion of new lettings went to BAME households in Newham (Inside Housing, 2014b).

If waiting lists have reduced since 2012, the same cannot be said about homelessness or use of temporary accommodation, as Fig. 4.4 indicates. While the numbers of households living in temporary accommodation declined in the 2009–11 period, they have been on a firmly

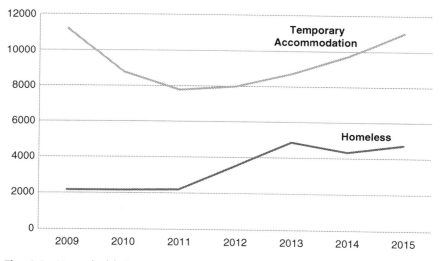

Fig. 4.4 Households in temporary accommodation, and accepted as homeless and in priority need in Host Boroughs, 2009–15

Source: Department for Communities and Local Government: Detailed local authority level homelessness figures (accessed from Shelter Housing Data Base, http://england. shelter.org.uk/professional_resources/housing_databank, December 2015

Note 1: temporary accommodation data taken from Q1 in each year.
Note 2: homeless data is based on annual totals.
Note 3: the 2015 homeless figure is a hypothetical approximation since it is based on doubling the first half-year figures, i.e. Q1 and Q2; Q3 and Q4 were unavailable at the time.

Table 4.4 Temporary accommodation in Host Boroughs and London, 2012–15

	Q1 & Q2 2012 Average	Q1 & Q2 2015 average	N increase 2012–15	Percent increase 2012–15
Host Boroughs				
Barking & Dagenham	1,115.5	1,389	274	25
Greenwich	240.5	385.5	145	60
Hackney	1,359	2,088	729	54
Newham	2,261	3,419.5	1,158	51
Tower Hamlets	1,783.5	2,025.5	242	14
Waltham Forest	1,312	2,059	747	57
Total Host Boroughs	**8071.5**	**11,366.5**	**3,295**	**41**
Total London	36,965	48,935	11,970	32

Source: Department for Communities and Local Government: Detailed local authority level homelessness figures. Section 6, Column e69c (accessed from Shelter Housing Data Base, http://england.shelter.org.uk/professional_resources/housing_databank, 10 December 2015).

upwards trajectory since. The numbers of households accepted as home-less and in priority need by the Host Boroughs have also increased considerably since 2011, albeit with a less even trajectory.

From the standpoint of assessing 'convergence' (see Introduction), we can compare these figures with their London-wide counterparts. Tables 4.4 and 4.5 do this with reference to the period just before the 2012 Games (first half of 2012), with the first half of 2015. This three year-period provides a picture of what's happened post-Games to those at the bottom of East London's failing housing system. Each table shows a negative result; the gap between the Host Boroughs and the rest of London has *widened* not reduced. Table 4.4 shows that across London the number of households in temporary accommodation increased by 32 per cent from 2012 to 2015, but by 41 per cent in the Host Boroughs with above-average increases in four boroughs (except Tower Hamlets and Barking and Dagenham). In relation to Table 4.5, the gap in terms of the numbers of households accepted as homeless and in priority need is even wider since the increase across London was 23 per cent whereas it was 63 per cent in the Host Boroughs and a huge 122 per cent in Newham. If ever there was a set of data which negates all three of the Olympics aims in relation to housing – Legacy, Convergence and

Table 4.5 Households accepted as homeless and in priority need in Host Boroughs and London, 2012–15

	Q1 & Q2 2012 Total	Q1 & Q2 2015 total	N increase 2012–15	Percent increase 2012–15
Host Boroughs				
Barking & Dagenham	247	398	151	61
Greenwich	109	194	85	78
Hackney	424	547	123	29
Newham	192	426	234	122
Tower Hamlets	159	281	122	77
Waltham Forest	319	520	201	63
Total Host Boroughs	**1,450**	**2,366**	**916**	**63**
London	7,140	8,790	1,650	23

Source: Department for Communities and Local Government: Detailed local authority level homelessness figures. Section 6, Column e69c (accessed from Shelter Housing Data Base, http://england.shelter.org.uk/professional_resources/housing_databank, December 2015).

providing 'homes for all' – it is this. Three thousand two hundred and ninety five *additional households* were living in temporary accommodation in 2015 compared to 2012, a percentage increase considerably above the London norm.

Why are so many people experiencing such housing hardships in East London? One set of issues behind such hardships, as Shelter (2013) highlight, are the insecurities faced by tenants living in the PRS, notably that the majority are on either 6 or 12-month assured short-hold tenancies. The combination of relatively easy evictions by landlords coupled with their material interest in evicting lower-paying tenants if they are located in gentrifying areas, alongside chronic social rental shortages (Watt, 2009), is a toxic mixture which will inevitably result in landlord evictions and increased homelessness (Watt and Minton, 2016). These factors, alongside the greater upwards pressure on markets rents and house prices, especially noticeable in parts of Newham such as hyper-gentrifying Stratford, are all acute in East London.

The geography of the private housing market certainly suggests that there is greater housing-related insecurity in East London than the rest of the city. One indication of this is that rates of landlord and mortgage possession claims made to the Courts in the year up to

September 2014 are extremely high in the Host Boroughs (Shelter 2014: 7). Indeed, these boroughs are 'hotspots' in that five of them (except Tower Hamlets) appear in of the 'worst 10' slots with Newham and Barking and Dagenham the highest and second highest rates for the entire country. Annual claims' rates for landlord repossessions alone are around twice the England average (1 in 47) in Waltham Forest (1 in 22), Barking and Dagenham (1 in 23) and Newham (1 in 26).

The Shelter (2013: 9) report on Hackney, Newham and Tower Hamlets identified increasing numbers of private rental eviction warrants issued from 2009 to 2012, with particularly high increases in Newham. Later data for 2012–15, presented in Table 4.6, confirm this upward trend with levels beyond the London norm for four Host Boroughs (except Greenwich and Waltham Forest). The widening gap between the Host Boroughs and London is likely to be one of the factors behind the worsening homelessness and temporary accommodation data in Tables 4.4 and 4.5. The next section moves onto consider the experiential nature of the Olympics' legacy from the perspective of young East Londoners living in temporary accommodation, the very people for whom the regeneration of the area was supposed to be for (Kennelly, 2016).

Table 4.6 Possession claims issued by landlords in Host Boroughs and London, 2012–15

	Q1 & Q2 2012 Total	Q1 & Q2 2015 Total	N increase 2012–15	Percent increase 2012–15
Host Boroughs				
Barking & Dagenham	749	896	147	19.6
Greenwich	1,035	1,021	-14	-1.4
Hackney	1,031	1,203	172	16.7
Newham	1,161	1,294	133	11.5
Tower Hamlets	723	906	183	25.3
Waltham Forest	833	882	49	5.9
Total Host Boroughs	**5,532**	**6,202**	**670**	**12.1**
London	22,782	24,710	1,928	8.5

Source: Ministry of Justice Mortgage and landlord possession statistical data June – LA CSV (accessed from Shelter Housing Data Base, http://england.shelter.org.uk/professional_resources/housing_databank, December 2015).

Young People in Temporary Accommodation

During the period leading up to the Games, young people living at the Hostel in Newham expressed firm and profoundly prescient views that the new housing developments proliferating on the East London skyline (Figs. 4.1 and 4.2) were 'not for them', but were instead aimed at wealthy incomers (Kennelly and Watt, 2012; Watt, 2013). They were concerned that rents in their area were increasing to levels beyond their limited financial means, irrespective of whether they were in paid employment or not. A recurrent theme was that Newham, and Stratford in particular, was going upmarket in a way that did not include them and even threatened their capacity to remain in the area. They were therefore experiencing what Marcuse (1986) terms 'indirect displacement' – a feeling that the neighbourhood is gentrifying in a manner which symbolically excludes existing low-income residents such as themselves (Kennelly and Watt, 2012; Watt, 2013).

The post-2012 research findings corroborate the pre-Games picture, with the vital caveat that the young people's immediate housing prospects were if anything *even worse* than previously. Anxieties over local rents were again prominent. The new homes in the area, including those at the East Village, were considered out-of-bounds, as this extract from a 2013 focus group indicates.

Respondent 5: There's nothing gained out of the houses they've just built . . . they're expensive.

Respondent 6: I get £5.48 an hour plus 50p extra if I do my team leader shifts on top of that plus for doing a keyhole shift. I need benefits still anyway. I need to work at least 30 hours a week to be able to afford my rent, my electric.

Interviewer: That's here [Hostel]?

Respondent 6: That's here. So if I'm out there, because of my age I don't get . . . I can't have the best wage. I get minimum wage, so if nominations are coming up in April, if I get nominated [see below] and if I want to live there [East Village], I physically couldn't because I just couldn't earn enough. Being in retail or just working in general at the age we are, we can't afford much. So it's not really helping us by putting prices up here, there and everywhere.

As Respondent 6 says, renting 'outside', especially in the PRS, was extremely difficult since they either worked in insecure, minimum-wage jobs or were unemployed (as seen in Chapter 10 with a similar youth demographic). High rents put the young people off from even trying to get into the East Village: 'my friend's friends paying £1,400 a month in East Village, that's not affordable' (Aaron, aged 21, Black British, 2014). Consequently these young people's only genuinely affordable option was social renting. However, the sense that the East Village social rental homes were not for 'the likes of them' was a recurrent theme.

> Respondent 1: . . . there's not one person that I heard of that's from here, or from any [HA] places that have been moved there. I haven't heard of anybody that's been moved there, it's like a sold dream.

Scott (aged 23, White British, 2013) was keenly aware who the East Village flats were for and who they were *not* for – streetwise youth like him and his friends.

> Scott: I wouldn't mind living in the new place, the [East] Village, do you know what I mean, but they ain't going to give it to you. Even though 15 per cent of it are going to the council and that, but what people do I know that are going to get stuck in there, do you know what I mean?
>
> Interviewer: So you'd like to go there?
>
> Scott: No man, I ain't expecting no-one to get moved into there that I know.
>
> Interviewer: Why?
>
> Scott: Not unless you're in a top-paid job really or unless you work for the council. That's it. They just don't want to put no roughnecks there, it's a new area, it's even got a new post code, E20. Fucking hell, do you know what I mean? They want to make it top notch and all that stuff.

For the young interviewees living in temporary housing, the East Village is all-too literally a 'place beyond belief' (see Chapter 5) – a neighbourhood that is off limits to them and to similar 'undeserving poor' in Newham and East London generally.

As Watt (2013) argues, during the pre-Olympics period, young people were cushioned from any immediate *direct displacement* pressures associated with gentrification – rising rents and/or landlord evictions – by the fact that they were physically located in the Hostel itself which meant they had some degree of security, as well as support, albeit that this accommodation was of a temporary nature. Importantly the Hostel also operated several schemes, in co-ordination with its parent housing association and Newham Council, which meant that the young people could potentially access social housing via four routes: firstly nomination rights whereby around 15 single people annually could obtain a council flat; secondly mothers being able to obtain a council tenancy; thirdly bidding rights for around five tenancies a year at the housing association; lastly applying for council properties via the normal bidding system. In addition, the Hostel had a bond scheme which assisted residents with obtaining a deposit for the high-cost PRS.

Obtaining a social tenancy was by no means easy for the youth, as Watt and Kennelly witnessed over the 2010–13 period. Nominations for council flats were highly sought after and were the subject of jealous discussion as to who got them and whether they 'deserved' them or not. Despite their scarcity, some young people *did* obtain social tenancies during 2010–13. Indeed of the twelve, 2013 interviewees, four had moved out of the Hostel by the time of the interviews, three into social housing in Newham and Tower Hamlets and the fourth into another supported temporary hostel in Newham. A few others had been nominated and were waiting for their keys. Nevertheless changes to local authority housing priorities (mentioned previously) were beginning to percolate down causing considerable trepidation, as one of the 2013 focus group female participants says.

When I moved here, they led us to believe that if you stay here for a year and a half and then you get a council flat in the Newham area. Now that I've spoken to a key worker and I've been here a year and a half, and I've been like 'what's going on'? They're saying it's up to three years now, and so they've changed it and now it's not necessarily in the Newham area. So they could move you to a completely different area, whereas I've based my life here, everything around – like I've got my doctors, I've got my work, everything I do is around here, now I could be moved like on the other side of London, so they kind of give you false promises.

By 2014 young people's immediate housing prospects had drastically worsened. As a worker at the Hostel explained, not only did the PRS bond scheme no longer exist, but the routes into social tenancies had either ceased (council nominations and tenancies for mothers), or had become much tighter (council bidding and housing association nominations). Faced with such a shrinking set of options, the 2014 interviewees had only vague or unrealistic plans as to what to do next. Jason (aged 21, Black British) had been in the Hostel two and half years; he regularly bid for council homes, with no luck, and 'guessed' that if he stayed long enough then he would eventually get his own house. Jourds (aged 21, Black British) was waiting for an offer of a flat from the housing association, but his tenancy had been terminated six months previously and he was frustrated with how long it was taking.

Austerity welfare cuts plus changes to Newham's waiting list policies had brought about this worsening situation; the number of people the Hostel could support was falling and it was generally downsizing. New admissions ceased in early 2014 and a programme of evictions was underway related to rent arrears. A self-fulfilling prophecy was also happening whereby the young people expected to be evicted and therefore stopped paying their rent – which then led to their eviction. By September 2014, the number of people who were funded was half the Hostel's capacity, while the staff had also been halved, according to a worker. By the end of 2014, a general air of decline and frustration was descending in contrast to 2010–13 period when the Hostel was fully occupied, properly staffed and had a general hubbub of purposeful activity. Staff were caught in the process of 'managed decline' and one worker described how she was only too well aware that this was inadequate in terms of supporting the young people in their care, several of whom were vulnerable.[6] She estimated that

---

[6] The worker was made redundant and eventually left. The Hostel was closed as a dedicated supported housing unit for youth in 2016.

only 10 per cent of the young people were happy to leave the unit. Some tried to patch up their relations with their parents or guardians and return home, but as the worker repeated several times, 'private renting is basically the only option'.

As a consequence of all these changes, young people's cushion against gentrification-induced displacement was being dismantled. They were far more likely to experience *direct displacement*, not only in the short-term due to being evicted from the Hostel itself for rent arrears, but also in the medium-term since they would more than likely end up in the insecure PRS and suffer subsequent evictions and moving on as the rents increased beyond their limited capacity to pay for them.

Displacing the Homeless

A combination of welfare and housing 'reforms' and austerity cutbacks – the housing benefit (HB) cap, introduction of the bedroom tax and changes to housing allocations (Hodkinson and Robbins, 2013), as well as cuts to local housing allowance (LHA)[7] in the PRS (Powell, 2015) – have resulted in London councils exporting their homeless families to temporary accommodation in cheaper areas either within or outside London. London councils are increasingly turning to the PRS to provide temporary accommodation and housing their homeless populations (Shelter, 2013) – ironically at the very same time that private landlords in London are increasingly financially unable (or more accurately unwilling) to sustain such placements because of LHA cuts (Powell, 2015). These displacement pressures form part of wider processes of what housing campaigners have, not without good reason, dubbed 'social cleansing', whereby London councils remove the 'undeserving poor' from their areas (Watt and Minton, 2016).

The Bureau of Investigative Journalism (2013) found that 32,643 households were moved out of London boroughs from 2009–10 to 2012–13. Shelter (2013) identified 11,513 homeless households placed in temporary

[7] LHA is 'the regime for administering HB in the private rented sector' (Powell, 2015: 321).

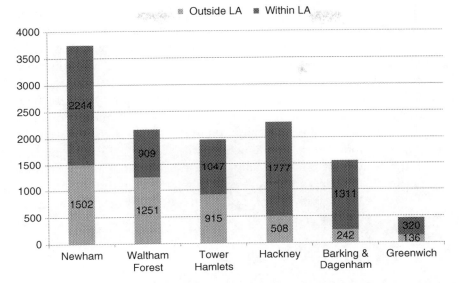

Fig. 4.5 Households in temporary accommodation located within and outside local authority, Host Boroughs, July–September 2015, N.

Source: Homeless Statistics – Statutory Homelessness, July-September 2015, Detailed Local Authority Level Responses, Section 6, 17 December 2015, available at: https://www.gov.uk/government/statistical-data-sets/live-tables-on-homelessness

accommodation outside their home borough in 2012; of these 580 households (5 per cent) were placed outside London with 120 relocated 20 miles or more away. Figure 4.5 provides later data on households living in temporary accommodation within and outside the local authority for the individual Host Boroughs from July to September 2015. The 1,502 in Newham and 1,251 in Waltham Forest in fact represent the highest and third highest numbers living in temporary accommodation in another local authority in London. In total, 4,554 households were living in temporary accommodation outside each individual Host Borough, while the latter's average of 37 per cent was above the 34 per cent London average.

In order to better understand the sociological processes and impacts involved in these out-of-borough displacements, we will draw upon ongoing ethnographic research with people living in temporary accommodation in East London and also in Welwyn Garden City

(WGC), a town around 25 miles north of London. These people were mainly, although not exclusively, female lone parents and from BAME backgrounds. They had approached their respective council as being homeless because they suffered from landlord evictions, family disputes, domestic violence, as well as overcrowding (see Watt, 2017).

Assistance by the council included being offered temporary housing both inside and outside of the borough. Stressful and complex enforced mobility patterns were common. Amran (aged 20s, Black British, 2015), for example, was ejected from her brother's over-crowded home when she became pregnant. Newham Council initially relocated her to temporary accommodation in Wandsworth in south west London, nearly 10 miles from her family, before they eventually placed her in a bed and breakfast hostel in Forest Gate back in Newham. Sade (aged 40s, Black British, 2015) approached Waltham Forest Council as homeless in 2012 after she left her violent partner. She and her daughter were first relocated to temporary accommodation in the adjacent borough of Redbridge; from there they were moved to Enfield, followed by sofa surfing at Sade's adult son's flat back in Waltham Forest, and then eventually they were sent to WGC.

The block of 45 self-contained 'studio flats' in WGC where Sade lived – Boundary House – is located about two miles from the town centre, and was being used as temporary accommodation by several London councils, but especially Newham and Waltham Forest. Although this accommodation was nominally 'temporary', several residents had been there for well over a year, the longest having been there nearly four years. Rhianna (aged 20s, Black British, 2016) lived at Boundary House with her two young children and despairingly said:

> I feel trapped, I don't know how to get out of this place. [. . .] I was told by the council that I'd be here a couple of months and its two and a half years, and now they're saying there's nothing we can do for you.

The sense of abandonment – both social and spatial – for Rhianna and others like her was palpable. Michael (aged 40s, Black British, 2016) was a single parent who had been at WGC nine months: 'we should not be up here, it's ridiculous, they [council] want us to go into private renting, they want us out of their responsibility'. Michael was desperate to get back to London, as most Boundary House residents were; London was where family and support networks were, where they could buy their own ethnic food (e.g. Halal meat), and where they had a better chance of obtaining paid work.

Living conditions at Boundary House were reminiscent of Dickensian London in terms of over-crowding and quality (see Belgrave, 2016). Each family lived and slept in a small studio flat. One woman slept with her two children on beds while her husband slept on the floor in front of the sofa and they had been doing so for two years (Fig. 4.6). Parents described how their children were repeatedly falling ill because of damp and mould which kept coming back because they had to cook, wash and dry clothes in the same small room. Not only were living conditions appalling, but tenants/HB paid exorbitant rents to the managing

Fig. 4.6 Welwyn Garden City – studio flat for two adults and two children (kitchen and washing in background), June 2015

Source: Paul Watt

agents/landlord of the block. Krista (aged 37, White Eastern European, 2015) paid a monthly rent of £1,300 excluding electricity; most of this amount was covered by HB, but still paid over £120 herself.

The process of applying as homeless typically involved applicants having to wait until the day they were evicted before going to the council offices for assistance, and then more or less having to take whatever was offered to them, often on the same or following day (cf. Shelter, 2013). Not accepting the offer, no matter how unsuitable it might be, would result in them having made themselves 'intentionally homeless' and then consequently the council would have no further duty to assist them. Interviewees mentioned being offered places in Hastings, Walsall, Birmingham and Manchester, as well as Welwyn and Basildon. The combination of their dire living conditions and the conditional nature of the 'support' they were being given placed enormous psychological stress on all the interviewees which some said affected their mental health. One young mother (Adriana, aged 20s, Black British, 2015) had been offered a house in Bexhill-on-Sea, a coastal town 50 miles south of London. Adriana reported 'pleading' with housing officials not to have to go there and leave her family in Newham, but was told that she should think herself 'lucky' that she was not being sent to Birmingham.

It is important to recognise how the London housing market operates in relation to welfare and housing reforms and cuts (Powell, 2015). While central London boroughs such as Westminster have exported their homeless populations elsewhere to cheaper London areas for many years, a combination of rising private rents with recent 'reforms' and cuts have rendered traditionally cheaper London areas, such as East London, increasingly out-of-bounds for private tenants relying upon LHA, as Powell (2015) illustrates and East London councils admit. At the time of the interview, Ousman (aged 40s, Black African, 2015) was living with his wife and young children in two adjacent flats in a large block being used as temporary accommodation in Newham. The family had rented a private house in the borough for five years, but were evicted because the landlord sold the property. Despite earning an above-average salary, Ousman still needed to claim some HB/LHA to afford the increasing private rents. However the Newham estate agents and land-lords Ousman approached refused to let him a property because he would claim HB; such refusals are increasingly common in London (Powell, 2015). Ousman therefore had no option but to turn to the council for assistance. At first he was offered two separate flats at opposite ends of his current block. Having refused this, because of its sheer impracticality, the family went to stay at friends for a few days. Ousman went onto describe how he was offered his present accommodation.

> We were coerced into accepting this, because the [homelessness] manager told me that if you don't go in the next 10 minutes, you are going to lose that property and you will not have any place to live in. I said to her, 'don't threaten me, I work like you'.

Following six months at the block, Ousman and his family were moved by the council to a three-bed house in Manor Park, but the contract was on a week-by-week basis with, as he said, no security whatsoever.

Housing Campaigns: 'Social Housing Not Social Cleansing'

In and amongst the maelstrom of intertwined systemic housing failures and personal tragedies in post-Olympic East London, several campaigns have formed to challenge the neoliberal political consensus around housing including, in no particular order, Tower Hamlets Renters, DIGS – Hackney Renters, and Action East End (all affiliated to the London-wide Radical Housing Network; http://radicalhousingnetwork.org/), plus the campaign to save the TUSH housing co-operative in Tower Hamlets (https://towerhamletsrenters.wordpress.com/tag/tush-housing-co-op/). Probably the most famous is the Focus E15 campaign which formed around a group of young mothers who were threatened with eviction from the Focus E15 foyer in Stratford (Watt, 2016). Because the rules regarding allocations had been changed by Newham Council, the mothers' capacity to access council housing was reduced. However instead of dutifully accepting their allotted fate, the mothers and their supporters mounted a high-profile campaign which resulted in the mothers being successfully re-housed in East London near their support networks, albeit largely in the PRS. The Focus E15 campaign has subsequently expanded its remit to embrace the cause of 'social housing not social cleansing' in London. One of the campaign's major actions was the temporary occupation of the two-thirds empty Carpenters Estate in Stratford, a council-built estate; Dennison Point, one of the estate's largely empty tower blocks, can be seen in Fig. 4.1. This estate has been gradually 'decanted' (emptied) since 2005 in lieu of the Godot-like 'regeneration' which has never arrived (Watt, 2013); the last regeneration partner, University College London, pulled out in May 2013.

The Focus E15 campaign held a weekly Saturday stall in Stratford since autumn 2013. This regular stall is located a few yards from many of the new out-of-reach, but in-site Stratford upmarket housing developments, including Stratford Plaza discussed before (Fig. 4.1). The stall functions as a hub for housing activists, but even more importantly as a place that those suffering from housing deprivation can come to tell their stories and receive empathetic advice, support and solidarity (Watt, 2016). Although people come to the stall from all over London and even beyond, most are East Londoners and especially from Newham – those very same people who are supposedly basking in the golden glow of the 2012 Games housing legacy. Figure 4.7 illustrates one such story from a stall visitor.

To return to the question of social housing provision in post-Olympic Newham – or to be more precise, lack of provision – the development plans for the Upton Park home of West Ham United Football club (see Chapter 9) have prompted considerable local opposition. The initial development proposal for the Boleyn Ground site, included 6 per cent affordable housing but no SRH element. Two campaigns – 'Campaign for 100 per cent Social Housing for the Boleyn Ground Development' (boleyndev, 2016) and 'Newham Citizens' (Citizens UK, 2016) – opposed this, albeit with the former aiming for 100 per cent social rental properties and the latter lobbying for 35 per cent affordable housing, i.e. at the

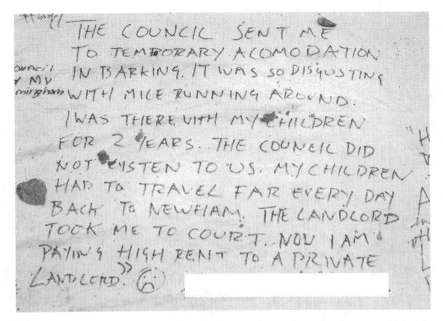

Fig. 4.7 Visitor's written testimony at the Focus E15 stall, Stratford Broadway, August 2014

Source: Paul Watt

bottom end of Newham Council's borough-wide affordable housing target of 35–50 per cent. Whilst the council negotiated an increase in the affordable housing element to 25 per cent, it accepted plans for 842 new homes in March 2016 – with 125 at affordable rent and 84 shared ownership homes (Newham Recorder, 2016). This outcome fell well short of what campaigners lobbied for and is yet again indicative of Newham Councils' apparent reluctance to expand social housing provision in the borough.

> Despite over 700 objection letters submitted by our campaign and 11 objecting speakers, the Strategic Planning Committee approved plans for the Boleyn Ground development with only 25 per cent so called 'affordable housing' and no social housing, woefully failing to

meet the minimum 35 per cent required by Newham's Core Strategy. (boleyndev, 2016)[8]

Conclusion

Our findings in this chapter do not unfortunately lead us to alter our previous assessment that the 2012 Games' housing legacy is high on hyperbole but low in terms of genuinely tackling the manifold housing problems of East London. While the LLDC and Host Boroughs can point to the East Village tower blocks and the other new housing developments in and around the QEOP as the visible results of staging the 2012 Games, these have at best merely dented long-term unmet housing needs in East London, such as large numbers on waiting lists for social housing and high levels of homelessness, overcrowding and poor quality homes (see also Thompson et al., 2017).

At the present time, the transformation of Stratford, the 2012 Games investment epicentre, is well underway as we have discussed. There appears to be no shortage of private-sector developers interested in building in the area and capturing the value uplift from significant public-sector investment (Financial Times, 2013; Savills, 2014). This area, indeed Newham as a whole, has also become a place for BTL investors wishing to cash in on rising rents, a process which is transforming an already-insecure PRS into a veritable minefield of tenant repossessions and evictions. Ironically even if those people who are experiencing upward mobility wanted to stay in Stratford, they probably couldn't afford to do so as the area moves upmarket at a rate of knots. Ultimately the bulk of new-build East London housing is not intended to meet needs (enabling of homes as use values), but rather with maximising investment returns (exchange values) at a time of record low interest rates. As such these housing developments are far divorced from those families and individuals living in housing need whose plight was

---

[8] Paul Watt was one of the 11 objectors (Newham Recorder, 2016).

exploited to justify Team GB winning the bid, including rhetoric about transforming the area for 'everyone who lives there'.

This 'everyone' includes the young people living in temporary accommodation, such as Leroy quoted at the head of this chapter. Their cynicism towards the 2012 Olympics' regeneration ('It's not for us'; Watt, 2013), and arguably towards rich incomers and the political class generally ('them'), can only deepen as they move from one cramped, dingy private bedsit to another via way of friends' sofas, if they're lucky, or shop doorways if they aren't. The 'undeserving poor' will grow in size, as more of them struggle to eke out an existence at the margins of East London's broken housing system. At the same time, while East London as a whole is increasingly attractive to housing investors, this attractiveness, allied with austerity cuts, housing 'reforms' and long-run shortages of social housing, has meant greater displacement of homeless populations to the city's marginal spaces and beyond (cf. Powell, 2015). One can argue that these worsening displacement processes mean that assessing the Games legacy by walking around the East Village and QEOP – as so many official and unofficial tours of post-Olympic East London do – is both socially and spatially myopic. If one really wants to look for the underside of the Games housing legacy, one should travel out to those suburban towns, such as Welwyn and Basildon, where the ex-East London homeless populations are being decamped via subliminal processes of social cleansing (Watt, 2017).

We are left with the question of how we explain this slippage between original policy intentions and outcomes. In one sense, the convergence outcomes were always chimerical since an absence of specific budgets meant they could be 'perceived as a "wish list" rather than a viable strategy for the reduction of deprivation in east London' (Bernstock, 2014: 88). On housing, there was also a profound mismatch between the grandiose head-line pronouncements – 'homes for all' – and their related measurable indicators of which there was only one – delivery of total and affordable housing units (Host Boroughs Unit, 2009). Thus right from the very start, the Host Boroughs did not develop a robust and consistent battery of adequate indicators for housing in the same way that they did for other outcomes such as education, health and employment (Host Boroughs Unit, 2009).[9] It is also worth reiterating how 'off message' (i.e. negative) housing needs' trends, such as overcrowding and homelessness, are downplayed or even erased in official legacy reports (Growth Boroughs Unit, 2015; UEL, 2015). Thus the Olympics' housing legacy can receive an official green light for progress because new homes are being built, some of which are 'affordable', despite the fact that the living circumstances of those at the bottom of East London's broken housing system are even worse than they were before the Games.

The wider policy context has of course made an unsatisfactory situation worse. Key components of planning and regeneration in 2005 have been all but dismantled. Planning gain even in 2005 rarely achieved 50 per cent affordable housing, but nevertheless levels were much higher than currently (Bernstock, 2014). Ironically in the early 2000s, Newham Council argued that there was a need for more market housing to balance what was perceived as too much social housing. However this has aided the opposite trajectory and the problem now is that we are confronted with huge concentrations of wealth, as seen in the plethora of new apartment blocks on the Stratford skyline, alongside mounting housing deprivation and associated human misery, anger and frustration on the streets below. It is noteworthy that even some Newham Labour Councillors, albeit somewhat belatedly, have come to accept that the Olympic housing legacy is less than satisfactory in relation to affordable housing provision (Gardiner 2016).

We will leave the final words to Amran, a homeless female lone parent with a young child, who had grown up in Newham. Amran had worked in catering in the Olympic Park during the Games and received free tickets as a result, and she described being 'really excited' by the Olympics. Once the Games ended, however, 'everybody went back on benefits, because it was all temporary jobs'. At the time of the interview (summer 2015), Amran was living in trepidation of imminent eviction from her temporary accommodation coupled with being declared

---

[9] For example, the Host Boroughs Unit (2009) report contained five educational and six health and well-being indicators.

'intentionally homeless' by the council because she had refused an offer of a property in Basildon, many miles from her East London support networks, and a place where she had experienced Islamophobic/racial abuse.

> It's gone really bad, like Newham [Council] used to be a place where, as it says on their slogan, 'You can live'... but they've taken that away, it's become a money making thing, you can see it, on every corner there's brand new houses being built but it also says you can buy them, it talks about how much it is to lease and what you pay upfront. It's not like you can go through them to rent it, they won't do it, no-one that's on benefits or... And even if you're not on benefits, even if you're working, you can't afford it, the rent is like a grand something and you're probably getting that at work anyway so it's not just like people are on benefits it's affecting, it's affecting everybody. [...] It's going to be everybody soon, it's going to be if you can live in the area, you have to earn £40 k, £20 k a year, you cannot earn the normal £25 k, £20 k, £12 k a year and live here, it's getting really bad. [...] The place you grew up, the place you call your area, your home, is getting taken away from you.

Acknowledgements   Paul Watt's 2014–17 research was funded by the School of Social Sciences, History and Philosophy, Birkbeck, University of London. Thanks to all the interviewees who took part in the research, and to Phil Cohen, Debbie Humphry and Jacqueline Kennelly for their helpful comments on earlier drafts of this chapter.

References

Belgrave, K. (2016) 'This is how you and your kids can expect to live if you lose your home', *Kate Belgrave: Talking with People Dealing with Public Sector Cuts*, 24 January 2016, http://www.katebelgrave.com/2016/01/this-is-how-you-and-your-kids-can-expect-to-live-if-you-lose-your-home/.

Bernstock P (2014) *Olympic Housing: A Critical Review of London 2012's Legacy*. Farnham: Ashgate.

boleyndev100. (2016) 'Campaign for 100% Social Housing for the Boleyn Ground development', https://boleyndev100.wordpress.com/.

Bowie, D. (2010) *Politics, Planning and Homes in a World City*. London: Routledge.

Brownill, S., Cho, Y., Keivani, R., Nase, I., Downing, L., Valler, D., Whitehouse, N. and Bernstock, P. (2015) *Rethinking Planning Obligations: balancing housing numbers and affordability*. York: Joseph Rowntree Foundation.

Building construction design. (2015) 'Tower Hamlets builds highest number of affordable homes in country', 25 June 2015, http://www.buildingcon structiondesign.co.uk/news/tower-hamlets-builds-highest-number-of-afford able-homes-in-country/.

The Bureau of Investigative Journalism. (2013) 'Infographic: price of UK's escalating housing crisis', 20 May 2013, https://www.thebureauinvestigates. com/2013/05/20/info-graphic-the-price-of-britains-escalating-housing-crisis/.

Burns, T. (2014) 'An update on East Village, E20: a legacy neighbourhood for London'. Presentation at The Housing Forum, 15 October 2014.

Butcher, M. and Dickens, L. (2016) 'Spatial dislocation and affective displace-ment: youth perspectives on gentrification in London', *International Journal of Urban and Regional Research*, 40(4): 800–816.

Chobham Manor E20. (2016) 'Destined to be one of London's most sought after addresses', http://chobhammanor.co.uk/, accessed at 20 May 2016.

Citizens UK. (2016) 'Community demands 300 homes on the Boleyn Development', http://www.citizensuk.org/community_demands_300_homes.

Council of Mortgage Lenders. (2015) 'Buy-to-let: the past is no guide to the future', http://www.cml.org.uk/news/buy-to-let-the-past-is-no-guide-to-the-future/.

DCMS. (2013) *Report 5, Post-Games Evaluation: Meta Evaluation of the Impacts and Legacy of the London 2012 Olympic Games and Paralympic Games*. London: DCMS.

Delancey. (2015) 'East Village, London E20: press release', 2 October 2015, http://www.delancey.com/east-village.html.

Easier Property (2014) 'Raft of measures mean Chobham Manor homes are accessible for all', *Easier Property*, 30 August 2014, http://www.easier.com/125099-raft-of-measures-mean-chobham-manor-homes-are-accessible-for-all.html.

East Thames Group. (2011) *Impact of the Affordable Rent Model: Newham*. London: East Thames Group.

Financial Times. (2013) 'Post-Olympics developments in Stratford', *Financial Times*, 15 March 2013.

Flynn, J. (2016) 'Complete control: developers, financial viability and regeneration at the Elephant and Castle', *City* 20(2): 278–286.

Gardiner, J. (2016) 'Olympic games: keeping the legacy alive', *Building.co.uk*, 28 July 2016, http://www.building.co.uk/analysis/olympic-games-keeping-the-legacy-alive/5082800.article.

Generation Rent (2015) 'East Village tenants face Olympic rent rises', 3 April 2015, http://www.generationrent.org/east_village_tenants_face_olympic_rent_rises

Growth Boroughs Unit. (2014) *Convergence: Annual Report, 2013–2014*. London: Growth Boroughs Unit.

Growth Boroughs Unit. (2015) *Convergence: Annual Report, 2014–2015*. London: Growth Boroughs Unit.

Guardian. (2013) 'Young mothers evicted from London hostel may be rehoused 200 miles away', *The Guardian*, 14 October 2013.

Halifax Press Team. (2015) 'Newham is UK's top house price performer in 2015', *Press Release 28/12/2015*. Leeds: Halifax Press Team.

Hodkinson S. and Robbins, G. (2013) 'The return of class war Conservatism? Housing under the UK Coalition Government', *Critical Social Policy* 33: 57–77.

Host Boroughs Unit. (2009) *Strategic Regeneration Framework: An Olympic Legacy for the Host Boroughs*. London: Host Boroughs Unit.

Inside Housing. (2012) 'The last social homes', *Inside Housing*, 29 June 2012.

Inside Housing. (2013) 'Prices revealed for transformed Olympic village properties', *Inside Housing*, 18 September 2013.

Inside Housing. (2014a) 'Locked out', *Inside Housing*, 2 May 2014.

Inside Housing. (2014b) 'Ethnicity and new social housing lets', *Inside Housing*, 16 July 2014.

Jowell, T. (2015) 'Olympic legacy failure: Tessa Jowell attacks 'wicked' Coalition Government', *The Guardian*, 5 July 2015.

Kennelly, J. (2016). *Olympic Exclusions: Youth, Poverty and Social Legacies*. London and New York: Routledge.

Kennelly, J. and Watt, P. (2011) 'Sanitizing public space in Olympic host cities: the spatial experiences of marginalized youth in 2010 Vancouver and 2012 London', *Sociology* 45(5): 765–781.

Kennelly, J. and Watt, P. (2012) 'Seeing Olympic effects through the eyes of marginally housed youth: changing places and the gentrification of east London', *Visual Studies* 27(2): 151–160.

LBN. [London Borough of Newham] (2012a) *Newham New Housing Allocations Scheme – Equalities Impact Assessment*, 17 September 2012. London: London Borough of Newham.

LBN. (2012b) 'Armed services and people in employment to be prioritised for social housing', LBN website, accessed 19 August 2015:.

LBTH. [London Borough of Tower Hamlets] (2010) *Tower Hamlets Housing Strategy 2009–2012: Annual Report – 2009/10*. London: London Borough of Tower Hamlets.

LLDC. (2014a) *LLDC Local Plan Background Paper: Housing, August 2014*. London: LLDC.

LLDC. (2014b) Legacy Communities Scheme Accelerated Delivery 14/00035/AOD, 22 April 2014.

London Tenants Federation. (2012) *The Affordable Housing Con*. London: London Tenants Federation.

LSE Housing and Communities. (2014) *Facing Debt: Economic Resilience in Newham*. CASE Report 83. London: Centre for Analysis of Social Exclusion, London School of Economics.

Marcuse, P. (1986) 'Abandonment, gentrification and displacement: the linkages in New York City', in N. Smith and P. Williams (eds.), *Gentrification and the City*. London: Unwin Hyman.

Minton, A. (2012) *Ground Control. Fear and Happiness in the Twenty-First-Century City*. London: Penguin.

Newham Recorder. (2016) 'Boleyn Ground development approved with minimum of 25% affordable housing', *Newham Recorder*, 11 March.

ONS. (2014a) *Overcrowding and Under-Occupation in England and Wales*. London: Office for National Statistics.

ONS. (2014b) *Overcrowding and Under-Occupation by Ethnic Group, 2011*. London: Office for National Statistics.

OPLC [Olympic Park Legacy Company]. (2011) *Legacy Communities Scheme*. London: Olympic Park Legacy Company.

OPLC. (2012) *Legacy Communities Scheme: Regulation 22: Response and Additional Information Submission: Addendum, Housing and Social Infrastructure Statement*. London: Olympic Park Legacy Company.

Powell, R. (2015) 'Housing Benefit reform and the private rented sector in the UK: on the deleterious effects of short-term, ideological knowledge', *Housing, Theory and Society* 32(3): 320–345.

Rightmove. (2015) '3 bedroom apartment for sale, shared ownership', http://www.rightmove.co.uk/property-for-sale/property-50986831.html, accessed 3 August 2015.

Savills. (2014) *London Development: Building opportunities East of City*. London: Savills World Research, Autumn 2014, http://pdf.euro.savills.co.uk/uk/residential-other/east-of-city.pdf.

Shelter. (2013) *When the Golden Dust Settles: Housing in Hackney, Newham and Tower Hamlets after the Olympic Games*. London: Shelter.

Shelter. (2014) *Repossession and Eviction Hotspots – September 2014*. London: Shelter.

Slater, T. (2014) 'The Myth of "Broken Britain": welfare reform and the production of ignorance', *Antipode* 46(4): 948–969.

Somerville, P. (2016) 'Coalition housing policy in England', in H. Bochel and M. Powell (eds.), *Coalition Social Policy*. Bristol: Policy Press.

Telegraph. (2015) 'Buy-to-let: hotspots for 2015 revealed', *The Telegraph*, 28 May 2015. http://www.telegraph.co.uk/finance/personalfinance/investing/buy-to-let/11633681/Buy-to-let-hotspots-for-2015-revealed.html.

Thompson, C, Lewis, D.J., Greenhalgh, T., Smith, N.R., Fahy, A.E. and Cummins, S. (2017) '"I don't know how I'm still standing": a Bakhtinian analysis of social housing and health narratives in East London', *Social Science & Medicine* 177: 27–34.

Triathlon Homes. (2014) 'Demand sky high at East Village', 24th March 2014.

UEL [University of East London]. (2015) *Olympic Games Impact Study – London 2012 Post-Games Report*. London: University of East London.

Watt, P. (2009) 'Social housing and regeneration in London', in: R. Imrie, L. Lees and M. Raco (eds.), *Regenerating London*. London: Routledge.

Watt, P. (2013) '"It's not for us": Regeneration, the 2012 Olympics and the gentrification of East London', *City* 17(1): 99–118.

Watt, P. (2016) 'A nomadic war machine in the metropolis: en/countering London's 21st century housing crisis with Focus E15', *City* 20(2): 297–320.

Watt, P. (2017) 'Gendering the right to housing in the city: homeless female lone parents in Post-Olympics, austerity East London', *Cities*, online, http://www.sciencedirect.com/science/article/pii/S0264275116302165

Watt, P. and Minton, A. (2016) 'London's housing crisis and its activisms', *City* 20(2): 204–221.

Wessendorf, S. (2014) *Commonplace Diversity: Social Relations in a Super-Diverse context*. Basingstoke: Palgrave Macmillan.

Paul Watt is Reader in Urban Studies at Birkbeck, University of London. He has published widely on topics including the London housing crisis, social rental housing, urban regeneration, suburbanization, and the 2012 Olympic Games. He is co-author (with Tim Butler) of *Understanding Social Inequality* (Sage, 2007), co-editor (with Peer Smets) of *Mobilities and Neighbourhood Belonging in Cities and Suburbs* (Palgrave Macmillan, 2014) and co-editor (with Peer Smets) of *Social Housing and Urban Renewal: A Cross-National Perspective* (Emerald, 2017). He sits on the Editorial Board of City (Taylor & Francis) and is Board Member of the Research Committee on Sociology of Urban and Regional Development (RC21), International Sociological Association.

Penny Bernstock is Reader In Urban Regeneration at the University of East London and is Director of the Centre for East London Studies. She has published extensively on housing and urban regeneration in East London. She has previously worked as an Action researcher for the Docklands forum and a Research Officer at the London School of Economics. She has recently published *Olympic Housing: A Critical Review of London 2012's Legacy* (Ashgate, 2014).

5

A Place Beyond Belief: Hysterical Materialism and the Making of East 20

Phil Cohen

As a microcosm of what we hope to achieve, look at the Olympics and their Legacy . . . a city that looked extraordinarily good, diverse, welcoming, at ease with itself. . . . .Unlike virtually, any other post-Olympic park we are turning London's site into a pole of attraction for tourists and employment . . . The bedrock of infrastructure is fast being accelerated and directly as a result of the Olympics. . . . The social and cultural legacy is real . . . We have set ourselves the goal of 'convergence'. The idea is that kids growing up in East London should have the same life chances as anywhere else. There is no reason why the kids of East London should not benefit from, say, rugby, as much as the kids from Richmond. After two hours of hard physical exercise such as scrumming and tackling around the ankles, a 16 year old is less likely to want to get into a gang fight.

P. Cohen (✉)
University of East London, London, England
e-mail: pcohen763@hotmail.co.uk

139

P. Cohen, P. Watt (eds.), *London 2012 and the Post-Olympics City*,
DOI 10.1057/978-1-137-48947-0_5

Fig. 5.1 Newham poster celebrating winning the 2012 bid

Boris Johnson – *2020 Vision. The Greatest City on Earth: Ambitions for London*

In dreams begin responsibilities W.B. Yeats[1]

---

[1] This is an epigraph to a collection of Yeats' poems published in 1916, but written before the Easter uprising in Dublin. It refers to the poet's attempt to distance himself from the romantic nationalism associated with the 'Celtic Twilight' and engage with contemporary political realities, including the Workers strike of 1913. The epigraph was used by Delmer Schwarz as the title for his most famous short story, published in 1919 in which the protagonist dreams he is watching a film featuring his parents courtship and vocally intervenes in a row between them on screen, resulting in his being expelled from the cinema. In his dream the narrator thus throws a spanner in the works of the dream factory, and is promptly evicted from its mise en scene. The hero acts as if the screen depiction was happening in real time, and as if his intervention possessed a magical power of performativity and could actually stop his parent rowing, and possibly breaking up. His eviction from the cinema – and by implication from the dream – illustrates the issue of hysterical materialism being addressed in this chapter.

Living the Dream

The Olympics are the stuff that dreams are made of, as the opening ceremony with its central reference to Shakespeare's *Tempest* and to Britain as an enchanted isle so winningly demonstrated. But if the Olympics are a dream factory or a dream machine, what it produces is a very material dream, a dream realized in terms of material infrastructures, and not just spectacle. Although its encoding follows specific rules of condensation and displacement, dream material may, of course have many sources. Psychoanalysis insists that its navel, where its meanings are mostly tightly knotted together and difficult to unravel and where its narrative reaches down into the unknown, derives from its relation to a primordial architecture: the maternal body as our birthplace and first homeland we have left behind, become cut off from but continue to hold unconsciously in mind, if only as a commemorative scar, so that it serves as a template for our modes of worldly inhabitation and quasi-umbilical attachment to place (Balint, 1964; McDougall, 1989).[2] The unconscious drive to possess an ideal replacement for this original home, once liberated from material constraint, leads to the building of palaces, vanity projects and follies of every kind, like the Arcelor Mittal Tower in the Queen Elizabeth Olympic Park, so many megalomaniac exercises in navel gazing designed to win the plaudits of an admiring crowd (Damisch, 2001; Konings, 2015). The construction of this 'other scene' of regeneration does not follow the rational calculus of urban planning, with its benchmarks and milestones, but rather operates its own subliminal logic of repetition, reversal, and disavowal, a logic submerged within the analytic rigours of cost/benefit analysis, the gloss of promotional hype and the architectural sublime (Pile, 2005).[3] By

---

[2] This primary process of environmental attachment is virtually ignored by psycho-geographers who are more influenced by the French situationists, who in turn draw on Bachelard's phenomenological 'topo-analysis' as advanced in his book *The Poetics of Space* (1994), in which he completely rejects the Freudian Unconscious. The psycho-social geography advanced here draws on Michael Balint's Kleinian model of spatial object relations supplemented by an ethno–cartographic approach to understanding how mental maps are formed through cultural processes.

[3] It was difficult for modernist architects and planners to recognise this 'other scene' of urban regeneration because their professional training predisposed them to emphasise the creation of a

the same token, the dream materialities of the Post-Olympic city, like the narrative legacy of Games Time itself, are subject to nostalgic reminiscence and cynical dismissal as well as narcissistic elaboration or foreclosure.

What I shall call 'hysterical materialism' involves a particular involution of this process, through a play of substitutions between the social imaginary, the symbolic and the real. Material things (artefacts, instruments, devices and technologies of every kind), instead of being treated as products of labour, as affordances or hindrances to human projects, are magically invested with an autonomous power of efficacy, a mysterious capacity to condition or compel human actions which in fact substitutes itself for them. The displacement effect can go the other way, symbolic action being substituted for a material intervention which is interdicted. In both cases changeable social relations between things take on a phantasmagoric form and are treated hysterically *as if* they were fixed physical relations between people (Appadurai, 1986; Latour, 2014).

It has recently been argued that hysterical materialism is symptomatic of the emotional logic of late capitalism, and its enrichment economy, an economy in which the financialisation of personal assets (not only houses and possessions but social, cultural and intellectual capacity) has become a prime driver of wealth creation and its transmission between the generations (Konings, 2015; Boltanski and Esquerre, 2016). In a society dominated by what Karl Marx called 'fictitious capital', 'money talks', while people without it are robbed of a voice in economic affairs, and even the most ephemeral objects of consumption become collectibles and acquire additional market and status value (Hudson, 2010; Haiven, 2014). Hysterical materialism is fictitious capital in ideological action; at a political level it involves substituting a material problem which the political class has neither the will or capacity to solve (viz. structural inequality in a capitalist society)

---

rational spacial order. The shift to a post-modern aesthetic encouraged greater experimentation with urban form, and opened up room for the utopian and phantasmagoric, albeit at the service of fictitious capital.

for a problem which is resolvable through purely symbolic means which may become financialised (viz. winning an Olympic Games bid through lobbying, PR and sometimes bribery) and then passing that off as a way of tackling the deeper disavowed issue. Olympic urbanism involves a double substitution: of the object (the urban fabric) for what it is made to represent (the fabrication of the Olympic vision), and of the subject (the architectonic drive of the master plan) for a consensual discourse (the Olympic compact) in which it is magically realised. Social engineering, underpinned by environmental or technological determinism, so prevalent in the Olympic bid and civic compact discourse is a prime example of hysterical materialism at work.

There is no doubt about the hysterical nature of Boris Johnson's vision of the 2012 Games as a model for London's future regeneration. His text alternates between purple prose lyricism and boastful claims (Johnson, 2013). His panegyric to the 'Legacy Games' reiterates the Panglossian script of the original Olympic compact: London's citizens are invited to 'live the dream' of being in the best of all possible worlds, where they can enjoy the fruits of capitalism and the delights of consumerism, whilst saving the planet, loving their neighbour and engaging in strenuous physical activity designed to sublimate their well-known tendency to riot, engage in gang fights and generally let the side down. It is that carefully arranged marriage between commerce and communitas which made the 2012 Olympics such a gift for New Labour and also for the neoliberal brand of coalition politics that followed. Like all arranged marriages, what seems to be a mutually beneficial merger of interests was in fact a takeover bid in which the moral economy of gift exchange was effectively marketised: 'buy one get one free' became the *mot d'ordre* of the bonanza promised to Londoners as part of the Olympic legacy compact. Yet, as it turned out, the real payoff was ideological not economic. For here after all was the prospect of an opportune truce to the rancorous divisions of an increasingly unequal and divided civil society, to become one nation under the Olympic flag, as we all let our hair down with one hand and tightened our belts with the other.

Yeats's epigraph reminds us that the personal capacity to imagine and dream is never not political and is often appropriated by those who can only imagine and dream in the idioms of wealth or power. We are, after all, living in the age of urban imagineering and brandscaping populated by smart cities, creative cities, linear cities, Olympic cities. Corporate visionaries and evangelical bureaucrats now occupy the platform once commanded by poets and artists and indeed often employ them to write their scripts and design their logos. Between the closed symbolic order of speeded up regeneration (always the same old story of gentrification or NIMBYism), and the mash up of its diverse heterotopic features in futuristic scenarios, everything that was hitherto real and solidary about the urban fabric – the life-time estate, the shared memoryscape, the capacity to sustain struggles of long duration – is made to dissolve into the thin air of its simulation. The city of flesh is magically turned to stone, while its rhythms are taken over by a networked infrastructure whose space of circulation is as immaterial as the informatic mode of production it sustains, just another circuit of fictitious (i.e. financial) capital, a dream you can live and profit by (Poynter, 2012; Cohen, 2017).[4]

Yet, of course, the task of translating the Olympic legacy dream into reality, 'to provide lasting material benefits to the people of East London' requires more than impression management or wishful thinking. The ex-Mayor of London's idea of a level playing field may have been formed in the same school as the Eton Mission, whose civilising ambition was to inculcate public school values of fair play into generations of deprived East End children from their 'Wilderness' sports ground on the edge of Hackney Wick; nevertheless the goal of convergence, suitably bracketed here in scare quotes, has become

---

[4] Fictitious capital was a term coined by Marx in *Capital: Volume 3* to refer to the ideological impact of an economy burdened with property and financial claims in the form of interest and dividends, fees and commissions, exorbitant management salaries, bonuses and stock options, and where 'instead of explaining the self-expansion of capital out of labour-power, the matter is reversed and the productivity of labour-power becomes itself this mystic thing, interest-bearing capital' (cited in Hudson, 2010).

the touchstone of debate on whether or not 2012 has delivered for those working-class and minority ethnic communities in whose name the Games was won.

It is possible to demonstrate that some of the claims made for the 'catalytic effect' of 2012 are entirely bogus. For example, Johnson cites Westfield Shopping Centre and the International Stratford station as major outcomes, but both would have been built anyway, even if London had not won the bid. Even where such direct effects can be shown, they are not necessarily altogether positive. Many of the jobs for local people created in and around Stratford were short term and those that have proved more sustainable are mainly low-wage, low-skill, and concentrated in retail services (Poynter, 2016), Similarly the housing gain has been largely offset by rises in land values and house prices (see Chapter 4), while rising education standards are partly due to the influx of middle-class professional families, in other words to accelerated gentrification. Equally the so-called health dividend has not been reflected in falling rates of obesity amongst young people in the Host Boroughs even if participation rates in some sports have increased (see Chapter 11). More rugby, even of the non- contact variety, is unlikely to do the trick.

There are researchers busy working away at making detailed empirical rebuttals of each and every legacy claim; however in the war of facticities between the positivists and the negativists, the Olympophiles for whom the Games can do no wrong and the Olympophobes for whom they can do no right, a priori positions coupled with empirical myopia combine to ignore the central issue: what are the limits and conditions of local redistributive intervention in a global city established by a 'mega event' (Sassen, 1991; Porter, 2009). The navel of the Olympic dream, the rational kernel inside its mystical shell, turns out to be about existential principles of hope for a better life and a fairer society, principles not easily quantified or represented in social statistics but which are nevertheless active in shaping popular perceptions of the project's success or failure (Cohen, 2013).

So how and how far is the original compact of the 2012 bid being conserved in its post-Games iteration? How is the legacy transition actually being negotiated, managed and lived, by those who are responsible for delivering it on the ground in East London, and even more importantly by local citizens who are supposedly its main beneficiaries. We need to know more about the pattern of discontinuity which opens up between the road maps to the future which planners and property developers are so busily constructing and the ways in which ordinary folk go about navigating and narrating their way about this new piece of city. That was the starting point for the series of projects reported in the following sections.[5]

East Village: An Estate of Exceptions

This chapter takes its title from a temporary installation erected in Victory Park, in East Village in 2015. The artwork is by Nathan Coley, who was shortlisted for the Turner Prize in 2007 and who, his biography states, 'is interested in the idea of "public" space, and exploring the ways in which architecture becomes invested – and reinvested – with meaning'. The scare quotes around 'public' are for once fully justified since as we will see the relation between public and private space in East Village is both ambiguous and contested. The work takes the form of a large neon sign on scaffolding situated outside the offices of Get Living London (GLL) who commissioned it (Fig. 5.2).

GLL is in charge of letting the private rental flats in East Village on behalf of Quatari Diar, the international property arm of the Quatari Royal family, who own the entire estate, including the public space on which the sign was situated (see Chapter 4). 'A Place beyond belief', like all post-modern art is intended to problematise its own meaning and to be read in a number of different ways: as a self-referential statement about its location, as an ironic comment on the kind of modernist architecture associated with Olympic urbanism and its utopian aspiration; as an invitation to suspend judgement or mobilise our capacity for

---

[5] The projects took place in 2014/15 and were funded by a consortium of local agencies: The London Legacy Development Corporation, Share East, and Triathlon, and delivered by The Building Exploratory in partnership with LivingMaps. Chapter 6 by Debbie Humphry in this book describes one of the projects in detail.

Fig. 5.2   Installation East Village

Source: Author

wonder against the incredulity generated by some of the more extravagant Olympic Legacy claims; and, finally, as a sceptical meta-statement about the process of urban imagineering of which it is itself an example. However we take it, we are invited to consider the intricate dialectic between fact and fiction, epistemic trust (what you see is what you get) and distrust (nothing is quite what it seems) as this operates in the transformation of the Olympic Athletes Village into an experiment in multi-tenure rental housing.

That dialectic is already present in the choice of a new post code for the district. East 20 was chosen not only because it was free from an unwanted legacy of association with post coded 'gang cultures' in Hackney and Newham, but because it was, of course, the fictional address of Britain's favourite soap, BBC's *East Enders*. The script writers responded in kind and have changed the casting, if not the story line, to reflect the changing demographic of the New East End: hipsters have yet to take over leading roles, but at least they are now part of the crowd in the New Vic. Urban fact and fiction morph seamlessly into a single mythography of the real (Dench et al., 2006; Cohen, 2013).

The report on East Village commissioned by GLL from the Smith Institute is a curious document in this regard (Chevin, 2012). It is based on interviews with planners, architects, designers and housing experts, and is supposed to identify the potential 'challenges' posed for management by the new development. In fact it is largely an exercise in branding and promotion, full of glowing images and recommendations designed to reassure any doubts or anxieties about the viability of the project, as in this quote:

> East Village has inevitably drawn parallels with the Millennium Village at Greenwich, built in the early to mid 2000s. Both are large-scale communities with mixed tenure – though the privately rented dimension in Greenwich comes from owners subletting.

But Ralph Luck, ODA director of property who has had a hand in both developments, remarks: 'At Stratford, I think we'll see a community created far faster. And with a greater feeling of place within the wider community'.

Similarly the challenge of bringing together tenants with different life styles and socio-economic circumstances in a single rental development is recognised but even when a cautionary note is sounded, it is framed by a reassurance:

> . . . unlike the high-density estates of the past, there are plans to ensure the estate is tightly managed and maintained. This is made affordable by the presence of a landlord with a long-term commitment to renting. Get Living London and Triathlon Homes will establish a joint management company to handle potential social friction as diplomatically as possible – although ensuring its staff don't grate on the neighbours with overzealous balcony policing, for example, won't always be easy.

From the very outset the East Village announced itself as an exceptional place, in so far as it exemplified the Olympic Dream:

> Imagine the best of London, all in one place. Tradition and innovation, side-by-side, in a landscape of quality family homes, waterways, parklands and open spaces – anchored by the London 2012 Olympic and Paralympic venues. The residential neighbourhoods will take the best of 'old' London – such as terraced housing inspired by Georgian and Victorian architecture, set in crescents and squares, within easy walking distance of a variety of parks and open spaces. It will take the best of 'new' London – whether in terms of sport, sustainability or technology – to create a new destination for business, leisure and life. Above all, East 20 will be inspired by London's long history of 'villages', quality public spaces, facilities and urban living, learning from the best of the past – to build successful communities for families of the future. (LLDC Website, 2012a)

The motif of the urban village is central to the whole construction. It is very much an invented metropolitan tradition and refers primarily to working-class neighbourhoods in the inner cities that either have become gentrified, or are where the 'gentry' have always lived – at least since the eighteenth century (Jacobs, 1964).[6] More recently, environmentalists have adopted the urban village as a symbol of historical individuality threatened by the culturally homogenising pressures of globalisation, as well as a model of local democracy and sustainable community development (Magnaghi, 2005). Under this rubric the ideal of 'inclusive insularity', a post-Imperial version of a larger 'island story' has increasingly informed attempts at neighbourhood renewal, as a way of reaffirming the viability of the local while still subsuming it under the global. Against this background the rhetorical use of urban village imagery to promote a mega–development representing everything that the concept was originally designed to oppose is an exceptional piece of ideological recuperation which indeed merits incredulity.

---

[6] Jane Jacobs, the American urbanist, was an apostle of 'spontaneous un-slumming', and saw the urban village as a model of piecemeal urban renewal in inner-city areas threatened by 'slash and burn' redevelopment – an alternative regeneration strategy led by small businesses rather than large corporations.

We are used to thinking about the special powers of securitisation mobilised to protect Olympic venues from terrorist attack as representing an unwarranted suspension of civil liberties, but in the transition to a post-Olympic city these powers may be not simply relinquished or carried over into the new context but actively transformed, along with the function of the venues themselves. A case in point is the Athletes Village which has evolved into an estate of exception where the normal limits and conditions of urban planning, governance and accountability have been swept aside in the name of a higher public good, in this case the realisation of an Olympic compact which promised to deliver exceptional benefits to the people of East London. The promise of the renamed East Village was to realise the Olympic dream of *convergence;* it would bring together people from different social backgrounds, income levels and life styles and create a community in which these status and class distinctions were held in abeyance in a kind of permanent truce (see Introduction). This was to be achieved through a tenure-blind housing allocation policy and a strategy of estate maintenance and securitisation that kept the area safe and in pristine condition: a form of social engineering guided by environmental determinism which offers a hysterical materialist solution to the intractable problem of class division.

How far has this exceptionalism worked out in practice? Has it proved beneficial to the incoming inhabitants of East Village? How has it shaped their emergent sense of place identity and patterns of belonging? How has it affected their perception of the adjoining communities of Stratford and Hackney Wick? These were some of the questions we took with us into our research.[7]

---

[7] The projects included an ethnographic field study, youth video and community photography workshops and a Young Persons Guide to the Olympic Park produced with students from Chobham Academy School, one of the Legacy flagships. I would like to thank all the East Village residents who took part in the ethnographic study for their permission to reproduce extracts from interviews. A report on the whole project is available from www.livingmaps.org.uk and www.buildingexploratory.org.uk.

Speaking Out of Place

Let us begin with a brief walk around the manor. As we have seen it is an area heavily populated with large public expectations. But it is also haunted by the ghosts of 2012. The baptismal naming of the streets evokes the euphoria of Games Time, the cheering, the victory parades, the sporting heroes, the festive conviviality: Cheering Lane, Prize Walk, De Coubertin Street, Victory Park. As we walk down Celebration Avenue, dreaming of Gold with eyes open, we might get a glimpse of Tom Daley slipping into Sainsbury's for a diet coke after his training session at the Aquatic Centre. And was that Mo Farah we just saw gliding past on an invisible hover board? Yet the streets thus named remain eerily silent, they compose an oneiric townscape more reminiscent of a Chirico painting or an architectural model than a real live place. There are few people about at any time of the day or season. Over several months, I spent two hours a day sitting on the same bench in one of the main thoroughfares observing what was happening around me. I found so little human traffic to record that I ended up noting the number of passing cars and buses. I began to long for a few stray cats or even a passing pigeon or two. There is currently a resident population of nearly 7,000 souls, but apart from a short period when school is out, the tree- lined streets and avenues are virtually deserted. One reason, of course, is that the young professionals who make up over half the resident population are out at work, they leave early and come back late. There is a pervasive sense of emptiness which can turn alarming as in this story told by one of the residents:

> It was really hot last Summer and I was cleaning my flat one day and I was just wearing a vest and shorts, not particularly decent but I was just cleaning and I went outside my door and I went to pop something outside just to remind me later, and the door slammed and locked behind me. And there I was half undressed. So I went up upstairs and knocked on everyone's door and there was no–one home, so then I went to the floor below and knocked on everyone's door and again there was no one in. So I went down to foyer and waited and waited and no one came in. I was there about an hour and no one came. I was getting hungry and tired and embarrassed, it just shows how empty those blocks can be. The block

where I live is the busiest one, it was the first one that was filled and would have had the most people in.

There is also an absence of visitors. Few of the thousands of shoppers who throng the malls of Westfield less than half a mile away venture forth to explore East Village, a fact that it is a strong disincentive to small businesses who rely on passing trade. Partly as a result, there has been a slow retail uptake which contributes to the lack of urban buzz. There is a gourmet pizzeria, a coffee shop specialising in artisan bread, a wine merchant selling craft beers, a Sainsbury's and a great barn of a pub misnamed 'the Neighbourhood' which is as far away from the cosy Queen Vic of East Enders fame as it is possible to get. Get Living London seem keen to establish an up-market image for the neighbourhood, they opt for busi-nesses that have already succeeded in hipster areas like Dalston, and filter out enterprises that might 'lower the tone', an anticipatory form of gentri-fication which is embedded in its promotional literature. So there is no bookies, no laundrette, no late night convenience store, no cash converter, no mini cab firm, no Aldi and Lidl, and definitely no fish and chip shop.

Above all there is not a graffito to be seen. There is not even chewing gum on the pavement, except outside Sainsbury's where the school kids at nearby Chobham Academy School (one of the Olympic Legacy flagships), go to get their daily fix. Moreover if such minor acts of vandalism as dropping gum or litter or creating a piece of street art did occur, the perpetrators would quickly be spotted by the omnipresent CCTV cameras and apprehended by the private security staff who patrol the estate 24/7, or by the police on their bikes who are also uncharacteristically thick on the ground. The eyes on the street belong not to neighbours but to those who are employed by a special public/private partnership to establish ground control.

This intense securitisation, underpinned by an enhanced policing service paid for by the landlords, has undoubtedly paid off. If you look at a crime map of East London, E20 is, at present, a virtually crime-free zone in a region of London still notable for its knife and gun crime. Moreover if our tagger or gum chewer did get away with it, all trace of the 'crime' would be quickly removed by the maintenance staff who ensure that all facades and walkways are kept spotlessly clean. Symptomatic of the tight estate management is what happened when local skateboarders turned up in the forecourt outside Chobham Academy, perhaps as much inspired by the marble street furniture which provided an ideal affordance for their moves as by the Tennysonian injunction 'to strive, to seek, to find and not to yield' inscribed on it, only to discover that it was out of bounds to them and were forced to look elsewhere for a place to demonstrate their commitment to Lord Alfred's injunction.

Those residents we interviewed were unanimous in saying how safe they felt in walking around the area, but some of them also commented unfavourably on the unusually sanitised nature of the environment and this perception was even shared by some of those responsible for estate management. One housing manager commented:

> I have got a 22 year old and 25 year old who are both living at home and I don't think I would recommend them to move to East village. I don't think either of them would want to live there, because, frankly, there is something about it that is not quite working, it's actually a bit dull. In and of itself it doesn't have much sense of being a vibrant community, such as you would find in Clerkenwell or Dalston, Peckham, Notting Hill where the rental prices won't be that different.

The creation of such a sterile environment can be interpreted in part as a carry-over from the strategy of ground control which was applied in the run up to and during the Games (Fussey et al., 2011; Kennelly and Watt, 2012; Minton, 2012), but in a post Olympic context this could also serve as a disincentive to a 'creative class' in search of a new urban buzz. This perhaps partly explains the slow take up of the private rental accommodation. Hipsters like a bit of grime as part of their metro-sexual life style, as long as it does not interfere with their amenities, and they might well prefer Hackney Wick, with its funky street art, boho cafes, and Lowryesque industrial landscape (see Chapters 7 and 8). Yet some of the community leaders who emerged in the first 'pioneer' stage of East Village's inhabitation did come from precisely this background. One of the private tenants describes his trajectory like this:

> We moved to Fish Island [in Hackney Wick] because of the vibrant culture. Amy Whitehouse used to live just two doors down from us, another next

door neighbour was Jamie Cullum, the jazz singer, it was the last outpost of the contemporary artist and as an illustrator working in the music business, it was the right place to be. But it was quite cut off… The Olympics coming to town was very exciting for me personally, this unique opportunity, to be part of the whole regeneration process. There were a lot of people, mainly hipsters, who didn't like sport, who were opposed to the Olympics, but I was up for it. So when my landlord refused to renew our lease, moving to the Athletes Village was a no brainer. I had decided even before I moved in that I wanted to set up some kind of community network, create a skills based data map of the area but when I actually moved in I found that community was more important than skills, finding out who my neighbours were.

Motivations for moving and modes of selective attachment to place are complex mixes of rational calculation and gut feeling, coercive pressure and aesthetic or sentimental appeal (Savage, 2010). But it was possible to distinguish two patterns of cultural inhabitation which correspond to basic forms of dwelling in the world, as well as articulating personal histories and geographies (Appleton, 1996; Ingold, 2000). There were those I call the *Prospectors*, who saw the move to East Village as a platform of opportunity, a launch pad for realising personal ambitions, the next step up on the housing or career ladder, and who saw its physical location and legacy narrative as offering a prospect on a brighter future. And there was others, whom I call the *Refugees* for whom their tenancy represented a haven from uncertain or precarious circumstances, a welcome source of security in the midst of a rapidly changing and increasingly incomprehensible world. These are, of course, ideal types, but they provide a grammar and sometimes a vocabulary for many of the stories we were told.

For a young investment banker, from a well-off professional Indian family, now working in Canary Wharf, living in East Village offered a prospect on a world that was very much his oyster and a stepping stone towards a more settled and stable lifestyle. He described his transition in these terms:

I was so engrossed in my job I hadn't really thought about the future, I was spending about £2,000 a month on rent and I was caught up in the expensive life style of a Wharfer, clothes, clubs, late nights etc. I was living beyond my means, I was young and silly, but then one day my Dad took me aside and said, 'look you are growing up, you are nearly 30, one day you might have kids and a wife, you need to look around for a place to buy as an investment'. I listened to my Dad and I started saving, living more frugally and in a year I saved up a lot of money. So I was looking around to buy something and then one day near Liverpool Street I saw this stall advertising East Village, as the Olympic Athletes' Villages. I had been mesmerised by the Olympics, I had been to some of the minor events and I thought it was great, it made me proud to feel British, the Union Jacks everywhere, all the medals. It was a good time to be British. So I came here to look at a flat, and I was amazed at the thought of living in a flat that the Olympic athletes had once used. Actually it was the South African athletes who lived in my blocks and some of them even engraved their names on the windows. So I was part of the legacy.

So for him the Olympic legacy represented a surrogate inheritance, at once a personal *patrimony* (he follows his father's advice and takes his symbolic place as an adult), an *endowment* of British identity (pride in the Union Jack) while the flat itself was an Olympic *heirloom* (the athletes' inscription), as well as an *investment in* the future through shared ownership.

One of his neighbours, with whom he became close friends, could not have had a more different trajectory into East Village. He was a retired manual worker who described himself as an 'East Ender born and bred'; he had lived on the once notorious Kingsmead Estate in Hackney, known locally as 'Devils Island' and went to what he described as a 'dockers school' in Poplar. He had been an active trade unionist but had become disenchanted with the labour movement, and especially with the Left, during the time he worked for the Greater London Authority under 'Red Ken' Livingstone. For him and his wife, East Village offered a safe haven from an intrusive world that had changed around them, as well as financial security via shared ownership.

I've got no time for all this romantic Olympic legacy rubbish – the whole thing was a ploy to leverage investment into the East End. What attracted us to the Village was the fact that it was all new, it was a fresh start, it was near the Park and the transport links. Me Mum is 82 and lives just down the road. I am still an East Ender, after 60 years I think I qualify even though the East

End has changed beyond recognition. There was a feeling when I was young that Homerton where I lived was a village, like Clapton and Hackney Wick, they were entities unto themselves. The area lost the feeling of that when they built these giant tower block housing estates in the 1960s and 70s, and demolished all the Victorian housing. And the people changed. The old East Enders moved out to Essex and all points east for whatever reasons. I suppose I hoped that East Village might in some way re-create a sense of community, and it is a bit of an island, an entity to itself but with all mod cons.

Moving to East Village for this couple was thus quite a complex manoeuvre, in which some links to the past and the old East End were retained, whilst its legacy of struggle was rejected; equally, some aspects of the New East End were embraced, whilst others were held at arm's length. And while there was no sense of elective affinity with East 20 as the materialisation of the Olympic ideal, its rhetoric of community could still be deployed to give a positive spin to its insulation from the rough and tumble of life in the working-class city.

A more integrated journey from the old to the new East End was also possible. One of the most dynamic community actors in East Village had grown up on the Carpenters estate, the last major surviving landmark of Stratford's pre-Olympic existence, increasingly depopulated of residents (council tenants and leaseholders), threatened with demolition, but also a site of local resistance to Newham Council's regeneration plans (Watt, 2013). Here is an extract from her story.

I grew up in Dennison Point, which is one of the blocks they want to demolish now, but in those days, it was fine. There were issues but generally it was a good place to grow up in, you could walk to school without crossing road, there were local shops, as well as Stratford mall and the market and there was a community centre. We had a view over the whole of what was to become the Olympic site, there were breakers yards, disused factories, garages, there was a lot of dumping went on. It was an industrial site. There was a club, near where the Copper Box now is, where we used to go, also everyone used to go clubbing in Hackney, the Four Aces. For my generation of black youth, the trend was always to go to Dalston, hang around the market. It was the scene for the whole of London. We had lots of house parties. We went around in groups of girls. It was quite a safe area, there wasn't so much youth

crime. So when I look at the Carpenters estate now and what they want to
do to it, it makes me quite sad.

After a spell working in the sales and marketing division of New Nation,
a newspaper aimed at London's black community, she records that
she became involved in youth and community projects in Plaistow in
the build-up to the Olympics, particularly around gun and knife crime
issues which were prioritised in the wake of the 2011 riots, while at the
same time Newham Council were making cuts to after-school and youth
clubs, as a result of the government austerity programme, cuts which
were only partially compensated by the advent of Olympics-funded
youth sports participation schemes. Her story continues tracing her
love/hate relationship with the Olympics.

> I became involved in the opening ceremony. I carried the flag for Bosnia.
> I was living the dream. We were all very enthusiastic and excited about it
> but the local shops and businesses who all got geared up, didn't get any
> footfall. The potential for the local economy just was not realised. All the
> local people got were the security cordons, the noise from the construc-
> tion, they didn't even get tickets for the Games.

It was not all bad news. She went on:

> Newham definitely was put on the map because of the Olympics. Before
> when people asked where we came from we would say Hackney or maybe
> East London, but now the youth say we're from Stratford or Newham. I had
> this love affair with the Olympics, I had come so far in my journey and
> I wanted to be involved in the legacy, to make sure there is a positive
> outcome for local people. So I got a job with a local community development
> agency to promote local use of Olympic Park. I had this love affair with the
> Olympics, I had come so far in my journey and I wanted to be involved in
> the legacy, to make sure there is a positive outcome for local people. So I got
> a job with Community Links to promote local use of Olympic Park.

In making this journey from the old to the new East End an Olympic
one, she was thus also able to merge the values of commerce and
communitas, legacy as dividend and endowment, and subsume both

moral and market economies of worth under an overarching commitment to civic accountability.

Trajectories of involvement with East Village did not stack up neatly in terms of indicators of class, ethnicity, or gender. There was a correlation with housing tenure, although this had less to do with income as with perceived social status and associated life style and with physical location on the estate. However, as we will see, these 'floating' signifiers could under certain circumstances become embedded in a vernacular discourse of class distinction and invidious comparison.

Aversive Geographies

To understand how this played out we, have to grasp the intricate relationship between the physical layout and design of the estate and its emergent social geography. The architectural uniformity of the blocks certainly gives

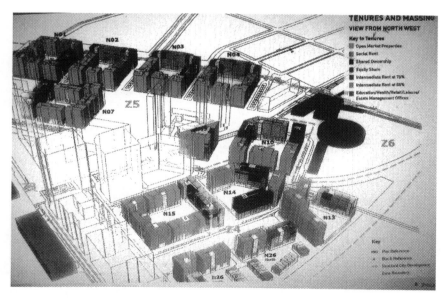

Fig. 5.3   East Village tenures

Source: Triathlon Homes

physical expression to a 'tenure blind' approach; it is indeed impossible to tell private, intermediate, shared ownership and social rental apartments from the outside, and this is underscored by regulations preventing tenants from using the balconies in any way that would express cultural or social identities. However that was not the end of the story. A number of social tenants housed at lower levels told us that they rarely went out onto the balconies because they didn't like private tenants upstairs 'looking down on them'. The ready way in which physical features – door colours, knockers or signage, the presence or absence of curtains, the type of dustbin etc. – can be mobilised to support a narcissism of minor difference and articulate social divisions is the despair of architects who subscribe to the view that people who live in the same built environment will evolve a common culture. Although the hysterical materialism of high modernism, with its ambition to build the New Jerusalem around 'vertical streets' and 'defensible spaces', has been largely discredited, the idea that community can be socially engineered by environmental or political means dies hard (Hatherley, 2009; Wallace, 2010).

In the case of East Village, during the initial phase of people moving in, shared concerns about snagging issues, and the sense of being pioneers in a brand new development with such a high public profile ensured that a sense of common predicament prevailed. But as tenants began to compare notes, differences in treatment between GLL and Triathlon tenants began to emerge. Social tenants complained that they had carpeting instead of wooden floors, did not have pre-installed washing machines and dish-washers, and had less cupboard space than the private tenants. The latter retorted that they were paying three or four times as much for the same accommodation and were surely owed a few perks. The main forum for this early conversation was Facebook, as there were few places to meet, except online. At the same time the blocks were being classified into 'GLL' or 'Triathlon' and certain social typifications attached to them. This was possible because of the 'pepper potting' arrangement adopted and the way the spatial identity of the estate was scaled. The basic unit was the block, and private GLL tenants were concentrated in some blocks, sharing lifts and foyers, and Triathlon tenants (social and intermediate tenants and shared ownership) in others (see Chapter 4). Each block had its own personalised name (viz. Tuscana, Mimosa, Camelia, Vesta), and quickly developed distinctive foyers. Blocks are grouped around courtyards, enclosing a green space on all sides. This 'commons' was to be shared by all tenants, irrespective of status, a space, neither public or private, where they could socialise informally and hopefully mix. On the official plans these spaces are called 'plots' and identified by abstract impersonal geo-locations (viz N.10, S.5). Yet it was here that the Olympic dream of conviviality and communitas was to be realised, despite the ban on barbecues and partying. Finally the block clusters are grouped into residential zones, primarily for management and logistical purposes, these units having little significance in the social geography of the estate.

To understand what follows, it is important to realise that it was the block and not the courtyard which constituted the primary structure of place identity and belonging while the courtyard became contested space and provided a platform for the enactment of latent social tensions. It is also important to know that the two-storey townhouses at ground level were occupied either by social tenants with large families, or by house-share groups of young single professionals. The rear patios lead out directly into the courtyards so that it was easy to see them as an extension of domestic space. The final piece of the jigsaw is provided by the enclosed design of the courtyards which ensured that sound generated at ground level was funnelled upwards and became amplified en route.

If the reader has ever lived in a high density housing estate, or has a basic grasp of the spatial dynamics of social interaction, it is not too difficult to imagine the situation that emerged once the honeymoon period of settling in was over. Here is how the issue was described by a focus group of tenants, all of them from the same block where shared ownership predominates, and hence with above-average incomes. Members of this group played a key role in defining the community politics of East Village at this point:

First speaker: When we first came here we had high expectations reading the tenants charter. We were promised a nice quiet environment, there would be no washing on the balconies and so on. And then the large families started moving into the town houses and the kids started coming into the courtyards with bikes and balls, playing football, knocking little kids over, screaming their heads off from 8 o'clock in the morning till 10 o'clock at night, they trashed the courtyards. We got in touch with the management but they totally ignored us. The families renting the town houses are mostly social tenants. The old idea was that if they mixed social tenants with people who bought their houses, then it would bring the social tenants up to their standard – that was their words, not mine. But it doesn't work. We had a lot of 'them and us' on Facebook.

Second speaker: Someone said it was like living in a council estate, it certainly wasn't what we had been led to expect from the GLL brochures. My biggest thing is that it's down to bad parenting. They should be out there with their children, keeping an eye on them, stopping them misbehave. They encourage them, they throw balls down to them. They treat the courtyards as an unsupervised crèche.

Third speaker: I think the main problem is a lack of enforcement of the prohibition – because if it's not enforced the parents are just going to do the easy thing and let their children play out unsupervised while they stay indoors and watch the television.

Fourth speaker: The realistic solution is for some kind of curfew, at 7 pm and instead of well-meaning community engagement people coming round with a bar of chocolate, have the security staff saying you are in breach of your tenancy agreement and we will have to report you if you don't stop your children playing out. If this was a purely private estate then it would be a 'three strikes and you are out' policy.

Third speaker: I am afraid it is part of the culture on council estates. People live in fear of gangs whom they think are controlling the area, the authorities turn a blind eye and people are resigned to it. But in this area it's different, you have a lot of people who are paying a lot of money to live here and are used to living in areas where people are more responsible and having arrived here and seen what's going on, they are horrified and are insisting that something is done about it. You have got the problem of middle-class expectations coming up against people who are used to very different conditions.

First speaker: The community engagement officers just stand around, they even encourage the children, they are like trolley dollies and some of them even stir it. They are supposed to have said to the social tenants 'Oh it's just them GLL people, they don't have any kids, they don't understand, they are just stuck up snobs'.

Fifth speaker: Yes, but it's not just the social tenants. Some of the people paying the highest rents are the least considerate and have the noisiest parties, like they think 'we are paying all this money we can do what we like'.

Third speaker: One tension in our courtyard is that the people who live in the town houses are able to use our stairwell to bring their rubbish through to our basement and their bags often drip rubbish so they leave a trail of debris and some of my neighbours feel that people who are not in the building physically are less careful in avoiding spillages. We wrote to East Village management to try to get access rights withdrawn from the courtyard dwellers. That created a great furore because some people felt it was discriminating against the social tenants and we shouldn't be ghettoising neighbours, whereas others felt that if it was making a mess then we have got to do something about it.

The first speaker describes a sense of culture shock that an estate marketed to young professionals, as an aspirational lifestyle choice, comes to be inhabited by people on low incomes. And because the social housing was rapidly filled, while, as we noted, the occupancy rate for private rentals was much slower, the initial demographic favoured this definition of the situation. As the discussion develops and the scenario of an 'enemy within' the gated community is established we can see how easily a noise war can turn into a culture war, and sound amplification morph into deviancy amplification. This is another example of hysterical materialism at work, this time around the definition and defence of physico-moral boundaries (Virilio, 2005). What is perceived as an unresolvable issue of material design (how to get rid of noise pollution without knocking down one of the blocks to open up the courtyard) is magically transformed into a soluble problem through a form of symbolic action with all too material consequences: get rid of the people whose presence is regarded as polluting an otherwise purified environment.

The transformation of the commons into a children's playground turned it into a no-go area for some, while the social tenants ended up being stigmatised as 'bad parents', an ascription often associated with a feckless life style and general anti-social behaviour and attitudes. Litter dropped in the courtyard or urine in the lifts (another example cited) became tell-tale signs of the unwarranted presence of an urban underclass and led to social tenants being categorised, by association, as rubbish, human matter out of place. The language of class is deployed both directly and indirectly for this purpose, and at moments takes on a racialised connotation. But it really is a matter of class not race. In fact the ethnic diversity of the estate was widely welcomed as a desirable social mix, with the presence of significant numbers of Chinese, African, Indian, Russian, Filippino and other foreign professionals, business people and students being seen as a welcome sign of the cosmopolitan and inclusive character of this 'global' village.

The members of this focus group were certainly self-conscious pioneers, but they also express some ambivalence about exerting a civilising influence over the social tenantry, a role which they assume they are expected to play and which represents another version of the convergence project. They were all too aware that in these noise wars, late night hipster parties were as much of a problem as unregulated children's play, and indeed could be regarded as an adult version of it.

For some of the tenants we interviewed, the interior of East Village was becoming perceived as what one described as a 'hellish inferno', an Olympic dream turned nightmare; yet, as others pointed out, it was one full of the real stuff of high-density urban living, where affluent and poor coexist, chic by growl. Meanwhile outside on the street an inert form of social peace and quiet prevailed, a mirror image of the pacification process orchestrated by the neo-liberal urban order, where the privatisation of social conflicts and their resolution within a domesticated inner sphere is supposed to provide a principle of civil defence against the intrusion of chaos and disorder from outside.

The housing authorities responded to the social tensions by appointing six community engagement officers whose job was to work with parents and children in the courtyards, in an attempt to reduce the noise and get them to observe a 'play curfew' after 8 pm. At the same time they were charged with pacifying those residents who were now beginning to demand punitive action against the 'noise vandals'. Yet official opinion about the nature and seriousness of the courtyard situation was not unanimous. In fact there has been a continuing debate between the two landlords about the best kind of estate management strategy to pursue. Get Living London have been in favour of tight micro management whereas Triathlon (who are responsible for the social, intermediate and shared ownership tenants who make up 49 per cent of the resident population), prefer a more laissez-faire approach as outlined by this housing manager:

> We need to allow a community to self-calibrate, to enable people from different backgrounds and socio-economic circumstances to learn to live alongside each other without friction, and to find a way of doing that that does not require a lot of intervention, or scrutiny or caretaking. East Village has had a phenomenal amount of management input, more than anything I've seen. My working hypothesis is that this these interventions might get in the way of the community naturally finding its own forms of internal self-regulation, rather than having that imposed from outside.

The Inoperable Community

One word dominates discussion about East Village: community. Community real or imagined, absent or present, as event or process, as a euphemism for managed consensus or an expression of human solidarity (Keller, 2003; LLDC, 2012b). Of course this obsession with community is hardly new. Nor is it confined to those who see in it an organic metaphor of a body politic in which 'all though all differ, all agree', and a panacea for social ills of every kind).[8] The quest for community is just as much part of the discourse of the Left, and underpinned New Labour's regeneration discourse especially in its more populist and moralising tendencies (Wallace, 2010; Cohen, 2016b).

---

[8] The phrase is Alexander Pope's from his poem *Windsor Forest*. The full quatrain is:

Not Chaos like together, crushed and bruised
But as the world, harmoniously confused
Where order in variety we see
And where, tho things differ, all agree.

See the discussion in Cohen (2013, Chapter 9) on the implications of this model of an organic body politic for the 2012 version of the Olympic dream.

In the early 1990s in the aftermath of the end of the Cold War, and the collapse of Communist Parties both east and west, Jean-Luc Nancy, a philosopher formed in the intellectual hothouse of Parisian post-structuralism, wrote an influential essay entitled 'The Inoperative Community' (Nancy, 1989). In an early passage of this text he wrote: 'The gravest and most painful testimony of the modern world, the one that possibly involves all other testimonies to which this epoch must answer (. . .) is the testimony of the dissolution, the dislocation, or the conflagration of community'. Nancy is describing the death of communism, or more precisely the French Communist Party as both a community of political activists and working-class militants, and as an intellectual community, a community of scholar activists. We sometimes forget that comradeship, before it became a corpse in the mouth, had for many, the sweet taste of fellowship. It was this existential sense of belonging and the principle of collective hope afforded by mass social democratic parties, that enabled their members to weather so many storms of history and have the resilience to face political defeats and sets backs, with a sense that theirs was a struggle of long duration in which ultimate victory was assured by a good teleology to which they had privileged access (Cohen, 2016b).

The intellectual and emotional vacuum created by the collapse of this dream has been filled by all manner of surrogate faith communities, a communitarianism which is both religious and secular; indeed much of the contemporary appeal of the Olympic Ideal comes from the fact that it offers a universal language of sport and a vision of international solidarity, that appears to transcend ideological divisions and class struggle. Yet once the official communist party was over, people became more aware of what David Graeber has mischievously called 'actually existing communism', the cultures of mutual aid, symmetrical reciprocity and gift exchange occupying the gaps which still exist amidst the apparently frictionless circulation of commodities and without whose existence the wheels of capitalist production would quickly grind to a halt (Graeber, 2002). I have argued elsewhere that the Olympic compact offers a potential point of purchase for this moral economy, but that it also provides a platform for its marketisation, and its subsumption – and stifling – by bureaucratic norms of civic governance (Cohen, 2016a).

In East Village there was indeed an attempt to establish just such a moral economy as a strategy of community development. Share East was set up Community Links, a long-established organisation in East London, as a means of exchanging skills and services and in the process building links between the new residents. It uses a currency called 'echoes' which people earn or spend in trading these skills and services. But what does this pseudo- currency actually echo? Some residents we interviewed were in no doubt:

First Resident: I think there is a bit of a problem with it. Echoes is essentially money, it is a currency, it's about exchange values as much as use values, and so it's going to bring up some of the same systemic problems we have with the market economy. If I was to spend one hour of my time, giving a face to face tutorial and earn one Echo, so it would be valued at that. But there have been some people in Share East who have worked the system to their own advantage. One person made an on line video tutorial for one echo per view, so actually in return for one or at the most two hours time, they could rack up any number of Echoes. So it is treated like a commercial enterprise, to get more out of it for doing less, which is what capitalism is all about. This is dissolving the whole ethos of the sharing economy which the project is supposed to be about.

Second Resident: I think the problem is with the way it has been set up. I think communities are built on trust and good will. So, yes, if you have a lawn mower and a neighbour approaches you to borrow it, you are not going to say 'Well OK but can you trim my hair next week'. That's not how community is built. You might watch to see that they use your mower safely, but that's the end of it. Next week they might invite your round for a meal to say thanks, but that's not part of the deal.

The first speaker suggests that this attempt to formalise moral economy ends up echoing the mechanisms of the market, whilst the second asserts the informal principle of mutual aid, one that it is based on voluntary, and non-obligatory reciprocity. Those tenants who were enthusiastic about the scheme had the skills and confidence to benefit from it, although in most cases they also had sufficient disposable income to pay for the services they needed. Those who lacked these assets viewed the scheme with suspicion, since they thought they had little to offer, and would end up owing a lot of 'echoes' that they could not possibly earn back. The spectre of debt reared its ugly head in the shared economy because symmetrical exchange simply does not work if there is asymmetrical capacity amongst participants. A scheme that was designed to build links between different groups of tenants thus served to underscore the inequalities between them.

This project highlights the importance of social and cultural capital in shaping patterns of stake holding in 'community' and modes of attachment to place. Following Putnam (2000), we can distinguish two types of stakeholding, which are strongly correlated with the positions of 'prospectors' and 'refugees' previously discussed. *Bridgers* have the cultural and social capital to create formal structures of networking, whether through social media or actual organisations; they are highly proactive and, for example, looked on the advent of the Olympics as creating an opportunity for advancing their own, or their organisation's interests through various forms of partnership.

In East Village, on the whole (and with some notable exceptions) bridgers were concentrated amongst young professionals irrespective of their tenancy status; their intimate social networks were often distributed across the metropolis and linked to both personal and professional affinities. Many were actively engaged in the residents association and were concerned to establish a distinctive identity for East Village. They saw the multi-tenure character of the estate as a positive asset, creating a rich mix of life styles and saw themselves as pioneers in building a community which honoured the Olympic ideal of bringing together people from different backgrounds and walks of life in a common purpose. As one of them put it, 'one of the good things about East Village is that it wasn't an established community, we were all moving in together, and we have a chance to define what the place meant'.

Bonders with less cultural and social capital to spread around tend to concentrate their energies on creating little niches of neighbourliness from which they can assert moral claims of ownership over wider amenity or resource. One East Villager described the process like this: 'it's only when you can begin to trust the people next door to take in your mail for you, or borrow some milk when you've run out, that you can begin to think you have neighbours, and then you begin to look around and think how could this neighbourhood be improved for everyone'.

Bonders emphasised the importance of having neighbours with whom they had something in common sociologically, in terms of background and life experience, and these elective affinities tended to be highly selective. Their sense of place rested largely on informal, highly localised networks and often revolved around child care. These networks may not register on the official radar of community building but through them many people were slowly but surely making the area into their kind of town; as we have noted, some aspects of this came to be seen as problematic, if not actually anti-social by some of the bridgers, as a failure to live up to the wider communitarian aspirations of the Olympic Dream and its exceptional prides of place. There was an implicit class difference being registered here. Those social tenants who were able to take on a proactive bridging role, for example via the residents association, often drew on social skills and confidence gained in dealing with members of a diverse public through responsible jobs in the service industries or the public sector. In contrast private tenants who either 'kept themselves to themselves' or created exclusive little niches with people from similar class and ethnic backgrounds did so because they did *not* recognise in East Village a potential space of 'community', or feel the need for any wider frame of social support.

The Other Scene

How was the exceptionalism of East Village and its prides of place actually lived and represented? A clue was to be found in the way the neighbourhood was defined in relation to its surroundings. Very few residents likened it to a village, but a number did refer to it as an island, or an oasis, one described it as a moat and yet another as a gated community without the gates. One phrase cropped up again and again in relation to nearby Stratford which was frequently referred to as the 'dark side'. So have we got hold of a nice juicy bit of hipster racism directed against the local working-class peasantry who literally live on the wrong side of the tracks – the railway lines which separate what one resident referred to, half-jokingly as 'Ye Olde Stratford' from Westfield Shopping Centre and East Village? Before we jump to conclusions, it is worth considering the locally situated provenance and meaning of this term in the mental maps of local residents as they negotiated the topography of East 20.

The East Villagers who frequented the Olympic Park drew a distinction between the south park which they referred to as 'the light side', because it is brightly illuminated at night and the north park, which is much less lit for the sake of the wild life concentrated there; both parts of the park are under 24/7 CCTV surveillance, and indeed the overall design brief was built on the combined principle of open access and total ground control; there is no unmonitored space, but there is clear demarcation in terms of landscape, the north being 'rural' and the south 'urban'. The north park is a careful approximation of the English countryside, with meadowland, treescapes and ponds; it is more frequented by East Villagers and other locals and residents reported that it was 'their kind of place', somewhere they felt at home. In contrast the south side, where the Olympic landmark venues are concentrated, is modelled on a metropolitan pleasure gardens; it has wide boulevards and broad vistas designed to cater for large crowds and is regarded by locals as the province of tourists and other visitors to the area. So in this context we have the association of 'dark' to the familiar, the safe, the homely and the natural world, whereas 'light' is linked to the foreign, the threatening, the unhomely and the Other, the opposite of the normal connotations.

In nineteenth century painting and early photography, the chiaroscuro effect was often used to symbolise the great divide between the respectable and the dangerous classes in depicting the moral topography of the Victorian City; street lighting is linked to social improvement and its absence associated with the underworld (Nead, 1995; Edensor, 2016). In the case of East Village, the principle is turned upside down and put to work to draw the line between insiders and outsiders. Yet no sooner stated than the distinction is normalised as it is transposed from the Park and mapped onto Stratford; here darkness comes to signify not safety and familiarity but danger and disorder. In fact it was a relatively simple act of translation. For the contrast now struck is between different standards of public hygiene, between cleanliness and dirt, purity and impurity. Stratford market was frequently described as full of rubbish and detritus whereas East Village as we've seen was spick and span. Of course dirt is often racialised and deployed as a derogatory epithet addressed to pariah groups but that did not happen in this case. Although within East Village itself, as we have seen, the physical condition of the habitat <u>was</u> indeed strongly associated with the moral status of the inhabitants, this anatomy of distinction was <u>not</u> used as an othering device in relation to outsiders. In fact, a significant number of East Villagers shopped on the so called 'dark side' in Stratford market, rather than go to Westfield Shopping Centre because it was both cheaper and more fun. Especially for hipsters it was an act of revolt against their sanitised environment and they actively enjoyed the buzzy urban multiculture apparently so lacking in their own area. It was their very own 'Other Scene'.

Rethinking the Post-Olympic City: From Mega-Event Analysis to Micro-histories of Transition

In this project we aimed to capture a specific moment in the transition to a post-Olympic city, and in this account I have deliberately focussed on some of its more problematic aspects.[9] It is important to record that while some of the East Villagers who were mobilised around the 'noise war' saw it is as potentially chronic source of conflict, many did not, referring to as 'teething problems', a kind of social snagging process, and believed that 'things will settle down' as people learn to rub along together and the estate 'matures'.[10] This chapter of the East Village story suggests that instead of trying to impose a one-size-fits-all model of organic community, derived from an Olympic Legacy Ideal, we need a

---

[9] The research was part of a longitudinal ethnographic study which began in 2007 and is scheduled to finish in 2020. The aim is to chart the unfolding narrative of the 2012 legacy outside the evaluative framework imposed by the official legacy narrative and its mode of deferral.

[10] The use of principles of periodicity and predicament derived from the life course provides a reassuring naturalising framework for understanding the micro-histories of neighbourhoods and underscores an organic model of urban regeneration.

multivocal model that sees community emerging in and through conflict, complaint and contradiction, as a platform for democratic debate, dialogue and dissent. That is what truly creating an urban commons and a civic (rather than an ethnic) nationalism of the neighbourhood is surely all about (Rogaly and Taylor, 2009; Cohen, 2016b).

So will East Village evolve into a life time estate? Will its social geography polarise between a hard core of social tenants and shared owners, who for different reasons have a long term investment in the place, and a rapidly changing population of young professionals and students? Will the advent of a new neighbourhood of owner occupiers (Chobham Manor) finally tip the demographic of East 20 decisively in favour of middle-class gentrifiers? Will 'convergence' come to mean that the West End came and saw and conquered the East End? Or will a generation of New East Enders be formed by a genuine redistribution of social, cultural and intellectual capital?

These are some of the research questions we will be taking forward into the next stage of the research which will take the form of a participatory exercise in social cartography and citizen social science (Cohen, 2016c).[11] Premonitory views of these possible legacy outcomes are inevitably over-determined by attitudes to the Olympic project as such. For Olympophiles legacy is about the attempt to live up to the ideals of the original bid and the high expectations it aroused. They remain haunted by the past and the promises made. For the Olymophobes it is about trying to forget the past, to recover from the post traumatic stress induced by the Games and minimise or mitigate its negative impact in the long aftermath. To some extent the two positions require and feed off each other, and like all phantasmagoric constructs both can find support in the realities of the situation. Yet neither singly or taken together do these narratives quite capture the surreal ambition of Olympic urbanism and its tragic-comic consequences, the principles of hope and despair which it animates.

---

[11] The objective is to train some of our key East Village informants as do-it-yourself ethnographers, so that the research story ends by being told in their own idiom.

For this purpose we need to abandon mega-event analysis, which treats the host city as a *tabula rasa* on which the master plan is imprinted, and instead trace the vicissitudes of the regeneration project through site specific micro-histories of transition from the pre to post Olympic city. To conclude here are three brief example of this process, each with a very different trajectory of meaning.

One: For the host communities in and around Stratford, the epicentre of 2012 Games, we can document an initial phase of de-familiarisation from 2007 to 2012 as the local memoryscape is progressively 're-branded' or erased and local people living near the construction site begin to feel that they are in a foreign country. As in this story from a resident who lived on the edge of Draper's Field, a long-established local park adjacent to the Olympic site:

> It was quite disturbing. We had this quiet place and now we find ourselves suddenly living next to this massive building site and they used to work up to 11 or 12 at night. They cut down the trees, tarmacked the whole place, and got rid of all the grass. They destroyed the wildlife of that park and it never came back. It became a big security exercise. There were three fences, a wire fence, an electric fence and one made of wood, then they had turnstiles installed at the gate, and they checked your ID, it was like leaving the country! The Olympics created a new kind of internal border, it was really strange. It was like the military had moved in and set up a base camp, but it was for laundry! It was really uncanny. They invited the locals to take a tour of the place, and we had to take our passports to prove who we were.

Draper's Field has now been reinstated as a multi-purpose recreational space and a new generation of residents, mostly young people from East Village, are busy rendering the strange familiar, carving their own memoryscapes out of the site. On their mental maps, Draper's Field figures far more prominently than the over-regulated and, from their point of view, under-resourced Olympic Park, partly because Drapers is the location of a popular Soccer Academy which is the only youth provision so far available to East Villagers and partly because if offers the kind of safe but relatively un-policed space that teenagers need to hang out with their friends beyond parental ken (Rathzel and Cohen, 2007). So in this legacy game of two halves, initial losers do indeed come out as eventual winners, on condition that the resentment and alienation experienced in the run up to the Games is transmuted into an active appropriation of its legacy, whether as an heirloom or dividend.

Two: Near Draper's Field is the site of the Clay's Lane Estate which was demolished to make way for East Village with a loss of over 400 homes (see Chapter 4). This involved the dispersal of a self-managed housing co-operative composed of mostly young people on low incomes living a more or less alternative life style and who were not otherwise able to afford to get on the housing ladder, a prototype of 'generation rent'. The only remaining trace of the estate is the name given to one of the East Village blocks, which is largely inhabited by well-off young professionals. It could be argued then that this micro-history represents a classic instance of social cleansing, the displacement of a precariat by a salariat, a process which is now occurring across London and other cities in the UK (Watt and Minton, 2016). However Clays Lane also offers a more hopeful precedent in its form of governance. This could well provide a model for the rehabilitation and re-population of Carpenters Estate, which could be set up as co-operative to be managed by the local community groups who have campaigned so successfully to preserve low-rise homes and resources for local people on the site (Watt, 2013). So here what appears to be a loss of amenity and a political defeat may yet be reversed into its opposite, on condition that what was once a cause for despair is transformed into a principle of hope.

In the process another kind of legacy, a rich heritage of community activism and democratic struggle, comes into view and challenges the dominant regeneration narrative of East 20. According to the official narrative, before the Olympics, Stratford was a semi-derelict and heavily polluted industrial wasteland, while after the Olympics it has been transformed into a vibrant commercial and cultural centre fit for purpose as part of a global twenty-first century city. It is a story of progress, a transition from poverty to prosperity led by enlightened public servants in alliance with Big Business. Yet once Hegel's old mole of history is allowed into the account, the path of progress becomes less smooth, more irregular and intermittent, more subject to reversal. We do not have to make mountains out of these molehills, and deny that *any* progress has been made (the Olympophobic position), but we do have to recognise that not everyone is a winner. As we noted in the case of Draper's Field, the slash-and-burn regeneration strategy adopted for 2012, as for most mega-events, not only bulldozes buildings but provokes a certain return of the repressed. Instead of consigning these structures of feeling to the dustbin of history, or deodorising the stink of the past so that everyone comes up smelling like roses, we need to create a living archive in which the past, present and future of the city can be properly documented and debated (Cohen, 2017).

Three: My final example concerns a reversal of spatial rather than temporal fortunes. The steps which lead down from the bridge connecting Westfield Shopping mall to 'old Stratford' were designed to expedite human traffic between the station and the Olympic Park. However they form a kind of amphitheatre facing onto a large pavement 'stage' and during the Summer months large numbers of young people have taken to congregating there, sitting on the steps to watch performances from buskers and a wide variety of street entertainers. The area has become a kind of Piccadilly Circus of the East End where local youth mix with visitors from all over the world; it is an example of unplanned do- it-yourself urbanism in the form of a pop-up commons where various lines of desire, not unconnected with drugs, sex and rock n roll (or rather rap) intersect and where for once East End boys and West End girls can meet on something like equal terms. This scene does not, of course, figure on any of the official maps of East 20 but, it could be argued, it represents a form of convergence that perhaps has more to tell us about the creative potential of the post-Olympic city than any amount of statistics about youth participation rates in sport.

Unless we begin to trace through such micro-histories in which flows of capital, structures of private ownership and public control and procedures of urban planning intersect with the life stories, livelihoods and life styles of those in whose name Olympic-led regeneration is carried out, and until we embed that account in a wider angled and longer term view of East London's development, we are only telling half the story and perhaps not the most interesting or important half at that.

References

Appadurai, A. (1986) *The Social Life of Things: Commodities in Cultural Perspective*. Cambridge: Cambridge University Press.

Appleton, J. (1996) *The Experience of Landscape*. London: Wiley.

Bachelard, G. (1994) *The Poetics of Space*. Boston: Beacon Press.

Balint, M. (1964) *Thrills and Regression*. London: Tavistock.

Boltanski, L. and Esquerre, A. (2016) 'The economic life of things', *New Left Review* 98: 31–54.

Chevin, D. (2012) *New Urban Living: The Making of East Village*. London: Smith Institute/Get Living London.

Cohen, P. (2013) *On the Wrong Side of the Track: East London and the Post Olympics*. London: Lawrence and Wishart.

Cohen, P. (2016d) *Archive That, Comrade: Left Legacies and the Ruses of Remembrance*. Oakland, CA: PM Press.

Cohen, P. (forthcoming 2017) *Material Dreams: Maps and Territories in the Un/making of Modernity*. Basingstoke: Palgrave Macmillan.

Damisch, H. (2001) *Skyline: The Narcissistic City*. Stanford: Stanford University Press.

Dench, G. (2006) The New East End: kinship, race and conflict Profile Books.

Edensor, T. (2016) (ed) Geographies of Rythm: nature, places, mobilities, bodies. London: Routledge.

Fussey, P., Coaffee, J., Armstrong, G. and Hobbs, R. (2011) *Securing and Sustaining the Olympic City: Reconfiguring London for 2012 and Beyond*. Aldershot: Ashgate.

Graeber, D. (2002) *Towards an Anthropology of Value*. Basingstoke: Palgrave Macmillan.

Haiven, M. (2014) *Cultures of Financialisation: Fictitious Capital in Popular Culture and Everyday Life*. Basingstoke: Palgrave Macmillan.

Hatherley, O. (2009) *Militant Modernism*. New Alresford: O Books.

Hudson, M. (2010) 'From Marx to Goldman Sachs: the fictions of fictitious capital, and the financialization of industry', *Critique: Journal of Socialist Theory* 38(3): 419–444.

Ingold, T. (2000) *Perception of the Environment*. London: Routledge.

Jacobs, J. (1964) *The Death and Life of Great American Cities*. Harmondsworth: Penguin.

Johnson, B. (2013) *2020 Vision. The Greatest City on Earth: Ambitions for London*. London: Greater London Authority.

Keller, S. (2003) *Community: Pursuing the Dream, Living the Reality*. Princeton: Princeton University Press.

Kennelly, J. and Watt, P. (2012) 'Seeing Olympic effects through the eyes of marginally housed youth: changing places and the gentrification of east London', *Visual Studies* 27(2): 151–160.

Konings, M. (2015) *The Emotional Logic of Capitalism*. Stanford California: Stanford University Press.

Latour, B. (2014) 'On some of the affects of capitalism', Lecture www.latour.com

LLDC [London Legacy Development Corporation]. (2012a) *Community Engagement Policy*. London: LLDC. http://queenelizabetholympicpar.uk/~/media/lldc/policies/1197539591lldccommunityandengagementpolicy nov2012.pdf

LLDC. (2012b) *Inclusive Design Strategy*. London: LLDC. http://queeneliza betholympicpar.uk/~/media/lldc/policies/lldcinclusivedesignstrategy march2013.pdf

Magnaghi, A. (2005) *The Urban Village: A Charter for Democracy and Sustainable Development*. London: Zed.

McDougall, J. (1989) *Theatres of the Body*. London: Free Association Press.

Minton, A. (2012) *Ground Control. Fear and Happiness in the Twenty-First-Century City*. London: Penguin.

Nancy, J.-L. (1989) *The Inoperable Community*. California: Semiotext(e).

Nead, L. (1995) *Victorian Babylon: People, Streets and Images in 19th Century London*. London: Kala Press.

Pile, S. (2005) *Real Cities: Modernity, Space and the Phantasmagorias of City Life*. London: Routledge.

Porter, L., et al. (2009) 'Planning displacement: the real legacy of major sporting events', *Planning and Theory* 10(3): 395–418.

Poynter,G. (2012) 'The global recession', in G. Poynter, I. MacRury and A. Calcutt (eds.), *London after Recession*. Farnham: Ashgate.

Poynter G. (2016) 'Olympics inspired inward investment – transforming East London?', in G. Poynter, V. Viehoff and Y. Li (eds.), *The London Olympics and Urban Development*. London: Routledge.

Putnam, R. (2000) Bowling Alone: the collapse and revival of American Community Simon and Schuster.

Rathzel, N. and Cohen, P. (2007) *Finding the Way Home: Race, Gender and Belonging Amongst Young People in London and Hamburg*. Hamburg: V & R Publishing.

Rogaly, B. and Taylor, B. (2009) *Moving Histories of Class and Community*. Basingstoke: Palgrave MacMillan.

Sassen S. (1991) *The Global City*. Princeton: Princeton University Press.

Savage, M. (2010) 'The politics of elective belonging', *Housing, Theory and Society* 27(2): 115–161.

Virilio, P. (2005) *City of Panic*. London: Berg.

Wallace, A. (2010) 'New neighbourhoods, new citizens: challenging "community" as a framework for moral and social regeneration under New Labour', *International Journal of Urban and Regional Research* 34(4): 806–819.

Watt, P. (2013) '"It's not for us": Regeneration, the 2012 Olympics and the gentrification of East London', *City* 17(1): 99–118.

Watt, P. and Minton, A. (2016) 'London's housing crisis and its activisms', *City* 20(2): 204–221.

Phil Cohen is Professor Emeritus at the University of East London, Visiting Professor at Birkbeck, University of London, and a Research Fellow at the Young Foundation. He is the founder/research director of the LivingMaps Network and the editor-in-chief of its online journal *LivingMaps Review*. His ethnographic fieldwork over the last 30 years has been based in East London and has dealt with issues of racism and multiculturalism, public safety and danger, the role of the cultural economy in urban regeneration, and popular participation in planning. His research with young people has developed new methods of visual ethnography, social mapping and dialogic engagement with informants. Most recently he directed a multi-project initiative examining the Post Olympic Legacy in East 20. He is the author of *On the Wrong Side of the Track? East London and the Post Olympics* (Lawrence and Wishart, 2013). Other books include *Knuckle Sandwich: Growing up in the Working Class City* (with Dave Robins, 1978), *Rethinking the Youth Question* (1997), *New Ethnicities, Old Racisms* (2001), *London's Turning: the Making of Thames Gateway* (edited with Mike Rustin, 2008). He has also published a memoir *Reading Room Only: Memoir of a Radical Bibliophile* (Five Leaves, 2013) and a book of poetry and prose, *Graphologies* (Mica Press, 2014). A collection of his new research, *Material Dreams: Maps and territories and the un/making of Modernity* is forthcoming from Palgrave Macmillan. www.philcohenworks.com

6

'The Best New Place to Live'?
Visual Research with Residents in East Village and E20

Debbie Humphry

Introduction

This photo-essay emerges from an ethnographic research project, *Speaking Out of Place*, that examines experiences of living in the Post Olympics' East Village residential development in E20 (see also Chapters 4 and 5). This images series and accompanying analyses aim to expand and complicate existing East Village and E20 narratives. The ethnographic images, loosely-speaking, are environmental portraits, but they evade easy categorization as intimate close-ups are mixed with anonymous distant shots, single people with groups, and eyes-to-camera portraits with documentary moments. The shifting perspectives demand varying responses from the audience, so the viewer is led through a 'dis-coherent' experience aimed at eliciting a questioning and critical response to the Olympic legacy story.

D. Humphry (✉)
University of Kingston, London, England
e-mail: debbiehumphry@btinternet.com

© The Author(s) 2017
P. Cohen, P. Watt (eds.), *London 2012 and the Post-Olympics City*,
DOI 10.1057/978-1-137-48947-0_6

Fig. 6.1 East Village E20

Photo by Debbie Humphry

East Village (Fig. 6.1) is the former Athletes Village for the 2012 London Olympic and Paralympic Games, now converted to provide 2,818 homes that are delivered by two separate housing providers, Triathlon Homes and Get Living London (see Chapter 4 for details). Triathlon Homes own and manage 1,379 'affordable' properties (split between social rent, intermediate affordable rent, shared ownership and shared equity), while Get Living London (GLL) is a real estate development and investment partnership established by Qatari Diar and Delancey (QDD), and they manage and let the other 1,439 properties as private rents at the full market rate.

Imaging the legacy has always been important for the London Olympics (Cohen, 2013). The plethora of texts and images, from the bid to the Games and now for the legacy, has produced a heavily represented space, with the predominant pubic representations of the Olympic legacy in East Village and Queen Elizabeth Olympic Park

Fig. 6.2 Get Living London sign 'Winner Best New Place to Live London Planning Awards 2014', in East Village apartments' foyer window

Photo by Debbie Humphry

(QEOP) produced by official sources. These official representations are unsurprisingly celebratory, given the interests of their authors in the legacy project being an unequivocal success (GLL, 2014; East Thames, 2015; East Village London, 2015; Delancey, 2015; LLDC, 2015; Triathlon Homes, 2015a; Qatari Diar, 2015). Much quoted by these interested parties were the 'Planning Excellence' and 'the Best New Place to Live' awards that East Village won at the 2014 London Planning Awards (Fig. 6.2). However, it is worth noting that the ex-Mayor of London, Boris Johnson, was a partner in delivering these awards (Gov.uk, 2015), and that as a personal champion of the legacy, and having tasked the London Legacy Development Corporation (LLDC) to deliver the physical, social, economic and environmental legacy regeneration, he is deeply invested in the legacy's success (London.gov.uk, 2015; LLDC, 2015).

While there is an emerging critical literature on the 2012 Olympics' legacy project, as the chapters in this book attest (see also Armstrong et al., 2011; Kennelly and Watt, 2011; Watt, 2013; Vijay, 2015), there is little on the East Village (with the exception of Bernstock, 2014). The critical response to the Olympic legacy has included drawing on visual data, across academic, activist and cultural texts (Kennelly and Watt, 2012; Powell and Marrero-Guillamon, 2012; GamesMonitor, 2015), but none directly focused on East Village, as might be expected since residents only started moving there in November 2013. This photo-essay therefore adds to the debate on the Olympic legacy, by focusing on East Village, and by presenting visual data in this context. As photographs are more accessible to a lay public than written academic texts, the images are also well-positioned to counter and complicate the hegemonic official representations of East Village and E20 for a wide audience.

The multiple perspectives generated by the ethnographic photography echo the methodological approach of the larger research project of which it is part. *Speaking Out of Place*, led by Phil Cohen, explores a multi-faceted story of living in the Olympic legacy site, drawing in the subjective viewpoints of East Village residents (see Chapter 5). The research team used mixed methods, including ethnographic observation and photography, in-depth interviews with residents, and three participative visual projects (photography, video and mapping). My primary role was leading the participative and ethnographic photography strands of the research[1] and, with Phil Cohen, conducting the ethnographic and interview fieldwork and analysis. Whilst this photo-essay focuses on the ethnographic photographs I took in East Village and E20, they cannot be completely separated from my involvement with the other research strands. Over time, I developed relationships with the residents, and drew on interview

---

[1] For the participative element I delivered photography workshops with residents to explore their experiences of living in East Village. These culminated in a joint photography exhibition entitled 'MyPlaceYourPlaceE20' shown in E20 and E15 venues from November 2015–April 2016.

material to inform the photography. The images, therefore, emerged from my evolving relationship with the people and the place of East Village and, as such, can be understood as inter-subjective data (Humphry, 2013).

Taken over the period of a year (October 2014–October 2015), the images represent several phases of photography that reflect different physical and emotional distances from the place and its inhabitants. In the early months relatively few residents had moved to East Village, and the first retail unit did not open until March 2015. So in contrast to the many symbolic representations made of East Village, the material place appeared almost empty, both of inhabitants and the meanings produced by their everyday practices. East Village, and to an extent QEOP, felt more like empty film sets waiting for the characters and stories to arrive. In this context the photography began with me walking the territory, camera in hand, waiting to see what kind of actions and meanings would unfold. The images changed as a result of my own deepening relationship with East Village, but also in tandem with a place that was itself only gradually becoming, as its inhabitants started to make lives there.

As a method, ethnographic photography was a useful way for me to think through the meanings being produced in the material, lived place, because taking photographs demanded a physical engagement with the people and place, and the resulting photographs provided a trace of the real to further reflect on (Berger, 2008). In this photo-essay I explore what these photographic representations of East Village and E20 can tell of the Post-Olympic story. In the first section, I draw on the more distant images I took in the first phase of photography, picking up Watt's (2013) question of who the Olympic legacy is for. The images disrupt official claims that the legacy is for the benefit of East London residents, and suggest instead several other possible beneficiaries. In the next section I focus on the more intimate shots of East Village residents taken in the second phase of the photography. These images suggest diverse subjective experiences and provide a more complex and ambiguous story of the Olympic and Paralympic legacy than represented by official sources. Therefore overall, across the two sections, official representations are complicated and contested.

Distance and Disjunction: Landscapes of E20

In the first phase of photography the distant shots of the new-build landscape reflect my own newly-arrived distant position (Fig. 6.3). The clean architectural lines, scarcely broken by human presence, present a sharp contrast not only to the over-representation of the official legacy discourse, but also to the traditional image of a busy, over-crowded and disadvantaged East London (Widgery and Holborn, 1991; Koutrolikou, 2012; Cohen, 2013; Vijay, 2015). At a first reading this photograph appears to confirm a transformed East London landscape of physical renewal as promised by the Olympic legacy discourse. However, the image's idealized aesthetic, produced by the clean lines and space, is created by absence, raising the question of who is missing from this landscape. Whilst this image was taken during the early stages of residents moving into East Village, it

Fig. 6.3   The sparsely populated E20 landscape

Photo by Debbie Humphry

nevertheless raises the question of how many of Newham's E15 residents are accessing this legacy space. This is pertinent because, as Bernstock argues (2014: intro), 'One of the distinguishing characteristics of London's bid to host the games was its commitment to legacy where it was argued that "the legacy would lead to the regeneration of an entire community for the direct benefit of everyone who lives there"'.

With so few residents visible on the streets, the presence of workers was especially evident. The photographs include images of East Village security employees and community engagement officers, police, gardeners, builders, maintenance workers, jet-washers, a lift operator, a minister, a marketing manager and owners and employees of the new retail spaces. Whilst on the one hand this seems to affirm the increased employment opportunities promised as part of the legacy project, on the other hand the viewer is directed to question what purpose this multitude of workers serves. The overall impression is that huge amounts of public resources have been used to ensure the smooth running of the legacy space, and that they variously serve the purposes of security, spectacle and capital (Armstrong et al., 2011; Kennelly and Watt, 2012).

The photograph of three police with their bicycles standing in front of large images of Olympic and Paralympic athletes suggests ambiguity (Fig. 6.4). The police are lined up in a row, echoing the row of athletes behind them, and this works to blur the distinction between representation and the material, image and reality. This leads the viewer to question whether the police are serving the purpose of security or spectacle, or both. The photograph evokes the village bobby on their bike, a representation that is distanced from the image of a busy 'dangerous' metropolis generally associated with a disadvantaged East London borough. It is easy to surmise that the police on their bikes are part of the branding of this new urban village, rather than solely there to counter crime. As the policeman on the right looks straight into the camera, a certain collusion with the act of image-making is implied.

Similarly the photograph of gardeners landscaping, planting and watering outside of the Get Living London offices mixes the symbolic

Fig. 6.4   Police on bikes outside Sainsbury's in East Village

Photo by Debbie Humphry

and the substantive (Fig. 6.5). Who is the landscaping for? Perhaps to clothe the global real estate corporation in an arcadian neighbourhood attire.

Another shot depicts jet-washers cleaning the pavement outside the new East Village Sir Ludwig Guttman Health and Wellbeing Centre on the day of its public launch event (Fig. 6.6). Again the eyes-to-camera style of the portrait suggests the workers as self-consciously part of a publicity event, whilst the woman who is passing by in the background, unidentified and unaware, appears as merely an extra to the main event. Both images intimate versions of the Olympic rhetoric and display noted by Vijay (2015), aimed at representing the Olympic

Fig. 6.5 Landscape gardeners at work in the Get Living London forecourt

Photo by Debbie Humphry

legacy in a positive light to the wider public. The images remind us that this is a place in the making, constructed with deliberation and intent.

A further series of images suggests possible benefactors of the E20 legacy. In one shot a group of people are being led on an Olympic Park tour by a man in a suit (Fig. 6.7). Again we are reminded that QEOP serves the purpose of spectacle, representing the legacy achievement. We can just see the symbolic Olympic rings behind the trees. But the image of a man in a business suit is somewhat unexpected for a tour leader, leading the viewer to question who has organised the tour. What is being shown and told? The ambiguity of the image invites the viewer to

Fig. 6.6 Jet washers cleaning the pavement outside the Sir Ludwig Guttman Health and Wellbeing Centre on its launch day

Photo by Debbie Humphry

engage in their own analysis, with an implication of business and commerce in the story.

This theme is re-iterated in Fig. 6.8 as a blue- and white-collar worker walk and talk together in a location near Pudding Mill Lane station, where one of the five new neighbourhood developments is planned (LLDC, 2015: 224). We might ponder the relationship between the manual and professional workers, juxtaposed in their different hierarchical roles, questioning how racialised and gendered labour relations play out in the legacy regeneration.

Both these images point to the idea that commercial and political interests drive the Olympic legacy, as noted by critics. (Kennelly and Watt, 2011; Armstrong et al., 2011; Bernstock, 2014; GamesMonitor, 2015; Vijay, 2015). Figure 6.9 further emphasises this idea as a group of Asian professionals cluster around a central figure in the Sir Ludwig

Fig. 6.7 A tour group head towards the Olympic rings in QEOP

Photo by Debbie Humphry

Guttman Health and Wellbeing Centre, who gestures into the gleaming architectural space, implicating the purpose of spectacle as intertwined with the purposes of commerce and care.

These figures are compositionally paired with the lone figure of a patient waiting for service, suggesting variant purposes of the legacy venture. The patient tells us that the Health Centre provides a useful service for local people, whilst the Asian professionals hint at global, commercial or career interests, suggesting Olympic legacy benefits beyond the local community. East Village may be indicated as 'the Best New Place to Live', for where else in London would you find an almost empty doctor's waiting room? But it may also be the best new place to invest in. Therefore the everyday is pictured within wider socio-spatial relations (Massey, 1994). Overall the image can be interpreted as a symbol of the public-private partnership delivery mode of the legacy regeneration. Bernstock (2014) argues that the London Olympic legacy has weakened its commitment to a public-private

Fig. 6.8 Workers near Pudding Mill Lane station, one of the five new planned neighbourhood developments in E20

Photo by Debbie Humphry

partnership by shifting away from an equal partnership with the state towards a more market-led model, and the single patient outnumbered by the professionals reiterates this idea.

Armstrong et al. (2011: 3169) argues that the positive legacy discourse focusing on the benefits to the local community is deliberately used by the Olympic Legacy power brokers to validate their own interests in shaping land deals, contracts and developments. This renders this research project with a particular responsibility as regards representing the residents and East Village community. So in the next section I reflect on the photographs of the residents, exploring what they say of diverse identities and experiences and how this reflects on the social legacy aims, including the promise to develop community (LLDC, 2012).

Fig. 6.9 Professionals and a patient in the Sir Ludwig Guttman Health and Wellbeing Centre in East Village

Photo by Debbie Humphry

Close Up Contradictions: East Village Residents

The image series of East Village residents develops the theme of interrogating representation versus reality. As with Fig. 6.4, some the images of residents include Olympic signage, such as the Olympics Rings cushion on a resident's bed in Fig. 6.11, and the 'Back the Bid' poster in Fig. 6.16. Thus there is an ongoing reference to symbols and branding mixed in with experience and the material. In Fig. 6.10 the real couple in the midground are echoed by the idealized couples on the background hoarding, nudging the viewer to compare what is real to what is represented. The sense that the E20 post-Olympic landscape is a manufactured film set awaiting action is felt even in these portraits of the residents. The couple stand watchfully in the depopulated landscape, as if waiting for the

Fig. 6.10 Couple on the Velopark bike track, in front of Chobham Manor residential development hoardings, with East Village in the background

Photo by Debbie Humphry

director – or the photographer – to impose meaning. They hold their bikes rather than riding them, as if waiting for stage directions. The scene is at once formally balanced yet symbolically disjunctive. The distant line of grey East Village flats echoes images of communist-period, Eastern European mass-produced housing blocks. This is then disrupted by the modern marketing hoardings in the mid-ground that conjure intimate encounters. Both these versions of the urban are further disrupted by the seemingly rural landscape in the foreground. However the caption indicates that this natural landscape is in fact a constructed bike track. Along with the rest of the E20 landscape, nature is built in as part of the master plan. The image thus speaks to the idea that both the Olympic legacy concepts and the material landscape are constructed representational spaces.

As the camera lens comes in closer to the subjects, my deepening relationship with East Village and its residents is reflected. Most of the resident images are shot as eyes-to-the-camera portraits, indicating a mutual awareness between the subjects and myself. This draws attention to the fact that my images are also constructed representations. I photographed the residents in their homes, and also invited them to choose a location that was meaningful to them. Whilst this enabled a wider window onto their identities and shifted some control in their direction, the image is still a representation – albeit an inter-subjective one.

The images of the residents speak to the social heart of the legacy promise because the mixed-tenure housing provision in East Village is designed to address the housing needs of people from diverse socio-economic groups. This mixed-tenure character was one of the reasons East Village won 'the Best New Place to Live' award (GLL, 2014). And in fact the images of residents in their apartments do indicate an equality of access, as diverse people are depicted as settled and at home in similar quality spaces (Figs. 6.11 and 6.12). Just as the properties are designed to be tenure-blind, so too are the images, because without captions it is impossible to tell what tenure-type we are looking at. The images therefore capture something of the Olympic legacy promise to address housing needs, especially as further residential developments in E20 are planned to be delivered with lower levels of social rented housing (see Chapter 4).

The mixed community arising from this unique mixed-tenure development is part of the social legacy commitment to construct community (LLDC, 2012, 2015; Bernstock, 2014: 121–124). The concept of community has been much problematized in relation to previous UK political projects, such as New Labour's New Deal for Communities (Rogaly and Taylor, 2009; Wallace, 2010) and 'community cohesion' (Amin, 2002). In this context, the photographs offer an insight into how residents' experiences compare to political rhetoric.

During the fieldwork, I observed community-building, through residents' own efforts and via official channels (Triathlon Homes, 2015b). Community events, for example, were funded by the housing providers and LLDC. Indeed, given that the ethnographic photographs and other elements of the *Speaking Out of Place* research were sponsored by LLDC,

Fig. 6.11 Resident in shared ownership flat in East Village

Photo by Debbie Humphry

Fig. 6.12 Resident in social rented flat in East Village

Photo by Debbie Humphry

Fig. 6.13 Residents in East Village play area

Photo by Debbie Humphry

the images themselves can be regarded as part of the legacy efforts to construct community. The exterior shots in Figs. 6.13 and 6.14 depict residents accessing and using community infrastructure. However, the different distances and amounts of space in the two images throw the viewer back and forth between a sense of busyness and emptiness, activity and stasis, nudging the viewer to question how much the facilities are used, and by whom. Most of the exterior images depict the residents in depopulated landscapes (Figs. 6.10, 6.14 and 6.16), which again suggests that these legacy places are not regularly accessed by wider Newham and East London residents (as in Fig. 6.3). At the same time not one East Village resident has chosen a space outside of the green and pleasant land of E20 as their meaningful location. So we are led to question not just who is missing from these places, but also what places are missing for these people. A crossover between the pre-existing Olympic Stratford E15 and this new Stratford E20 is absent from the images,

Fig. 6.14   East Village Family in Wetlands, QEOP, E20

Photo by Debbie Humphry

and this 'best new place to live' is represented as a world unto itself, far from the madding crowds.

Despite a degree of equity across tenure types, the images do indicate some differences experienced by diverse East Village residents. The concept of living in a bubble, set apart from the less privileged, is echoed in Fig. 6.15 as a family is pictured in their penthouse apartment, at some distance across their rooftop garden, and removed from the density of flats and residents below them. Thus the earlier suggestion of equivalent access to similar housing is disrupted.

A look at images of disabled residents tells us the more about contradictions in the context of the Paralympic legacy. Figure 6.16 suggests that the public spaces are well-designed to meets the needs of disabled people, as a resident in a wheelchair moves freely across the bridge from East Village to QEOP, her mobility on a par with the cyclist. However,

Fig. 6.15   Family in a penthouse flat in East Village

Photo by Debbie Humphry

this image is then disrupted as the subsequent photograph shows another visibly disabled woman unable to open a door in her block of flats (Fig. 6.17)[2]

Following this, the resident in Fig. 6.18 is not visibly disabled but the overall impression is that she is tired and not altogether happy. Her pose, nevertheless, is alert and dynamic, not waiting for meaning but rather as if she has a story to tell – which indeed she had. She told me that she had become seriously ill and unable to work since moving into her intermediate rented apartment, and without the same protection and security offered by the social rented apartments, shortly afterwards she had to move out of her flat and out of London altogether. A sense

---

[2] At the time of writing, this resident has tried and failed for over two years to get Triathlon Homes to adjust the door so that she can open it.

Fig. 6.16   Disabled resident crossing the bridge from East Village to QEOP

Photo by Debbie Humphry

of impermanence is communicated as her 'Back the Bid' picture is in its wrapping and unhung. Whilst the image cannot communicate the details of the situation, it nevertheless suggests that something is amiss, implicating different and unequal experiences.

The emphasis on the Olympic legacy arguably fails to adequately interrogate a commitment to the Paralympic legacy, and overall the images of disabled residents present a discoherent Paralympic legacy story. The individual stories are incomplete, but the photographs as a group, of three women each with different forms of disability, indicate differences in their access to security, mobility and independence. Any idea of a smooth or straightforward Paralympic legacy is disrupted, as is the more general legacy claim for '(d)iversity in housing provision to meet requirements' (LLDC, 2015: 11).

The sense of ambiguity throughout the photo-series suggests that both positives and negatives can emerge from this place that has

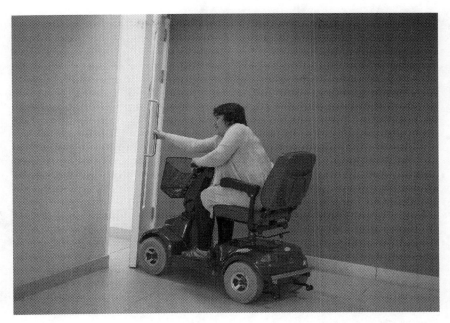

Fig. 6.17 Resident unable to open a door in her block of flats, East Village

Photo by Debbie Humphry

deliberately sought to bring difference together. This is symbolized in Fig. 6.19, which conveys a sense of the dissonance between different people's experiences and connections. Two young black men are depicted looking into the window of the East Village Neighbourhood pub, at me, a white older female photographer. The young men have variant expressions of connection and reserve, and as they make eye contact there is a sense of the different and dynamic modes of negotiation that encounters across boundaries of difference evoke. The image series overall indicates that a diversity of cultural groups live in East Village, but how this plays out, through cross-fertilisation or conflict, equivalence or inequality, may depend on how far the officials in charge of the legacy are prepared to look beyond their own celebratory representations.

Fig. 6.18   Intermediate tenant in her flat

Photo by Debbie Humphry

Conclusion

Overall this photo-series disturbs a simplistic representation of East Village as the 'Best New Place to Live'. As the various perspectives across the image-set disrupt each other, a simple celebration or a straightforward critique is therefore undermined. There are echoes and repetitions throughout, but overall the ambiguities and absences provide no definitive answers and instead raise questions. Images function in a different way to other kinds of data, but whilst secondary or supporting data could fill gaps and add clarity, the effect of their absence is to draw the viewer in to the debate. The viewer is thus encouraged to question representations made of the Olympic Legacy, including those made by these photographs.

Just as the essay refutes the idea of an objective, coherent representation of East Village and E20, equally it refutes the idea of a coherent

Fig. 6.19 Two young men looking into the Neighbourhood Pub, East Village

Photo by Debbie Humphry

community, or a definitive place. In fact the divide between the represented and the real is itself troubled, as the images blur the divide between the material and the symbolic. The sense of East Village and E20 being a film set, onto which action is constructed and meanings can be inscribed, is a theme that runs across the images. East Village and E20 is at once something concrete in the process of being made, a spectacle to be looked at, and a complex of representations drawn by variant interests and viewpoints.

This does not mean, however, that important material, representational and structural question are not raised, nor that the images fall short of addressing issues that impact materially on people's lives. For the key issues raised through the photo-essay are substantive and significant: from the importance of equal access to housing necessary to meet needs and build a diverse community, to the suggestion of exclusions for both the residents and wider Newham demographic. There is also a suggestion of the wider role that power, capital and their representations play in how the legacy is unfolding. Overall the images offer a series of ambiguities and differences, within and without the East Village community, structured variously by identity, housing tenure, planning design and diverse interested parties. By exploring these variant viewpoints via the camera, both the close-up everyday and the more distant sense of the structural contexts, the images are able to speak of the lived relations of place within wider socio-spatial discourses and relations.

This is a place that is more complicated and unformed than the phrase 'Best New Place to Live' implies. There is a sense throughout the images that E20 is a place both over-signified and under-populated, struggling to find its own meaning in the midst of the Olympic hype. This photo series is in itself an attempt to fill the place with something other than official hegemonic narratives. We are left with the sense of the beginnings of a place that has not yet been fully inscribed with meaning, of a place that is still waiting to see if its promise can be fulfilled. As an emerging community and place there is much to play for – positives to be protected and negatives to be addressed – and in this context the residents and other beneficiaries of the legacy seem to be watching and waiting, poised for action perhaps, or already agent, all party to this beginning process of place-making.

References

Amin, A. (2002). 'Ethnicity and the multicultural city: living with diversity.' *Environment and Planning A* 34(6): 959–980.

Armstrong, G., Hobbs, D. and Lindsay, I. (2011) 'Calling the shots: the pre-2012 London Olympic contest', *Urban Studies* 48(15): 3169–3184.

Berger, J. (2008) *Ways of seeing* (Vol. 474). London, UK: Penguin.

Bernstock P (2014) *Olympic Housing: A Critical Review of the 2012 Legacy*. Farnham: Ashgate.

Cohen, P. (2013) *On the Wrong Side of the Track: East London and the Post Olympics*. London: Lawrence and Wishart.

Delancey. (2015) 'East Village', http://www.delancey.com/east-village.html, accessed 6 November 2015.

East Thames. (2015) http://www.east-thames.co.uk/projects

East Village London. (2015) http://www.eastvillagelondon.co.uk/

GamesMonitor. (2015) 'GamesMonitor: debunking Olympics myths', http://www.gamesmonitor.org.uk/, accessed 6 November 2015.

GLL [Get Living London]. (2014) 'East Village named "Best New Place to Live" in double win at London Planning Awards', 5 February 2014, http://www.getlivinglondon.com/pressmedia/east-village-named-best-new-place-to-live-in-double-win-at-london-planning-awards.aspx

GOV.UK. (2015), 'East Village big winner at London Planning Awards', https://www.gov.uk/government/news/east-village-big-winner-at-london-planning-awards, published 5 February 2014.

Humphry, D. (2013) 'Inside out: a visual investigation of belonging in a London neighborhood', in M. Kusenbach and K. E. Paulsen (eds.), *Home: International Perspectives on Culture, Identity and Belonging*. Frankfurt am Main: Peter Lang Publishing.

Kennelly, J. and Watt, P. (2011) 'Sanitizing public space in Olympic host cities: the spatial experiences of marginalized youth in 2010 Vancouver and 2012 London', *Sociology* 45(5): 765–781.

Kennelly, J. and Watt, P. (2012) 'Seeing Olympic effects through the eyes of marginally housed youth: changing places and the gentrification of east London', *Visual Studies* 27(2): 151–160.

Koutrolikou, P. (2012) 'Spatialities of ethnocultural relations in multicultural East London: discourses of interaction and social mix', *Urban Studies* 49 (10): 2049–2066.

LLDC [London Legacy Development Corporation]. (2012) *Community Engagement Policy*. London: LLDC. http://queenelizabetholympicpark.co.uk/~/media/lldc/policies/119753959lldccommunityandengagementpolicynov2012.pdf

LLDC. (2015) *Local Plan: 2015–2031*. London: LLDC. http://queenelizabetholympicpark.co.uk/~/media/lldc/local%20plan/adoption%20july%202015/lldc_localplan_2015_interactive100dpi%20(4).pdf

Massey, D. (1994) *Space, Place and Gender*. Cambridge: Polity Press.

Powell, H. and Marrero-Guillamón, I. (2012) *The Art of Dissent: Adventures in London's Olympic State*. London: Marshgate Press.

Qatari Diar. (2015) 'Our projects: East Village, http://www.qataridiar.com/English/OurProjects/Pages/East-Village.aspx

Rogaly, B. and Taylor, B. (2009) *Moving Histories of Class and Community*. Basingstoke: Palgrave MacMillan.

Triathlon Homes. (2015a) 'Triathlon Homes: about us', http://www.triathlon homes.com/about-us/, accessed 6 November 2015.

Triathlon Homes. (2015b) 'The community', http://www.triathlonhomes. com/residents/the-community/, accessed 6 November 2015.

Vijay, A. (2015) 'After the pop-up games: London's never-ending regeneration', *Environment and Planning D: Society and Space* 33: 425–443.

Wallace, A. (2010) 'New neighbourhoods, new citizens: challenging "community" as a framework for moral and social regeneration under New Labour', *International Journal of Urban and Regional Research* 34(4): 806–819.

Watt, P. (2013) '"It's not for us": Regeneration, the 2012 Olympics and the gentrification of East London', *City* 17(1): 99–118.

Widgery, D. and Holborn, M. (1991) *Marketa Luskacova: Photographs of Spitalfields.* London: Whitechapel Art Gallery.

Debbie Humphry is a human geography lecturer at Kingston University, Research Fellow at the Centre for East London Studies (CELS) University of East London, and web editor for CITY journal (Taylor and Francis). She has published widely in academic, educational and media publications on housing/ home, urban neighbourhoods, inequality and visual methods. As a photographer she has also published and exhibited widely, including at The National Portrait Gallery, London, The Royal Festival Hall, London, and the Watershed, Bristol. www.debbiehumphry.com

7

Expert Knowledge and Community Participation in Urban Planning: the Case of Post-Olympic Hackney Wick

Isaac Marrero-Guillamón

Introduction

The Post-Olympic period in Hackney Wick has been characterised by the enactment of new structures of local governance, increased development pressure and sustained community advocacy. My interest in this chapter is to explore the relationship between local authorities, private developers and community groups in the context of planning and development. In particular, I focus on the issues and interfaces around which the different groups have coalesced, as well as the strategies by which community groups have tried to influence the process, especially in relation to the deployment of expert knowledge and the recourse to lobbying. The discussion is framed around the process surrounding the development of a new local plan for the area, and a concomitant grassroots campaign for affordable workspace. I will focus on the actions of a local group – The Unit – and describe their

I. Marrero-Guillamón (✉)
Goldsmiths, University of London, London, England
e-mail: i.marrero@gold.ac.uk

© The Author(s) 2017
P. Cohen, P. Watt (eds.), *London 2012 and the Post-Olympics City*,
DOI 10.1057/978-1-137-48947-0_7

205

participation in two parallel participatory processes: the first was a series of non-statutory, informal meetings with local officials and developers; the second refers to the official mechanisms of planning consultation. These two forms of community participation, in their differences and similitudes, raise important questions about the relationship between expert knowledge and democratic politics.

I employ the concept of 'ecology of affordability' to refer to the material and immaterial infrastructure that sustains access to affordable workspace.[1] This would include the availability of cheap and flexible industrial spaces; the commitment to retaining industrial use designations; and long-term leases that provide security of tenure. In addition, in the case of Hackney Wick, workspace affordability has been achieved through a rich tradition of self-building and self-managing practices aimed at tailoring large industrial spaces to the needs of the end-users. The legal status of some of the latter interventions, for instance those involving live/work conversions, is shaky to say the least: they are technically illegal, yet tolerated by landlords and authorities – or at least they were during a period in which the possibility of bigger returns on those industrial properties (e.g. though mix-use developments) wasn't yet so tangible. Hackney Wick's ecology of affordability, then, involved a wide range of factors, from government regulations regarding land uses to private lease contracts; from local authorities turning a blind eye on certain uses, to the landowners' limited business expectations.

A second key concept for the argument here pursued is the notion of 'para-democratic' structures, by which I mean instruments of community participation *adjacent to* statutory democratic mechanisms, which achieve some form of legitimacy in practice but whose representativeness remains uncertain. The term is not intended to be derogatory, for two reasons: first, to the extent to which these structures represent the enactment of *actually operational* spaces of community participation, they are to be welcomed. Secondly, I do not wish to imply that existing democratic procedures (such as consultation events or directly contacting your local

---

[1] One of the particularities of the Hackney Wick context is that the discussion around affordability does not revolve mainly around housing, as it is most often the case, but around workspace.

councillor) are necessarily more democratic (Maginn, 2004). The development of bottom-up para-democratic structures could, at least in principle, produce *more* and not less opportunities for local involvement in decision-making. The experience discussed in this chapter, however, shows some of the barriers for this, in particular in relation to the reliance on technical knowledge. One of the defining features of these para-democratic structures in Hackney Wick is that they take the form of 'technical forums' (Callon et al., 2009), in which participation – as well as the possibility of making a difference – is based around the capacity to leverage expert knowledges (i.e. limited to a few).

The chapter is based on ethnographic fieldwork conducted in Hackney Wick between 2011 and 2015. My involvement with the area started with a postdoctoral project looking at the role of art in the production of spaces of dissent in relation to the London 2012 Olympics. Over time, the research became a wider exploration of the politics of urban regeneration. I was actively involved in some of the processes discussed in this chapter, and details of my participation are provided below.

The Fallow Is Over: Post-Olympic Hackney Wick

Up until the end of the 1990s Hackney Wick was a semi-secret, unregulated and cheap (post-) industrial area in East London. It attracted artists, raves, black markets, discarded white goods and burnt cars (Gill, 2007). The converted factory buildings (turned into artist studios, live/work units, lofts or performance spaces) coexisted with the remaining industries, including notably a concentration of printing and finishing businesses (muf, 2009), while poor transport connections and a network of canals and motorways isolated the area from its surroundings.

Then, during the first half of the 2000s, a first wave of development materialised in the form of generic waterfront new builds and loft conversions. The departure of industry accelerated. Artists, makers and others seeking affordable workspace continued to settle in the area, an influx partly due to displacements from increasingly gentrified nearby areas such as Hoxton and Shoreditch (Pratt, 2009). A survey conducted in 2009 found 700 artist studios, making Hackney Wick one of Europe's largest concentrations of such spaces (muf, 2009). Counterintuitively, when the Olympic bid was won in 2005 development in Hackney Wick slowed down[2] and then came to a virtual halt following the 2008 financial crisis. This unexpected respite, or development fallow, lasted until the Games were over.

Walking around in 2015 one could see an amalgam of vacant plots, trendy venues, graffitied walls, brand new Overground trains, Legible London maps, unfinished buildings, artist studios, light industries, abandoned factories, car mechanics, co-working spaces, vintage shops, converted factories, new residential developments, art galleries, social housing bungalows, and hardware shops. This juxtaposition would be mirrored in the kind of pedestrians one would encounter any given (work)day: older residents, creative types, skateboarders, hipsters, workers, high-school youth, men in suits, young mothers, university students on a tour of the area, and tourists. Looking at the less visible layer of land ownership would reveal a very fragmented landscape, with more than 90 plots of land, mostly owned by different private real estate companies. An analysis of planning applications would be more revealing: no less than 17 active proposals, mostly for mix-use developments in ex-industrial locations. In addition, a new Local Plan for the area, detailing land uses and development targets, was adopted in July 2015 (LLDC, 2015). Even a quick look at social media and discussion forums would show a local community concerned with the sustainability of the area as they have known it. Hackney Wick is on the verge of a great transformation, all of the above seems to indicate (Fig. 7.1).

The Olympic period was characterised by a harsh separation between Hackney Wick and the Olympic Park; apart from the natural boundary

---

[2] It is difficult to explain why the development of the Olympic Park hindered, rather that promoted, developers' interest in Hackney Wick at this early stage. One hypothesis is that developers expected even bigger returns could be achieved after the Park was completed and the area possibly re-zoned. Or perhaps the demand for high-end housing was not strong enough yet to justify the risk.

Fig. 7.1 General view of Hackney Wick from the Overground Station, 2014

Source: Author

provided by the canal, the authorities' concerns with securing the Olympic site translated into the deployment of a variety of military urbanism strategies, including an electric fence, widespread CCTV surveillance, and access restrictions on roads and bridges (Fussey et al., 2011). Once the Games were over, re-connecting the Park with its surroundings – 'stitching the fringe' in the official lingo (Design for London, 2013) – became one of the main priorities for the authorities. Undoing this hard boundary has represented a huge urban design challenge, involving the construction of bridges, parks, public realm interventions, etc., plus numerous artistic and cultural projects designed to bridge other, more immaterial 'gaps'.

This concern with 'reconnection' is closely connected to an important change in the governance of the area. The London Legacy Development

Corporation (LLDC)[3] was introduced in 2012 to oversee the transformation of the Olympic Park and its surroundings and deliver the promised legacy of 'convergence' with the rest of the city. The LLDC is a Mayoral Development Corporation (MDC), a type of entity introduced by the Localism Act 2011, and in many respects modelled after the pioneering London Docklands Development Corporation (see Brownhill, 1999 for a critical assessment of the latter). Similarly to previous Urban Development Corporations, the mission of MDCs is to lead great transformation projects and, in theory, are temporary structures linked to delivering those. The LLDC was enacted by, and responds to, the Greater London Authority; it exists in *parallel* to local boroughs, and in issues such as planning, *above* them. The LLDC took over all urban planning responsibilities in the Olympic Park and its surroundings (previously under control of four different boroughs: Hackney, Tower Hamlets, Newham and Waltham Forest) and developed a Local Plan for the whole area (a process I return to below). One of the particularities of this local authority-cum-development company is that it is non-elected – its democratic accountability is at best indirect, through the GLA and the Mayor (who is the chairman of the LLDC's Board). We may say that the 'legal architecture of exception' of the Olympics (Marrero-Guillamón, 2012: 22), initially justified on the grounds of temporary needs related to security and delivery, has been prolonged by the introduction of the LLDC, itself legitimated through a rhetoric of efficiency. As Mike Raco (2012, 2015) has argued, there is a widespread belief within policy circles in the idea that, free from democratic interference – i.e. provided that both the government and the wider public are kept at arm's length – experts will 'get the job done' more effectively. I will return below to the question of how the reliance on the discourse and practice of expertise has interesting parallels with

---

[3] This is the latest in a series of QUANGOs specifically created to manage the urban transformation of the area in relation to the Olympics. The LLDC replaces the Olympic Delivery Authority (ODA) and the Olympic Park Legacy Company (OPLC), and also inherits the functions (and properties) of the London Thames Gateway Development Corporation (LTGDC), an experimental body introduced for the acceleration and coordination of the development of this part of East London.

the way in which community groups in Hackney Wick have gone about making their case.

In parallel to this spatial and institutional restructuring led by local authorities, private developers switched gears soon after the Games were over, and starting in late 2012 a steady stream of development proposals were put forward for Hackney Wick. Most were rather predictable plans for replacing industrial buildings or vacant lots with cheaply produced, high density residential or mix-use developments (Fig. 7.2).

The 'development fallow' was clearly over in the mind of developers, who undoubtedly recognised the existence of a massive 'rent gap' (Smith, 1987) ready to be actualised: rents extracted from industrial properties, even when converted into artist studios, are indeed significantly lower than those potentially extracted with residential developments. To an extent, these proposals responded to expectations created by the Hackney Wick and Fish Island Action Area Plans (AAPs), prepared, respectively, by the London Boroughs of Hackney (LBH, 2012) and Tower Hamlets (LBTH, 2012) before the LLDC came into being. These documents identified the need to release land previously

Fig. 7.2 Initial proposal for Neptune Wharf (detail)

Source: Neptune Group, 2012

defined as Strategic Industrial Location and 'promote a more flexible approach to land use . . . in order to assist in creating sustainable communities [and] maximise the benefits of the Olympic Legacy' (LBTH, 2012: 44). This re-zoning effectively opened the way for substituting industrial venues with mixed-use and residential developments.[4]

Community Responses

The development of the Local Plan and the surge in private development interest became parallel and tangible forces in post-Olympic Hackney Wick. At one level, legal requirements meant that public notices were disseminated and community engagement meetings organised. These formal 'participatory devices' produced their own responses in the form of questionnaires, comments, objections, etc. Other local initiatives, such as *The Wick* newspaper (of which I was the editor), art/architecture studio public works' *Wick Sessions* (a series of public talks) and Richard Brown's campaign for affordable workspace provision, *Affordable Wick*,[5] strived to make these processes more widely public by publishing relevant articles, organising debates, explaining things in lay terms, and generally encouraging people to get involved in the area's future (Fig. 7.3).

However, rather than taking for granted the existence of a community that then mobilises against 'external' threats, my argument is that the urban plans and development proposals affecting the area became issues with the capacity to generate public involvement (Marres, 2007). In other words, *a* community was enacted as a *result* of coming together to tackle the proposed changes to the built environment and their

---

[4] These AAPs were replaced in July 2015 by the LLDC's Local Plan. The latter, however, was developed in continuity, rather than rupture, with previous planning legislation (LLDC, 2013: 32).

[5] Originally his final project for an MA in Architecture at the RCA, *Affordable Wick* took the form of a 3 m[2] cabin, or 'roaming workspace', and a website. Through both outlets, current development proposals were made public and explained, as well as Brown's own proposals for a grassroots model of development based on existing self-build practices in the area.

Fig. 7.3   Richard Brown's *Affordable Wick* cabin in campaign mode, 2013

Source: Courtesy of Richard Brown

perceived effects. As Noortje Marres puts it (cited in Harman, 2014: 168): 'members of political communities are not in the first instance connected by way of shared or opposing opinions and interests, but by issues'. Drawing from Deborah Martin's (2003) work on the concept of neighbourhood, we could say that this local community was *enacted in practice* through the residents' actions against a threat to their conditions of existence. This performative understanding of community is a long way from the use (and abuse) of the concept in policy, where it has routinely been deployed – both by New Labour and the Coalition Government – to denote bounded, homogeneous and consensual groups at the centre of welfare reform (Raco and Flint, 2001; Wallace, 2010; Hancock, et al., 2012).

In this section I want to focus on how one particular group was formed to give response to both the public authorities and private developers' plans. 'The Unit' emerged originally out of the Cultural Interest Group (CIG), 'an independent local networking organisation … with the aim of helping to establish a permanent, sustainable, creative community' (Chamberlain, 2013: 18). The CIG was founded in 2008 by William Chamberlain, a lawyer who had been part of the team preparing the London bid for the Olympics and who subsequently moved to the area. As he recounts:

> Disillusioned by my legal career, I handed in my notice with a vague idea about wanting to be involved in helping to deliver some sort of [Olympic] legacy in East London. I was particularly interested in the idea of rewarding artists for being the pioneers of urban regeneration and felt that the best way to avoid gentrification would be to try and empower the existing community in such a way that regeneration was done by the people living there rather than having it done to them – hopefully a more sustainable inside-out approach rather than top-down. (Chamberlain, 2013: 18)

The CIG materialises in an open, itinerant monthly meeting. Amongst its regulars one finds artists and other professionals from the cultural sector, residents, businessmen and local government representatives. The matters discussed are extremely heterogeneous: urban planning, art funding opportunities, business openings and closings, street signalling, transport issues, street safety, etc. The group perceives itself mainly as a forum for sharing relevant information, making connections, and making sure that local residents and businesses are part of the opportunities and processes taking place in the area.

For the purposes of this chapter, I'm mostly interested in the ways in which the CIG organised itself to provide a response to the development pressure in line with its remit to fight for the sustainability of the creative community. In 2012, a 'Planning and Development Subgroup' (subsequently rebranded as 'The Unit') was created. It was led by two residents with interest and experience in these issues (architect Richard Brown, mentioned above, and planner Lee Wilshere) and included a larger group of collaborators (amongst them, myself). The Unit set to articulate a local vision for Hackney Wick and lobby for it through various channels.

One such channel was a close relationship with the Design Team at the LLDC. The latter was led by a group of architects that had been working in the area since the mid-2000s with Design for London.[6] This team, responsible for overseeing the design of the Park and its surroundings, identified in The Unit a key local actor with valuable knowledge useful for informing their guidance documents. Both the Design Team and The Unit shared a worry about the potential harm that the kind of proposals that were being put forward by developers (disproportionate, uninterested in the area's qualities and history, and of poor architectural quality) would cause to the neighbourhood if left unchallenged. They agreed that gathering a strong evidence base highlighting the versatility of the existing building stock and its role in sustaining the local ecology of affordability was an important part of 'steering' development in the right direction. Moreover, the Design Team hoped to be able to influence the local plan from inside the LLDC. Apart from frequent communications and sharing information, the Design Team commissioned two reports, on live/work and self-build practices in the area, from The Unit's co-chair, Richard Brown (2012, 2013).

From the point of view of The Unit, collaborating with the LLDC was a welcome opportunity to influence those in charge of planning the future of the area. But it wasn't the only available strategy. We were also interested in the new possibilities for community-led planning that the Localism Act 2011 had opened. Forming a neighbourhood forum and pursuing a locally-grounded vision for the area through a neighbourhood plan seemed a potentially worthwhile project, as well as a strategy that would guarantee autonomy from local authorities (see Sturzaker and Shaw, 2015). In the end, however, it was decided that taking into account the limited time and resources available to the group, it was wiser to use the good rapport with the Design Team to try to influence the local plan – in many ways the single most important document for the future of the area.

It was around that time that the collaboration with the Design Team took a new turn, as the latter started to point at The Unit as key local

---

[6] Design for London was an experiment of the Labour GLA, which tried to introduce the idea of strategies and principles of design in the fragmented landscape of urban regeneration in London.

interlocutors in their conversations with potential developers. The Unit accepted to meet face to face with them, and indeed showed a great capacity to provide useful feedback and criticism to development proposals – as well as to use those meetings to introduce issues that weren't necessarily on the agenda, such as affordable workspace or live/work. These meetings gained notable traction, to the point that after a while it became almost standard practice for developers to contact The Unit and meetings moved forward to the pre-submission stage – that is, before the proposal is official and public. Arguably, The Unit was becoming an 'obligatory passage point' (Callon, 1986), that is, a necessary mediation between actors, a negotiation space interested parties cannot afford to bypass. To be sure, the emergence of this space was aided by the difficulties developers were encountering in having their plans approved. The LLDC had rejected most of the applications it had received on the basis that they ignored existing regulations (e.g. maximum building height) and didn't respect the area's character (e.g. its industrial architecture features). This news must have run like wildfire among developers: resubmitting an application is expensive; anticipating problems is cost-effective.

As a collaborator of The Unit, I attended several of these meetings, in which the developers' team (mainly architects) would explain their proposal, aided by plans and images, and members of The Unit (and others they had invited) would respond with questions, feedback and comments. One of the things I found most surprising was the ductility of the proposals during the process. I will provide an example. The initial, pre-application proposal for a site known as 415 Wick Lane consisted on two large blocks of flats between 7 and 13 stories. In the first meeting with The Unit, the height, massing, orientation and design of these blocks was severely criticised: they blocked the view of a historic industrial chimney, they didn't respect the preferred pedestrian route to the Greenway, and their relation to the street was questioned. Models of affordable workspace and live/work provision were also discussed. Some of these comments were quite readily taken on by the developers, who said that there was room to move buildings around and rethink their connection to the immediate environment. The issue of height was peculiar: the then current Action Area Plan was clear that the maximum height was six stories, and yet the developers were ignoring that on the basis that Tower Hamlets had allowed taller student housing buildings. They hoped that the provision of affordable housing and workspace could be used to 'negotiate' the extra height.

Several months later, the same parties met again to discuss the fourth iteration of the project. The whole development was now between six and eight stories, the orientation of the blocks had changed, and the connection with the Greenway reworked via a passageway leading up to it. Affordable workspace was part of the proposal too – it occupied the ground floor of both blocks and there was a preliminary agreement with artist Gavin Turk, who would take most of it. The developers said they were also aiming to include 'as much affordable housing as possible' (i.e. without affecting their target profit) taking into account the new limitations they were working with (meaning the reduced height).[7] Most of the discussion during the meeting centred around the workspace component, and in particular on its 'active frontage' (i.e. shopfront) design. It became apparent that this wasn't the kind of artist workspace most in the room had in mind. The architects responded that the full height windows facing the street could be rethought to let light in but also allow privacy. Anna Harding, from Space Studios,[8] questioned the soundness of the plan, arguing that there were plenty of empty shopfronts in the area: artist studios required a different approach, and a provider capable of successfully managing them. The developers and Turk, however, seemed less worried about this. The former, in particular, insisted the design could be tweaked to accommodate Turk's studio needs.

A number of things happened in these meetings. Developers seemed to go into them looking to test the grounds and/or legitimise their projects. My impression is that they perceived The Unit to be *representative* of the area's 'sensibility', and therefore able to quickly flag up an application's shortcomings or the conflicts it may cause in the

---

[7] I have, on various occasions, heard developers wield variations of this argument, according to which planning restrictions (e.g. maximum height) are directly responsible for the lack of affordable housing provision. The idea of developers spontaneously self-regulating in the interest of the common good seems to me to be, at the very least, implausible.

[8] Space Studios, established in 1968, are one of the biggest artist studio providers in London.

community. Developers encountered in them a local group with the technical expertise to examine, and occasionally challenge, their designs. For The Unit, the meetings were an opportunity to inspect the quality of the proposals, but also to lobby for certain issues. As I showed above, there is a surprising amount of room for change at this stage: buildings may contract, move or change orientation; use allocations reconsidered; boundaries between public and private areas redrawn; alternative work-space management models discussed. My impression is that as long as their bottom line was preserved, developers were quite ready to accept changes, and that the speed and smoothness of the planning application process was more valuable to them that any design principle. Far from immobile objects, buildings are, at this stage, extremely 'elastic' – their imprint being a dynamic reflection of the diffused authorship at play, and the changing relations between the actors (Weizman, 2007).

These meetings acted, quite literally, as interfaces between the actors, as spaces of negotiation. And yet, there is the peculiarity that, strictly speaking, they were only informal meetings: they aren't a procedure recognised as part of the consultation process, and The Unit has no legal status or mandate to represent the community. Even so, the meetings produced some form of legitimacy-in-practice, inasmuch as the decisions taken in them were then carried forward. Compared to the rigidness and limited scope of formal consultation, this 'para-democratic' interface became a productive space of negotiation, a flexible protocol tactically convenient for those involved and capable of making divergent interests converge around the table.

At the same time as these meetings were taking place, The Unit was also busy advocating for wider public involvement in key planning issues: using Brown's *Affordable Wick* as the main platform (both online through its web and offline through the roaming cabin), the group was campaigning for the extension of the conservation zones in Hackney Wick and Fish Island, and making public the developers' planning proposals and their comments on them. Local Facebook groups were also used to this end. This work was an important counterbalance to the small-group, close-doors dynamic of the meetings with the developers, and in my opinion speaks highly of The Unit's commitment to use their access to these spaces of negotiation for making things more widely public.

The Local Plan

The LLDC published the first draft of the local plan in December 2013 (LLDC, 2013). Rather than looking at the entirety of this long and complex document, here I will focus on The Unit's response to the section on Hackney Wick, as it provides a good opportunity for evaluating the impact that the collaboration with the Design Team had had in the Plan itself. The response was a collective effort, with contributions from several members of The Unit and close collaborators (including myself). It opened with the following statement:

> We believe that the development of the Local Plan provides an excellent opportunity to foster a creative, affordable and sustainable neighbourhood. As detailed below, we think the current Draft does not appropriately address some of the key issues concerning the future of the area. We would like to see greater emphasis in policies that work towards the sustainability of an affordable ecology that over the years has allowed the development of a thriving artistic and cultural scene spanning several generations of practitioners. Supporting such community-led regeneration, we believe, could provide a blueprint for similar scenarios across Britain and the world – one which feeds from, rather than overtakes, grassroots dynamism. (The Unit, 2014: 1)

The response articulated three main areas of criticism. Firstly, it highlighted the insufficiency of the valorisation, protection and support for existing spatial and social dynamics. The omission of live/work was openly criticised: it was an open secret that many of the area's factories had been unofficially converted into live/work units, and that they were a key component of Hackney Wick's ecology of affordability. Moreover, the LLDC had commissioned a report on this very practice from Richard Brown – that evidence needed to be integrated into the Plan, and a new use designation for live/work introduced.

A second area of critique was affordable and managed workspace. First, it was demanded that the policy in question that the Plan introduced (BEE.6) was applied to all areas with Hackney Wick, and not limited to larger studio providers. The Unit also demanded that the workspace provision strategy became a planning requirement in order to ensure appropriate design and costing, as opposed to an aspect left to be detailed via later Section 106 agreements.[9] Special emphasis was put on the importance of appropriate management schemes for these spaces, and the necessity of creating flexible structures that allowed collectives to self-build their space, as had happened informally in the area for years.

A third area of concern had to do with a more general question, the lack of emphasis the plan put on the existing social fabric. It was demanded that an explicit recognition of the local community's vitality was introduced, as well as a consideration of how future development would contribute to its sustainability. For example, it was highlighted that the area had built its success as a creative hub based on a diverse mix of uses and spatial adjacencies – it was important that the impact of residential development on this ecology was addressed.

On the positive side, The Unit was pleased to see explicit mention of the particularity and value of the industrial architecture of the area, and the idea that it should inform future proposals. In this sense, the plan to extend the conservation area to include more recent buildings (some without great architectural merit) was welcomed, particularly as it pointed towards the protection of the material base of the area's ecology, rather than the singling out of singular buildings.

These comments, variations of which were submitted by many individuals who were enlisted to the cause by The Unit during their advocacy campaign, were part of the materials that had to inform the second draft of the local plan, the Publication Version, which went through consultation between August and October 2014. It is very difficult, if not impossible, to precisely gauge the extent to which The Unit's response informed this second draft, which obviously had to address a much wider set of comments. Nonetheless, it is interesting to discuss the differences between the two versions in relation to the demands mentioned above.

---

[9] Section 106 of the 1990 Town and Country Planning Act refers to planning obligations linked to a planning application decision. For instance, it may require a proportion of affordable housing, or a compensation for loss of open space.

The overarching emphasis of the Local Plan's approach to Hackney Wick continued to be on developing a 'balanced' mix of uses and creating better connections within the area, and between the area and its surroundings. However, the Area Priorities included, at the top of the list, the following two: 'Heritage-led regeneration and high-quality design: Ensuring that proposals for development are designed to respond to heritage assets, and where possible, restore and reuse those assets in a way that reinforces and celebrates their historic significance'; and 'Creative and productive employment: Protecting creative and cultural industrial uses that support the continuation of Hackney Wick and Fish Island's entrepreneurial and enterprising work culture'. This was connected to the introduction of two entirely new policies. Policy 1.1, 'Managing change in Hackney Wick and Fish Island', was introduced 'to protect the exiting industrial and economic base of the Sub Area', and established that proposals for development would be acceptable when they maintained 'the overall amount of existing employment floorspace . . . including that used by creative and cultural industries and operating as low-cost and managed workspace' (LLDC, 2014: 151). Policy 1.2, 'Promoting Hackney Wick and Fish Island's unique identity and appearance', argued that development proposals should 'reference and reinforce [the area's] local distinctiveness and use it as a driver for economic, environmental and heritage-led regeneration. The overall aim is to deliver place-specific development that is well designed for its context' (LLDC, 2014: 152).

This seeming rapprochement of views between the two parties (the live/work issue notwithstanding), was partly confirmed by The Unit's response to the Draft. Rather than questioning the overall approach, it suggested partial amendments, such as the affordability criteria specifications. It was also a more technical document, prepared with the support of the London Tenants Federation and Just Space,[10] which had organised several workshops with local groups to help them prepare their responses. These

---

[10] The London Tenants Federation is an umbrella organisation of social housing tenants associations. It sends delegates and provides support in many planning consultations and examinations (see http://www.londontenants.org/). Just Space 'is an informal alliance of community groups, campaigns and concerned independent organisations'. Its aim is 'to improve public participation in planning to ensure that policy is fairer towards communities' (see http://justspace.org.uk/).

comments were submitted during the consultation period, and added to the evidence to be considered during the Plan's independent examination by a designated Planning Inspector. The latter's report set the parameters of the public hearing which took place in March 2015; it established, based on all the evidence submitted, the issues to be discussed and, based on the latter, the parties that were invited to speak.

The hearing took place over two weeks at the LLDC offices in Stratford. The Planning Inspector presided the meeting, sat on her own at one end of the table and surrounded by piles of documents. To her right sat the representatives from the LLDC and the developers; to her left were the community groups. Opposite the Inspector, completing the square, there were further seats, allocated to developers and/ or community groups if needed. Only those sat around the table had the right to speak, which is awarded based on having submitted a written response during the consultation. The audience sat in rows of seats at the other end of the room, facing the Inspector. The hearing is a public event, anybody can attend – and yet, there were never more than 10 people in the two days I was there. Hard copies of the Plan and the documents it referred to, amounting to several thousand pages, were available for consultation on a table by the window; see Fig. 7.4.

Each day was organised in morning and afternoon sessions, in which the questions raised by the Inspector in her Examination Report were addressed. As she explained on the first day, the aim of the hearing was to test whether the plan was 'sound',[11] i.e. compliant with the regulations. This greatly limited the scope of the discussion, which as I will show below was overall rather technical. In addition, only those parties whose comments had been selected by the Inspector had the right to sit on the table. I will provide an example that illustrates the dynamic, the discussion around Policy B.4, on affordable workspace (see Fig. 7.5).

First to speak was Daniel Watney, representing local landowners and developers Roypark and Newstates Ltd. He argued that the policy wasn't sound: first, it wasn't clear how historic rent was calculated or what

---

[11] The National Planning Policy Framework establishes that to be sound, a Local Plan should be 'positively prepared'; 'justified'; 'effective' and 'consistent with national policy' (DCLG, 2012: 43).

Fig. 7.4 The LLDC's Draft Local Plan and supporting evidence, as seen at the public hearing

Source: Author

counted as workspace. Second, the demands placed on developers in terms of providing affordable workspace *and* affordable housing were simply too great – it was 'impossible' to do both, with the difference that good indicators existed for the latter, as well as a tried and tested methodology for delivering it. Hence, it was preferable that the Plan stuck to affordable housing in terms of planning requirements.

A Space Studios' spokesperson made clear that they were in support of the policy, but with some questions. They wanted to suggest changes to the wording: 'where viable' and 'acceptable where' should be removed; instead, the onus should be on the developers to justify why workspace should not be retained. Point 3 should be amended and read 'loss of employment *space*' instead. The rent review should

Existing managed and low-cost workspace shall be retained where viable and where it complements wider plans for the area. New managed workspace and/or low-cost workspace will be acceptable where it:

1. Is flexible and able to meet the needs of various end users within B Use Classes;

2. Includes an appropriate management scheme secured through Section 106 Agreements; and

3. Does not result in a net loss of employment.

Low-cost provision will be supported and secured through Section 106 where:

4. Rents are up to 75 per cent of historic market rent for the previous year for the equivalent floorspace in the same area for an equivalent B Class Use;

5. It is secured at the current market rate for cultural or creative purposes;

6. It is subsidised to reduce the cost to the user for charitable purposes; or

7. It establishes robust management links with a registered workspace provider.

Fig. 7.5 Policy B.4: Providing low-cost and managed workspace

Source: LLDC (2014: 34)

be conducted through an external expert, and not include office space. Space Studios also questioned the 75 per cent of historic rent affordability criteria; they used 50 per cent in their business model. Also, the time period under consideration should be longer, three to five years, to minimise the risk of distortions. The policy didn't currently address the question of the length of leases, but it was fundamental that the provision of affordable workspace was tied to longer contracts, no less than 20 years. Finally, links with established providers should be strengthened.

These comments and suggestions were echoed by representatives from ACME Studios, Mother Studios,[12] and Just Space. They spoke of great difficulties in securing longer leases, and the need to retain *existing*

---

[12] ACME Studios and Mother Studios both run artist studio spaces in Hackney Wick. The former was established in 1972 and is one of the largest providers in London, together with Space Studios. Mother Studios is an independent organisation and runs one building in the area since 2001.

affordable workspaces – new built 'affordable' workspace was always 20–40 per cent more expensive. Just Space also highlighted that the wording of points four to seven was unclear: were these either/or criteria? If so, a loophole was being created, in which proposal could go through meeting only partially the criteria for affordability.

Watney spoke again, and argued that there was 'a cost' to this policy; there needed to be subsidies if it was to succeed. He also reiterated that the requirement should be to provide *either* affordable workspace or affordable housing in areas such as Hackney Wick.

The LLDC responded that they considered the policy was sound and needed no changes. The representatives briefly addressed some of the comments above, first by emphasising that the role of this policy was to create 'favourable conditions' for the provision of affordable workspace. The inclusion of 'where viable' was a recognition that there would be circumstances in which retaining workspace would not be possible. Points 4–7 were indeed designed to provide flexibility of delivery. And with regards to the length of the leases, this was not something that the Local Plan had the remit to address.

Just Space responded that it was within the remit of the plan to consider how the proposed rezoning affected existing uses, and the length of leases clearly fell within this. Furthermore, the many caveats on the policy had the risk of raising expectations in terms of mix-use developments. Point 4 could not be optional; it had to be clear that it had to apply to all schemes.

The LLDC then reiterated that there was nothing they could do legally to address the length of leases – they were not in a position to dictate the terms of these private contracts. However, it would be possible to negotiate this with a willing developer through Section 106 agreements. Regarding the possible negative impacts produced by the policy's flexibility, they wanted to highlight that this policy referred back to Policy B1 on the protection of employment – therefore, there was no such risk.

A thorough analysis of the public hearing is outside the scope of this paper, but I will offer some analytic observations to end this section. The main dynamic I observed during the hearing was the LLDC's reluctance to engage with any of the arguments presented by either developers or community groups. As far as they were concerned, the Draft Plan was 'sound' and required no substantial changes. The other parties' attempts to steer the document in the direction of their interests were by and large unsuccessful. This meant that the public hearing was not a space of negotiation, but rather a staging of disagreements. It was left to the Planning Inspector to decide, in her final report, whether any changes were needed.

Also of interest are the conditions of 'participation' in the public hearing. Not only there was hardly any public; more fundamentally, the right to participate was limited to those whose comments to the draft Plan that had been selected as worthy of further discussion by the Inspector. Moreover, once on the table, successful 'participation' depended on being able to understand and deploy a highly technical language. Indeed, most of the people around the table had some kind of training that facilitated this: lawyers and planning consultants in the case of the developers and the LLDC; architects, community organisers or urban studies scholars in the case of the community groups.[13] It is well documented in the planning literature that the very nature of certain participatory mechanisms is exclusionary along class, gender and ethnic lines, clearly favouring the 'habitus' of well-educated professionals (see Imrie and Raco, 2003; Maginn, 2004; Dillon and Fanning, 2011). The 'quasi-judicial' (Raco and Flint, 2001) nature of both planning documents and the public hearing itself acted as a huge barrier to inclusive participation. As a participatory device, it was clearly a very limited exercise.

Following the public hearing, the Planning Inspector wrote her final report, in which only minor changes and clarifications were demanded of the LLDC. The Local Plan was subsequently adopted in July 2015 (LLDC, 2015). Policy B.4 was included without any changes.

---

[13] As a further, if anecdotal, example of this, I had to sit in for The Unit in one of the sessions and found it impossible to actually intervene. After hearing the articulate presentation of a Just Space colleague, in particular, I felt there was nothing I could possibly contribute to the discussion of a rather technical aspect of the Plan.

Conclusion: On the Expertification of Participation

I will conclude by briefly teasing out some of the wider implications of the processes described above in relation to democratic politics. Community participation in the planning process has been led in Hackney Wick by The Unit, a self-appointed group (part of a larger interest group, the CIG) whose leverage has relied on their technical expertise and local knowledge (see Tironi, 2015). The Unit is not a representative entity and doesn't aspire to become one (there are no elected members, for instance, or mechanisms to gauge how shared their 'vision' is within the community). It is rather a group structured around common *interests* (in this case, broadly speaking, the sustainability of the cultural sector in the area), the defence of which takes the form of advocacy and lobbying. The Unit's 'successes' in terms of, for example, changing the design of buildings, or introducing certain ideas in local planning policy, have depended on its capacity to convince others through expert discourse. It was their situated knowledge, as both local residents and architects/planners, that enabled the emergence of certain informal spaces of dialogue with the authorities and developers in the first place, and the defining quality that made them tactically convenient for those involved. To reiterate, in these technical forums the Unit did not speak on behalf of the local community, but rather advocated for a particular idea for the area they had developed and promoted. This is not to say that The Unit is entirely without legitimacy. I would argue that it has indeed developed a form of authority in practice, which emanates from its ability to articulate a 'vision' for the area, gather support for it, and use this to exert pressure on influential others. The 'para-democratic' structures generated in the process have, to be sure, contributed to steering both the discussion and actual development in Hackney Wick in a more community-oriented direction in relation to the goal of sustaining the area's 'ecology of affordability'. The Unit has indeed shown remarkable effectiveness as a kind of lobby. Furthermore, inasmuch as the 'local community' cannot be said to pre-exist the issues that brings it together, it can be argued that through its advocacy, The

Unit has contributed to the enactment of *a* Hackney Wick community – imagined or otherwise.

The dynamics within these 'para-democratic' structures stand in sharp contrast with the statuary participatory process associated with the local plan. Here, as described above, the involvement of The Unit and other local organisations was mostly reactive and increasingly narrow. They had to respond to specific documents, and do it in the latter's own terms. The scope of the consultation became more and more limited in each step of the process – to the point that, during the public hearing, the discussion of the Plan's 'soundness' translated mostly into disagreements about phrasings and percentages. The 'quasi-judicial' (Raco and Flint, 2001) character of participation was apparent: in the trial-like mise-en-scène; in the division between those with the right to speak on one side of the room and a mute audience on the other; and in the expectation that the parties will adhere to a technical and precise language. In this sense, the official democratic participatory process proved to be more rigid and restricted than the informal, para-democratic structures mentioned above.

If, following Jacques Rancière (2014), we define democracy as 'the government of anyone and everyone', and understand that the democratic process is triggered when those who aren't entitled to be part of public life (because they are not considered citizens, or because their concerns aren't considered legitimate) demonstrate the arbitrariness of this partition and partake in what they have no part in, then the participatory process surrounding the Local Plan in Hackney Wick has been anything but democratic. On the one hand, The Unit's reliance on expert knowledge and semi-closed meetings is, in and of itself, an inscription of entitlement and a barrier for incorporating 'the part with no part' (Rancière, 2014). On the other hand, the official democratic structures of participation, in theory open to all, are in fact effectively limited to those with the necessary expertise to navigate them.

The situation is no doubt tricky: by deploying technical expertise The Unit has been able to put itself in a position to make a difference – although at the cost of perpetuating the performance of politics as the domain of experts. Without their lobbying tactics, however, local residents and groups would be relegated to official participatory devices, which are extremely limited in scope and impact (see Dinham, 2005).

Moreover, the 'expertification' of the participatory process I have observed in Hackney Wick seems to mirror the ongoing redefinition of local democracy in the area, apparent in the governance structures introduced to deliver the Olympic legacy (namely the LLDC). In both cases, traditional democratic concerns with representativeness, accountability and inclusion are secondary to notions such as effectiveness and efficiency (Raco, 2015).

References

Brown, R. (2012) *Made in HWFI: The Live-Work Collectives*. London: See Studio.

Brown, R. (2013) *Creative Factories: Hackney Wick and Fish Island*. London: See Studio.

Brownhill, S. (1999) 'Turning the East End into the West End: the lessons and legacies of the London Docklands Development Corporation', in R. Imrie and H. Thomas (eds.), *British Urban Policy: An Evaluation of the Urban Development Corporations*. London: Sage.

Callon, M. (1986) 'Some elements of a sociology of translation: domestication of the scallops and the fishermen of St Brieuc Bay', in J. Law (ed.), *Power, Action and Belief: A New Sociology of Knowledge*. London: Routledge & Kegan Paul.

Callon, M., Lascoumes, P. and Barthe, Y. (2009) *Acting in an Uncertain World: An Essay on Technical Democracy*. Cambridge, MA: MIT Press

Chamberlain, W. (2013) 'The cultural interest group', *The Wick* (3): 18.

DCLG. (2012) *National Planning Policy Framework*. London: Department for Communities and Local Government.

Design for London and LLDC. (2013) *Stitching the Fringe: Working Around the Olympic Park*. London: London Mayors Office.

Dillon, D. and Fanning, B. (2011) *Lessons for the Big Society: Planning, Regeneration and the Politics of Community Participation*. Farnham: Ashgate.

Dinham, A. (2005) 'Empowered or over-Powered? The Real Experiences of Local Participation in the UK's New Deal for Communities.' *Community Development Journal* 40(3): 301–12.

Fussey, P., Coaffee, J., Armstrong, G. and Hobbs, R. (2011) *Securing and Sustaining the Olympic City: Reconfiguring London for 2012 and Beyond.* Aldershot: Ashgate.

Gill, S. (2007) *Archaeology in Reverse.* London: Nobody.

Hancock, L., Mooney, G. and Neal, S. (2012) 'Crisis social policy and the resilience of the concept of community', *Critical Social Policy* 32(3): 343–364.

Harman, G. (2014) *Bruno Latour: Reassembling the Political.* London: Pluto Press.

LBH [London Borough of Hackney]. (2012) *Hackney Wick Area Action Plan.* London: LB Hackney.

LBTH [London Borough of Tower Hamlets]. (2012) *Fish Island Action Area Plan.* London: LB of Tower Hamlets.

LLDC. (2013) *Local Plan: Draft Version.* London: LLDC.

LLDC. (2014) *Local Plan: Publication Version.* London: LLDC.

LLDC. (2015) *Local Plan: 2015–2031.* London: LLDC. http://queeneliza betholympicpark.co.uk/~/media/lldc/local%20plan/adoption%20july% 202015/lldc_localplan_2015_interactive100dpi%20(4).pdf

Maginn, P. J. (2004) *Urban Regeneration, Community Power, and the (In)significance of 'Race'.* Hants and Burlington: Ashgate.

Marrero-Guillamón, I. (2012) 'Olympic state of exception', in H. Powell and I. Marrero-Guillamón (eds.), *The Art of Dissent: Adventures in London's Olympic State.* London: Marshgate Press.

Marres, N. (2007) 'The issues deserve more credit: pragmatist contributions to the study of public involvement in controversy', *Social Studies of Science* 37(5): 759–780.

Martin, D. G. (2003) 'Enacting neighborhood', *Urban Geography* 24(5): 361–385.

muf architecture/art. (2009) *Creative Potential: Hackney Wick and Fish Island.* London: Muf publications.

Pratt, A. C. (2009) 'Urban regeneration: from the arts "feel good" factor to the cultural economy: a case study of Hoxton, London', *Urban Studies* 46(5–6): 1041–1061.

Raco, M. (2003) 'Remaking place and securitising space: urban regeneration and the strategies, tactics and practices of policing in the UK', *Urban Studies* 40(9): 1869–1887.

Raco, M. (2012) 'The privatisation of urban development and the London Olympics 2012', *City* 16(4): 452–460.

Raco, M. (2015) 'Sustainable city-building and the new politics of the possible: reflections on the governance of the London Olympics 2012', *Area* 47(2): 124–131.

Raco, M. and Flint, J. (2001) 'Communities, places and institutional relations: assessing the role of area-based community representation in local governance.' *Political Geography* 20(5): 585–612.

Rancière, J. (2014) *Hatred of Democracy.* London: Verso.

Smith, N. (1987) 'Gentrification and the rent gap', *Annals of the Association of American Geographers* 77(3): 462–465.

Sturzaker, J. and Shaw, D. (2015) 'Localism in practice: lessons from a pioneer Neighbourhood Plan in England', *Town Planning Review* 86(5): 587–609.

Tironi, M. (2015) 'Modes of Technification: Expertise, Urban Controversies and the Radicalness of Radical Planning.' *Planning Theory* 14(1): 70–89.

Wallace, A. (2010) 'New neighbourhoods, new citizens: challenging "community" as a framework for moral and social regeneration under New Labour', *International Journal of Urban and Regional Research* 34(4): 806–819.

Weizman, E. (2007) *Hollow Land: Israel's Architecture of Occupation.* London: Verso.

Isaac Marrero-Guillamón is Lecturer in Anthropology at Goldsmiths, University of London. He has done research on the resistances to urban renewal in Poblenou, Barcelona, and on the relations between the 2012 Olympics, the transformation of East London and critical artistic practices. He's the editor, with Hilary Powell, of *The Art of Dissent: Adventures in London's Olympic State* (Marshgate Press, 2012). His recent work has appeared in *Ethnography, Qualitative Sociology* and *Visual Studies*.

8

Contesting Community on London 2012's Olympic Fringe

Francesca Weber-Newth

Introduction

The smell of freshly baked pizza wafts out of the door of a smart, newly refurbished, former industrial printworks. People congregate on beer-garden benches, drink craft beer, peer across the canal at the street art and catch the last rays of sun before they retreat behind the White Building (see Fig. 8.1). An artist clambers up the metal staircase to her studio on the second floor. This is the sensitive community-orientated legacy that Olympic planners imagined: the renovated building has been re-imagined as a cultural hub where the artistic community, local residents and visitors can intermingle. The White Building is a low-budget Olympic intervention into the neighbourhood Hackney Wick Fish Island. The neighbourhood is located directly adjacent to the Olympic site, part of the so-called Olympic Fringe, and is therefore an important space to showcase London 2012's 'legacy'. While the White

F. Weber-Newth (✉)
Humboldt University of Berlin, Berlin, Germany
e-mail: fwebernewth@gmail.com

Fig. 8.1 A community-oriented legacy as London 2012 authorities imagine it: Lea Navigation canal with the White Building on the left, July 2013

Photograph: author

Building gives an insight into 'community legacy' as imagined by its initiators and funders, the London Legacy Development Corporation (LLDC), it is only part of how 'community'[1] is lived, post-London 2012.

Through three empirical cases – a housing estate, a rowing club and a new cultural centre – this chapter delves a little deeper into what community on the Olympic Fringe meant before 2012 and what it means now. It documents and analyses how community is understood, defined, constructed and idealised within the London 2012 regeneration process – and why different definitions reveal the tensions, and crucially,

---

[1] When I use the term 'community' I describe the way various social actors imagine and use the concepts: I see these as shifting categories with contested meanings and do not intend to reify the terms. In the proceeding discussion I omit the inverted commas so as not to distract the reader.

the power dynamics at play within the 'Regeneration Games'. Community is not only an important pillar within policy documents and political rhetoric, but also within the language of activists and residents. Identifying which of these constructions are included in formal policy – which are dominant and which are marginal(ised) – reveals which individuals and groups benefit and which lose out in urban development.

How has community been written into the planning of Olympic-led regeneration? How do London 2012 authorities define community? How has community rhetoric changed since the bid was won in 2005? Have formal definitions been contested at ground level? By answering these questions, this chapter uses community as a lens to reveal *for whom* exactly London 2012's urban regeneration is conceived.

Community as a Lens

The language of community has common appeal for policymakers of all kinds. Community provides a tangible bridge between micro and macro, individual and society, identity and Culture (Deas, 2013). Within a post-Fordist context in which governance replaces government, community rhetoric is particularly relevant in regenerating cities: community conveys a sense of 'the local' and therefore fits into the picture of shared responsibility of state and citizen. Scholars have pointed out that re-building local community is seen as the solution to area-based economic hardship (Amin, 2004): a way to nurture small economies, stimulate entrepreneurship and eventually catalyse economic growth. Consequently, alongside economic vitality, community is perceived within policy as an indicator (and even evidence) of the successful regeneration of space, especially in the context of large-scale regeneration schemes (Wallace, 2010). Community is used to show that regeneration is being created on a human scale, for 'the people', an antidote to the so-called White Elephant developments, which fail in their everyday use and haunt planning professionals. In other words, weaving a narrative of community into the technical details of strategic plans is a way to make regeneration appear tangible and valuable to individuals.

Community has, in this way, become celebrated within urban regeneration, particularly as it chimes with the new paradigms of citizen participation and inclusion within the planning process. Community rhetoric can be analysed as a strategy to neutralise the corporate flavour of Olympic commercialism; a means through which London 2012's interventions in East London's neighbourhoods via 'regeneration' are justified. However, as this chapter shows, the kinds of social groups that are bestowed the official label of community indicates that not all 'communities' were equally celebrated within the process of London 2012's urban regeneration: some were deemed valuable and worth saving, others, in the worst case, were displaced. By focusing on the construction of community in and around the Olympic Fringe neighbourhood of Hackney Wick Fish Island, the dynamics, tensions and ambiguities of urban regeneration are revealed.

Olympic Fringe Neighbourhood: Hackney Wick Fish Island

Hackney Wick Fish Island is located adjacent to the London 2012 Olympic site (see Fig. 8.2), straddling the London boroughs of Hackney and Tower Hamlets. Wedged like an island between the Lea Navigation canal and the busy A11 duel carriageway, the neighbourhood was left largely without investment for decades and became known for its difficult socio-structural conditions. The 2011 Census shows that over half of the households in the neighbourhood live in social housing, unemployment is above the borough average and health indicators score the residents of Hackney Wick ward as worse than the borough average (London Borough of Hackney Policy and Partnerships, 2014: 4). Since London won the bid to host the Olympic Games in July 2005, it is one of the areas particularly affected by Olympic-led changes. In physical terms this has meant investment in re-paving roads, laying new pavements and installing street furniture, but the initiative with the biggest impact has been the construction of new bridges over the Lea canal, connecting the neighbourhood with the Olympic site. As part of the

Fig. 8.2 View over Hackney Wick Fish Island with Olympic stadium and ArcelorMittal Orbit sculpture visible in the background, March 2012. The letters HW stand for 'Hackney Wick'

Photograph: author

Olympic Fringe, there has been an emphasis in London 2012 documentation on the communities of this neighbourhood benefitting from the 'Olympic legacy' – providing a rich basis for research on the *process* of regeneration from the vantage point of this area.

The problem of poverty has historically defined the development of Hackney Wick, the northern half of the neighbourhood. This is evident in Charles Booth's East End poverty maps (*Survey into Life and Labour in London*, 1889), in which many of the residential streets in Hackney Wick are classified as dark blue, representing inhabitants who are 'very poor' with 'chronic want'. These terraced streets were demolished after World War II bomb damage and replaced by the Trowbridge Estate, comprised of low-rise bungalows and, most strikingly, seven 21-storey tower blocks. The towers were built by London County Council in the late 1960s, who envisioned working-class community lived out in 'streets in the sky'. However, in the 1980s and 1990s (as little as 20 years after they had been constructed), the flats were perceived as high-rise slums and were demolished, replaced by low-rise housing. This brief sketch of the area's history demonstrates that urban professionals have been concerned about poverty (and moral disorder) in the neighbour-hood since the 1880s, in each phase hoping that urban planning could remedy the situation. Crucially, this history also indicates the recurring problematisation of (working-class) community in the neighbourhood by urban planners – a theme that is reflected in current development discourse, especially in ideas of creating movement through the neigh-bourhood enclave via bridges.

Community in London 2012 Planning

Strengthening and building community was key to London 2012 plan-ning. In the 2005 Olympic bid, London itself was represented as 'a community', communicated through images of its multi-cultural history and the notion of unity and harmony through this diversity (Falcous and Silk, 2010). As Angharad Closs Stephens puts it, in the Olympic narrative 'difference is celebrated as part of the community's postmodern identity' (2007: 9). However, there are inconsistencies in the definition of community throughout official London 2012 documents, specifically the scale at which it is conceptualised. This highlights the slippery nature of the term community and the way it has been used to suit a range of different agendas over time.

The success of London's Olympic Bid (submitted to the IOC as a pitch) rested on its commitment to building a lasting social legacy for the existing communities of East London. The bid document states: 'The most enduring Legacy of the Olympics will be the regeneration of an entire community for the *direct benefit of everyone who lives there*' (LOCOG, 2005: 19, emphasis added). An LLDC report shows a clear reading of community as spatially bounded to East London, specifically relating to the 'communities that border the park' (LLDC, 2012a: 12), and temporally bounded to the present, because the emphasis is on benefits for people who *currently* live in the East End. London Mayor Boris Johnson confirms that 'existing communities' surrounding the Park site are central to his legacy vision (Design for London and LLDC, 2013: 4). This conceptualisation of community equated to *existing* social groups is relevant because the existing population in and around Stratford have continually been defined as chronically deprived (Davies, 2012). Consequently, including these marginalised groups within the Olympic vision was seen as the necessary benchmark for Olympic success. Crucially, given the area's 'social problem' status, community groups of Hackney Wick Fish Island were explicitly referenced as benefitting from the momentum of Olympic development (Design for London and LLDC, 2013: 43). By focusing Olympic-led regeneration and legacy on the concept of community, London 2012 planners sought to distance themselves from the planning mistakes of the nearby Docklands and Canary Wharf, in which top-down planning and a strong neoliberal agenda (Lees and Ley, 2008: 2380) created a wide gulf between mobile employment cultures and existing working-class lives.

While the bid documents imply a commitment to existing communities, there is a shifting conceptualisation of community in official Olympic planning documents, with a growing emphasis on *new* community. It must be stated that definitions of community as *existing* residents or *new* residents are not mutually exclusive. However, the two definitions indicate a new agenda that has developed since 2005. One of the five 'Olympic Promises' of the Department for Culture, Media and Sport (DCMS) was 'transforming communities'. This was to be achieved by 'build[ing] over 9,000 new homes, a large proportion of which to be affordable; and provid[ing] new sport, leisure, education and health facilities that meet the needs of residents, business and elite sport' (DCMS, 2008: 8). The 'new homes' are to be delivered within the frame of the Legacy Communities Scheme. The scheme very clearly defines community in terms of the five new residential areas – Chobham Manor, East Wick, Sweetwater, Marshgate Wharf and Pudding Mill – to be built in the Queen Elizabeth Park before 2040 (queenelizabetho-lympicpark.co.uk). This indicates not only a definition of community as new residential neighbourhoods, but also suggests that Olympic planners imagine community over a long time frame, hence the projection of community into the future. This perspective is reflected by Sir Robin Wales (Mayor of the London Borough of Newham), when he states: 'We need to develop communities' (Wales, 2008). This indicates that community is seen as an aspiration rather than something tangible that already exists.

While this inconsistency in definitions of community does not necessarily reflect inadequate planning, or strategic manipulation, it does indicate mixed agendas. The changing definition and use of community by London 2012 officials can be seen as a strategic manoeuvre: benefits for 'the community' were staged in a certain way during the bid process in order to gain IOC favour and trigger funds, and later amended to suit the priorities of the competitive urban growth machine. This demonstrates the power of language within urban regeneration, with institutions employing certain words appropriate for certain contexts, toying with meanings to promote changing agendas.

Clays Lane Estate: Failed Community or Absent Voice?

Clays Lane, a residential estate, was once located where the London 2012 Olympic site now stands (see Chapter 4). It has been described as an 'experiment in building close-knit communities' (Bishopsgate Institute). Officially, it was the Clays Lane Peabody Estate (formerly Clays Lane Housing Co-operative), once the UK's largest purpose-built housing estate, constructed in the Borough of Newham in 1977 for vulnerable single people. Reflecting this ethos of mutual support was its motto 'A community – not just a housing estate'. Founded jointly by Newham Council Housing Cooperation and the University of East London (formerly Polytechnic of East London), the estate comprised 57 shared houses (in which 4, 6 or 10 people lived), and 40 self-contained bungalow flats. However, rather than being labelled as productive or dynamic, this group of residents was represented by Olympic officials as a dysfunctional community and on these grounds was displaced from what is now the Olympic site. The story of Clays Lane shows how conflicting definitions of community, specifically the language of 'failing community', were used to justify the demolition in the case of Clays Lane.

Clays Lane was set in semi-wild green space neighbouring a gypsy-traveller site and Park Village, the two UEL student-residence towers (demolished in 2005). In total there were between 420 and 500 people living on Clays Lane estate; all contractual tenants who were members of the co-operative, a high percentage of whom were black and ethnic minority. The idea of the co-op was to help integrate the marginalised residents back into social life, with its courtyard system encouraging social interaction and mutual support between residents. Social relationships were fostered through self-governance within the co-operative system. After the estate was subject to a Compulsory Purchase Order by the LDA in 2006, it closed in July 2007 and was demolished in September 2007. Scrutinising the years leading up to the residents' eviction and their subsequent relocation provides a valuable insight into the contested nature of community within London 2012's regeneration. The difference between London 2012 planners' conception of community and how community was lived and experienced by the residents provides an insight into the dynamics of urban regeneration and power of the concept community.

London 2012 planning professionals regarded Clays Lanes Estate as a socially and economically dysfunctional community, backed up by the findings and conclusions of the Audit Commission's Inspection Report in 2005. The report stated: 'We have assessed Clays Lane Housing Co-operative as providing a "poor, no-star" service that has poor prospects for improvement' (Audit Commission, 2005: 5). When the Compulsory Purchase Order of Clays Lane Estate was decreed in 2006 (the first step towards the demolition of the estate), many residents took up the offer of relocation without further negotiation. This seemingly confirmed the Audit Commission's assessment that community in Clays Lane was fleeting, or even non-existent. However, when considering the political ideals on which the estate was conceived (the co-operative model), combined with the perspectives of some long-term residents, another image of the estate emerges that challenges notions it was a 'failing community'.

The views of two former Clays Lane residents juxtapose the formal Olympic planners' perspective. Long-time resident Julian Cheyne was resident in Clays Lane for 16 years and played a central role within the Clays Lane Former Tenants Association. Cheyne was not only committed to fighting the CPO on a full-time basis but also campaigned for increased compensation for residents' relocation and represented the estate's residents at various public meetings. When asked whether he considered Clays Lane a community, Julian states: '[the Olympic authorities] had community and they demolished it ... [T]hey say that they're sad, but that's the price of progress'. Interestingly, Julian's account of Clays Lane does not idealise community in defence of the co-op as one might expect. He is frank in admitting that the estate was not an especially inviting place, a surprising admission in the context of defending its existence. As Cheyne describes it, the estate stood at the top of a hill, was fairly run-down, surrounded by cars and rubbish; an industrial estate was located further down on the same road. This view of bleak and unwelcoming surroundings is confirmed by John Sole, another Clays resident, who describes his first experience of the estate:

> I walked [into Clays Lane Estate] and the gypsies were burning off cable in their paladin bins, and the community centre in Clays Lane was bathed in smoke. And I thought to myself, here are all these sort of small Rottweiler dogs breathing through the smoke and sort of feral children. I thought this really looks like downtown Beirut, so that was my first impressions of going there. That was 1991. (Interview, 26 August 2011)

According to Cheyne, residents did not make the best use of the facilities, especially the community centre, which he describes as 'under-used', a laundry room that became defunct as people increasingly bought their own washing machines, and a small shop that could not support itself. John Sole also highlights that the co-op committee was fraught with disagreements. Sole himself was taken to court by another committee member after an unsuccessful coup: 'I used to call it "co-op wars", you know, going to the committee meetings. Lots of people withdrew from them because they were very combative meetings... a system of perpetual revolution' (interview, 26 August 2011). Nevertheless, both John Sole and Julian Cheyne describe their attachment to the estate. John Sole explained that, 'On Clays Lane, there was a complete social context within to live, and the availability of that, I thought, was a godsend'. Sole explicitly describes Clays Lane as a community, referring to the sense of loss he felt when moving out of the estate and the value he placed on the social relationships fostered there:

> The real reason that I think it's a tragedy [the closure of Clays Lane] is an emotional one. Because on the day before I left Clays Lane I was living in a community of around 450 people of which I probably knew a third of them by name, and certainly could recognise all of them, or at least most of them, but definitely there were 30 or 40 people who I'd recognise fairly well. The next day I'm living on my own in a purpose-built bedsit... And so for a few weeks I felt really that I'd been robbed of, well, 400 people. (Interview, 26 August 2011)

Julian Cheyne's definition of the Clays Lane community rests almost entirely on the close-knit social relations between residents and a sense of mutual support and everyday reliance on neighbours. Cheyne juxtaposes his reading with the legal definition of community as proposed by a London Borough of Hackney Councillor, explaining how their views diverge:

> I think community is a very difficult concept... If you have a community, does it need to be supported? In a sense the whole idea of community is that it is self-sustaining. What the [Clays Lane] community consisted of was people going to each other's houses and talking to another and helping one another if they needed to get to the shops or whatever. That was actually what made the community work. The bits which in a sense were add-on, often didn't work, were the administration and the maintenance... In our case, we were specifically told 'you are not a community'. [Andrew] Gaskell [Hackney Councillor] actually said: 'you're not a community. The travellers are a community, because they have legal status, you don't have that legal status'. Even though we were an

incredibly diverse community, I counted 40 different nationalities amongst people I knew, there were probably more. But no, [they suggested] we weren't a community, just a collection of individuals who would be dispersed. (Interview, 11 August 2011)

One of the striking points mentioned here is Cheyne's suggestion that a local authority employee defined community purely by legal status, as a means to justify the Clays Lane evictions. While Cheyne's statement should be analysed within the context of a long-standing political battle charged with high emotions, and while the councillor has not been granted a right to reply (or explain), the suggestion that community could be understood purely on legal grounds is important. Community in this sense is failing if it cannot display inner cohesion or prove its legal status. Yet, when Clays Lane residents were initially approached by the LDA about possible relocation in 2003, Fluid Architects conducted a survey (in August 2004). One of the aims of the survey was to discern whether there were residents who would like to move 'as a community'. The Fluid Survey shares some of the Audit Commissions concerns about the Estate, highlighting that personal security, sharing space and anti-social behaviour contributed to 'existing issues'. The estate suffered under mismanagement and a dysfunctional complaints procedure. However, the Fluid Survey also emphasises the unique character of Clays Lane, which is largely overlooked and disregarded by Olympic authorities:

> What emerges very strongly from the consultation process, both from the Residents Survey findings, and from the experience of the Fluid team working intensively on the ground for many, is the unique character of Clays Lane. This is of particular importance because many of its qualities are greatly cherished by residents, but will not be easily replicated elsewhere. (Fluid Survey, 2005: 51)

Despite the existing issues and conflict between residents in the estate – divided opinions on the Olympics, Olympic-led development and subsequent need for relocation – this residential community provided 500 marginalised people with homes at a rate lower than market value, and, crucially, a housing structure that encouraged mutual support through its design. In the Fluid survey (2005: 26), two important questions stand out. When asked why they moved to Clays Lane, 125 (57 per cent) of the 296 respondents specified that they lived in Clays Lane due to 'housing need', which commonly refers to homelessness. When asked what the pros and cons of being part of the co-operative were, the most common 'pros' were related to the social life on the estate: 'community spirit/sense of community' (169 from a total of 294 responses) (Fluid, 2005: 28). The survey responses suggest that residents felt that Clays Lane Estate provided some form of community. While discourse on the London 2012 legacy centred on sustaining community, it seems that the type of community at Clays Lane was not legitimate or valuable in the eyes of Olympic authorities.

The tensions between the group of former Clays Lane members and Olympic Authorities can be seen as the struggle around defining community intersecting with claims to space. Cheyne articulates his views on the politics surrounding the language of community:

> I think that when these programmes [like the Olympics] are put forward, they always have the kind of publicity blurb . . . this thing about 'supporting sustainable communities'. But what does it exactly mean? What is a community? What does it mean to sustain them? I think it's just language which they feel obliged to use . . . We were a fantastic community in the sense of getting together, mixing and all the rest of it, but that didn't count in their definition, but even then I just think it's a meaningless concept – 'sustaining communities' – because it's entirely a planning-economic definition. (Interview, 11 August 2011)

The dispersal of the Clays Lane residents after the demolition was a complex and drawn-out procedure, including attempts to organise a joint move, initially for 30 residents, later 7. During the Olympic Games, the site where Clays Lane once stood housed the Athletes Village, which has since been refitted as residential accommodation, 'creating a real mixed community' (East Village London, 2014: 2) (see Chapters 4–6). The dispersal of the co-op residents, which marked the end of a communal social housing experiment, can be analysed as the demolition of an economically unstable social institution (which would have required vast investment) to make space for residential units that will ultimately create profit – exemplifying the privatisation of space within neoliberal growth agendas. Clays Lane, while not representing an outwardly cohesive and conflict-free community, ticks all the boxes for an 'existing community' worthy of support: local, diverse and fulfilling a crucial role in providing social housing. The fact that the estate put into practice experimental communal living, albeit with tensions and failures, made it a unique housing initiative in London, and even Europe. The fact that the individuals living in the estate were denied the label community – a lifeline that might have helped to house some residents as a group – is an important part of understanding the process of London 2012's urban regeneration.

Eton Mission Rowing Club: NIMBY Enclave or Valuable Community Asset?

Clashing definitions and visions of community have been the cause of conflict between Olympic authorities and members of the Eton Mission Rowing Club in Hackney Wick. Similar to the Clays Lane case, *who* and *what* constitutes community are key issues. Eton Mission Rowing Club is a small privately run club, which has had its two-storey boathouse located at the Lea Navigation canal since 1934. A dispute erupted when a bridge was planned and then constructed directly next to the club (see Fig. 8.3). Planners see the bridge as a means to relax the hard borders that the canal has defined, loosening the feeling of the neighbourhood as an enclave. The bridge opened in July 2013, giving residents in Hackney Wick direct access to the Olympic Park and sports facilities. Vice versa, the bridge is hoped to encourage future residents from the five newly constructed neighbourhoods on the Olympic site to access Hackney Wick. The Eton Mission Rowing Club primarily objects to the bridge on the grounds that it is a subversive act of displacement, threatening their very existence.

A member of the rowing club argues that the bridge is a means to squeeze the rowing club out of existence. He suggests that the LLDC's

Fig. 8.3 The Eton Mission Rowing Clubhouse next to the 'legacy' bridge, during the construction of the wheelchair accessible lift, February 2014

Photograph: author

vision for the canal's future doesn't include rowing, prioritising the idea of a public canal sidewalk and café culture:

> I've come to the conclusion that they want this building for some other purpose. They're just chipping away, take this, take that, devalue this, and devalue that. Working away so that eventually, they hope, that they can just grab it for as cheap as they can, because all its facilities and amenities have been taken away. (Rowing club member, interview, 19 August 2012)

The club member explains that building the bridge has already meant the Compulsory Purchase of 1 metre of Rowing Club land, a significant amount considering the lack of space. Public access of the bridge would result in health and safety problems, as the eight-person rowing boats are so long that passers-by might be hurt in their transportation from the boathouse into the water: 'Space is our problem. They've squeezed a bridge into a space that was never ever going to be big enough, and now other people have to shrink to accommodate their "planning folly" as I call it'. When considering the existential fears of the rowing club, the celebration of legacy bridges' claim to space by Commission for Architecture and the Built Environment (CABE) is stark:

> We think these bridges will set a high quality precedent for landscape interventions along the river that knit the existing communities into the Olympic Park after the Games. In particular, we support the generosity of space provided for pedestrians and cyclists at the bridge landings. (CABE, cited by LLDC, 2013b: 59)

Presenting these two positions – existential fears pitted against an inclusive community future – simplifies the dispute and flattens the detail. However, it does lay a useful basis for further discussion on how the bridge debate highlights divergent conceptions of community and how these conceptions then are employed within Olympic legacy. It becomes evident that while LLDC planners frame Olympic legacy around 'community inclusion' – that this version and vision of community does not synchronise with existing groups in Hackney Wick.

The history of the Eton Mission Rowing Club plays a significant role in their narrative and claim to space. The Club was founded in 1885 as part of the Eton Mission. The Mission comprised of a group of philanthropists from the well-known public school Eton, who came to Hackney Wick in the early twentieth century with the intention of providing the deprived local population with an escape from poverty. Through the Eton Manor Boys Club, of which the rowing Club was part, poor Hackney Wick boys aged 13–17 were served the idea of 'self-help' via after-school sports and camaraderie. This historical context shows that the rowing club's facilities were part of a social reform narrative that aligns almost perfectly with the rhetoric of the Olympics using sport (in combination with urban regeneration) to alleviate the deprivation of East London communities. The physical structure of the boathouse and its role in the construction of community and place in Hackney Wick are striking. From this perspective, if the central aim of London's Olympic Legacy is to nourish 'existing communities' and encourage health and fitness (Girginov and Hills, 2008), the Eton Mission Rowing Club could provide an ideal contender as flagship project. However, this is the point at which the divergent conceptions of community play a role, and we see that for the LLDC community is more to do with attracting *new* communities.

One aspect of the debate is that until now the rowing club was able to function unchallenged, using their own land, but also spilling onto public land if needed, precisely because this was a forgotten corner of London. Consequently, criticism of the club might be that its members merely want to keep the status quo: safeguarding their secluded corner of Hackney Wick, rather than embracing change and democratising access, potentially for a large amount of bridge users. Yet, the member's perspective on the 'new communities' that are planned for the Olympic Park in the future show that his view is more differentiated; he is quietly optimistic that the Olympic-led housing developments and new communities could be harnessed, providing the opportunity to gain new members. If the Club were to get permission for their planned building extension that incorporates dual facilities (male and female changing rooms), the club hopes it could be a new phase of existence for the rowing club:

> That will make a nice legacy project for them [the LLDC]. If they've got all that money for bridges to nowhere, then they can fund our extension too. This is our answer to them. You can either have a rowing club that's going to work for the future, and you can still have your bridge . . . or if you don't want that, you better move us somewhere else then, and you can have this site and do whatever you want with it. (Rowing club member, interview, 19 August 2012)

The question of 'planning futures' is important at this point as it links with consultation and transparency as a second point of contention. When asked how the rowing club had been informed of development plans, the member stated:

Basically we need them to tell us what they're going to do, but they wont, because they know we wont like it. So they just sit there and the months just roll by. We had a meeting with the LLDC two years ago, and absolutely no feedback at all. Well that's good communication isn't it(!).

This indicates an important point about the timeframe and perspective of the LLDC, who in their desire to 'plan for the future' are leaving current users excluded. If we consider the LLDC's claims that 'Development should . . . maximise opportunity for community diversity, inclusion and cohesion; should contribute to people's sense of place, safety and security (Policy 7.1)' (LLDC, 2012b: 22), then it seems, with the case of the rowing club, that this ideal falls short. Not only is community at centre of LLDC claims, but there is also direct reference to the value of boating: 'This [waterside] environment has been successful elsewhere in Hackney, and with the activity created by residential uses, boating and other leisure activities next to the canal, this will provide a vibrant and pleasant place to live' (LDA, 2009: 44). While 'boating' may not be directly referencing the rowing club, this statement indicates that the atmosphere achieved through water sports and boats on the canal is desirable. However, the emphasis on the 'atmosphere' that this achieved, rather than on the activities, social relationships that this forges, shows the narrow conceptualisations of 'community legacy' narrative: in its focus on design and image it overlooks the existing social fabric and bonds that have been forged over decades.

While on the abstract level existing communities are very much part of the Olympic legacy agenda, the vision for the future use of the canal, and *who* exactly constitutes community is the sticking point. The crux is whether the canal is deemed a space for consumption and public leisure activities – potentially for existing *and* new users – or rather a place for rowing sport is undertaken. Rowing is the bond that holds users of the club together, so then it has to be acknowledged as 'existing community', whether or not it fits into the image of community that the LLDC have. And it seems there is not the space for the two visions to coexist. Olympic rhetoric states that regeneration in East London will be based on 'community inclusion', with an emphasis on 'the local', yet the Eton Mission Rowing Club, which embodies 'local sport' and local history, is excluded in planning. The bridge dispute highlights that LLDC planners use community in a flexible way. Community is bent in order to suit the particular needs of a particular point, at a specific time. While the rhetoric of 'nurturing existing communities' won London the Olympic bid, the bridge dispute shows how the overriding aim in this particular corner of the Olympic fringe was to make the boundaries between the old and new more porous. Yet, it is precisely the 'pores' or openings between existing social groups and 'new communities' of the future that leave some existing communities feeling excluded, and at worst case, in an existential battle.

Negotiating 'Global' and 'Local' Interests

Complicating the story of community on the Olympic Fringe is that many LLDC planners and local borough employees are themselves cynical of wholesale Olympic regeneration; not only aware of the tensions between citywide strategic goals and local needs, but also critical of the contradictions within planning. Many see the limited Olympic timescale as adding to the pressure to deliver 'legacy' and plan for sensitive regeneration. One Hackney Borough Councillor candidly explains the problem: 'The great thing is that [development] happens in four years. The downside is that's fucking shit because it's happening so quickly . . . You lose the soul, you come back to the world of market economics' (interview, 8 September 2011). This perspective illuminates a central issue: the dominance of a 'global' growth imperative, often over the more specific, localised needs, such as supporting social structures and initiatives that do not generate profit but provide valuable services to residents (such as community centres, public spaces and improvements in infrastructure).

During the planning stage, many planners and politicians were in an ambiguous role; having to abide by the rules of the IOC, yet trying to use the Olympics as an opportunity to deliver and consolidate policies developed before the London Bid was won. This strain was vocalised by an officer of Hackney Council:

In theory you should be able to exploit [the Olympics]; sponsors, media stories, whatever else we'd like to do. There's just that disconnect I think, between running this mega global event and the real micro level area. You even ring up LOCOG and say 'can you do a talk' and they'll say 'oh yeah, it's a host borough talk, is it?' I'm like, 'no it just here, your neighbours in Hackney Wick', and they'll be like 'oh, well that's too small an area'. It's just amazing really. (Interview, 22 September 2011)

While the intersection between 'global' and 'local' has been analysed by many scholars, who demonstrate that the dichotomy is not always a useful construct (Robertson, 1995), in this case the tensions between satisfying the various agendas of the Mayor of London, the government, the London Organising Committee of the Olympic and Paralympic Games (LOCOG) and large businesses, with interests in the neighbourhood, demonstrates a disjuncture of scale. It indicates that the range of Olympic planning authorities (LDA, LOCOG, LLDC) had to weigh up and choose between interests. While the 'global' and 'local' interests may not always clash, the empirical cases discussed earlier suggest that interests are often in competition. Put simply, the priorities for Olympic-led regeneration as presented within the discursive realm of the competitive 'global city' London are often different to the needs and desires of urban regeneration for existing social groups living on the Olympic Fringe. Consequently, the idea of who and what constitutes community often aligns with one of these two camps. As indicated, planning professionals and council employees are often caught in a position where 'global' forces dictate the frame, whereby only concessions can be reached by trying to negotiate (and subvert) well-worn planning paradigms, such as property-led regeneration.

The White Building in Hackney Wick Fish Island, introduced at the beginning of the chapter, is a good example of how these ambiguities play out. The White Building is testament to a U-turn in London 2012 planning policy for the neighbourhood, specifically the commitment of some LLDC employees to value existing social structures. As the funders and initiators of the project, the LLDC put it: 'The White Building Cultural Hub is an initiative born out of the need to give the artistic community a public face and to provide a place where local residents, artists and visitors can connect' (Design for London and LLDC, 2013:

66). The project represents a change from perceiving Hackney Wick Fish Island as an appendage of the Olympic site to be regenerated through classic property-led development of residential high-rises, to valuing the importance of existing local cultures and communities in the neighbourhood and wanting to preserve its idiosyncratic social and architectural forms. In planning terms, the White Building symbolises a change to culture-led regeneration in the neighbourhood.

Delivering this new, culture-led vision of regeneration is achieved through key features: the building is 'for communities in the area' (thewhitebuilding.org), it was developed at a relatively low construction cost of £550,000 and its day-to-day running is organised by SPACE, a charity and studio manager working locally since 1968. While Bloomberg is the commercial sponsor of the arts programming and studio residencies, SPACE have a lease on the venue for 10 years, renting out affordable spaces to artists. Yet, while the White Building shows a shift in Olympic-led regeneration strategy – towards a more inclusive understanding of existing community – the marketable value of the creative community must also be taken into account. However 'inclusive' the initiators intentions, the White Building nevertheless works *with* rather than *against* the grain of neoliberal development agendas, framed around interurban competition, gentrification, middle-class consumption and place-marketing (Peck, 2005: 741). It could therefore be argued that the White Building is an attempt to 'de-risk' the neighbourhood through a very particular reading of community.

While the White Building represents a new planning path for Olympic-led regeneration that works against the wholesale demolition of an industrial neighbourhood – and is valuable in its role as such – the project nevertheless uses the creative communities of Hackney Wick Fish Island as a sign to attract new consumers and cultural entrepreneurs to the area. In doing so, the 'sensitive' community legacy articulates *which* communities and *whose* social worlds have a place in the regenerated future of the neighbourhood. The White Building therefore provides a useful lens to understand the contradictions and ambiguities of 'community-orientated legacy', which may be experienced throughout the Olympic Fringe. The Hackney Councillor explains the difficulty of trying to use the Olympics as a catalyst to implement local change, a perspective that helps to understand the dynamics of urban regeneration in Hackney Wick Fish Island, and elsewhere:

> I made it very clear to my political colleagues, and council officer colleagues that this is an opportunity of such a ferocity, of such a scale, that it must be understood that . . . we are on this wagon and we decide to get off, we will never get back on it. If you try to stop this wagon, it will squash you. You cannot stop it . . . the challenge for the people who are organising it, is to try and always insure that they never ever lose sight of the local in amongst the global. (Interview, 8 September 2011)

This statement is a clear indication of the different agendas of politicians, planning professionals and bureaucrats, working to create 'local legacy'. However, as the quotation demonstrates – 'you cannot stop it' – the challenge of negotiating global pressures with local needs is an almost impossible task. Definitions and understandings of community which align with a growth agenda – and a discourse that emphasises London as a strong global player – will continually win in the London 2012 narrative.

Conclusion: London 2012 Fostering or Displacing Community?

As this chapter demonstrates, Clays Lane, Eton Mission Rowing Club and the White Building give us an insight into the power dynamics of regeneration on the Olympic Fringe – revealing important aspects of the relationship between global interests and the local arena. The case studies show that the language of community has powerful repercussions that play into and steer the dynamics of urban regeneration. The social groups that cannot or refuse to present themselves as vibrant, cohesive and economically valuable assets within London's citywide development are often overlooked or deliberately excluded within the process of urban regeneration. This chapter illustrates that far from being the arbitrary result of policy needs, the concept of community is embedded in concrete political-ideological visions. Definitions of community are always in movement, with actors employing different meanings over time. Each definition is about *including* some groups and *excluding* others.

The story of Clays Lane Estate demonstrates the messy and complicated nature of how community is lived and contested. The way that the Clays Lane community was described as 'failing' indicates a process of pathologising its residents and suggests a reading of the space that overlooks the social bonds between people, focusing instead on economic viability. The residents of Clays Lane did not constitute a cohesive or homogenous group, nor did they form a consensus regarding their relocation, compensation, nor their attachment to place. However, this residential enclave did represent a functioning community in the sense that single people, many relying on state support, were able to live independently, with the help of support networks that were largely constructed through the architectural form of courtyards and shared flats. Analysis suggests that Clays Lane residents – denied the label of community by authorities – stood in the way of the neoliberal logic of Olympic-led regeneration, and consequently were displaced. Similarly, the bridge built next to the Eton Mission Rowing Club indicates precisely which are the priority 'communities'. While London 2012 policy emphasised the support of existing social structures (particularly during bid stage), the construction of the bridge illustrates that in this corner of the Olympic Fringe new communities have precedence.

Current developments in Hackney Wick Fish Island reveal which 'communities' are celebrated and imagined as shaping the future of the neighbourhood. As the White Building cultural hub demonstrates, the language of community is used to justify certain interventions. Olympic-led urban regeneration in Hackney Wick Fish Island – initiated by the LLDC – has in recent years integrated a culture-led approach whereby existing social structures, particularly the artistic community, have been acknowledged (to a certain extent) as a valuable basis for development. In this sense the White Building can be seen as a beacon for 'saving' the existing factory and warehouse structures in the neighbourhood from wholesale demolition and preventing a property-led regeneration strategy. However, a culture-led regeneration approach is not free of market pressures, and the commercialisation of existing artistic cultural communities is the concession. Importantly, London 2012 interventions in the

Olympic Fringe remain top-down interventions, and as such are embedded within the politics of competitive growth agendas, fought out on the global stage. If the Olympic promise to support and nourish existing structures in London's East End is to be taken seriously as something beyond rhetorical wordplay, then a community-orientated Olympic legacy must widen its conception of community and actively work to sustain existing bottom-up initiatives.

References

Amin, A. (2004) 'Regions unbound: towards a new politics of place', *Geografiska Annaler: Series B, Human Geography* 86(1): 33–44.

Audit Commission (2005) *Report on Clays Lane Housing Co-operative*. London: Audit Commission.

Booth, C. (1889) 'Life and Labour of the People in London', http://booth.lse.ac.uk/cgi-bin/do.pl?sub=Home, accessed 28 April 2014.

Davies, J. S. (2012) 'The impact of the Olympics: making or breaking communities in East London', *LSE Cities Blog*, 11 July 2012, http://blogs.lse.ac.uk/politicsandpolics/communi-ty-impact-of-the-olympics-davis/

DCMS [Department for Culture, Media and Sport. (2008) *Before, During and After: Making the Most of the London 2012 Games*. London: DCMS.

Deas, I. (2013) 'Towards post-political consensus in urban policy? Localism and the emerging agenda for regeneration under the Cameron Government', *Planning Practice & Research* 28(1): 65–82.

Design for London and LLDC. (2013) *Stitching the Fringe: Working Around the Olympic Park*. London: London Mayors Office.

East Village London. (2014) 'East Village named "development of the year" at 2014 RESI Awards', http://www.eastvillagelondon.co.uk/UploadedImages/Resi-east-village-press-release-15-05-14.pdf, accessed 12 January 2015.

Falcous, M. and Silk, M. (2010) 'Olympic bidding, multicultural nationalism, terror, and the epistemological violence of "Making Britain Proud"', *Studies in Ethnicity and Nationalism* 10(2): 167–186.

Fluid Survey. (2005) *Clays Lane Housing Co-op Residents Survey Report for the London Development Agency*. London: Fluid.

Girginov, V. and Hills, L. (2008) 'A sustainable sports legacy: creating a link between the London Olympics and sports participation', *The International Journal of the History of Sport* 25(14): 2091–2116.

Lees, L. and Ley, D. (2008) 'Introduction to Special Issue on Gentrification and Public Policy', *Urban Studies*, 45(12): 2379–2384.

LDA. (2009) *Legacy Masterplan Framework: Hackney Wick East Area Brief*, http://www.phase2.lda.rroom.net/userfiles/file/LMF_Hackney%20Wick%20East_Public%20Consultation_Full%20110209%20part%203.pdf, accessed 4 February 2015.

LLDC [London Legacy Development Corporation]. (2012a) *Community Engagement Policy*. London: LLDC. http://queenelizabetholympicpark.co.uk/~/media/lldc/policies/119753959lldccommunityandengagementpolicynov2012.pdf

LLDC. (2012b) *Inclusive Design Strategy*. London: LLDC. http://queenelizabetholympicpark.co.uk/~/media/lldc/policies/lldcinclusivedesignstrategymarch2013.pdf

LLDC. (2013b) *Report: Wallis Road Bridge (Bridge H10) – 13/00090/VAR*. London: LLDC.

LOCOG [London Organising Committee of the Olympic and Paralympic Games]. (2005) *2012 London Olympic Bid Candidate File*. London: LOCOG.

London Borough of Hackney Policy and Partnerships. (2014) *Hackney Wick Ward Profile*, http://www.hackney.gov.uk/Assets/Documents/hackney-wick-ward-profile.pdf, accessed 20 November 2014.

Peck, J. (2005) 'Struggling with the creative class', *International Journal of Urban and Regional Research* 29(4): 740–770.

Robertson, R. (1995) 'Glocalization: time-space and homogeneity-heterogeneity', in M. Featherstone, S. Lash and R. Robertson (eds.), *Global Modernities*. London: Sage.

Stephens, A. C. (2007) '"Seven Million Londoners, One London": National and urban ideas of community in the aftermath of the 7 July 2005 bombings in London', *Alternatives* 32(2): 155–176.

Wales, R. (2008) 'Delivering a usable local legacy', *GamesMonitor*, 7 February 2008, http://www.gamesmonitor.org.uk/node/563

Wallace, A. (2010) 'New neighbourhoods, new citizens: challenging "community" as a framework for moral and social regeneration under New Labour', *International Journal of Urban and Regional Research* 34(4): 806–819.

Francesca Weber-Newth is a British-German urban sociologist. Her PhD (University of Aberdeen) focused on urban regeneration in London and Berlin. She now teaches at the Humboldt University of Berlin. Her activities outside academia include collaborations with an architect (*Community Lover's Guide to Berlin*, 2013), poet (*Walking Is Not an Olympic Sport*, 2012) and documentary filmmaker (*Mauerpark Berlin*, 2010).

9

West Ham United in the Olympic Stadium: A Gramscian Analysis of the Rocky Road to Stratford

Jack Fawbert

Introduction

This chapter is about a particular aspect of the Olympic legacy; how to make best use of the main Olympic Stadium after the games; something that was not properly considered prior to planning the main Olympic site at Stratford, East London (Gibson, 2015). It was later conceded that it would only be financially viable if an FA Premier League football team moved there and used it as their 'home' ground on a regular basis (Gibson, 2013a). The 'natural' choice of club was West Ham United (WHU), a club generally regarded as 'representing' the East End of London; though for a much smaller number of football fans Leyton Orient represent some of the more northerly parts of the East End in the London Borough of Waltham Forest. This chapter looks at the process by which WHU did, indeed, become the Post-Olympic 'anchor', or main, tenants of the Stadium. In particular, using the Gramscian

J. Fawbert (✉)
Anglia Ruskin University, Cambridge, England
e-mail: jack@fawbert.net

© The Author(s) 2017
P. Cohen, P. Watt (eds.), *London 2012 and the Post-Olympics City*,
DOI 10.1057/978-1-137-48947-0_9

259

concept of 'hegemony' (Gramsci, 1971), it looks at cultural struggles between the club owners and its supporters during this process.

As a consequence of the game's specific history, rooted as it was in 'muscular Christian' missionary work by Victorian gentlemen in poor communities, in the late nineteenth and early twentieth centuries the 'Men from Uppingham . . . flocked in droves to the East End of London on missionary social work' (Korr, 1986: 24), using sport as a vehicle for moral instruction. Sport in general has since played a central role in the culture of the East End. More specifically, the whole area became 'football mad' (Korr, 1986).

The 'East End' is an amorphous term (Korr, 1986; O'Neil, 2001; Dench et al., 2006), although today it is generally agreed that, *culturally* at least, the 'East End' extends from the London Borough of Tower Hamlets in the west to the London Borough of Barking and Dagenham in the east with the London Borough of Newham in between (Farrar, 2008); the latter being the borough in which the Olympic Stadium was sited in Stratford. Since 1904 WHU's ground had been situated at the Boleyn Ground, Upton Park E13 in the middle of what is now the London Borough of Newham and had, thus, been seen to represent the East End as a whole (Fawbert, 2011a: 177).

The overwhelmingly working-class nature of the East End had always encouraged a *locale* characterised by counterhegemonic forms of mechanical solidarity as opposed to the more organic kinds of solidarity characteristic of the division of labour found in modernity in general (Durkheim, 1984). As a consequence, not only were the people of the East End ' . . . loyal and value[d] comradeship . . . ' (Belton, 1998: 11) but also they had a keen sense of 'territoriality' and a 'fierce local pride' (Clarke, 1976) rarely seen in middle-class culture and expressed as a 'cockney' identity (N.B. a 'cockney' is traditionally someone born within the sound of the bells of Bow church). This manifested itself in strong bonds of working-class solidarity and longstanding loyalties to trade unions, the Labour Party and to WHU.

Support for the latter was passed down from generation to generation. In such a *habitus* the club was an integral part of and a focus for the emotional loyalty of the whole East End. Korr went on to say that WHU:

. . . has touched the lives of tens of thousands of people in ways that have nothing to do with what happens on the field. The Hammers have been part of something much larger than the club, the League, or even the game of football. (Korr, 1986: 207)

The Great Exodus: Farewell to the East End?

Following World War II in which the Blitz destroyed large parts of the East End, the London County Council, and subsequently the Greater London Council, embarked on a policy of slum clearance and relocation of much of the East End population to council housing in New Towns and estates, mostly in Essex and Hertfordshire. As Watt et al. (2014: 121) say, Thurrock and Southend-on-sea in Essex in particular 'have long been identified as emblematic sites of the Cockney Diaspora'. As was found in much earlier research by Young and Willmott (1960), whilst most of the émigrés hankered after their lost milieu, their motivations for leaving were jobs, better accommodation with 'all mod cons', gardens and a generally better physical environment for their children to grow up in. This policy of state relocation lasted until the 1980s, but the exodus continued into the twenty-first century through private decision-making and choosing to buy rather than to rent.

In Watt et al.'s (2014) research, most of the affluent newcomers to the private housing developments of 'Eastside', an anonymised suburb of Thurrock, were 'white British who had been brought up in London, mainly East London'. Almost half of their survey respondents had left parents behind in London, mostly in the East End. One of the respondents to their survey, Kathy, described 'Eastside' as 'the East End haven for everybody' (Watt et al., 2014: 132). As a consequence of these changes, adopting a 'cockney identity' became less a matter of coming from a bounded territory and more a matter of self-definition (Fawbert, 2005, 2006) and of 'being in one place but identifying with another' (Watt et al., 2014: 121). For those who had moved outwards and, mostly, upwards, 'attachments to place in Essex [for example] remain[ed] an uneasy mix of aspiration, nostalgia and melancholia' (Watt et al., 2014: 142).

The exodus was further encouraged by pull factors, such as educational reforms that gave children from working-class families' opportunities not only for social mobility but also for geographical mobility (Young and Willmott, 1957; Greenslade, 1976; O'Neill, 2001), and push factors such as the decline of dock work and associated engineering factories (Lash and Urry, 1987; Crow and Allan, 1994; Massey, 1994; Fawbert, 2005).

At the same time as capital was relocating its manufacturing operations elsewhere, the 'control functions' of companies were increasingly being relocated to the South-East and this led to an influx of the professional-managerial class to the area (Deakin and Edwards, 1993; Savage and Warde, 1993). In a clear example of what Butler (2007) calls 'gentrification by capital' rather than 'gentrification by social action', this process was cemented by the Docklands Development project which resulted in significant numbers of new jobs going to middle-class 'outsiders' (Deakin and Edwards, 1993; Morris and Morton, 1998) because the jobs required higher qualifications than were held by most people in the area (Coupland, 1992). Other poorer areas of the East End, however, witnessed an influx of several waves of new, generally poorer, immigrants (Dench et al., 2006).

The Boleyn Ground as Surrogate for a 'Magical Recovery of Community'?

Despite the 'disappearance' from the East End of the old white working-class communities that supported WHU, attendances at the Boleyn Ground have increased considerably over the last 30 years (West Ham Statistics, 2015). This is not, however, due to the new minority ethnic fans swelling the numbers, because, for a variety of reasons, the proportion of match day attendees from minority ethnic groups was still only around 2 per cent by the end of the 2000s (Fawbert, 2011a: 178).

But neither is it a consequence of any significant increase in attendance by the new service class in the 'gentrified' areas of the East End. Like at most Premier League clubs, despite attempts at 'gentrification' of the football fan base, the vast majority who go to watch live games still come from working-class backgrounds (Fawbert, 2011b). As a result of the Docklands Development, the kind of life that Butler's (2007) 're-urbanising new-coming' interviewees were seeking did not include support for a football club who are more associated with traditional working-class communities.

By the turn of the twentieth century, the majority who attended matches at the Boleyn Ground came from outside the East End (Williams and Neatrour, 2002); a mixture of 'affluent worker' émigré cockneys and their offspring to whom they had passed on their East End traditions, including the tradition of supporting WHU, plus others attracted from across Britain and indeed the world since the televisual globalisation of the Barclays Premier League. For example, there are now not only 17 WHU-affiliated supporters' clubs from outside London across the United Kingdom but also there are a further 49 from across the globe (WHU, 2014). There are a considerable number of groups who organise trips to games on a regular basis from amongst the 28 affiliated supporters' clubs across Europe; often using *Eurostar* or budget airlines (WHU, 2014).

For the 'cockney diaspora' trips to Upton Park represent an attempt at a 'magical recovery of community'; part compensation for what Watt et al. (2014: 136) refer to as 'an underlying sense of melancholic loss'. The Boleyn Ground at Upton Park became a surrogate for a lost gemeinschaft. It helped keep alive not only very personal senses of history but also recreated the feelings of attachment to a community. To a great extent, ex-cockney fans of WHU are an émigré community that is constantly concerned with the quest for recreating their former 'homeland' in their imaginations. Though talking about Millwall FC, for Robson (2000: 149) 'such ritual visits to symbolically charged ancestral stamping grounds resonate with the voices and atmosphere of the past'.

As far as the 'globalised' fan base, who had no family or community connections to the Boleyn Ground, are concerned the location of the football club seemed, surprisingly, just as important. Their affiliation represented a search for a communal shelter and their lifelong commitment seemed to be as strong as that of any cockney émigré. For these Hammers supporters it was a 'magical *discovery* of community', or rather communion, that fuelled their search for 'authenticity' (Fawbert, 2005: 191).

The Rocky Road to Stratford: the Legal Wrangles

It is against this background that in May 2010 David Gold and David Sullivan bought 60 per cent of WHU shares and therefore a controlling interest in the club from the Icelandic company CB Holdings (Eurosport, 2010). Despite having owned Birmingham City FC for many years, both of them had grown up in the East End supporting WHU, declaring that ownership of WHU was what they had always wanted. They immediately installed the entrepreneur Karren Brady, who had worked for them at Birmingham City, as vice-chair.

In the summer of that year it was announced that the new owners, together with Newham Council, had launched a joint bid to buy the Olympic Stadium and to move the club 2.4 miles to it from their 'spiritual home' at the Boleyn Ground after the 2012 Olympic Games. Other bids came from Tottenham Hotspur jointly with the Anschutz Entertainment Group (AEG), Leyton Orient and several rugby and cricket clubs (BBC News, 2010). On 12 November 2010 it was announced that the two bids from WHU/Newham Council and Tottenham Hotspur/AEG had been shortlisted to buy the stadium post-Olympics.

On 11 February 2011 the Olympic Park Legacy Company (OPLC) unveiled WHU as the preferred stadium bidder (BBC News, 2011). However, a protracted legal dispute with Leyton Orient FC, and more particularly with Tottenham Hotspur FC, over the whole process resulted in several bitter High Court battles and complaints to the European Commission. This led to abandonment by the OPLC of talks with WHU on 11 October 2011. The OPLC announced that the stadium would remain in public ownership and be leased out to an 'anchor', or main, tenant following a new tender process (ESPN Soccernet, 2011). WHU immediately announced plans to bid for tenancy of the stadium

(WHU, 2011a). By February 2012, 16 bids for tenancy had been received (Inside the Games, 2012).

Further legal wrangles meant that it took until December 2012 before the London Legacy Development Corporation (LLDC) named WHU as the preferred bidder (BBC Sport, 2012) for tenancy, although there were conditions, mainly concerned with who pays for what with regard to the running costs because of the huge amount of public money, about £253.8 million (Gibson, 2015), that was to be spent on revamping the stadium for football use. WHU was given three months to improve the terms of their deal or lose the bid. On 22 March 2013 WHU were awarded a 99-year lease deal (BBC Sport, 2013a). The stadium would be revamped in preparation for the start of the 2016/17 football season. Work to convert the stadium for football use began in late 2013. It was announced by WHU that the Boleyn Ground at Upton Park, home to the club for 112 years, would subsequently be sold off to developers.

The Rocky Road to Stratford: The Cultural Struggle

Whilst all of these legal and financial wrangles were going on, a cultural struggle between the owners of the club and some of its supporters developed over the proposed move; whether or not the move should be undertaken in the first place and if so under what conditions. Gramsci's (1971) ideas are useful in understanding these cultural struggles. For Gramsci capitalist societies consist of a continual struggle over ideas. Owners of capital have to engage in such struggles in order to secure support for ideas that serve their interests; that is, they have to continually 'win consent' from subordinate forces for ideas that benefit themselves. Sometimes subordinate forces resist. At other times they acquiesce to the dominance of ruling ideas. The point is that complete ideological domination is very rare.

To express this struggle Gramsci used the concept of 'hegemony'. Describing ideas as 'hegemonic' means that they dominate social consciousness to the extent that they are taken-for-granted and regarded as 'common sense'; in this case, the 'common sense' business decision to move the club to the Olympic Stadium. It is therefore important to examine how moving to the Olympic Stadium became hegemonic or 'common sense', how such an idea was challenged from below and how subordinate challenges were incorporated into the 'common sense' of relocation.

For Gramsci, this continuing struggle results in various forces shifting alliances and forming 'historic blocs' in an effort to 'make safe' subordinate challenges and incorporate them into the body politic of, in this case, WHU. In other words, ruling groups have to find ways to accommodate resistance. In this 'war of position' it appears, on the surface at least, that the bourgeois rationale of 'good business sense' was forced to compromise with traditional fandom for 'consented coercion' or incorporation of dissent to be realised.

When the owners of WHU first launched their bid in August 2010 they enlisted the endorsement of a dozen influential cognoscenti including Lord Coe, chair of the London Organising Committee of the Olympic and Paralympic Games, Ed Warner, chair of UK Athletics and Patrick McGee, Vice-Chancellor and Chief Executive of the University of East London (WHU, 2010a). The club bombarded the fans with 'ebulletins' extolling the benefits to everyone of moving the club to the Olympic Stadium. They never mentioned the financial benefits to themselves as owners of the club and emphasised the benefits to the East End as a whole, proclaiming in one bulletin, for example, that 'we have the real interests of East London people at heart' (WHU, 2010b), in another that 'the club is run by supporters' (WHU, 2010c) and in another exhorting fans to 'remember this club is run by fans for fans' (WHU, 2010c).

Despite growing up close to the ground of WHU's biggest rivals, Tottenham Hotspur, in North London (Viner, 2000) and having no previous connection to WHU, the club's vice-chairman, Karren Brady, in another blog, also said:

> Not only is the stadium in our area but it's at the heart of our community in the East End of London and it's a symbol of our area and that's why it was important that we got it for our community, we got it for our football club and we got it for the people of the East End. (WHU, 2011b)

The multiple use of the possessive pronoun '*our*' was clearly a move in a semiotic guerrilla campaign for hegemonic control. Brady went on to try to woo the cockney diaspora by saying:

> Stratford is a great place to come to, it's got fantastic transport links and it's very important to all those West Ham supporters who have moved out to Essex and further afield that they can get here, reignite (sic) with the football club, come back and come home. (WHU, 2011b)

Furthermore, Brady later stressed that the views and feelings of Hammers supporters were the most important consideration and that it was imperative that the club engaged with them (WHU, 2011b).

In a move designed to demonstrate to fans their commitment to the East End in opposition to their East London neighbours Leyton Orient, protagonists in the dispute over who should move into the Olympic Stadium, WHU blogged on 11 October 2011:

> The club remain committed to east London and believe we are the right choice. In contrast, back in May 2009, our neighbours Leyton Orient were looking at a move away to Harlow or Basildon. The Olympic Stadium is in Newham and Leyton Orient is in Waltham Forest. We will not move away from Newham, after all it's our home borough. (WHU, 2011c)

Following the successful first bid for ownership of the Olympic Stadium, the club promised to 'step up consultation with supporters' (WHU, 2011d) which up until then had been solely conducted through a dedicated email address. The club also promised to respect fans' wishes with regard to the heritage of the club by making 'the Olympic Stadium a home from home' (WHU, 2011d). The 'John Lyall gates' at the entrance to the Boleyn Ground (Fig. 9.1), the commemorative bricks that held up the main stand that fans had paid to have inscribed with their names and the memorial areas at the front of the Boleyn Ground, amongst other pieces of 'heritage', were all to be relocated (WHU, 2011d).

Fig. 9.1   Outside the main 'John Lyall gates' at the Boleyn Ground

Source: Kara Louise Fawbert

Fig. 9.2 The 'Legends' statue opposite the Boleyn public house

Source: Kara Louise Fawbert

Later, the club promised to seek agreement for the 'Legends' statue in the Barking Road (Fig. 9.2) to be moved to outside the new stadium.

Most significantly, they promised affordability (lower ticket prices) and 100,000 free tickets per season for children in local schools and community groups; thus reconnecting with those who live in the area but, because it is one of the most deprived areas in the country, can't afford to go to games (WHU, 2011e).

Some commentators might speculate whether these were all genuine moves to preserve a cultural heritage for the fans and connection with the club's East End roots or a more cynical attempt at 'incorporation' of dissent and a chance to gain a commercial advantage over football rivals. It was the latter motive that some supporters thought predominated (KUMB, 2011). There was suspicion that the two owners were planning the move in order to 'fatten the calf' for a sell-off later on at a huge profit.

Table 9.1 WHU supporter polls, 2010–12

Organisation	Date of poll	% in favour of moving to the new stadium	% against moving to the new stadium	% undecided
KUMB	January 2010	54	21	25
KUMB	May 2010	18	72	10
KUMB	January 2011	57	32	11
KUMB	February 2012	22	60	17
Premier League (cited by WHU)	April 2010	87	–	–
WHU's View	May 2012	13	87	0
SMG YouGov. (for WHU)	December 2012	85	5	10

Nevertheless, in January 2010 an online poll of supporters (Table 9.1) undertaken by the influential WHU fanzine website *Knees Up Mother Brown* (KUMB) had shown 54 per cent of fans supported the board's plans to move WHUFC to the Olympic Stadium, 21 per cent voted 'no' and 25 per cent were 'undecided' (KUMB, 2011).

However, this poll was conducted prior to the revelation that a running track must remain at the Olympic Stadium; something that would have meant that fans would have been a long way away from the pitch and something that, on past experience at other clubs, kills the 'atmosphere'. On 14 May 2013 the former Labour sports minister, Richard Caborn, argued that the biggest mistake made in the run-up to the Olympic Games was not to design the Olympic Stadium with a future that combined football and athletics because any large stadium would only be financially viable with regular use as a football stadium (Gibson, 2013a).

Consequently, when KUMB carried out a poll with the same question in May 2010 (Table 9.1) once the plan to retain the running track had been revealed the result was very different. Only 18 per cent voted for the move with 72 per cent voting against and 10 per cent remaining 'undecided' (KUMB, 2011). This suggests that it was the terms on which a move was proposed that was more the issue, with WHU supporters supporting a move only if a 'magical recovery' of the Boleyn Ground atmosphere was feasible.

A further poll in January 2011 reversed the result yet again with 57 per cent voting for the move, 32 per cent voting against and 11 per cent being undecided (Table 9.1). However, this poll was conducted after Tottenham Hotspur, WHU's bitterest rivals, had revealed their own plans to move to the Olympic Stadium. Comments from supporters accompanying the poll were summed up succinctly by one respondent, who said 'Spurs moving into WHU and Orient territory cannot be allowed to happen' (KUMB, 2011). This demonstrates that divisions often cut across class lines and that alliances or 'historic blocs', as Gramsci called them, are not always determined by class and the bourgeois nature of society.

In February 2012, when WHU was named as one of the 16 bidders, KUMB carried out a further poll (Table 9.1) that revealed that only 22 per cent of respondents supported the move, 60 per cent were against and 17 per cent were unsure. However, the volatility of these results could also be ascribed to the fact that all these polls involved self-selecting samples (always problematic as 'no' voters were always more likely to participate), were restricted to KUMB members and involved under 1,000 respondents; only 808 supporters in the last one (KUMB, 2012).

But this was the best observers had to go on up to this point. Despite their rhetoric about the supporters' role in the club, up until April 2013, that is, after the bids for both ownership and tenancy had been accepted, there had been no widespread consultation with or attempts to seek the views of the vast majority of fans by WHU. WHU responded to criticism by stating that a Premier League survey (Table 9.1) carried out at the beginning of April 2012 'by an unknown number of various supporters online' (WHU's View, 2012) had shown that 87 per cent of supporters backed the proposed move. However, this was before details of the bid had been revealed and the number of respondents to the survey, as well as their status (whether they were season ticket holders or even match attenders), was not revealed (WHU's View, 2012).

In October 2011 a campaign group called 'WHU's View' was set up. Its sole aim was to persuade the club to commission an independent poll of match attending supporters prior to the club committing to any move to the Olympic Stadium. In total, 1,700 supporters registered their support and an open letter requesting such a poll was sent to WHU.

At a Christmas social meeting on 5 December 2011 a club representative stated that the club was willing to carry out a poll. On 12 December 2011 Karren Brady wrote back to WHU's View stating that the club was happy to commit to a poll '*ahead of taking a decision* [author's emphasis]' (WHU's View, 2012).

However, on 22 February 2012, in an interview with reporter Iain Dale, David Sullivan stated that the club would not hold a poll of supporters because 'we're not a democracy' (Dale, 2012); a reassertion of one of the guiding principles of 'free market' capitalism. Subsequent discussions took place between WHU's View and Karren Brady on 29 February 2012. 'WHU's View' advised the club that such a poll would only cost them in the region of £10,000; a small price to pay, considering that this was the most important decision the owners would ever make with regard to the club. The club, however, declined to commission such a poll. Brady stated that, due to 'confidentiality clauses', whatever that meant, they would not hold a poll or further consultation before the successful bidder was announced on 21 May. After then, of course, it could have been seen as a *fait accompli*, despite Brady's protestations that a successful bid did not commit the club to moving (WHU's View, 2012).

Subsequently, at a meeting held at the Supporters' Club on 4 April 2012, when representatives of WHU were in attendance, it was suggested from the floor that the club could carry out its own ballot at the turnstiles at forthcoming home matches. Again, the club declined to do this (WHU's View, 2012). On 10 April 2012 a statement was issued to the BBC stating that the club would hold a poll after 21 May 2012 when the results of the bids were to be announced and in her regular *Sun* column on 14 April 2012 Karren Brady tried to assure fans that there was 'no chance of a move there without wide consultation with all supporters' (Brady, 2012). The use of the term 'wide consultation' was, of course, a semantic move to demonstrate the commitment of the club to supporter involvement without committing it to a poll. She was keen to emphasise that legal restrictions before 21 May 2012 prevented the club from explaining the fullest details of the proposed move to the new stadium and that if a poll was carried out prior to that date, fans would be voting on the basis of imperfect information (WHU View, 2012).

The club, however, as promised back in February 2011 (WHU, 2011d), did set up a Supporters Advisory Board (SAB) of 100 members nominated from amongst supporters. This could be interpreted as the club keeping its promise to involve the fans as part of the club. However, it could also be regarded more cynically as an attempt at 'incorporation' of dissent, with the club owners being able to manage such dissent through what Gramsci called 'consented coercion'. Indeed, SAB meetings were invariably 'led' by at least two members of the board; either Gold, Sullivan, Brady or sometimes all three. The word 'led' could be interpreted as a euphemism for 'managed' or 'controlled'. Indeed, on social media critics of the proposed move often described the SAB as 'toothless' (KUMB, 2012).

In saying that they had the support of fans up until their poll, the club relied on a single meeting of 49 members of the SAB Olympic Group as their stated 'consultation'. At the SAB meeting on 23 February 2012 the club presented information about its bid for the Olympic Stadium. Those members present were required to sign a confidentiality agreement and so were unable to discuss the proposals with other supporters; not even with those who had sponsored their SAB membership. It was claimed that this was for legal reasons (WHU's View, 2012).

Prior to the bid for tenancy in 2011, the club did invite comments from supporters by email, but neither the number of emails received nor the views submitted were published and there was no indication from the club that supporters' comments were acted upon (WHU's View, 2012). The club appointed one SAB member to collate these comments, but did not make a request for feedback. Nevertheless, a confidential report supposedly containing a range of supporters' views was submitted to the club on 19 March 2012. The club stated that this report helped inform their decision in bidding for the Olympic Stadium (WHU's View, 2012).

On 3 April 2012 Karren Brady claimed that SAB members who had seen detailed proposals for the move were '100 per cent' behind the switch if the 99-year lease tender to become the anchor tenant succeeded (WHU's View, 2012). She claimed that after seeing the detailed plans no SAB member voted against the proposed move. However, there was no show of hands at the meeting in which SAB members could have voted against the plans. Indeed, the following day, 4 April 2012, David

Gold stated on LBC Radio that 70 per cent of fans, not 100 per cent, supported the move to Stratford. No supporting evidence was provided for this figure (WHU's View, 2012).

In frustration WHU's View carried out their own poll of supporters (Table 9.1) by mass leafleting at three consecutive home games and distributing a small number of leaflets at two away games during April 2012, asking fans 'based on all available information do you agree with West Ham United's proposed move to the Olympic Stadium?' (WHU's View, 2012). No duplication of voting was ensured by asking for names and patron numbers in the questionnaire. The intention was to gauge the views of regular match-attending supporters; something that distinguished it from all previous polls.

In this questionnaire each fan was asked whether they were a season ticket holder, an Academy Member (membership provides match ticket benefits), Box or Bondholder (the latter is a scheme to guarantee a seat for life) or simply a match day attendee. Polling was carried out in various locations around the ground(s) including local pubs, cafes and in the WHU Supporters' Club. Responses were received on the day, by post and online. A confidential list of all votes cast was produced that could be given to the club if they wished to receive it.

West Ham's View accepted that there were flaws in their poll, partly because they didn't have access to WHU's database of supporters and so could not be sure that their sample was representative of supporters in general and also that those opposed to any move were more likely to vote. Notwithstanding these reservations, on a return of 2,431 valid votes, only 13.4 per cent agreed with the question above with 86.6 per cent disagreeing; the results being announced on 11 May 2012 (West Ham's View, 2012). The club did not take up the offer of verifying the results.

Instead, once the LLDC had named WHU as the preferred bidder in December 2012 the club called an emergency meeting of the SAB, declaring:

> The time for supporters to have their voices heard is now and a more intensive consultation process will commence . . . The club stand by its commitment to conduct full supporter consultation regarding the proposed move, *including the polling of supporters* [my emphasis]. (WHU, 2012)

After revealing more detailed plans of the conversion including, significantly, a retractable seating system with seats over the running track to bring fans closer to the pitch, the club subsequently kept their word and commissioned an independent poll of supporters. The poll was carried out by the respected *SMG YouGov* polling company (Table 9.1). In total, 11,858 fans took part in the poll. Also, 85 per cent supported the Olympic Stadium move, 10 per cent said they would consider approving and only 5 per cent were against the move (BBC Sport, 2013b).

However, one could argue that there were methodological problems that reveal a bias in the way the main question was worded. Fans were asked to agree with one of six statements:

1. Support move as better fan experience.
2. Support move as will provide resources to improve squad.
3. Support move, will grow level of support.
4. Support move, trust club directors.
5. Consider support but need more information.
6. Against the move under any circumstances (BBC Sport, 2013b).

Four of these statements supported the move for different reasons, one stated 'consider support but need more information' and only one option was 'against the move' and this option restricted support to fans who were against the move 'under any circumstances'. Such obvious bias or simply poor design in a questionnaire seems suspicious for such a respected polling organisation as *SMG YouGov*.

Opposition to the move from some fans continued with Karren Brady declaring in frustration in her *Sun* column that 'I respect some fans would not move even if we had added Messi [Lionel Messi was voted the world's greatest footballer] to the bundle of benefits' (Brady, 2013). However, confident that the majority of fans were now 'onside', the club went ahead, signed the deal and in late 2013 work was started on the conversion of the stadium to make it suitable to host Premier League football by the start of the 2016/17 season. 2015–2016 saw the club play its last season at the Boleyn Ground (Figs. 9.3 and 9.4).

Fig. 9.3 The last season at the Boleyn Ground; the view from the Sir Trevor Brooking Stand Lower Tier

Source: Kara Louise Fawbert.

The Profit Motive and the Appropriateness of a Gramscian Analysis?

To what extent did the profit motive inform the enthusiasm of the club directors for a move to the Olympic Stadium? Conversion of the Olympic Stadium was going to cost around £272 million (Gibson, 2015), but WHU were only going to be paying £15 million of that, the rest coming from the public purse (Rumsby, 2013). The Exchequer put in £148.8 million, Newham Council loaned £40 million, the Department of Culture, Media and Sport supplied £38.7 million, £25 million came from the Department of Community and Local Government and the rest was loaned by the LLDC. As tenants, the club has to pay £2.5 million per season (half that if WHU get relegated from the FA Premier League) linked to the Retail Price Index over the

Fig. 9.4   The 'Party's Over'

Source: Kara Louise Fawbert

99-year lease and share the proceeds of naming rights and catering income with a special purpose vehicle set up by the LLDC and Newham Council (Gibson, 2013b; When Saturday Comes, 2015).

Following several Freedom of Information requests, in July 2015 the contract documenting the deal was finally released. It revealed that the LLDC will pay between £1.4 million and £2.5 million a year for match day security, ticketing, pitch maintenance, lighting and heating, maintenance of customer toilets and even goal nets and corner flags (When Saturday Comes, 2015); all usually paid for by football clubs themselves and inviting the possibility of litigation for breaching EU rules on fair competition in football. More worryingly for local people and taxpayers, huge amounts of the released contract were redacted because it was claimed by the LLDC that revealing the contractual details in full would be 'commercially damaging' to them in negotiations with other potential private legacy providers (Jones, 2015).

This further fuelled speculation that WHU was being fattened to make the club more attractive to potential buyers, especially as Gold had previously said that he hoped 'the stadium can help slash the Hammers' £110m debt' (Rumsby, 2013). Also, the sale and demolition of the Boleyn Ground, which was on prime building land, would offset a large proportion of the cost. At the time of writing the club were still keeping the sale price to property developers *Galliard Homes* a closely guarded secret (When Saturday Comes, 2015), although it was rumoured to be £30–50 million.

Nevertheless, Sullivan claimed that '99 out of 100 fans' in the SAB were in favour of moving to the Olympic Stadium under these terms. Anecdotal evidence on the internet and social media suggested that fans were still more evenly split (Gibson, 2013b). However, 'the road to Stratford' was much more complex than a simplistic Marxist analysis might suggest. Indeed, Gramsci provides us with the tools to reflect on a more sophisticated understanding of what was going on.

To start with, the protagonists of labour and capital are largely absent. Firstly, fans are not employees. They are not even 'consumers' in the bourgeois sense; that is, people who have no loyalty and behave totally rationally by seeking out the best products at the most competitive prices. As Rogan Taylor (cited in Davies, 1995) pointed out many years ago:

> There's a huge difference with the football consumer and the product he [sic] consumes. Nobody's spreading their grandfather's ashes down the central aisle of Tesco's. But every day of the week somebody is spreading someone's ashes on a football pitch in England . . . the relationship is not that of a simple consumer. In fact, it is more like a disciple going to a temple.

However, it could be argued that the relationship of fans to their clubs has changed since the early 1990s. There used to be a more 'organic' relationship. By the new millennium it was being argued (Giulianotti, 2002) that the relationship of many fans, or rather 'post-fans', to their football clubs was more through what they bought as 'consumers'. Nevertheless, the nature of the relationship between fans and their clubs is still only 'quasi-capitalist' (Kennedy, 2012) and there is a high degree of resistance to the full commercialisation of football by fans across Europe (Kennedy and Kennedy, 2012). Indeed, for WHU fans, moving to the Olympic Stadium was not simply a rational economic decision; it was a social, cultural and emotional one.

More pertinently, whilst bourgeois economic imperatives are indeed very important in a capitalist context, directors of football clubs were, until recently, not always like rational capitalists. It is true that since the early twentieth century most top clubs were incorporated as limited liability companies with boards of directors who dominate the running of them (Mason, 1980; Tischler, 1981; Vamplew, 1988). However, a century ago shareholders were 'overwhelmingly drawn from the local populace' (Vamplew, 1988: 158–161) and they remained so during the 'golden age' of football which lasted at least until the 1960s and was still thriving to some extent in the early 1990s. The motive of football club directors in the past was not profit maximisation but utility maximisation in terms of playing success on behalf of their communities.

During the 'golden age' directors were more like paternalistic public benefactors who had deep-rooted links with the communities that their clubs represented, regarding their roles as defenders of the local football team. Service to the community was a more dominant ethos than profit maximisation and most of them kept standard business ethics at arm's length. Investment in a club was for emotional reasons, not for financial return.

However, since the 1960s and certainly since the Taylor Report (Lord Justice Taylor, 1989), the establishment of the new FA Premier League and its symbiotic relationship with the BskyB deal to televise live games, the football *fin-de-siecle* of the twentieth century was nothing less than a commercial revolution in the game. A new entrepreneurial elite running football clubs emerged; one that

> ...aggressively 'sells' the sport and its products...This new elite has a late-modern and 'global' view of the sport's marketability and, unlike those men who used to run top clubs, the new order sees profit and routine tenets of business as integral elements in the practice of sports governance and sports administration.... (Williams, 1999: 17–18)

This late 'bourgeoisification' of ownership of football clubs, especially in more recent years with American, Russian, Arab and Far Eastern oligarchs taking over many of the Premier League's top clubs, has led to a great deal of scepticism by fans of the motives of club directors (Olatawura, 2006; Millward, 2011, 2012). However, in any revolutionary change, at the very least, traces of the preceding order remain; anachronistic as they may sometimes seem. Football is no exception. Football loyalties cut across lines of class, gender, race and ethnicity, sometimes uniting fans and owners in a relationship based on *topophilic* associations with specific places and sentimental, nostalgic attachments to particular football clubs.

Both Gold and Sullivan had supported WHU as children and both of them have been lifelong fans. They have stated their intentions to hand the club on to their children to be kept in safe hands for the people of the East End when they depart this world. Under the heading 'Is there a danger the current owners will sell up?' the WHU website claimed:

> David Sullivan and David Gold have waited their whole lives to 'come home' to West Ham. It is not about bricks and mortar for them but a commitment to helping their club to be the best it can be wherever they play. David Gold was born in the East End [in Green Street where the Boleyn Ground is situated], and David Sullivan went to university here [He was also brought up in Hornchurch; part of the extended East End]. They know the

area, they know the people and they have a long-term vision. Our owners are supporters and no-one will work harder than them to ensure the success of the new stadium and the club as a whole. (WHU, 2011e)

Indeed, commenting on the speculation that he might 'cash in' after moving WHU to the Olympic Stadium, in 2013 David Gold said 'I can understand the speculation, but I'm the only one who really knows, in here' (Gibson, 2013b) as he pointed through his sheepskin coat to his heart; or was he pointing to his wallet?

Conclusion

What the foregoing demonstrates is that any social or cultural theory cannot be applied rigidly; it has to take account of the nuances and particularities of specific circumstances. This is why Gramscian theory is so applicable to the specificities of the relationship between the owners of WHU and its supporters. The term 'hegemonic struggle' in particular can be applied to the struggle for hearts and minds between the club and its fans over relocation of the club to the Olympic Stadium.

Indeed, Gramsci eschewed arguments that issues and movements outside the concerns of labour and capital should be scorned or treated as inferior satellites, as an infantile 'Marxist' reading might suggest. Such infantile 'Marxist' economism reduces all political, social, cultural and ideological phenomena to a real or imagined economic base. Gramsci was opposed to such mechanistic determinism and economism and insisted that political battles took place on many fronts and with regard to many issues. The use of Gramsci's concept of hegemony is thus entirely justified in understanding the struggles that took place between the owners and the supporters over the proposed moving of the club to the Olympic Stadium.

References

BBC News. (2010) 'Tottenham and West Ham lead London 2012 Stadium bid', 12 November 2010, http://www.bbc.co.uk/news/uk-england-london-11746496.

BBC News. (2011) 'West Ham chosen as preferred Olympic Stadium tenant', 11 February 2011, http://www.bbc.co.uk/news/uk-england-london-12424549.

BBC Sport. (2012) 'West Ham United are preferred bidder for Olympic Stadium', http://www.bbc.co.uk/sport/0/olympics/20611708, accessed 20 December 2014.

BBC Sport. (2013a) 'Olympic Stadium: Barry Hearn calls for Judicial Review', http://www.bbc.co.uk/sport/0/football/21684372, accessed 20 December 2014.

BBC Sport. (2013b) 'West Ham: 85% of fans support Olympic Stadium move in Club Poll', http://www.bbc.co.uk/sport/0/football/22525290, accessed 20 December 2014.

Belton, B. (1998) *The First and Last Englishmen.* Derby: Breedon Books.

Brady, K. (2012) 'Karren Brady's Football Diary', http://www.thesun.co.uk/sol/homepage/sport/football/4255902/Karren-Bradys-football-diary.html, accessed 20 December 2014.

Brady, K. (2013) 'Karren Brady's Football Diary', http://www.thesun.co.uk/sol/homepage/sport/football/4255902/Karren-Bradys-football-diary.html, accessed 20 December 2014.

Butler, T. (2007) 'Re-urbanizing London Docklands: gentrification, suburbanization or new urbanism?' *International Journal of Urban and Regional Research* 31(4): 759–781.

Clarke, J. (1976) 'The skinheads and the magical recovery of community', in S. Hall and T. Jefferson (eds.), *Resistance Through Rituals: Youth Subcultures in Post-War Britain.* London: Hutchinson.

Coupland, A. (1992) 'Docklands: dream or disaster', in A. Thornley (ed.), *The Crisis of London.* London: Routledge.

Crow, G. and Allan, G. (1994) *Community Life: An Introduction to Local Social Relations.* Hemel Hempstead: Harvester Wheatsheaf.

Dale, I. (2012) 'The telegraph online', http://www.telegraph.co.uk/sport/football, accessed 20 December 2014.

Davies, H. (1995) *Without Walls: J'Accuse Manchester United,* Channel 4, 4 April.

Deakin, N. and Edwards, J. (1993) *The Enterprise Culture and the Inner City.* London: Routledge.

Dench, G. et al (2006) *The New East End: Kinship, Race and Conflict,* London: Profile Books.

Durkheim, E. (1984) *The Division of Labour in Society.* London: Macmillan.

ESPN Soccernet. (2011) '2012 Stadium Bid Collapsed',http://soccernet.espn.go.com/news/story/_/id/967950/west-ham's-olympic-stadium-ownership-dealcollapses?cc=4716, accessed 20 December 2014.

Eurosport. (2010) 'Gold and Sullivan take over West Ham', http://uk.euro sport.yahoo.com/19012010/58/premier-league-gold-sullivan-west-ham. html, accessed 20 December 2014.

Farrar, M. (2008) 'Analysing London's "New East End": how can social science make a difference?' *Sociological Research Online* 13(5), http://www.socreson line.org.uk/13/5/7.html.

Fawbert, J. (2005) 'Football fandom, West Ham United and the "cockney diaspora": from working-class community to youth post-tribe?', in P. Bramham and J. Caudwell (eds.), *Sport, Active Leisure and Youth Cultures*. Eastbourne: Leisure Studies Association.

Fawbert, J. (2006) 'Replica football shirts: serious or casual leisure?', in S. Elkington, I. Jones and L. Lawrence (eds.), *Serious Leisure: Extensions and Applications*. Eastbourne: Leisure Studies Association.

Fawbert, J. (2011a) '"Wot, no Asians?" West Ham United fandom, the cockney diaspora and the "new" East Enders', in D. Burdsey (ed.), *Race, Ethnicity and Football: Persisting Debates and Emergent Issues*. London: Routledge.

Fawbert, J. (2011b) 'Social inclusion and social exclusion: "gentrification" of football fandom?', in J. Long et al. (eds.), *Delivering Equality in Sport and Leisure*. Eastbourne: Leisure Studies Association.

Gibson, O. (2013a) 'Richard Caborn: time for rethink on role of sport and government', *The Guardian*, 13 May 2013.

Gibson, O. (2013b) 'West Ham get their move but must convince fans it is the right one', *The Guardian*, 22 March 2013.

Gibson, O. (2015) 'Back in business: the £701m stadium', *The Observer*, 19 July 2015.

Giulianotti, R. (2002) 'Supporters, followers, fans and flaneurs: a taxonomy of spectator identities in football', *Journal of Sport and Social Issues* 26(1): 25–46.

Gramsci, A. (1971) *Selections from the Prison Notebooks*. London: Lawrence and Wishart.

Greenslade, R. (1976) *Goodbye to the Working Class*. London: Marion Boyars.

Inside the Games (2012) 'West Ham among 16 interested in London 2012 Olympic Stadium as deadline passes', http://www.insidethegames.biz/ Olympics/summer-olympics/2012/15706-west-ham-among-16-bidders-for-lon don-2012-olympicstadium-as-deadline-passes, accessed 20 December 2014.

Jones, D. (2015) 'What a stench: it's an icon of national pride. So, how on earth were two porn barons and their protégée Baroness Brady allowed to take over the Olympic Stadium in a deal almost entirely financed by you the taxpayer?' *The Daily Mail*, 15 August 2015.

Kennedy, P. (2012) 'The football industry and the capitalist political economy: a square peg in a round hole?' *Critique: Journal of Socialist Theory*, 40(1): 73–94.

Korr, C. (1986) *West Ham United: The Making of a Football Club*. Trowbridge: Duckworth.

KUMB. (2011) 'Supporters Back Olympic Stadium Move', http://www.kumb.com/story.php?id=125110, accessed 10 December 2014.

KUMB. (2012) 'The Olympic Stadium: Poll IV', http://www.kumb.com/forum/viewtopic.php?f=2&t=138708 accessed 10 December 2014.

Lash, S. and Urry, J. (1987) *The End of Organised Capitalism*. London: Polity.

Lord Justice Taylor. (1989) *The Hillsborough Stadium Disaster*. London: HMSO.

Mason, T. (1980) *Association Football and English Society 1863–1915*. London: Harvester Press.

Massey, D. (1994) *Space, Place and Gender*. Cambridge: Polity Press.

Millward, P. (2011) *The Global Football League: Transnational Networks, Social Movements and Sport in the New Media Age*. Basingstoke: Palgrave Macmillan.

Millward, P. (2012) 'Reclaiming the Kop? Analysing Liverpool supporters' 21st century mobilizations', *Sociology* 46(4): 633–648.

Morris, A. and Morton, G. (1998) *Locality, Community and Nation*. London: Hodder & Stoughton.

Olatawura, O. (2006) '"The "theatre of dreams"? Manchester United FC, globalization and international sports law', *Marquette Sports Law Review* 16(2): 286–317.

O'Neill, G. (2001) *My East End*. London: Penguin.

Robson, G. (2000) *'No One Likes Us, We Don't Care': The Myth and Reality of Millwall Fandom*. Oxford: Berg.

Rumsby, B. (2013) 'Olympic Stadium could have standing areas when West Ham move in, says co-chairman David Gold', http://www.telegraph.co.uk/sport/football/10068365/Olympic-Stadium-could-have-standing-areas.html, accessed 20 December 2014.

Savage, M. and Warde, A. (1993) *Urban Sociology, Capitalism and Modernity*. Basingstoke: Macmillan.

Tischler, S. (1981) *Footballers and Businessmen: The Origins of Professional Soccer in England*. New York: Holmes and Meier.

Vamplew, W. (1988) *Pay Up and Play the Game: Professional Sport in Britain 1875–1914*. Cambridge: Cambridge University Press.

Viner, B. (2000) 'Brady's injection of sense and sensibility', *The Independent*, 27 December 2000.

Watt, P., Millington, G. and Huq, R. (2014) 'East London mobilities: the Cockney Diaspora and the remaking of the Essex ethnoscape', in P. Watt and P. Smets (eds.), *Mobilities and Neighbourhood Belonging in Cities and Suburbs*. Basingstoke: Palgrave Macmillan.

West Ham Statistics. (2015) http://www.westhamstats.info, accessed 10 October 2015.

When Saturday Comes. (2015) 'Calls for inquiry into West Ham's Olympic deal', *When Saturday Comes: The Half Decent Football Magazine*. London: When Saturday Comes Ltd.

WHU [West Ham United]. (2010a) 'Backing the Bid', http://www.whufc.com/page/Olympics/0,12562~2126853,00.html accessed 20 December 2014.

WHU. (2010b) '12 Reasons', http://www.whufc.com/page/Olympics/0,12562~2197524,00.html, accessed 20 December 2014.

WHU. (2010c) 'Today is a momentous day', http://www.whufc.com/page/Olympics/0,12562~2124187,00.html, accessed 20 December 2014.

WHU. (2011a) 'West Ham – Newham Statement', http://www.whufc.com/articles/20111011/west-ham-newham-statement_22368842478075, accessed 20 December 2014.

WHU. (2011b) 'The hard work starts now', http://www.whufc.com/Olympics/0,12562~2293342,00.html, accessed 20 December 2014.

WHU. (2011c) 'Olympic stadium update', http://www.whufc.com/page/Olympics/0,12562~2124187,00.html, accessed 20 December 2014.

WHU. (2011d) 'What happens next', http://www.whufc.com/page/Olympics/0,12562~2295520,00.html, accessed 20 December 2014.

WHU. (2011e) 'Your questions answered' http://www.whufc.com/page/Olympics/0,12562~2393757,00.html, accessed 20 December 2014.

WHU. (2012) 'SAB to discuss olympic stadium move' http://www.whufc.com/page/Olympics/0,12562~3006547,00.html, accessed 20 December 2014.

WHU. (2014) 'Affiliated supporters clubs', http://www.whufc.com/page/affiliatedSupportersGroupsIndex/0,12562,00.html, accessed 20 December 2014.

WHU's View. (2012) 'Poll of West Ham United supporters on proposed move to the Olympic Stadium', http://www.campaign@whusview.com, accessed 20 December 2014.

Williams, J. (1999) *Is It All Over? Can Football Survive the Premier League?* Reading: South Street Press.

Williams, J. and Neatrour, S. (2002) *The FA Premier League National Fan Survey 2001: Summary Report*. Leicester: Sir Norman Chester Centre for Football Research.

Young, M. and Willmott, P. (1957) *Family and Kinship in East London*. Harmondsworth: Penguin.

Young, M. and Willmott, P. (1960) *Family and Class in a London Suburb*. Harmondsworth: Penguin.

Jack Fawbert is retired but remains active with some part-time teaching in Sociology at Anglia Ruskin University. After working as a carpenter for many years, Jack successfully completed the Certificate in Industrial Relations and Trade Union Studies at Middlesex Polytechnic in 1982. He went on to achieve a BA (Hons) in Sociology and Economics at Cambridgeshire College of Arts and Technology, after which he went into Further Education teaching at West Suffolk College where he successfully completed a Certificate in Education for FE. After going on to teach in Higher Education for Anglia Polytechnic University and subsequently Leeds Metropolitan University, De Montfort University and the University of Bedfordshire, he successfully completed an MA in Sociology at Essex University and a PhD at Leeds Metropolitan University. He has contributed articles to *Social Science Teacher* and *Sociology Review* as well as chapters to several Leisure Studies Association publications. He has also authored chapters in *The Bountiful Game? Football Identities and Finances* (2005) and *Race, Ethnicity and Football: Persistent Debates and Emergent Issues* (2011).

10

Youth Transitions and Legacies in an East London Olympic Host Borough

Anthony Gunter

Introduction

London 2012 was heralded as a once-in-a-generation 'game changer', it was 'officially' sold as being the catalyst that would finally transform the fortunes of East London and its residents, particularly with regard to housing, educational attainment and employment. Official UK Labour Market statistics since September 2011 have consistently shown that employment is continuing to rise whilst unemployment is continuing to fall. The quarterly figures for June to August 2014 indicated that the unemployment rate had fallen to 6 per cent ('the lowest since late 2008'), and that there were 538,000 fewer unemployed people than was recorded the previous year during June to August 2013. According to the Office for National Statistics (ONS, 2014c) this is the 'largest annual fall in unemployment on record'. Even taking into account regional variations, the figures suggest that in particular London and

A. Gunter (✉)
University of East London, London, England
e-mail: A.Gunter@uel.ac.uk

© The Author(s) 2017
P. Cohen, P. Watt (eds.), *London 2012 and the Post-Olympics City*,
DOI 10.1057/978-1-137-48947-0_10

287

the South East are performing well; indeed London (after Scotland) was the region with the largest decrease in the unemployment rate at 0.9 per cent since the previous quarter. These buoyant UK Labour Market statistics unfortunately mask a number of key issues that are contributing to firstly increasing numbers of people in work poverty and secondly entrenched worklessness and labour market disadvantage; both issues are disproportionately affecting particular regions, localities and BAME communities (Catney and Sabater, 2015; Fisher and Nandi, 2015).

According to a number of independent analyses, whilst London as a region is economically vibrant, youth unemployment and poverty are at crisis point particularly within the eastern boroughs of the capital (NPI and Trust for London, 2013; Crowley and Cominetti, 2014; Hughes and Crowley, 2014). Despite being a major laboratory for a myriad of regeneration programmes over the past 35 years, not least the Olympic 2012 project, East London's long history of social and economic exclusion continues into the present. As such this sub-region is blighted by acute levels of poverty, homelessness, overcrowding and associated ill health, and educational disadvantage amongst those poorer residents. It is of course also important to note the specific impact of recent coalition government spending cuts – indeed local authorities in England will see their budgets slashed by 'nearly 30 per cent in real terms between 2008-2015' (Hastings et al., 2013: 3) – and welfare reform on East London's poorer communities.

This chapter – which revisits and updates the author's previous research undertaken a decade earlier (Gunter, 2008; Gunter and Watt, 2009; Gunter, 2010) – draws on data from an ethnographic study of youth transitions and cultures in an East London borough.[1] It comprises in-depth biographical interviews with 66 young adults aged 14–24, as well as interviews with 34 practitioners and key stakeholders including police officers, youth workers, housing officers, local residents and parents. The majority of the young informants resided in the adjoining neighbourhoods of Gulley and Dungle[2] – the two primary research sites

---

[1] The research was undertaken in the London Borough of Waltham Forest between 2009 and 2014.

[2] All names referred to throughout the remainder of this chapter, including participants and places, are pseudonyms.

featured in this ethnographic study – which are amongst the 20 per cent of most deprived neighbourhoods in England (HM Government, 2010). Nearly two-thirds (64 per cent) of the residents of Gulley and Dungle are from a BAME background (ONS, 2012). In this study approximately 10 per cent of the young respondents 'self-identified' themselves as white British, 50 per cent as black British or mixed (black/white) heritage, with the remainder describing themselves as white Other, Pakistani, Bangladeshi, Moroccan, Iranian, Mauritian or Somalian. The chapter will also examine the way in which continued cuts to (and/or re-allocations of) public expenditure have resulted in the move away from a universalist to more targeted youth service provision. To this end it will include a locally situated account of the impact of local authority spending cuts and changing youth policy agendas on young people's services in East London just prior to, and two years after, the 2012 Olympics.

Youth and Social Exclusion

Since the late 1990s, the *Teesside Studies of Youth Transitions and Social Exclusion* have undertaken a series of qualitative research projects that have examined the long-term transitions of youth growing up in the poor neighbourhoods of North East England (see *inter alia* MacDonald, 1997; MacDonald and Marsh (2005); Johnston et al., 2000). Notwithstanding the many insights gleaned from the *Teesside Studies,* due to focusing largely on white youth in a predominantly 'white place', the question arises as to how relevant are the findings to 'super-diverse' cities and urban spaces in the UK (Gunter and Watt, 2009). It is within this context that both my current (and previous) research projects were undertaken; firstly, as a means to compare East London with the North East of England and, secondly, to revisit the same place and themes – the long-term cultures and transitions of youth growing up in two multi-deprived neighbourhoods in Waltham Forest.

According to the Index of Multiple Deprivation (HM Government, 2010), Waltham Forest is the 15th most deprived borough in England and ranks 6th in London and is also one of the most 'super diverse' (Vertovec, 2007; Wessendorf, 2014) areas in the country. The borough has a poor record regarding educational attainment; in 1996 all the schools in Waltham Forest were placed under an OfSTED accelerated inspection. This was due to major concerns being raised, during earlier inspections, about the possibility of large numbers of failing schools in the borough, indeed 'seven schools were made subject to special measures' (OfSTED, 2000: 4). As well as highlighting the poor strategic management of education within Waltham Forest, the report also went on to outline the other areas of poor performance, most notably:

> ... the proportion of primary and secondary schools where the quality of education and school management requires some or much improvement is above that of statistical neighbours and national figures ... The proportion of pupils achieving five or more GCSE passes at grades A*-C is well below statistical neighbours and national averages ... Attendance levels are below national rates and the number of exclusions is well above.... (OfSTED, 2000: 4)

As a consequence of the damning findings of this Report, Waltham Forest Council took the decision in 2001 – under pressure from the Department for Education and Skills – to contract out its education service to a private company, EduAction (BBC News, 2001; Becket, 2001). However, a performance assessment of the Council's education and children's social care services carried out by OfSTED and CSCI in 2005 still found that 'too many young people, particularly Black Caribbean boys, do not reach level 2 in their education/training by the age of 19' (OfSTED, 2005: 7). In 2007, a report about educational attainment in Waltham Forest at key stages 2 and 3 found that:

> Although there has been steady improvement across both key stages since the beginning of the EduAction contract in 2001, there is still a significant gap between results for Waltham Forest and our ambition to reach national averages. These two measures in English and maths are key to the success of young people in gaining employment. (LBWF, 2007: 1)

Nearly 15 years after the initial privatisation of its education service, 22 per cent of children in Waltham Forest are still leaving 'primary school without Level 4 in English and maths compared to just 10 per cent in Richmond upon Thames' (GLA, 2013: 10). Historically, low-level and no qualifications have underpinned much of the labour market exclusion and disadvantage in East London (Syrett and North, 2008) which has impacted disproportionately upon its youth population. Indeed, young people residing in East London are more likely to be recorded as 'NEET' (Not in Education, Employment or Training) when compared to those living in other parts of city (GLA, 2007). Research indicates that there is a high correlation between being NEET and 'later forms of disadvantage and poor welfare outcomes' (Coles et al., 2010: 7) including cyclical bouts of unemployment and under employment, mental illness, homelessness and persistent offending behaviour culminating in custodial sentences.

Regenerating East London

Since the 1980s, East London has experienced a long line of regeneration initiatives – beginning with the London Docklands – centred on private business, local government and third-sector partnership working. However, New Labour's programme of urban renewal created an even more ambitious and complex strategy to transform East London delivered through the Thames Gateway project and the London 2012 Olympic Legacy, as well as a host of smaller-scale regeneration initiatives. According to Mayor of London Boris Johnson we are already 'seeing massive economic payback for London and the UK' from the 2012 Games, and this 'is only the beginning of a process that will drive extraordinary regeneration in East London' (HM Government, 2013: 6). The proposed regeneration legacy of 2012 includes the building of 11,000 new homes and creation of 10,000 new jobs on the Queen Elizabeth Olympic Park and a further '70,000 jobs for workless Londoners' (HM Government, 2013). However, it is the Convergence policy framework that represents the greatest legacy ambition of 2012 (see Introduction):

> The Mayor of London and the elected Mayors and Leaders of the six Olympic Host Boroughs have already committed themselves and their

organisations to working toward achieving socio-economic Convergence between the Host Boroughs and the rest of London over the period to 2030. (Growth Boroughs Unit, 2011: 1)

According to the Convergence agenda, private and public investment in preparation for London 2012 provided the catalyst for change across East London, and for the next 25 years the sub-region will benefit from continued further investment and economic growth. The *Convergence Annual Report 2013–2014* (Growth Boroughs Unit, 2014) estimates that by 2030 the Growth Boroughs will have attracted 190,400 new jobs, £34 billion worth of additional investment; more significantly the residents of the Growth Boroughs will 'enjoy the same levels of employment, educational attainment, housing, health or safety as other Londoners' (HM Government, 2013: 4).

The 2012 Games represents both the latest and grandest regeneration project yet undertaken in East London and the UK, and whilst we are still more than a decade away from 2030 (when a more definitive assessment of its ambitious targets, and the Convergence Policy Framework, can be undertaken), it is worth assessing the research evidence gathered so far about the impact of nearly 40 years of area-based urban regeneration in East London. Established in 1981, the London Docklands Development Corporation (LDDC) was given the developmental authority to regenerate '8½ square miles of East London', encompassing the Docklands areas of the boroughs of Newham, Tower Hamlets and Southwark. At the end of its 17-year life span, the LDDC in its Final Annual Report in 1998 proclaimed that it had amongst many other achievements: secured £1.86 billion in public sector investment and £7.7 billion in private sector investment; overseen the construction of the Docklands Light Railway; created 85,000 new jobs in London Dockland; and built 24,000 new homes, 11 new primary schools, 2 secondary schools, 3 post-16 colleges and 9 vocational training centres (LDDC, 2014). Whilst the physical transformation of the London Docklands 'urban landscape' might be considered a success story, many local people were unable to access these new jobs (Deakin and Edwards, 1993; Rhodes and Tyler, 1998; LDA, 2006). Additionally, with nearly 80 per cent of the 24,000 new homes being directly sold to 'more affluent' owner occupiers, the LDDC regeneration project, 'rather than creating mixed/balanced communities there is considerable evidence of entrenched class/ethnic 'polarisation both in incomes and lifestyles' (Bernstock, 2014: 22; see also Cohen, 1996; Back et al., 1999; Foster, 1999).

Since the LDDC, East London has been a major laboratory for a large number of government-led area-based regeneration programmes including City Challenge, Single Regeneration Budget, Neighbourhood Renewal Fund, Sure Start, Children's Fund, Youth Inclusion Programme, Education Action Zones, Health Action Zones, Housing Action Trusts (HAT) and the New Deal for Communities (NDC). All have been concerned in one way or another with improving the life chances and experiences of those children, young people and adults deemed 'at risk' from social exclusion, by implementing preventative programmes that physically renew neighbourhoods as well as tackle employability, poor skills, high crime rates, poor health outcomes and educational under-achievement. Despite four decades of a myriad of regeneration programmes, Britain is still characterised by deep-rooted poverty as well as broader socio-economic disadvantage which in addition to being largely concentrated in 'urban, metropolitan, and (post)industrial areas' has also widened considerably during the past 40 years (Fahmy et al., 2011: 594).

Whilst various national governments have been fixated by regeneration area-based initiatives (ABIs), research evidence points to the inherent limitations of ABIs with regard to tackling poverty and wider social disadvantage (Atkinson and Kintrea, 2002; Lupton, 2003; Rhodes et al., 2005; Lawless, 2012). Fundamentally, 'locality managerialist approaches' (Ball and Maginn, 2004: 757) to poverty and inequality fail to address the complex structural contributory factors – global economic pressures combined with national government policies – which impact upon housing, labour markets and the provision of welfare services like health and education. Whilst ABIs that rebuild and redesign dilapidated housing stock and surrounding estates 'might encourage local people to be more positive about their local environment . . . they are unlikely to sustain change with regard to people based outcomes' (Lawless, 2012: 325).

The London 2012 Legacy will more than likely fail in its grand ambitions since this latest and largest area-based regeneration initiative, like many others before it, cannot address deep-rooted structural and social/economic problems of East London's communities, which have only been further exacerbated by the current Conservative (and previous Con-Lib Coalition) government's austerity programme. Indeed London 2012 Legacy is more likely to lead to further gentrification and exclusionary displacement (Butler et al., 2013; Watt, 2013) by 'addressing primarily the housing and consumption needs of the expanding' number of high- and middle-income households (Poynter and MacRury, 2009: 148). Area-based regeneration initiatives in whatever guise or permutation are inherently piecemeal and problematic as they distract from addressing the ongoing issue of poverty and the worsening social and economic inequities within British society. These deep-rooted inequalities require radical social policy interventions (Goldson and Muncie, 2006; Dorling, 2010; Rogowski, 2010) and 'solutions focused upon a sustained commitment to the redistribution of wealth' (Fahmy et al., 2011: 612).

Poor and Extended Youth Transitions

The research findings outlined in this chapter are very similar to those presented in my previous study (although undertaken a decade earlier), characterised by continuities with regards to the young people's poor educational experiences/outcomes and subsequent poor/extended post-16 transitions. The majority of young informants in this study[3] left school with no or low qualifications – did not achieve five or more GCSE A–C grades including English and Maths – and described their experiences of school in largely negative terms, most still went on to post-16 full-time study at a sixth form or further education college:

Tyra:	I got kicked out of school when I was fifteen
INT:	Did you manage though to get any GCSE's
Tyra:	No, but I did some other like courses when I was at the centre [Pupil Referral Unit] before coming to college.
INT:	What are you studying at college?

---

[3] Current study was undertaken during the immediate lead up to, and 2-year period following, the London 2012 Olympics.

Tyra: BTEC in Catering and Hospitality
Kem: I left when I was sixteen.
INT: Yeah.
Kem: . . . and I got, only got one GCSE. . .
INT: Yeah.
Kem: . . . and that was in Maths.
INT: Okay and how about you?
Solomon: I left school when I was sixteen.
INT: Yeah and what kind of qualifications did you get there?
Solomon: I got nine A to C's.
INT: Okay and yourself?
Karl: And I was sixteen as well and I got, erm, three, erm, C's.
INT: Three C's okay and did you all kind of leave school and come
            straight to college or did you kind of do anything else in
            between?
Karl: No, straight to college.
Solomon: Yeah, I came straight to college.

Whilst the majority of young informants were attending – or at some
point had attended – college, there was small segment of white young
males in this study who managed to find entry-level jobs in the construction industry (usually through family contacts). As noted in the
previous study (Gunter and Watt, 2009: 521), there is still a 'residue of
traditional male manual jobs available in London, at least for those males
"in the know" and with the right social networks' (see Watt, 2003):

INT: Do you go to work or college?
Matty: I work
INT: Ok what do you do?
Matty: I'm a builder . . . erm I do like loft extensions, erm cement work
          just any type of building work that we get like . . .
Scott: I do bit of roofing, done scaffolding . . .
INT: Since you left school?
Scott: Yeah, but I'm gonna do plumbing, eventually like, get more
          money. That's my plan.
INT: So you thinking ahead?
Scott: Nah, not really, but my uncle he does it like, so I know like about
          the money [laughs] like and the job.

Many of the young people were acutely aware of the link between poor educational outcomes at school and alternative post-16 transitions such as 'working on road' (see Gunter, 2008, 2017; Gunter and Watt, 2009). Consequently, 'going to college' was viewed by the young people as an opportunity – not provided within the school environment or curriculum – to obtain the vocational skills and qualifications that might enable them to obtain professional and high salaried jobs in IT, finance, construction, hospitality, engineering, health and social care, and the creative industries:

> Jamal: Well I don't think hopeful kids would be on the streets. I think, if a person left school with good, like more than five As to Cs, I don't think they'd want to be on the streets. I think that like the systems have failed them. Because the way how schools are, it's only now that they've brought in like diplomas and stuff, but you see that many people aren't used to them yet, like because there's BTECs now and stuff but normally it's just like GCSEs. And I don't think many people like that formal education, like people work in different ways. I think if they made like more jobs and training available, something that will actually help us, I think that would be better.

College and Training: Get On [and Off] the Bus

Whilst the young people's post-16 education and training experiences were largely positive, there was though a high drop-out rate resulting in their post-school experiences mirroring a Hoppa[4] bus ride; in that the informants continually failed to complete their college course or training placement (journeys) and would eventually start another course/placement which they would again not complete:

> Emms: Yeah, I done lots of things. I went L . . . College. I done IT, then I flopped that. Then I went, erm to some training place and I done

---

[4] Smaller-sized shuttle buses used by passengers (who are constantly 'hopping off' and 'hopping on') only for very short journeys.

erm, motor skills. I got CSC card. And then after that erm I went some training place in . . . for some IT course, and I passed that. And then after that I went N. . . . College, sorry, to do thing, engineering. Then I done half of year, half of the year. Then after that, erm, yeah nothing after that.

Maria: At first I was doing hair and beauty at college. I did that for a little while, but I don't know, just couldn't be bothered with it and that. It just wasn't me. So I left that.

INT: What did you do after that?

Maria: I didn't do nothing really for quite a bit. I used to just be on road . . . doing whatever. Now though I'm doing a Health and Social Care course.

INT: What you want to do after you've finished?

Maria: Youth work most probably.

Sami: First I done a construction course, I passed the level one . . . And secondly I done administration . . . This was like administration in retail, it was three courses in one . . . After that I went to work, I was working in a coffee shop in. . . . So I worked there for a couple of Months . . . I got redundant then I looked for another job better job.

INT: Are you working now?

Sam: No I'm still unemployed.

Mo: But I done like training at that Leap programme at TGB [name of local vocational training provider] centre.

INT: Okay yeah.

Mo: And a retail training course, it was all right once we were there but it was just full of like broken promises because you're supposed to be paid up to £200 and we haven't got that, or our certificate so, it was like a waste of time.

These early college/training patterns of the young people mirror much of the later employment experiences of East London's poorer adult residents (see also Johnston et al., 2000; MacDonald and Marsh, 2005). As discussed earlier in this chapter, regeneration of the Docklands resulted in the creation of new professional-managerial jobs – particularly in the financial services sector located in Canary Wharf – that locals have been unable to access due to no or low skills and qualifications (Deakin and Edwards, 1993; Rhodes and Tyler, 1998; LDA, 2006). What has been available to them are the many new post-industrial service jobs that have been created in London over the past 30 years, but which are characterised by low pay, insecurity, short-termism, part-time and zero-hours contracts (Abrams, 2002; Watt, 2003; Smith, 2005; Syrett and North, 2008). This is the precarious labour market context that schools and colleges in East London are not – according to some young people – adequately preparing many of their students to enter:

Jay: I do think the school, as I just said, the way they are set up, it isn't good. How can I put it? There is no structure to it. It is like people don't know where they are going, basically school doesn't prepare you for life, it just is teaching you subjects or how to count to ten but, and that is all well and good. If you want to go down and do maths when you are older, which a lot of people do, or economics or you want to be able to count, then obviously you need to learn how to count. But there is a million other stuff that is not related to counting that they don't teach you.

Alex: No all I think they do they come in and they tell you 'go to college, college is great, you have to go to college. After college you have got so many opportunities'. Then when you go to college they tell you 'oh you have to go to Uni, if you don't go to Uni you haven't got a life, Uni will give you so many opportunities'. Then when you go to Uni they tell you 'oh yes you have got to do your masters degree, if you don't do your masters degree you haven't got a life. There is a load of opportunities if you do your masters'. There is no other options, all they talk and you can't decide either.

Assessing the school and post-16 experiences of the informants, it is clear that the formal education and training curriculum's provided by schools and colleges are still preparing too many young people to fail within East London's post-industrial economy. Moreover, the combination of neoliberal policies and post-industrialisation and the 'recomposition of class have given education a new role in social control as the age of entry into the labour market has been raised' (Allen and Ainley, 2007: 40). Education has always been linked to social control; however, it now plays an even more significant role in the lives of young people whose experience of the labour market are very different when compared to previous generations. Rather than the traditional route into waged labour – as was the experience of school-leavers during the 30-year period of 'full employment' after 1945 (see Willis, 1977) – many 14–19 years olds are warehoused in extended schools/colleges and placated with a plethora of foundation level vocational courses – and the 'promise of often receding eventual employment' (Allen and Ainley, 2007: 34).

Young People's Services and Austerity

The impact of neoliberal government social policies on young people's services over the past four decades – specifically the continued cuts to public expenditure – has resulted in the move away from universalist to targeted provision (Davies, 2013). Multi-agency partnership working and the commissioning and delivery of early intervention programmes for 'at-risk' youth is central to this model of current practice. In a climate of austerity many third-sector service providers, who have been particularly affected by these funding cuts, are compelled to engage with central government initiatives that have ring fenced funding attached. Similarly, local authority service providers (who on one hand implement these cuts to frontline services) have to buy into national programmes like 'Ending Gang and Youth Violence' (HM Government, 2011b) in order to bring in extra resources. In March 2015 Waltham Forest Council proudly proclaimed, in its weekly newspaper, 'SINCE 2010 WE HAVE SAVED £68 MILLION, BUT WE NOW NEED TO SAVE £57 MILLION MORE BY 2018' (LBWF, 2015: 2); however, these savings have particularly impacted upon frontline services such as housing, adult care, children and youth services. Interestingly, whilst acknowledging its new approved budget for the 2011/12 financial year included savings totalling £35 million, the Council boasted that it had found an extra £1 million for its gang prevention programme 'Enough is Enough' as well as £500,000 for 16 extra police officers (LBWF, 2012). It has become evident that the Council – and confirmed in all of its annual budgets since March 2011 – is prioritising control and punishment rather than welfare and support for its vulnerable residents (Wacquant, 2009); this is emphasised particularly by the decimating £5.9 million cuts (77 per cent of total budget) to its youth services (BBC News, 2014):

Mark [*Youth Work Practitioner*]:	You know there hasn't been a youth service in this borough for years. I mean I don't want to get political on you, but going back to the 90s they've cut it to the bone, and now this latest one, well this now is officially the end. How can a service go from 60 FTEs [full time equivalent posts] to 12 in one week and still expect to deliver any kind of service.
INT:	But they have invested in gangs youth work?
Mark:	Don't get me started on that one. That's another thing, every day we are picking up the pieces from all this over policing of our young people, and plus with all this talk about 'cleaning things up for the Olympics' things are getting worse, if you can believe that.
INT:	You mean stop and search?
Mark:	Yeah. They don't learn, and like they continue to target and be heavy handed with our youth, you know everything's about drugs and gangs and what have you. All this targeted youth work stuff, it's like we can only work with young people if they are in a 'gang'. I mean what the hell is a gang anyway? As my young people love to tell me, the biggest gang around here are the 'feds' [police]. All that generic youth work stuff, working with young people where they are at, empowerment, forget about that, its now all about disempowering young people. Basically we are now working for the police and the justice system.

Whilst targeted and multi-agency working has had a profound effect on the Management and delivery of youth services, clearly not all beleaguered practitioners – whether in housing, youth offending teams or youth services – are happy about their new role as 'junior partners' to the police and other justice sector agencies:

INT:	Is your work targeted?
Marvin [*Youth Work Practitioner*]:	Yeah, it is now. My job used to be around youth achievement, where I used to work with young people across the borough. but because of the high profile cases of two young men being stabbed in the south [of the borough], all the councillors started jumping up and down about the youth service needs to be doing more. So then my job got changed and I was deployed to the south to work on the crime prevention project.
INT:	So you work closely with the police and gang prevention team?
Marvin:	I don't know about the gang team, they're supposed to be working round here, but I've never come across them and nor have the young people I work with. But I hear they have a bigger budget than we do [laughs]
INT:	What about the police?
Marvin:	I mean our job was to a certain extent to prevent crime, but the police I just found they got in the way. They just really did get in the way. We did a SUS panel, like workshop, and we called in some police and then we got some young people to come in and address them, do you know what I mean, and speak to them. And it was just really interesting that they, the police, had no idea what was going on, do you get what I mean? And then when the young people actually said to them, well, we want a place where we can ride our bikes, we want a place where we can play football late at night, we want a place where we can play basketball. These were the sort of questions, and they just danced around it. They, say they're interested in crime prevention but really they're not. They just come in and cause problems and leave, there is no come back for them, so they feel they can act how they like. The way I see it if you police properly, you know going back to the old community

policing, where you had your community officer who walks the beat that builds relationships locally, you then wouldn't have these problems. But now it's like they want to use the police to solve everything. You know, like, what's that saying, just papering over big cracks, because the problems that are there were set in motion many years ago. You're looking at people living in extreme poverty, you know you got poor schooling, poor health, followed by things like high levels of crime. So trying to prevent it, you know, is a problem. You need to change the conditions that people are living in, then that would help to prevent the other things, so it's very easy for them to go in and over police certain areas for their crime figures.

Whilst the Council was proud of its award winning gangs project and constantly boasted about the increased investment in policing and crime prevention, there was an increasing amount of frustration and cynicism amongst many practitioners and community stakeholders:

Janice *[Housing Association Worker – Community Engagement Team]:*

Gang crime prevention. It's just politics. They're not interested in the young people, because if you was you'd change the conditions they're living in. Do you get what I mean? There's no point throwing millions at it. It's just ways for people to stay in office. They don't actually do anything. Do you know what I mean? How can I come in as a youth worker and have a young person for three hours, all right, and change the way that young person thinks, when they're going back to their situation straight afterwards.

Conclusion

Since the early 1980s various national governments have attempted to tackle East London's entrenched poverty and urban decay via the deployment of area-based regeneration programmes such as the LDDC, City Challenge, HAT, NDC and latterly London 2012 Legacy. With regards to the outcomes of nearly 40 years of regeneration in East London, research evidence indicates that in certain instances these schemes have provided some benefit to local communities with regards to the physical transformation of localities; and this particularly relates to those ABIs – such as Hackney NDC or Waltham Forest HAT – with a remit to redevelop dilapidated housing stock/estates and the surrounding environments. Overall though, many other studies point to the fact that the long line of regeneration programmes deployed in East London have failed to deliver on jobs for poorer local residents and instead have largely served to fuel gentrification and exclusionary displacement. Moreover, poverty and socioeconomic inequality in 'austerity' Britain has become more entrenched and widespread, impacting disproportionately upon particular regions/localities, including East London, and demographic populations such as young people and those from BAME communities.

This chapter has sought to provide a situated account of the post-16 experiences of young people growing up in Waltham Forest – and is set within the broader context of East London's political economy, particularly with regards to the implications of poverty and post-industrialisation – as well as the impact of coalition government austerity policies upon youth services in this 2012 Olympic host borough. Many of the young people in this study had left school at 16 with less than five A–C GCSE grades (including English and Maths), and even those that did achieve this national minimum standard still found their post-16 education and training experiences to be unsatisfactory. Consequently, this resulted in too many of the young respondents failing to complete their training schemes and/or college courses; however, within a short space of time they would embark upon a new scheme or course only to drop out from that. This pattern was being constantly repeated so much so that the respondent's descriptions of their post-16 experiences might best be described as a series of unplanned bus journeys that never seemed to arrive at the intended destination.

In many respects schools and colleges in East London are not able to adequately prepare or equip many of its young people – particularly those from poorer and disadvantaged backgrounds (Allen and Ainley, 2007) – with the high-level skills and qualifications required for entry into those growth areas of the East London economy, such as banking, finance and ICT [Information and Communication Technology]. Rather, many of these young peoples' future working lives will be characterised by entry-level jobs, short-term, part-time and zero-hours contracts largely within the retail and service sectors, in addition to a shortage of genuinely affordable housing, notably social housing (see Chapter 4; Kennelly and Watt, 2012). Nearly 40-plus years of UK urban regeneration (and social exclusion) policies have been unable to achieve the desired outcomes, largely because they have all failed to acknowledge exactly what the issue is; namely poverty and the deep-rooted societal inequalities that require redistributive and welfare-oriented social policies that are focused upon people-based outcomes. It is highly unlikely that the 2012 Olympic Legacy will filter down and improve things in East London for the better, if anything it will more than likely continue to change things for the worse with regards to the ongoing exclusionary displacement of its poorer residents.

References

Abrams, F. (2002) *Below the Breadline: Living on the Minimum Wage*. London: Profile Books.

Allen, M. and Ainley, P. (2007) *Education Make You Fick, Innit? What's Gone Wrong with England's Schools, Colleges and Universities and How to Start Putting It Right*. London: Tufnell Press.

Atkinson, R. and Kintrea, K. (2002) 'Area effects: what do they mean for British housing and regeneration policy?' *European Journal of Housing Policy* 2(2): 147–166.

Back, L., Cohen, P. and Keith, M. (1999) *Finding the Way Home: Working Papers 2, 3 and 4.* London: Centre for New Ethnicities Research, University of East London.

BBC News. (2001) '£200m education service contract', 23 July 2001, http://news.bbc.co.uk/1/hi/education/1453157.stm

BBC News. (2014) 'Youth services spending down by one-third', 25 March 2014, http://www.bbc.co.uk/news/uk-26714184

Becket, F. (2001) 'Is privatisation the best solution for Waltham Forest?' *The Guardian*, 26 June 2001, http://news.bbc.co.uk/1/hi/education/1453157.stm

Bernstock P (2014) *Olympic Housing: A Critical Review of the 2012 Legacy.* Farnham: Ashgate.

Butler, T., Hamnett, C. and Ramsden, M. J. (2013) 'Gentrification, education and exclusionary displacement in East London', *International Journal of Urban and Regional Research* 37(2): 556–575.

Catney, G. and Sabater, A. (2015) *Ethnic Minority Disadvantage in the Labour Market.* York: Joseph Rowntree Foundation.

Cohen, P. (1996) 'All White on the night: narratives of nativism on the Isle of Dogs', in M. Rustin and T. Butler (eds.), *Rising in the East: The Regeneration of East London.* London: Lawrence and Wishart.

Coles, B., Godfrey, C., Keung, A., Parrott, S. and Bradshaw, J. (2010) Estimating the life – time cost of NEET: 16–18 year olds not in Education, Employment or Training Research Undertaken for the Audit Commission. York: University of York Undertaken for the Audit Commission.

Crowley, L. and Cominetti, N. (2014) *The Geography of Youth Unemployment: A Route Map for Change.* London: The Work Foundation [Lancaster University], http://www.theworkfoundation.com/Reports/360/The-Geography-of-Youth-Unemployment-route-map-change

Davies, B. (2013) 'Youth work in a changing policy landscape: the view from England', *Youth & Policy* 110: 6–32.

Deakin, N. and Edwards, J. (1993) *The Enterprise Culture and the Inner City.* London: Routledge.

Dorling, D. (2010) *Injustice: Why Social Inequality Persists.* Bristol: Policy Press.

Fahmy, E., Gordon, D., Dorling, D., Rigby, J. and Wheeler, B. (2011) 'Poverty and place in Britain', *Environment and Planning A* 43(3): 594–617.

Fisher, P. and Nandi, A. (2015) *Poverty Across Ethnic Groups Through Recession and Austerity.* York: Joseph Rowntree Foundation.

Foster, J. (1999) *Docklands: Cultures in Conflict, Worlds in Collision*. London: UCL Press.

GLA [Greater London Authority]. (2007) *Research as Evidence: What Works in Preventing and Re-Engaging Young People NEET in London*. London: Greater London Authority.

GLA. (2013) The *London Annual Education Report* 2013. London: Greater London Authority.

Goldson, B. and Muncie, J. (2006) *Youth Justice and Crime*. London: Sage.

Growth Boroughs Unit. (2011) *Convergence Framework and Action Plan 2011 – 2015*. London: Growth Boroughs Unit.

Growth Boroughs Unit. (2014) *Convergence: Annual Report, 2013–2014*. London: Growth Boroughs Unit.

Gunter, A. (2008) 'Growing up bad: black youth, road culture and badness in an East London neighbourhood', *Crime Media Culture* 4(3): 349–365.

Gunter, A. and Watt, P. (2009) 'Goin' college, goin' work and goin' road: youth cultures and transitions in East London', *Journal of Youth Studies* 12(5): 515–529.

Gunter, A. (2010) *Growing Up Bad: Black Youth, Road Culture and Badness in an East London Neighbourhood*. London: The Tufnell Press.

Gunter, A. (2017) *Race, Gangs and Youth Violence: Policy, Prevention and Policing*. Bristol: Policy Press.

Hastings, A., Bailey, N., Besemer, K., Bramley, G., Gannon, M. and Watkins, D. (2013) *Coping with the Cuts? Local Government and Poorer Communities*. York: Joseph Rowntree Foundation.

HM Government. (2010) *English Indices of Deprivation 2010*. London: Department for Communities and Local Government, http://data.gov.uk/dataset/index-of-multiple-deprivation, acessed 2 October 2013.

HM Government. (2011b) *Ending Gang and Youth Violence: A Cross-Government Report*. London: The Stationery Office.

HM Government (2013) Inspired by 2012: The legacy from the London 2012 Olympic and Paralympic Games. A joint UK Government and Mayor of London report.

Hughes, C. and Crowley, L. (2014) *London: A Tale of Two Cities Addressing the Youth Employment Challenge*. London: The Work Foundation (Lancaster University).

Johnston, L., Macdonald, R., Mason, P., Ridley, L. & Webster, C. (2000) *Snakes and Ladders: Young People, Transitions and Social Exclusion*. Bristol: Joseph Rowntree Foundation/Policy Press.

Kennelly, J. and Watt, P. (2012) 'Seeing Olympic effects through the eyes of marginally housed youth: changing places and the gentrification of east London', *Visual Studies* 27(2): 151–160.

Lawless, P. (2012) 'Can area-based regeneration programmes ever work? Evidence from England's New Deal for Communities Programme', *Policy Studies* 33(4): 313–328.

LBWF [London Borough of Waltham Forest]. (2007) *Waltham Forest Council Children & Young People's Services Overview and Scrutiny Sub-Committee. Educational Attainment at KS2 and 3.* London: Waltham Forest Council

LBWF. (2012) *Enough Is Enough: The First Nine Months. Waltham Forest Council Gang prevention Programme.* London: Waltham Forest Council.

LBWF. (2015) We've all got less to spend. Waltham Forest [Council] News, 9 March 2015.

LDA [London Development Agency]. (2006) *Targeting Worklessness in London – Socio-Economic Analysis (Technical Annex).* London: LDA.

LDDC. (2014) *About LDDC: A Brief Overview,* http://www.lddc-history.org.uk/lddcachieve/index/html, accessed 21 November 2014

Lupton, R. (2003) *Poverty Street: The Dynamics of Neighbourhood Decline and Renewal.* Bristol: Policy Press.

MacDonald, R. (1997) *Youth, the Underclass and Social Exclusion.* London: Routledge.

MacDonald, R. and Marsh, J. (2005) *Disconnected Youth?: Growing Up in Britain's Poor Neighbourhoods.* Houndmills; New York: Palgrave Macmillan.

Maginn, P. J. (2004) *Urban Regeneration, Community Power, and the (In) significance of 'Race'.* Hants and Burlington: Ashgate.

NPI and Trust for London. (2013) *London's Poverty Profile 2013.* London: New Policy Institute and Trust for London.

OfSTED. (2000) *Inspection of Waltham Forest Local Education Authority.* London: Office for Standards in Education, https://www.ofsted.gov.uk/sites/default/files/documents/local_authority_reports/waltham_forest/023_LocalAuthorityInspectionas.pdf, accessed 28 October 2014.

OfSTED and Commission for Social Care Inspection. (2005) Annual Performance Assessment of Waltham Forest Council's Education and Children's social Care Services 2005, https://www.ofsted.gov.uk/sites/default/files/documents/local_authority_reports/waltham_forest/018_AnnualPerformanceAssessment.pdf

ONS [Office for National Statistics]. (2012) *Ethnicity and National Identity in England and Wales in 2011*, http://www.ons.gov.uk/ons/rel/census/2011-census/key-statistics-for-local-authorities-in-england-and-wales/rpt-ethnicity.html

ONS. (2014c) 'Statistical bulletin: UK Labour Market, August 2014', http://www.ons.gov.uk/ons/rel/lms/labour-market-statistics/august-2014/sty-lms

Poynter, G. and MacRury, I. (2009) *Olympic Cities: 2012 and the Remaking of London*. Aldershot: Ashgate.

Rhodes, J. and Tyler, P. (1998) 'Evaluating the LDDC: regenerating London's Docklands', *Rising East* 2(2): 32–41.

Rhodes, J., Tyler, P. and Brennan, A. (2005) 'Assessing the effect of area based initiatives on local area outcomes: some thoughts based on the national evaluation of the Single Regeneration Budget in England', *Urban Studies* 42(11): 1919–1946.

Rogowski, S. (2010) 'Youth offending: towards a radical/critical social policy', *Journal of Youth Studies* 13(2): 197–211.

Smith, D. M. (2005) *On the Margins of Inclusion: Changing Labour Markets and Social Exclusion in London*. Bristol: Policy Press.

Syrett, S. and North, D. (2008) *Renewing Neighbourhoods: Work, Enterprise and Governance*. Bristol: Policy Press.

Vertovec, S. (2007) Super-diversity and Its Implications. Ethnic and Racial Studies 30(6): 1024–1054.

Wacquant, L. J. D. (2009) *Punishing the Poor: The Neoliberal Government of Social Insecurity*. London: Duke University Press.

Watt, P. (2003) 'Urban marginality and economic restructuring: local authority tenants and employment in an Inner London Borough', *Urban Studies* 40(9): 1769–1789.

Watt, P. (2013) '"It's not for us": Regeneration, the 2012 Olympics and the gentrification of East London', *City* 17(1): 99–118.

Wessendorf, S. (2014) *Commonplace Diversity: Social Relations in a Super-Diverse context*. Basingstoke: Palgrave Macmillan.

Willis, P. (1977). *Learning to Labour: How Working-Class Kids Get Working-Class Jobs*. Farnborough: Gower.

Anthony Gunter is a Principal Lecturer in Criminology, Royal Docks School of Business and Law, University of East London, United Kingdom. His teaching and research interests are in the areas of youth cultures and transitions, race/ethnicity and crime, and ethnography. He is the author of *'Growing up*

Bad: Black Youth, Road Culture & Badness in an East London Neighbourhood' (Tufnell Press, 2010), and 'R*ace, Gangs and Youth Violence: Policy, Prevention and Policing* (Policy Press, 2017). During the past decade he has undertaken a number of ethnographic research projects in East London exploring youth lifestyles and transitions, serious youth violence, policing and community-led Third and Statutory Sector responses. Prior to his career in academia, Anthony worked for over 14 years in both South and East London, within a variety of community settings, as a detached community and youth worker and Project / Area Manager.

Part III

Sporting Chances? The Social and Health Legacies of 2012

11

Are the Olympics Good for Your Health? Physical Activity, Sports Participation and Health Before, During and After London 2012

Mike Weed

Introduction

Hosting an Olympic and Paralympic Games is expensive. The public sector budget for Games delivery was set at £9.3 billion, and an investment of public funding on this scale clearly requires a return on investment beyond the four weeks of sporting competition and spectacle that the Olympic and Paralympic Games themselves provide. While host countries have long espoused the legacy benefits of the Olympic and Paralympic Games, these have mostly tended to focus on assumed economic benefits such as, *inter alia*, increased investment, inward tourism flows, urban regeneration and employment. However, as the cost of hosting the Games has grown, along with scepticism about some of the economic legacies, Games hosts have begun to consider the possibility that a wider range of social and cultural legacy outcomes could be delivered.

M. Weed (✉)
Department of Policy Sciences, Canterbury Christ Church University, Canterbury, UK
e-mail: mike.weed@canterbury.ac.uk

© The Author(s) 2017
P. Cohen, P. Watt (eds.), *London 2012 and the Post-Olympics City*,
DOI 10.1057/978-1-137-48947-0_11

Among such wider legacy considerations has been that an Olympic and Paralympic Games might have a positive impact on population health.

Some Games hosts have claimed an impact on health through an assumed impact on national well-being associated with hosting the Games and through a positive impact on wider determinants of health such as improved urban infrastructures, housing and the environment. However, a comprehensive systematic review of evidence for an impact on these factors could locate no evidence for such legacies (McCartney et al., 2010). Furthermore, in terms of demonstrable health legacies from the Games they are somewhat distal and ephemeral. Hence legacies have tended to focus on increasing physical activity and sport participation, which is demonstrable and measurable, and is widely assumed to have a positive impact on public and population health.

However, in relation to potential Games legacies, as with public health policy more generally, there is a tendency to conflate physical activity and sport participation. Specifically, to assume that the same processes of engagement that are used to seek to deliver increased sport participation can also be used to deliver increased physical activity levels among those not engaged in sport, and that these processes are universal across different segments of the population. This assumption is particularly strong in relation to the impact of the Olympic and Paralympic Games, where legacy policy and strategy is dominated by the sport sector and where sport and physical activity are assumed to be the same thing.

This chapter therefore seeks to explore the extent to which an Olympic and Paralympic Games might have a net positive effect on population health, specifically focusing on the Olympic and Paralympic Games in London in 2012. In doing so, the chapter asks three questions: first what evidence exists that it is possible to improve physical activity, sport participation and health through an Olympic and Paralympic Games; second what evidence exists that London 2012 had any impact on physical activity, sport participation and health; and third was London 2012's strategy and approach to improving physical activity, sport participation and health through the Olympic and Paralympic Games effective?

What Evidence Exists That It Is Possible to Improve Physical Activity, Sport Participation and Health Through an Olympic and Paralympic Games?

Governments, event organisers and sport professionals have long suggested that it is self-evident that sport mega-events inspire others to take part in sport and, by extension, physical activity. The assumption has been that sport mega-events inherently and automatically inspire people and stimulate an increase in demand to participate in sport or to become more physically active. Consequently, it has been assumed that all that is required to secure an increase in participation is to ensure that there is an adequate supply of sport participation opportunities and sport facilities to provide for what is assumed to be an inevitable increase in demand associated with sport mega-events. These assumptions have also tended to be extended to physical activity, with the same assumed processes of inspiration.

Prior to the London 2012 Olympic and Paralympic cycle, there had been no real attempt to systematically investigate whether evidence from previous sport mega-events supported these assumptions. However, two systematic reviews of worldwide evidence, with slightly different remits, conducted in the years before the London 2012 Games, show that while sport mega-events can impact upon sport participation, and may have the potential to impact upon physical activity, the potential effects are far more nuanced than governments, event organisers and sport professionals have suggested. In 2010, a systematic review published in the *British Medical Journal* (McCartney et al., 2010) concluded that 'the available evidence is not sufficient to confirm or refute expectations about the health or socio-economic benefits for the host population of previous major multi-sport events'. Possible impacts on sport participation or physical activity were among the aspects considered as a health benefit of sport mega-events by McCartney et al. (2010).

McCartney et al.'s (2010) conclusions would normally invite two possible interpretations: either that no effect on physical activity or sport participation should be expected from sport mega-events or that there has been no robust evidence collected that proves or disproves that there is such an effect. However, in the case of sport mega-events a third interpretation is suggested. It is certainly true that at the time of McCartney et al.'s (2010) review there was no evidence that sport mega-events had resulted in sustained increases in mass participation in sport or in population-level increases in physical activity. But it was also true that no previous sport mega-event had proactively and systematically attempted to use the event to raise population levels of physical activity and sport participation. Participation data had merely been examined ex-poste to explore whether simply hosting a sport mega-event had affected participation levels. Consequently, McCartney et al.'s (2010) review might most usefully be interpreted to mean that there is no evidence for an inherent effect on physical activity or sport participation, in which benefits occur automatically.

The second systematic review, conducted for the UK Department of Health and published in 2009, also showed that there was no evidence for an inherent effect on physical activity or sport participation from sport mega-events (Weed et al., 2009). In fact, this review went further in suggesting that there *is evidence* that inherent effects *do not occur*. However, focusing initially on sport participation, Weed et al. (2009) also suggested that there is evidence that mechanisms associated with sport mega-events have had a positive effect on participation where specific initiatives have been put in place to harness such mechanisms to stimulate demand. Furthermore, the evidence suggested that such mechanisms are most effective if initiatives seek to capitalise on antici-pation in the run up to a sport mega-event, rather than relying on memory after an event. As such, initiatives to increase sport participation should seek to proactively leverage anticipation in the pre-Games period, rather than relying on a memory-driven post-Games effect. However, the initiatives reviewed were largely more local interventions and were therefore not on a large enough scale to affect population-level sport participation demand, hence the lack of evidence for an inherent effect among wider national populations that had not been exposed to such initiatives in McCartney et al.'s (2010) review.

Weed et al.'s (2009) review showed that, for sport, there was evidence that a demonstration effect, in which people are inspired by elite sport, sports people and sport events to participate themselves, could be harnessed to impact on sport participation demand among two specific groups. Firstly, that sport mega-events might be harnessed to inspire those that are already participating in sport to participate a little more and, secondly, that sport mega-events might be harnessed to encourage those that have participated in the past to participate again. For each of these two groups, the effects were largely shown to be leveragable in the pre-Games period, driven by wider anticipation of the Games, rather than after the Games when the presence of the Games in public discourse quickly abates. In addition, and importantly, the evidence also showed that a demonstration effect did not occur in those who do not participate, and never have participated, in sport, and therefore the effect cannot be harnessed to stimulate sport participation demand among lifelong non-participants. This evidence was reinforced in the English context by further analyses of national participation data for England (Weed, 2010), which showed that responsiveness to a demonstration effect was most prevalent among non-sport club members who participated between once a year and twice a week. However, it had little effect on demand among those participating three times a week or more and had virtually no effect on those who had not participated in sport in the last year.

This evidence for the circumstances in which a demonstration effect might be leveraged also clearly shows that a demonstration effect will not impact upon the physical activity levels of those disinterested in sport. In short, sport cannot be used to inspire and stimulate activity among the least active who do not participate, and never have participated, in sport. In fact, more than this, the review uncovered evidence that seeking to use elite sport, sport people and sport events to inspire physical activity among the least active can have a negative effect. This is through something called a 'competence gap' (Weed et al., 2009), in which the achievements of elite sport people are perceived to be so detached from the lives of the least active, and so far beyond their capabilities, that it reinforces a view that sport and, by extension, physical activity is 'not for me'.

However, looking beyond the demonstration effect and the use of elite sport, sport people and sport events to inspire others, Weed et al.'s (2009) review also offered some interesting emerging evidence in relation to physical activity. The review suggested that a different effect, focusing on celebration rather than sport, could offer some potential to use the Olympic and Paralympic Games to positively impact upon engagement with physical activity.

Weed et al. (2009) found that major events such as London 2012 may, if promoted in the right way, generate a 'festival effect' that may have the potential to be harnessed to promote physical activity among the least active adults. This 'festival effect' derives from the promotion of the 2012 Games as a national festival that is bigger than and beyond sport, but that is also rooted in the lives of local and cultural communities, thus creating a strong desire to participate in some way in an event that is both nationally significant and locally or culturally relevant. Chalip (2006: 110–111) explains:

> The sporting outcomes may matter to some, but there is a sense that something more important – something that transcends the sport – is going on. . . . There is a heightened sense of community among those who are present. This alteration of communal affect has been much studied and documented by anthropologists who study public performances, including sport events . . . They call the sense of community that is engendered 'communitas'.

Chalip (2006) notes that celebration and camaraderie contribute significantly to the feeling that an event is bigger than and beyond sport, and this aspect of the festival effect is fostered by symbolism and iconography. For example, Kennedy et al.'s (2006) study of the London 2012 bid campaign showed that the symbols and icons of London and Britishness (e.g. the London Eye, Nelson's Column) were combined with athletic acts to create a campaign which was, in and of itself, a spectacle, a form of 'affective magnet', where 'affect is about our investment in something, a particular experience or practice' (p. 16). Kennedy et al. (2006: 19) describe how '[d]esire for "London 2012" was mapped onto people's existing sites of investment to steer their energy towards the campaign'. Such sites of investment were monuments, symbols and icons that transcended sport and helped to engender celebration, camaraderie and communitas (Chalip, 2006).

The key aspect of communitas is that the communality and community spirit that it describes creates a desire, if not an urge, to participate in some way, and that this desire is stronger if the event is perceived to be bigger than and beyond sport. This is the *festival effect*. However, local (or cultural) relevance remains important. Crompton (2004) and Sparvero and Chalip (2007) in describing the community impacts of sport teams and events each highlight similar phenomena that they describe respectively as 'psychic income' and 'community self-esteem'. Psychic income and community self-esteem are linked to perceptions that the team or event's value is not in sport, per se, but in what the event or team brings to the community in terms of its own and others views of its self-worth. This locates the importance of the event or team within community identity, rather than within sport.

Focusing on the celebratory and festival elements of the Games creates a feeling that they transcend sport, and thus has much greater potential to engage those who are not interested in the Games as a sporting competition. However, Weed et al. (2012) note that the goal and challenge for physical activity participation policy and strategy will be to satisfy the desire to participate through providing physical activity opportunities presented as fun community events or programmes, for which the achievement of a 'critical mass' of community engagement may be important. The key to generating a physical activity legacy through this process is likely to be to de-emphasise the sporting element of the 2012 Games and promote the festival element.

Clearly, the evidence for demonstration and festival effects suggests a need for a segmented strategy that differentiates sport participation goals, targets and, most importantly, processes, from those for physical activity. In short, the processes necessary to use an Olympic and Paralympic games to impact upon sport participation are different from those that might harness the Games to impact upon physical activity outside sport. Furthermore, seeking to use the elite sport inspiration of the demonstration effect to deliver physical activity outcomes among non-sporty populations is likely to not only be ineffective, but to do more harm than good. This is a particularly important message for sport policymakers, who often find it difficult to understand that sport does not universally inspire.

To help communicate the need for a differentiated approach in the run up to the London 2012 Games, the UK Department of Health commissioned *Active Celebration* (Weed et al., 2010), an evidence-based guide for local practitioners designed to capitalise on the specific messages and the need for targeted social marketing campaigns identified by Weed et al. (2009). Active Celebration outlined demand-focused strategies which tailored initiatives, approaches and messages according to the current participation level and the wider values and preferences of a range of target groups shown to be responsive to either a demonstration or a festival effect. Examples of initiatives harnessing a demonstration effect included *Generation Games*, which was targeted at lapsed participants with young families, and sought to re-engage participation through the activities and enthusiasm for the Games of lapsed participants' children. Another example, *Raise Your Game*, was targeted at sporadic and casual participants in the most common informal or pay-as-you-play Olympic and Paralympic sports (e.g. running, swimming, badminton) and sought to encourage such participants to formalise their participation through playing or participating more regularly as members of a club. Examples of festival effect initiatives included *Going for Green*, which was targeted at those with an interest in eco-issues, and sought to enhance physical activity in the outdoors through sustainable living projects in local communities. Another example, *Chance to Dance*, was targeted at those who were starting to contemplate physical activity, but were not interested in sport, and sought to link to the Cultural Olympiad to promote dance in all its forms as a way of becoming active and joining in the Games celebrations.

In summary, the evidence that an Olympic and Paralympic Games can impact upon health is focused on the assumed health benefits of sport participation, and the contribution to public health made by increased population levels of physical activity. In terms of the former, and in contrast to the suggestions of governments, event organisers and sport professionals, the evidence shows that there is no inherent effect on sport participation demand from simply hosting sport mega-events. However, it also shows that sport participation demand among current and lapsed participants in sport has been increased where specific initiatives and strategies have been put in place to harness a demonstration

effect from sport mega-events to stimulate demand and increase participation in the pre-Games period. The evidence also shows that seeking to
use sport-related inspiration to increase physical activity among the non-
sporty is not only likely to be ineffective, but to do more harm than
good. Thus to achieve health gains through physical activity among the
least active, a strategy that is clearly segmented and differentiated from
that targeting sport participation is required, in which the festival and
celebration elements of the Games are promoted whilst the competitive
sport element is de-emphasised. That this is counterintuitive to many
sport policymakers and, indeed, to politicians in general, both of whom
tend to conflate sport participation and physical activity goals, targets
and processes, is evident in the analysis of the London 2012 Games that
follows.

What Evidence Exists That London 2012 Had Any Impact on Physical Activity, Sport Participation and Health in London and Across the UK?

The London 2012 Olympic and Paralympic Games was the first sport
mega-event to explicitly set out to increase mass participation in sport at
a population level across the host country. Initially in relatively vague
terms London 2012 aspired to reach out to people to '... connect them
with the inspirational power of the Games. So they are inspired to
choose sport' (Coe, 2005). Later, this became the first legacy 'promise':
'to make the UK a world-leading sporting nation. This means more
people of all ages playing more sport and being more physically active
than ever before' (DCMS, 2008: 18), and specifically 'a goal of seeing
two million people more active by 2012 through focused investment
in our sporting infrastructure and better support and information for
people wanting to be active' (p. 3). Operationally, the two million target
was split in two, with the Department for Culture, Media and Sport
(DCMS) taking responsibility for 'getting one million more people
playing sport [across England] by 2012' (Hansard, 2009: column
60W), whilst another one million people would be encouraged to
increase their physical activity levels to deliver the overall two million

target. However, while the target had been split in two, the assumed processes of inspiration through sport and investment in infrastructure, not to mention placing the physical activity initiatives under the top-line promise to make the UK a world-leading sporting nation, clearly indicated that there had been a conflation of sport participation outcomes and processes with those for physical activity.

The result for sport participation, as evidenced by the Active People survey in England, which provides official national statistics, was that despite an encouraging increase of 115,000 people doing sport three times a week in 2008–09, the following year (2009–10) the increase was only 8,000 (Sport England, 2009b, 2010a). This is perhaps because, despite repeatedly saying that the games would inspire one million more people to do more sport, by early 2010 there remained virtually no examples of initiatives to leverage sport participation from the Games. This thus reinforced the evidence from previous sport mega-events outlined earlier that suggests there is no inherent impact without effective initiatives and strategies to harness a demonstration effect to stimulate sport participation demand.

Similar to the Active People results, the Health Survey for England, which measures physical activity levels (albeit periodically rather than continuously), showed little change in population physical activity in a similar period (Scholes and Mindell, 2013). However, in 2009 the UK Secretary of State for Health, Andy Burnham, announced a raft of activities seeking to capitalise on the festival effect to use the London 2012 Games to increase physical activity. This followed the delivery of Weed et al.'s (2009) review to the Department of Health, with Burnham noting in his announcement that 'the festival effect – [is] crucial . . . This, for me, is the effect we need to maximise'.[1] Among the initiatives were the development of the Change4Life brand to include Dance4Life and Play4Life, the establishment of a Dance Champions Group, a Walking for Health 2012 campaign, and a national programme of city cycling

---

[1] Speech by Andy Burnham MP, Secretary of State for Health, 13 August 2009, 'Fit for the future – can we build a more active Britain?', http://webarchive.nationalarchives.gov.uk/+/www.dh.gov.uk/en/MediaCentre/Speeches/DH_104324.

initiatives. This was the first and, as it turned out, only time that physical activity was differentiated from sport in national legacy policy.

In May 2010, less than a year after Burnham's announcement, a General Election in the UK replaced the previous Labour government with a Coalition government committed to a range of austerity measures to stabilise the economy and the national debt following the global economic downturn. These measures included spending cuts that led to the cancellation of most of the initiatives announced by Burnham in 2009, many before they had begun. This, together with a later acknowledgement (Gibson, 2011) that the physical activity element of the two million target was 'quietly dropped' after the General Election, marked the end of the short-lived differentiated strategy to use the 2012 Games to deliver increased population levels of physical activity. In fact, more than this, it marked the end of any attempt to deliver physical activity outcomes from the Games at all. Thus, from mid-2010 the only health outcomes being sought as part of London 2012 legacy strategy were the assumed health benefits of increased sport participation.

In December 2010, the Coalition government published *Places People Play*, their London 2012 Mass Participation Legacy Plan (Sport England, 2010b). Places People Play comprised specific investments in sports supply and infrastructure totalling £135 million scheduled to take place between April 2011 and March 2015, thus shifting the emphasis from the pre- to the post-Games period. However, there were no specific ambitions set as to what these investments would achieve.

Six months after the launch of Places People Play, sport participation figures showed a fall of 4,000 in those doing sport three times a week (Sport England, 2011). At around the same time, perhaps unsurprisingly, the Secretary of State for Culture, Media and Sport gave an interview in which he disavowed the previous government's sport participation target which 'will shortly be dropped in favour of a "more meaningful" measure' (Gibson, 2011: 22). However, such a 'more meaningful measure' was never announced.

Post-Games data for England showed that the number of people doing sport at least once a month had increased by an average of 1 per cent per year in the four years since 2007–08, whilst those doing sport at least three times a week had increased by an average of 2.2 per cent per year in the four years since 2007–08 (Sport England, 2013). However, the context for this latter figure is that achieving the original participation target of one million people doing more sport set by the previous government would have required an average year-on-year increase of 3 per cent, and that the average increases in the two years prior to the period for which the target had been set (2006–07 and 2007–08) were 4 per cent per year (Sport England, 2008). Furthermore, in the year following the Games those participating at least once a month actually fell by 1 per cent (Sport England, 2013). By any measure this is not a successful outcome for population-level sport participation.

In addition to the countrywide ambitions, there were also more specific ambitions in London, where the Mayor of London and the Greater London Authority, together with the 33 London Borough authorities, were keen to use the Games to boost sport, physical activity and health. To this end, in 2009 the Mayor's Sport Legacy Fund was launched, setting out a £15.5 million programme of investment between March 2010 and December 2013 focusing on sport facilities, leadership and participation. In terms of participation, these investments sought to engage 250,000 Londoners, of whom 25,000 would be those not previously participating in sport. However, the wider London legacy offer included a large number of smaller investments made by the London Boroughs, as well as the London element of the national Mass Participation Legacy Plan.

In their supra evaluation of the impact of the London 2012 Games on places, people and policy in London, Weed et al. (2013) analysed 96 programme evaluations, reports, plans, strategies, policies and data sources to explore the imprint of the Games on London life. Within the people strand, Weed et al. (2013) specifically address sport participation, as well as wider physical activity and health outcomes. Their analysis of comparative data from the *Taking Part Survey* (DCMS, 2013b) shows that sport participation rates in London were higher than those across in England in 2010/11. However, during the following year London rates remained static whilst rates for England rose. In Games year sport participation rates in London rose again, but less than across England as a whole. However, it should be noted, firstly, that all of these changes were relatively small and, secondly, that such broad participation rates provide only a context to more specific data about the specific impact of initiatives on Londoners.

In terms of the Mayor's Sport Legacy Fund, since the start of 2011 and up to March 2012, over 140,000 people had been engaged across a number of programme strands (Ecorys, 2012; Weed et al., 2013), and as of March 2012 around 15,000 Londoners involved in the programmes (just over 10 per cent of those engaged) were previously inactive. However, at the time of their review, Weed et al. (2013) did not have access to systematic data on the extent to which participants were retained within programmes, or their subsequent sport participation, although within one programme strand, Freesport, it was estimated that almost a third of participants went on to join clubs.

Weed et al. (2013) also analysed London tracking data (GLA Intelligence, 2013), which is less specific but provides some post-Games insights, as well as an indication of how attitudes and participation in London changed across the pre- and post-Games periods. This data showed that in October 2012 a third of Londoners (up from a quarter pre-Games) felt the Mayor was offering lots of ways to participate in sport during 2012, with less than a quarter feeling that such opportunities were not being offered. However, Weed et al. (2013) also developed a bespoke segmented analysis of Londoner Groups that were differentially affected by the Games. One of these groups, comprising just under half (45 per cent) of the adult London population, was characterised by being highly engaged, having positive attitudes about the benefits of the Games for the city, and generally having felt a high level of personal impacts. Among this group, half thought the Games had brought more opportunities for Londoners to play sport, with almost the same number feeling that their personal opportunities to play sport had increased as a result of the Mayor's London 2012 sporting offer. Furthermore, 6 months after the Games, over three-quarters of this group said they had walked or cycled more, or that they were eating more healthily, or that they were using public transport more or were more engaged with their community, as a result of what they had seen or heard about London hosting the Games. Among Londoners as a whole, 40 per cent said they were walking or cycling more or eating more healthily 6 months after the Games.

In summary, it appears that the impact of the London 2012 Games on health was more positive in London than across the country. Undoubtedly national outcomes were affected by the initial conflation of targets and processes for sport participation and physical activity which, although segmented for a brief 9-month period before the General Election, were disrupted considerably by the resulting change of government. The cancellation of the previous government's physical activity initiatives, and the dropping of the physical activity target, meant that from May 2010 the only health outcome being sought by government from the Games was the health benefits that were assumed to derive from increased sport participation. However, data shows that such increased sport participation, and thus any health benefits assumed, did not materialise at national level, and so the next question is whether London did all that it could to deliver health benefits from the Games.

Was London 2012's Strategy and Approach to Improving Physical Activity, Sport Participation and Health Through the Olympic and Paralympic Games Effective?

The previous section suggests that London as host city for the 2012 Olympic and Paralympic Games appears to have been more successful than the host country in delivering outcomes for physical activity, sport participation and health. This is likely to have been because engagement was higher in London for two reasons: firstly, initiatives were more local and more locally tailored; secondly, the Games and their preparations were more proximate. However, sport participation and physical activity were identified very early on as a clear legacy area in which impacts could go beyond the host city.

From the outset, aspirations for the London 2012 Olympic and Paralympic Games were derived from a political position that included a belief in the efficacy of the demonstration effect, not just for sport, but also for physical activity. This is not surprising, as policymakers in the UK, the USA, Australia and New Zealand had previously provided the rationale for their sport policy by reference to such an effect (Weed et al.,

2015). However, while the evidence discussed earlier in this chapter suggests that some sport participation outcomes might be achieved through effectively leveraging the potential of a demonstration effect, there is also evidence that relying on an inherent demonstration effect to bring new participants into sport, or to get the least active more active, is unlikely to be successful.

Having explored the evidence for physical activity, sport participation and health outcomes from Olympic and Paralympic Games, and the outcomes that London 2012 did and did not deliver in the host city and the host country, the question now is how far did the evidence base inform policy and, more fundamentally, what exactly was policy and what was success envisaged to look like. The initial conflation of sport participation and physical activity aspirations and processes, and the subsequent dropping of physical activity aspirations altogether, meant that aside from the 9 months preceding the May 2010 UK General Election, there was no real policy in place to deliver wider health impacts from the Games nationally other than those assumed to derive from increased sport participation. However, even in relation to sport participation legacy efforts, there was ongoing confusion about what was being sought, particularly given the change of government in 2010, and little evidence that policy was evidence-based.

The public and the media in the UK clearly believed that sport participation aspirations for London 2012 were to get 'more Britons involved in sport' (*London Evening Standard*, 25 July 2008) or, more specifically, to encourage 'extra people into sport and physical activity by 2012' (*The Guardian*, 7 June 2008). Furthermore, statements from Lord Coe, the Chair of LOCOG, that 'the real challenge ... is how many people can you get into sport' (Coe, 2008b: para. 18), and Andy Burnham, at the time the Secretary of State for Culture Media and Sport, that 'Sport England [has a] commitment of getting 1 million more people playing sport by 2012' (Hansard, 2009: column 60W) supported this belief. However, the government's legacy action plan (DCMS, 2008: 19) contained a 'promise' to use the Games to 'help people in England to be more active by 2012', which Sport England later reinforced and clarified, stating 'Sport England are committed to delivering one million people doing more sport by 2012/13' (Sport

England, 2009a: 3). Furthermore, both the government and Sport England set a performance measure for this promise that one million more people in England would be participating in sport at least three times a week (DCMS, 2008; Sport England, 2009a). This would be measured by the Active People survey and would specifically be an increase from the 6.815 million adults who were participating in sport three times a week in 2007/8 to a target of 7.815 million adults participating at this frequency by 2012/13 (Sport England, 2009a). In short, this represented 200,000 adults per year increasing the frequency with which they participate in sport to three times a week or more in each of the four years before the Games and in the year after the Games. Clearly and unequivocally, this target does not measure new people participating in sport, but how often people participate, and the clearest route to achieving the target would be to encourage those who were already participating once or twice a week to participate a little more often. Thus, while the rhetoric of London 2012's sport participation aspirations was to get new participants to take up sport (which evidence suggests is not achievable), the detail showed that what was being sought was an increase in participation frequency (which evidence suggests is achievable). Either this was a deliberate political sleight of hand or a muddled and confused representation of policy. Whichever was the case, the specific target set for sport participation in 2008 by the then Labour government (DCMS, 2008) did align with evidence about what might be achievable. The specific target set for sport participation also aligned with the evidence that a demonstration effect is likely to be more powerful in the pre-Games pregnancy period, as the increases targeted were for the four years before the Games and for one year following the Games.

However, although participation policy was aligned with the evidence in seeking an increase in participation frequency largely in the pre-Games pregnancy period, one vitally important aspect of the evidence had been overlooked: there is no evidence to support an inherent demonstration effect. The evidence shows that the demonstration effect is a potential effect that must be leveraged. Unfortunately, while a very clear target for increases in sport participation frequency had been set, little had been put in place in the way of policies to leverage the

influence of the demonstration effect in which politicians so clearly
believed, and in which policy was so clearly invested. The UK government's Department for Culture Media and Sport (DCMS, 2008: 24)
tasked Sport England to 'create the infrastructure necessary to support
increased participation' and through the Grow strand of its Grow,
Sustain, Excel strategy (Sport England, 2008), to commission partners
to 'deliver a range of high quality sporting opportunities to increase
participation in sport'. Yet, almost unbelievably, Sport England's strategy for 2008–11, the all-important four years of London 2012's
pre-Games pregnancy period, made no mention of the Olympic and
Paralympic Games other than that hosting the Games in 2012 made it
'an appropriate time to take a clear look at the sport development system
and its fitness for purpose' (Sport England, 2008: 5). There was no
suggestion that the 2012 Games might be harnessed to inspire participation or any plans about how this might be done. In fact, if the references
noted earlier were removed, there was nothing in the strategy that
suggested the Olympic and Paralympic Games were taking place in
London in 2012. The strategy was entirely about how sport development programmes were to be managed, how funding was to be devolved
and what targets were to be achieved. This strategy was for investment in
supply, with little comment on how demand might be stimulated, and
no vision for how the London 2012 Games might be harnessed to
stimulate demand.

Having set very clear targets to increase participation through
the Olympic and Paralympic Games, but with no clear strategy
about how to harness the Games to do so, the inevitable outcome
was that progress towards the sport participation target was limited. As
noted earlier, while there was an encouraging increase of 115,000
people doing sport three times a week in 2008–09 (Sport England,
2009b), the following year (2009–10) the increase was only 8,000
(Sport England, 2010a), thus reinforcing the evidence that there is
no inherent demonstration effect without effective leveraging strategies. However, in December 2010 the new Coalition government
published *Places People Play*, the London 2012 Mass Participation
Legacy Plan (Sport England, 2010b), comprising specific investments
totalling £135 million.

While Places People Play appeared to align government policy more closely with the evidence by establishing strategies to harness the Games to increase sport participation, the reality was somewhat different. Firstly, the investments in Places People Play would commence in April 2011 and run to March 2015, thus shifting the focus significantly from the pre-Games pregnancy period where the evidence suggests opportunities to leverage a demonstration effect lie, to the post-Games period. Secondly, although Places People Play explicitly and extensively referenced the Olympic and Paralympic opportunity, the £135 million investment was almost entirely for supply; two-thirds for the supply of facilities, and the rest for the supply of 'provision capacity', leaders and opportunities. Places People Play contained no strategies to leverage a demonstration effect from the Olympic and Paralympic Games to stimulate demand. As such, it is little different from the previous government's plans to 'create the infrastructure necessary to support increased participation' (DCMS, 2008: 24). Both approaches appear to be based on the assumption that London 2012 will inspire participation increases through an inherent demonstration effect, and that the only role for sport participation policy is to ensure that there is sufficient supply to cater for an inevitable increase in demand. As such, while the Minister for Sport, Hugh Robertson, noted at the launch of Places People Play that, '[w]ith more Lottery money being invested in facilities, volunteering and protecting and improving playing fields, there will be opportunities for everyone to get involved', he said nothing about how 'everyone' will be encouraged to be involved, other than '[w]hen people talk about the legacy of the Games, we want them to talk about Places People Play – and then we want them to get out there and join in' (Robertson, 2010). But 'wanting them to join in' does not represent a strategy or a delivery plan to leverage a demonstration effect to stimulate demand. Therefore, whilst it remained clear that government and its Ministers retained its belief that an inherent demonstration effect would inspire people to take up sport, policy to harness the Games to increase sport participation had almost become the least aligned with the evidence as it was possible for it to be.

Fifteen months after the publication of the *Mass Participation Legacy Plan* (Sport England, 2010b) the government published *Beyond 2012:*

The London 2012 Legacy Story (DCMS, 2012). With only four months to go to the Games, this document contained, for the first time since the Coalition government came to power, an exposition of legacy strategy that included clear priorities and even some legacy targets, although most of these were not directly measurable (e.g. 're-energise competitive sport in schools'). Four headline areas were outlined (sport, growth, people, city), with a top-level 'legacy story' and a series of priorities provided for each.

In introducing *Beyond 2012: The London 2012 Legacy Story* (DCMS, 2012), the British Prime Minister, David Cameron, claims that 'the idea of legacy was built into the DNA of London 2012' (DCMS, 2012: 6), with the document presented as 'the story of the first ever Legacy Games, and of the many lives being transformed by it' (DCMS, 2012: 8). However, although *Beyond 2012* provided the first clear outline of the breadth of the coalition government's legacy strategy, it remained short on detail. Although priorities were listed, there was little other than single short paragraphs to explain how priorities were to be achieved. Furthermore, because few priorities were directly measurable the extent to which they have been delivered can be the subject of political interpretation and debate rather than being determined by a clear assessment of whether a targeted policy outcome has been achieved. One effect of failing to provide measurable outputs and outcomes for legacy priorities is that it becomes easier to claim success by measuring objectives and inputs, and this was one of the features of *Beyond 2012*, in which the 'story of the first ever Legacy Games' was presented as a retrospective with objectives and inputs presented as legacy successes already achieved. Supplementing the story of objectives and inputs were vignettes of 'the many lives being transformed', which amount to anecdotal accounts, such as that from an artist who received a commission as part of the Cultural Olympiad, or from a head teacher who believed the School Games would provide a powerful focus for sport. However, for sport there was virtually no data to show outputs and outcomes from the objectives and inputs claimed as legacy successes, and no evidence that programmes were enhanced by an association with the Games.

With physical activity aspirations for the Games having fallen by the wayside in 2010, the only health outcomes addressed in *Beyond 2012* were those implied by a focus on seeking to use the Games to increase sport participation. As noted earlier, although the previous Labour government's sport legacy target to get one million more people playing more sport by 2012 was disavowed by the Coalition government in 2011, the 'more meaningful national measure' (Gibson, 2011) that the Coalition claimed would replace it never materialised. In fact, the two participation focused priorities in *Beyond 2012* – 'address falling participation rates in sport' and 'tackle high numbers of young people turning away from sport' (DCMS, 2012: 12) – were presented almost as remedial measures rather than ambitions for increased participation. This suggests that the 'more meaningful national measure' that government was implying was to make sure that there are not fewer people playing sport after 2012 than were doing so before the Games. This was justified in the document by a claim by the Minister for Sport that 'When we embarked on this challenge, the backdrop could hardly have been tougher. Sports participation rates in the UK had been stagnant for many years' (DCMS, 2012: 13). Yet this is simply not true. The Active People survey shows that the average per annum increases in regular sports participation in the two years before the 4-year London Olympiad (2006–07 and 2007–08) were 4 per cent per year, with participation rates subsequently remaining relatively stable over the course of the London Olympiad (Sport England, 2012). As such, the available data hardly justified a claim of many years of stagnation in participation, and the data certainly did not indicate that there were 'falling participation rates in sport' to be addressed.

However, the 'legacy story' was one in which maintaining participation appeared to be the new 'more meaningful national measure', and the evidence offered that this would be achieved was the investment of an additional '£500 million in sport through government lottery reforms' (DCMS, 2012: 10–11), of '£1 billion in youth sport over the next five years through the new youth sport strategy' (DCMS, 2012: 16) and the '£135 million Places People Play programme to improve the nation's sports facilities' (DCMS, 2012: 19). Of course, all of these measures are programme inputs, and they were supplemented in *Beyond 2012* by reference to programme objectives, such as '6,000 community sports clubs will be created by local schools' (DCMS, 2012: 16) and

'100,000 adults will participate in multiple Olympic or Paralympic sports under a nationwide Gold Challenge programme by the end of 2012' (DCMS, 2012: 19), each of which were presented as legacy successes already achieved. Similarly, evidence for the achievement of the priority to re-energise competitive sport in schools was presented as the establishment of the School Games, to which '12,000 schools across England [have] signed up' (DCMS, 2012: 15), although there was no data about whether the quantity and/or quality of children and young people's participation had improved, nor about how the School Games performed in comparison to the previous School Sport Partnership programme, from which funding of £162 million was cut by the Coalition government in December 2010.

In total, *Beyond 2012* claimed over £1.6 billion investment in sport as part of legacy strategy. However, the vast majority of this (the £500 million from lottery reforms and the £1 billion for youth sport) was not new money, simply the detail of how sport funding was to be allocated, and as such there was little evidence that the Games was making a difference to sport programmes through additional financial resources. Furthermore, the youth sport strategy into which £1 billion was to be invested over the following five years contained no elements that were thematically enhanced by an association with the Games, nor was there any evidence that the £500 million of lottery funding would create such Games-enhanced programmes. As such, it seems that this £1.5 billion investment would have taken place, and that the programmes could have taken place, whether the Olympic and Paralympic Games were hosted in London or not. Thus the vast majority of the investment in sport participation claimed as legacy in *Beyond 2012* has been neither increased nor enhanced as a result of the Olympic and Paralympic Games and should therefore be considered business as usual rather than a 2012 legacy outcome.

In summary, the lack of evidence for a national physical activity, sport participation and health legacy from London 2012 is an indication of a policy failure to deliver that legacy rather than an indication that such legacies cannot be leveraged from an Olympic and Paralympic Games. It is clear that physical activity, sport participation and health legacy policy and strategy has been inconsistent over time, often unclear and lacking in a meaningful measure of success, detached from the evidence base and often more concerned with claiming legacy outcomes than with delivering them. Furthermore, much of the investment that has latterly been claimed as an Olympic and Paralympic legacy for sport participation has been neither increased nor enhanced by an association with the Games and thus, regardless of any outcomes that may or may not be delivered, it cannot be said to have delivered a legacy for physical activity, sport participation or health.

Conclusion: Are the Olympics Good for Our Health?

Are the Olympics good for our health? Unfortunately, the London 2012 Olympic and Paralympic Games does not help us to answer this question because at national level there has been a clear policy failure to implement strategies that could deliver legacy outcomes related to health, rather than a failure in the processes by which the evidence suggests there is potential for outcomes relating to health to be leveraged from an Olympic and Paralympic Games. Locally within the host city, evidence does suggest that outcomes relating to physical activity (e.g. walking and cycling), sport participation and even wider health outcomes such as healthier eating have been delivered, and that these were the result of more segmented and tailored policies, and of the closer proximity of those affected to the Games and its preparations.

The first national policy failing relating to the London 2012 Games and health was the failure to properly consider health as a potential legacy outcome. While two systematic reviews could not find any evidence that health outcomes other than those related to increased physical activity or sport participation might be deliverable from an Olympic and Paralympic Games, London as a host city appears to have had some success in some wider areas of health, such as promoting healthy eating (Weed et al., 2013). Nationally, however, potential health legacies were never able to emerge from the shadow of Lord Coe's promise at the bid stage that London 2012 would reach out to people to '. . . connect them with the inspirational power of the Games. So they are inspired to choose sport' (Coe, 2005). This pervasive narrative dominated policymaking such that potential physical activity legacy outcomes were doomed to failure because they initially became conflated with it and were later dropped as an aspiration just as bespoke initiatives were due to be implemented. Furthermore, the possibility of any health legacy beyond increased activity was never fully considered. This left the assumed health benefits of increased sport participation as the sole potential contribution of the Games to health.

The second national policy failing in relation to the potential health impact of the Games was the failure to develop an effective and evidence-based strategy to deliver the only remaining health-related outcome, an increase in sport participation. An ingrained belief among those in the sport sector, that was accepted without question by politicians seeking to deliver a sport participation legacy, that the mere hosting of the Olympic and Paralympic Games in London would automatically and inherently inspire an increase in sport participation demand, appears to be largely responsible for this failing. The result was a sport participation legacy policy that did not consider the need to leverage demand and that instead focused on enhancing supply of facilities, opportunities and coaching support. The outcome was very little change in sport participation at national level, and a change in approach to attempt to claim future investment in sport as a legacy of the Games. Neither of these outcomes can legitimately be considered to be a sport participation legacy.

In conclusion, despite some success in delivering some physical activity, sport participation and health outcomes in London as the host city, the London 2012 Olympic and Paralympic Games were not good for our health, although that is not to say that future Games do not have the potential to be.

References

Chalip, L. (2006) 'Towards social leverage of sport events', *Journal of Sport & Tourism* 11(2): 109–127.

Coe, S. (2005) London 2012: Candidate City to host the 2012 Olympic and Paralympic Games. Presentation to the 117th IOC Session, Singapore, 6 July.

Coe, S. (2008) 'We won't try to top Beijing – interview with Mihir Bose', *BBC News*, 20 August 2008, http://news.bbc.co.uk/sport1/hi/olympics/london_2012/7573227.stm

Crompton J. (2004) 'Beyond economic impact: an alternative rationale for the public subsidy of major league sports facilities', *Journal of Sport Management* 18(1): 40–58.

DCMS [Department for Culture, Media and Sport. (2008) *Before, During and After: Making the Most of the London 2012 Games*. London: DCMS.

DCMS. (2012) *Beyond 2012: The London 2012 Legacy Story*. London: DCMS.

DCMS. (2013b) *Taking Part: Statistical Releases*, https://www.gov.uk/government/organisations/department-for-culture-media-sport/series/sat–2, accessed 10 May 2013.

Ecorys. (2012) *Formative Evaluation of the Mayor's Sports Legacy Fund*. Report to the Greater London Authority.

Gibson, O. (2011) 'Jeremy Hunt admits London 2012 legacy targets will be scrapped', *The Guardian*, 29 March 2011.

GLA. (2013) The *London Annual Education Report* 2013. London: Greater London Authority.

Hansard. (2009) Written Answers for 26 January 2009 (pt 0011). London: HMSO.

Kennedy, E., Pussard, H. and Thronton, A. (2006) 'Leap for London? Investigating the affective power of the sport spectacle', *World Leisure Journal* 48(3): 6–21.

McCartney, G., et al. (2010). 'The health and socioeconomic impacts of major multi-sport events: a systematic review', *BMJ* 340: c2369.

Robertson, H. (2010). *London 2012 Mass Participation Sports Legacy Launched*. DCMS press release, http://www.culture.gov.uk/news/news_stories/7565.aspx, accessed 1 December 2011.

Scholes, S. and Mindell, J. (2013) 'Physical activity in adults', in R. Craig and J. Mindell (eds.), *Health Survey for England 2012*. London: Health and Social Care Information Centre.

Sparvero, E. and Chalip, L. (2007) 'Professional teams as leverageable assets: strategic creation of community value', *Sport Management Review* 10(1): 1–30.

Sport England. (2008) *Sport England Strategy 2008–2011*. London: Sport England.

Sport England. (2009a) *Briefing Note: Sport England's One Million Sports Target*, http://www.sportengland.org/idoc.ashx?docid=13d82781-85a9-4d49-a381-bc6e558ad03c&version=-1, accessed 20 October 2009.

Sport England. (2009b) *Active People Survey 3*, http://www.sportengland.org/research/active_people_survey/active_people_survey_3.aspx, accessed 10 January 2013.

Sport England. (2010a) *Active People 4*, http://www.sportengland.org/research/active_people_survey/active_people_survey_4.aspx, accessed 10 January 2013.

Sport England. (2010b) *Places People Play: Delivering A Mass Participation Sporting Legacy from the 2012 Olympic and Paralympic Games*, http://www.sportengland.org/about_us/places_people_play_-_deliverin.aspx, accessed 10 January 2013.

Sport England. (2011) *Active People 5, Quarter 2 Results*, http://www.sporteng land.org/research/active_people_survey/aps5/aps5_quarter_2.aspx, accessed 10 January 2013.

Sport England. (2012) *Active People 6*, http://www.sportengland.org/research/active_people_survey/active_people_survey_6.aspx, accessed 10 January 2013.

Sport England. (2013) *Active People 7*, http://www.sportengland.org/research/active_people_survey/active_people_survey_7.aspx, accessed 15 January 2014.

Weed, M. (2010) *The Potential of the Demonstration Effect to Grow and Sustain Participation in Sport*. Report to Sport England.

Weed, M., Coren, E., Fiore, J., Mansfield, L., Wellard, I., Chatziefstathiou, D. and Dowse, S. (2009) *A Systematic Review of the Evidence Base for Developing a Physical Activity and Health Legacy from the London 2012 Olympic and Paralympic Games*. London: Department of Health.

Weed, M., Coren, E., Fiore, J., Mansfield, L., Wellard, I., Chatziefstathiou, D. and Dowse, S. (2012) 'Developing a physical activity Legacy from the London 2012 Olympic and Paralympic Games: a policy-led systematic review', *Perspectives in Public Health* 132(2): 75–80.

Weed, M., Coren, E., Fiore, J., Mansfield, L., Wellard, I., Chatziefstathiou, D. and Dowse, S. (2015) 'The Olympic Games and raising sport participation: a systematic review of evidence and an interrogation of policy for a demonstration effect', *European Sport Management Quarterly* 15(2): 195–226.

Weed, M., Dowse, S., Brown, M., Foad. A. and Wellard, I. (2013) *London Legacy Supra-Evaluation*. Report to the Greater London Authority and London Councils.

Weed, M., Mansfield, L. and Dowse, S. (2010) *Active Celebration: Using the London 2012 Games to Get the Nation Moving*. London: Department of Health.

Mike Weed is Professor of Applied Policy Sciences and Pro Vice-Chancellor for Research and Enterprise at Canterbury Christ Church University. Drawing on a wide range of social science disciplines, including social psychology, sociology, economics, geography and policy sciences, his work has focused on informing, improving and interrogating policy in the applied domains of public health, physical activity, physical education, sport, tourism, transport, urban development and major events. Professor Weed is Strategic Director of the Centre for Sport, Physical Education & Activity Research (*spear*), Editor-in-Chief of the *Journal of Sport & Tourism* (Routledge), Editor of the SAGE Library of Sport & Leisure Management, and sits on the Editorial Boards of *Qualitative Research in Sport, Exercise & Health* (Routledge) and the *Journal of Global Sport Management* (Routledge). His research has been funded by, inter alia, the Department of Health, the Economic & Social Research Council, the National Health Service, UK Sport and the Mayor of London.

12

Observing Legacy: Ethnographic Moments in and Around the London 2012 Paralympic Games

P. David Howe and Shane Kerr

Introduction

In this chapter we explore the observable legacy of the London 2012 Paralympic Games. We do this by examining ethnographic material gathered by both authors as we were working as journalists during the games in London and by comparing the observations gathered to those taken by one of us during the 2004 Paralympic Games in Athens (Howe, 2008a). Some critics might suggest that we cannot compare the cultural contexts of Greece and England but we feel that the influence of the International Olympic Committee (IOC) in setting out the guidelines for how the games should be organised and managed trumps any local organising committee's provision. There is one similarity between these two venues that is significant when we discuss legacy. Greece is the spiritual home of the Olympic Games and England is the

P.D. Howe (✉) · S. Kerr
School of Sport, Exercise and Health Sciences, Loughborough University, Loughborough, UK
e-mail: p.d.howe@lboro.ac.uk

© The Author(s) 2017
P. Cohen, P. Watt (eds.), *London 2012 and the Post-Olympics City*,
DOI 10.1057/978-1-137-48947-0_12

spiritual home for the Paralympics as the first event that ignited the development of international disability sport took place in July 1948 on the same day as the opening ceremony for the post-World War II Olympics in London (Goodman, 1986).

One of the things that is distinctive about the UK is how the British mass media has embraced Paralympic sport. Over 20 years ago at the 1992 Barcelona Paralympic Games the British Broadcasting Corporation (BBC) televised a few events live on *Grandstand* their Saturday sport programme. At London 2012 we expected the spotlight to be much more intense since with every passing Paralympiad there has been an increased media presence and we were not disappointed. Coverage from host nations, notably Australia during the Games of 2000 and Athens during 2004, was good but no more compressed than the coverage provided by the British media. Since 2005 Britain has hosted the Paralympic World Cup in Manchester which has garnished a reasonable amount of media coverage and offered athletes a chance to shine in at least three of the flagship sport (athletics, swimming and wheelchair basketball) with often a fourth sport being added depending on availability of facilities. Events such as the World Cup and coverage of the London Marathon wheelchair race (which in 2013 hosted the International Paralympic Committee [IPC] Marathon World Cup) keep the British public mindful of Paralympic sport between Paralympiads.

The media frenzy surrounded towards London 2012 was even greater than we expected. There appeared to have been be very little let down in the carnival atmosphere at the Paralympic Games as compared to the Olympics. The host broadcaster Channel Four was different as the BBC was the broadcaster during the Olympics but the ownership was the same as the British government controls both organisations. Established in 1982, Channel Four is a British public service television broadcaster that is largely commercially self-funded, but is publicly owned. The volume of coverage in both broadcast and print media in Britain was unsurpassed at the Paralympic level. Stories that attracted the greatest media attention, however, still had the tone of inspiration about them. The Paralympics are in the eyes of the IPC designed to empower people with disabilities. Inspirational tone of reportage is a clear indication that media outlets are buying into the IPCs rhetoric but details of Paralympic culture are often sketchy. The media storm around the London 2012 Paralympics was much more comprehensive than has ever been the case. As a result we became interested in the legacy impact that hosting the Paralympics might have.

Unpacking Legacy

Legacy is a difficult and complex term. MacAloon (2008: 2065; italics authors' insertion) has argued that 'legacy talk is now all around the IOC [*and the IPC*] and the apparent simplicity of the concept . . . is the first thing to note in accounting for its attraction and ready diffusion among Olympic neophytes'. Statements like this substantiate the argument that legacy is one of the most pervasive phenomena of the contemporary Olympic and Paralympic Games. While it may be pervasive, simple questions such as 'what is legacy?' and 'what is Paralympic legacy?' continue to be sources of confusion for the sports field, even though it has been a decade since it was inserted into the Olympic Charter.

The difficulty of defining legacy was explicitly recognised in the report that came out of the IOC's (2003) International Olympic Symposium, entitled 'The Legacy of the Olympic Games 1984–2000', held in Lausanne in 2002, a year prior to Legacy's insertion into the Olympic Charter. If the contemporary persistence of this difficulty is doubted, Lord Harris of Haringey, the Chairman of the House of Lords Olympic and Paralympic Legacy Select Committee,[1] positing, 'What does legacy actually mean?',[2] as his opening question to the second oral evidence session provides at least some, if anecdotal, evidence. The arguments that London 2012 used the 'L word' more than any predecessor (Chappelet, 2012) and represented a shift in legacy strategy from a post- to a pre-games paradigm

---

[1] The Olympic and Paralympic Legacy Select Committee took place between 18 November 2013 and 19 March 2014.
[2] Uncorrected evidence available online from: http://www.parliament.uk/business/committees/committees-a-z/lords-select/olympic-paralympic-legacy/publications/

(Leopkey and Parent, 2012) heighten the efficacy of this example. The problem and difficulty of understanding exactly what legacy is in the sports field is paralleled in the academic literature. Preuss' (2007) sub-heading, 'Towards a Definition of Legacy', or Chappelet's (2012) description of his legacy definition as a 'working definition', offer further evidence of the difficulty of producing a *definitive* definition of legacy.

Girginov (2012) has articulated two sides of the term legacy, that is, prospective, the shaping of the future and retrospective nature of the term. This chapter will use the method of ethnographic participant observation to highlight the retrospective nature of legacy in so much as we will highlight the distinctive nature of the cultural of media reportage between the 2004 and the 2012 Paralympic Games. For one of the authors the Paralympic movement and its culture was not 'a foreign land' (Powdermaker, 1966) as he had represented his country in four Paralympic Games and subsequently gained access via media accreditation at the 2004 and 2012 events. Treading the Paralympic 'beat' in Athens, including the filing of good copy with the added aim of exploring the culture of sports journalism (Howe, 2008a), was a good way to gain insight into the issue that was perceived to be of importance to journalists but also key to unpacking the issues that the public think are newsworthy around the Paralympic Games. The second author also worked as a journalist during the London 2012 Games and has a particular interest in issues related to Paralympic Legacy. Before exploring what makes good copy in the newsroom we will briefly consider the concept of *habitus* as it relates to the world of sport and journalism. Once the cultural stage has been set we will venture into the newsroom in order to illuminate how the culture of media journalism production ultimately creates stories that are devoid of cultural understanding. The conclusion suggests how these 'inaccuracies' might be remedied.

Journalistic Habitus

The conceptual understanding of habitus outlined by Pierre Bourdieu is useful in examining the cultural milieu surrounding the production of media texts. To Bourdieu habitus informs action like grammar structures a language, which can allow for multiple forms of expression through the body whether it is how the body moves or how it is covered (Bourdieu, 1984). Habitus of the social agents involved in the production of the Paralympics, whether they are athletes, administrators or journalists recording the spectacle are 'players' in a game actively working towards achieving a goal with acquired skills and competence but doing so within an established structure of rules, which are only gradually transformed over time. Habitus predisposes action by agents but does not reduce them to a position of complete subservience.

The theory of practice developed by Bourdieu (1977, 1984, 1990a) identifies the nexus between the body and the social environment surrounding it. In a sporting context then the games metaphor that is employed by Bourdieu in both non-sporting and sporting contexts highlights the relationship between capital and field. The multiplication of a player's disposition, their competence (habitus) and the resources at their disposal (capital) in relation to the social environment highlights the social actors' position in the world. In the particular environment that is elite sport it is the embodied disposition or doxa that enables a social exploration of the distinctive character of sporting practice and body hexis that is the performative aspect of habitus. In a sense, embodied sporting practice is made up of the habitual disposition established through the training drills (either as athlete, administrator or journalist) that might be part of a traditional training regime and the desire actually to play the game. Paralympic practice is therefore structured at a number of levels with improvisation grounded in sediments of previous activities.

The structure of the Paralympic practice is also imposed in the form of rules and regulations that have been codified by sporting federations. Rules are imposed upon individuals who fall under the federation's authority including athletes, officials and journalists. The social environment of sport is determined by all three levels of structure but still allows room for improvisation on the part of the participants. This field or network configuration (Bourdieu and Wacquant, 1992: 97) therefore allows the social scientist to see beyond the body as object and allow for an appropriate conceptualisation within the sporting environment. Capital on the other hand allows for the exploration of the issues associated with assets both economic and cultural, which a disposition may have in a particular social field (Bourdieu, 1990b: 63).

The physical action of a participant within the Paralympic practice community is strategic and the better it is the more embodied cultural capital or physical capital a participant possesses (Wacquant, 1995; Shilling, 2003). For example, the qualities that are associated with sports journalism bodies such as the ability to forge an extensive network of contacts (informants), the ability to meet deadlines and innate ability to know the 'real' story in amongst the rumble of continuous press releases are all part of a continuum of performance, and when a journalist achieves highly in any or all of these categories they will possess capital in the sporting environment (field) where those qualities are revered. The physical act of working within the social environment of the newsroom requires the journalist to perform in the world of sports journalism. The embodiment of the habitus of a sport journalist enables the anthropologist to work at times in an unreflective manner, that is, without engaging in the 'how to' elements of the practice. This allows for access to sediments of past news beats to form the root of new improvisations. Likewise a journalist that is a new member of the Paralympic practice community (Howe and Jones, 2006) may also see the importance of acquiring good skills as part and parcel of this distinctive social environment.

In order to get accreditation to be a journalist at the Paralympic Games an individual is required to be 'working' for a recognised publication or media outlet. Once a position had been secured the journalist is also required to gain approval from the NPC. Accreditation was secured by both authors through their NPC. The NPC therefore was an important gatekeeper which controls access for journalists based in the Paralympic Media Centre to the world of newswork (Allan, 1999) at all IPC-sanctioned events.

Paralympic Community and Classification

In the social environment surrounding the elite sport for the disabled it is important to appreciate the habitus in order to fully understand the nature of the practice. The Paralympic movement led by the IPC see the essence of Paralympism as being 'to enable Paralympic athletes to achieve sporting excellence and to inspire and excite the world' (IPC, 2003: 1). It is however difficult to be inspired if the habitus of the sporting culture is not clearly articulated to the public. Primary to the habitus of Paralympic sport is a complex classification system that has been a staple in all discussions regarding future directions for elite sport for the disabled. However, the intricate nature of the classification system is seldom disclosed in media reportage.

Central to the commercialisation of high-performance spectacles for the disabled has been the closer ties the IPC has established with the Olympic movement. Benefits include long-term financial support, access to the high-quality facilities in which to hold the Paralympics and countless other commercial bonuses. An agreement between the IOC and IPC was signed in 2001 to formalise these ties. In 2003 this agreement was amended to transfer 'broadcasting and marketing responsibilities of the 2008, 2010, and 2012 Paralympic games to the Organizing Committee of these Olympic and Paralympic games' (IPC, 2003: 1). While agreements such as this will ease financial concerns for the IPC, it may force a restructuring of sport for the disabled. The IOC demands that the Paralympic Games are restricted in size to 4,000 athletes. Limiting the size of future Paralympic Games in the eyes of the IOC makes it a more manageable product to market. The marketing of the Olympics and Paralympics as a single entity may undermine the IPC's autonomy to use the Paralympic Games to educate the public about athletes with a disability. The erosion of this educational imperative is problematic because one of the IPC's explicit aims is the effective and efficient promotion of elite sport for the disabled. Moreover, the IPC's dictum 'empower, inspire and achieve'[3] suggests the Paralympic movement is concerned with empowering its athletes in hope that their performances will inspire others to great achievements. It is these tenets that form the foundation of the ideological movement of Paralympism. As a result anything that negatively impacts upon their successful achievement is likely to have a detrimental influence upon Paralympic sport.

---

[3] www.paralympic.org

The IPC desire to receive 'good ink' from media outlets where their 'product' that it can be 'sold' to the public means that it structures the retrieval of stories during the Paralympic Games accordingly, to the detriment of the Paralympic practice community. Moving into the field of Paralympic journalism requires the adoption of a distinctive habitus, one that almost negates the epistemological importance of classification within the field. It is the physical act of getting into the field that this chapter now turns.

London 2012 'Field of Vision'

Full media accreditation acts as a passport for Paralympic and city public transport as well as access to all areas associated with the Olympic venues (except those reserved for VIPs and the Paralympic Village). On visiting the Athens media centre that was in the bowels of the Olympic stadium it was here that the massive media machine that the Olympics create was starkly visible. The media centre could have housed an indoor 200 m athletics track it was so large. For the Paralympics perhaps not surprisingly the room was less than 20 per cent full. Due to the media centre's vastness journalists were given a map that traced the quickest route to the key media points including a 10-minute walk across the Olympic site to the International Broadcast Centre (IBC), where the studios were located for the broadcast media. This media venue was even more barren. NBC, the American broadcaster that had the televisual rights to the Olympic Games, had pulled out all its 3,500 staff after the closing ceremonies. One British journalist that had worked for a number of years on the Paralympic beat and as such embodied its habitus publicly criticised this move. The fact that NBC did not even leave a shadow broadcast team was highlighted as a negative for the New York bidding team for the 2012 games because all the other nations that were bidding for the games had maintained a degree of media presence during the Paralympic Games (Pryor, 2004a).

In spite of the empty space in both the media centre and the IBC there were journalists of every form covering the Paralympic Games, many of whom had also worked at the Olympics three weeks earlier. For the Athens Games, the BBC had doubled the amount of coverage it had shown in Australia four years earlier to an hour and a half every evening. By the standards of the Paralympics this is a high level of coverage but it falls well short of the coverage given by the same broadcaster during the Olympics game. On the print journalism front the British daily newspapers *The Times, The Daily Telegraph* and *The Daily Mail* all had journalists present on the Paralympic beat in Athens and all the broadsheets and tabloids in Britain had at least one journalist in the newsroom for the duration of the 2012 Paralympics.

The media centre on the Olympic Park was to be the hub of my newswork for the fortnight of the Paralympic Games. When holding a sporting event for athletes with a disability ease of access for those with mobility impairment should be well organised. In the case of the media centre it was not. There was only one lift to the heart of the centre and it could only accommodate one wheelchair. The fact that the lift was small made an explicit statement that disabled people were not expected to be members of the media. For those who did gain access, the area was full of other mobility pitfalls. In order to link up the stadium to the outside world thousands of miles of electrical and fibre optic cable were used. In the media centre most of this was on the floor and though it was covered by metal protectors these were several inches wide and several inches high. As a result these cable covers could be insurmountable barriers to a wheelchair user or an individual with a visual impairment (Howe, 2008a: 141).

Our observations and participation in the physical space of the media centre during the London 2012 Paralympics illuminated that accessibility was not regarded as an issue that would exclude journalists with impairments from using this space. While in Athens in 2004 only 5 per cent of had an impairment (Howe, 2008a) we estimate that 12–15 per cent of journalists working in London were impaired. One of the things that has changed between 2004 and 2012 has been the use of technologies that facilitate a virtual presence at sporting events. As a result many journalists who have mobility impairments do not have to physically attend events to report on them. The speed of journalist activity highlighted in the Athens research was no longer really an issue when, for example, copy can be uploaded all the time from websites.

Whether or not there should be a greater number of journalists with a disability working at the Paralympic Games is a contentious issue. Media outlets at the Paralympic Games did not more readily use disabled journalists and there seemed to be little concern about this imbalance (Howe, 2008a). Yet with the change in the media landscape means that the media has the potential to be more inclusive and it is less easy for a handful of institutions to control media outputs as it has been in the past.

Traditionally coverage of the Paralympics both in the written and visual press is laden with an appreciation for what the athletes have achieved before they get to the starting line (Silva and Howe, 2012). It is worth quoting an Australian journalist who tried to establish a more robust manner of reporting on the endeavours of Paralympians but encountered cultural difficulty in doing so. On one side, they will be dealing with athletes craving respect for their achievements, not merely acknowledgement of their courage and commitment. Yet, at the other extreme, the reporter who strays beyond the well-established territory of feel-good stories and heart-breaking profiles and dares to make a critical assessment risks automatic censure (Hind, 2000).

When in London 2012 the world's most celebrated Paralympian Oscar Pistorius behaved in an unsporting fashion many newspapers reacted against him. It was a sour reaction, cutting through the saccharine notes of so much of the Paralympic coverage. But Pistorius has always insisted that he wants to be known as an athlete, rejecting the labels other people have put upon him, whether they were that he was disabled, differently abled, a cheat, an inspiration or a role model. And this was an athlete's response to defeat, if a particularly ungracious one (Bull, 2012).

The loss of Pistorius to a talented young Brazilian named Oliveria was clouded with the spectre of cheating. Pistorius had wrongly suggested that his fellow competitor was wearing legs that were too long that therefore gave him an advantage. Commentators on Paralympic sport (Howe, 2008b, 2011) have illuminated the advantage that Pistorius has had over his fellow competitors and a moment from one of our ethnographic diaries highlights this issue.

I was called into the BBC World Service studio today. The topic of conversation was Oscar's 200m race yesterday. I was on a panel with 4 other experts though we were all in different locations. Basically everyone on the panel was against me. They said Oscar must have a point about the Brazilian cheating. Their view was he is such a role model that he would not get agitated for no reason at all. When I said that he was acting like a petulant child – as a lot of elite athletes do when they lose – it went over like a lead balloon and the other experts became very dismissive of me.

Subsequent events have shown that Pistorius was beaten fairly by the Brazilian and is not the sort of character who should be celebrated as a role model.

The key difference with the Paralympic beat is that because of the sensitive nature of the topic (Hind, 2000) journalists are not expecting to get a scoop. In fact most of the stories that were filed, or rather the stories that made it to press, were either reports on results of events or small biographies. Connections with inside sources established through long service to the beat are evidently more reliable than what can be obtained from within the press office, which is primarily an instrument of promotional culture (Wernick, 1991). Within this cultural milieu lines between entertainment and promotion become blurred. Constant promotion requires positive media coverage and advancement within this environment requires an agenda of press releases and news conferences.

Creating Newsworthy Copy: Contrasting Experiences of London in 2012

One of the distinctive features of London 2012 in comparison to Athens 2004 was the number of disability stories that ran alongside the sport coverage. Activists within the disability community in and around London used the games as an opportunity to highlight the liminal status of the impaired in British society. There were two particularly symbolic days during the summer of London 2012 that can be recounted here for the contrast they strike.

28th July 2012

The Counter Olympic Network (CON) was a mixture of different protest groups that collaborated to organise a peaceful protest on the opening day of the London 2012 Olympic Games at Mile End, near the Olympic stadium. Each group had its own issue or struggle which in some way challenged the legitimacy of the London 2012 Olympic and Paralympic Games.

I arrive at the meet point in Mile End just before the stewards are assembled. I declare myself as a researcher to the group. There are only a handful of people around at this point. A reporter is sent away from the steward's meeting. The leader begins outlining the 'rules of conduct' and assigning roles. I'm reluctant to volunteer for anything, I'm sure my hesitation is felt. The leader details the lengths they've went to cooperate with the police get to this point. Legal aid leaflets are distributed. One steward recounts the heavy-handedness of the police against the Critical Mass Ride[4] the previous night as the group came close to the Olympic stadium. More and more people begin to fill the area. There is now a swell of protest groups, CON affiliates, police officers, liaison officers and media reporters and crew, all being traversed by passers-by. There was a notice-able presence of foreign media, arguably reflective of the international media's skewed demand for this type of story. Within half an hour of the stewards meeting every CON affiliate is being engaged by some form of media. While waiting for the protest march to begin I converse with Adam, a member of Disabled People Against Cuts (DPAC). He tells me about DPAC's plans to organise a week of protests around the Paralympic Games. When the stewards gave the signal to make the short walk down towards the road to begin the protest march there was a scramble by media crew and photographers to get to the front to capture that picture. When the protest march began in earnest the police established a cordon around it, moving and stopping in tandem with the protest. Then each group began its own chants, 'Atos, get lost! Atos, get lost! Atos get lost!'. Whilst seeking to engage the public in their protest, the protest was not

---

[4] Critical mass ride was a group that would frequently organise mass cycles around London to promote cyclist rights.

autonomous from being engaged by the public. At a number of junctures passers-by verbally engaged the protests, challenging the legitimacy of the protest. But without regard, the protest marched on, and the chants with it, 'Atos, get lost! Atos, get lost! Atos get lost!'.

31st August 2012

I spent the morning of 31 August 2012 at the Aquatics Centre. I had agreed to cover Ireland's Lawrence McGovern, who was competing in the Men's S9 100 m backstroke, for an Irish newspaper. It was a good performance by Lawrence who managed to qualify for the evening's final. From the aquatics centre, a space defined by sport, I crossed London to arrive at Triton Square, a space defined by DPAC and other groups protesting outside Atos' headquarters. As I made my way closer to the protest the social energy, not too dissimilar from that I had just experienced in the aquatics centre, grew and grew. Many of the protestors held placards. Here are some examples of what they read:

'Atos out'; 'Atos Kills'; 'Unregulated capitalism (greed) has caused the economic crisis – not disabled people'; 'Cecilia Burns – R.I.P. Declared "fit to work" in February by Atos. Died this morning, "nil points" for her breast cancer. Atos is a sick joke'.

The protest, positioned between two high-rise buildings, created a space which heightened the intensity of the theatrical performance. For the main act, the protestors mocked Atos' magical ability to cure people of their ailments and be classified as 'fit to work'. After this performance, the protestors brought their stage to the offices of the Department for Work and Pensions, where they held a sit-in before being removed by the police. After the afternoon's protests I returned to the aquatics centre, where it seemed the sporting competitions and the cheering from the crowds had never ended.

The recounting of these two symbolic days brings forth many issues. DPAC's struggle against Atos' engagement with the Paralympic Games and the government's welfare reforms are of principal note. These struggles of DPAC, however, meet the unstoppable force which dictates that the Olympic and Paralympic 'show must go on'.

Atos is an international sponsor for the Olympic and Paralympic Games and during the games had a contract to carry out 'work capability assessments' for the UK Government Department of Work and Pensions and many protestors were drawn to the protest for at this time because of the Paralympic Games. As one informant suggested:

> Well I think, obviously it was a positive occasion, but I think that a lot of the spinning that has been done around it and particularly around the Paralympics and attitudes to disabled people is really very disingenuous because the disabled people who participate in the Paralympics are generally people who you would describe as disabled and well, so they're not ill. If they were ill they would not be able to participate in the Paralympics but unfortunately the government have collapsed it all together and given the impression that the Paralympics showed us what disabled people can do. The answer really is that it shows you what a few elite disabled sports men who are well can do and that's not usually included as a caveat. So I think it has given the government a very good excuse to say 'well you know all disabled people can do all these things' just because Paralympians can which is clearly absolutely rubbish. Unfortunately sound bites don't depend on the extent to which you can pull them apart, they gain a life of their own so I think that that is really unfortunate and I think it was always the danger of the Paralympics to be honest, that's my view.

Although this informant recognised the Games as being positive, her relation to the practices of the government challenges the legitimacy of their claims of disability legacy and their expressive use and leveraging of their investment and engagement with the Games. It is her social position that has produced this relation to the field and to see the conflation of disability and illness as a disingenuous strategy of the government. By challenging the legitimacy of the government's claims of legacy she is also challenging the legitimacy of the current government itself and its strategies and practices in the distribution of capital throughout society. The informant continued:

I didn't necessarily agree with all the campaigning around the Olympics in terms of . . . pinning a whole lot of blame on Atos as the people who deliver the WCA but also as the sponsors of the Games when actually it's the government's DWP [Department of Working Pensions] that is responsible for setting the parameters within which Atos work from, so whilst Atos is not totally innocent it's the monkey rather than the organ grinder and you know having a great big thing against Atos at the Games I actually think was a bit of a distraction.

Conclusion

For journalists who work for media outlets the ability to establish constructive relationships with those who have access to newsworthy information is a vital component of their habitus. While access to highly processed media releases is as simple as gaining media accreditation, insider stories are more difficult to obtain. Establishing a working relationship with gatekeepers is fundamental to the successful journalist regardless of the sporting practice they are exploring (Lowe, 1999). As a sporting practice becomes influenced by commercial concerns there is an increased likelihood that there will be access to both positive and negative stories. Mainstream able-bodied elite sport is full of news reports that highlight both positive and negative attributes associated with these sporting practices. Our current research highlights that the Paralympic Games are shifting slowly but surely towards the old adage that 'any publicity is good publicity'. As such there is greater control placed upon journalists to present positive coverage within the limited Paralympic spotlight.

Inside the newsroom information was controlled by both the IPC and its NPCs through their media liaison. Using press releases or the hexis of press conferences both the IPC and the NPCs were in a powerful position to control and shape stories through the use of these tools. Yet this control is waning as the technology for media professionals to work at a distance improves accessibility to journalists of all abilities. But what is the ultimate legacy of the 2012 Paralympic Games? From this small study we can clearly say that the development of a more diverse reportage of stories in and around the Paralympic Games will allow for more critical discussion of important social issues. Because England is the spiritual home of the Paralympic Movement (Howe, 2008b), issues of legacy were more apposite to the London 2012 coverage than has been the case in other Para Olympiads. Since 1992 the BBC has actively engaged in showing at least some of the Paralympics live. This is a tradition that has mushroomed to the point where Channel Four coverage of disability sport before and after as well as during the Games themselves should be celebrated.

It was not that long ago that there was an outcry when, during a live stand-up routine in Manchester, British comedian Jimmy Carr, who is known for his edgy humour, made the following joke: 'Say what you like about those servicemen amputees from Iraq and Afghanistan, but we're going to have a fucking good Paralympic team in 2012'. At the time the authors celebrated this gag, but perhaps not surprisingly there was a degree of public outcry regarding this line in the days that followed (see Moss, 2009). Yet times have changed. If a similar joke had been made when Channel Four held the Invictus Games, an international sporting event for wounded, injured and sick servicemen and women in September 2014, we believe it is safe to say that the public response would have been much more positive. Despite the caveats we have made, the 2012 Paralympics has had a positive legacy impact in terms of the publics understanding of disability as it relates to sport.

Bibliography

Allan, S. (1999) *News Culture*. Buckingham: Open University Press.

Bourdieu, P. (1977) *Outline of a Theory of Practice*. Cambridge: Cambridge University Press.

Bourdieu, P. (1984) *Distinction: A Social Critique of the Judgement of Taste*. London: Routledge.

Bourdieu, P. (1990a) *The Logic of Practice*. Cambridge: Polity Press.

Bourdieu, P. (1990b) *In Other Words: Essays Towards a Reflective Sociology*. Cambridge: Polity Press.

Bourdieu, P. and Wacquant, L. (1992) *An Invitation to Reflective Sociology*. Chicago: University of Chicago Press.

Bull, A. (2012) 'Oscar Pistorius angry at shock Paralympics 200m loss', *The Guardian*, 3 September 2012.

Chappelet, J. L. (2012) 'Mega Sporting Event Legacies: a multifaceted concept', *Papeles de Europa*. 25: 76–86.

Girginov, V. (2012) 'Governance of London 2012 Olympic Games legacy', *International Review for the Sociology of Sport* 47(5): 543–558.

Goodman, S. (1986) *Spirit of Stoke Mandeville: the story of Ludwig Guttmann*. London: Collins.

Hind, R. (2000) 'Sense and sensibilities: delicate balance of reporting the Paralympics', *Sydney Morning Herald*, 14 October.

Howe, P. D. (2008a) 'From inside the newsroom: Paralympic media and the "production" of elite disability', *International Review for the Sociology of Sport* 43(2): 135–150.

Howe, P. D. (2008b) *The Cultural Politics of the Paralympic Movement: Through the Anthropological Lens*. London: Routledge.

Howe, P. D. (2011) 'Cyborg and Supercrip: the Paralympics technology and the (dis) empowerment of disabled athletes', *Sociology* 45(5): 868–882.

Howe, P. D. and Jones, C. (2006) 'Classification of disabled athletes: (dis)empowering the Paralympic practice community', *Sociology of Sport Journal* 23: 29–46.

IOC [International Olympic Committee]. (2003) *The Legacy of the Olympic Games 1984–2000 – International Symposium Lausanne, 2002*. Lausanne: International Olympic Committee.

IPC [International Paralympic Committee]. (2003) *The Paralympian: Newsletter of the International Paralympic Committee*. No 2. Bonn, Germany: International Paralympic Committee.

Leopkey, B. and Parent, M. M. (2012) 'Olympic games legacy: from general benefits to sustainable long-term legacy', *The International Journal of the History of Sport* 29(6): 924–943.

Lowe, M. (1999) *Inside the Sports Pages: Work Routines, Professional Ideologies and the Manufacture of Sports News*. Toronto: University of Toronto Press.

MacAloon, J. (2008) '"Legacy" as managerial/magical discourse in contemporary Olympic affairs', *The International Journal of the History of Sport* 24(14): 2060–2071.

Moss, S. (2009) 'Jimmy Carr: "I thought my Paralympics joke was totally acceptable"', *The Guardian*, 5 November 2009.

Powdermaker, H. (1966) *Stranger and Friend: The Way of an Anthropologist*. New York and London: Secker and Warberg.

Preuss, H. (2007) 'The conceptualisation and measurement of mega sport event legacies', *Journal of Sport & Tourism* 12(3–4): 207–227.

Pryor, M. (2004a) 'Lack of coverage undermines US Bid', *The Times*, 22 September 2004.

Shilling, C. (2003) *The Body and Social Theory* (2nd ed.). Sage: London.

Silva, C. F. and Howe, P. D. (2012) 'The (in)validity of Supercrip Representation of Paralympian athletes', *Journal of Sport and Social Issues* 36(2): 174–194.

Wacquant, L. (1995) 'Pugs at work: bodily capital and bodily labour among professional boxers', *Body and Society* 1(1): 65–93.

Wernick, A. (1991) *Promotional Culture: Advertising, Ideology and Symbolic Expression*. London: Sage.

P. David Howe is Reader in the Social Anthropology of Sport in the School of Sport, Exercise and Health Sciences at Loughborough University. David is a leading figure in socio-cultural analysis of Paralympic sport and holds a guest professorship at Katholieke Universiteit Leuven, Belgium, and an adjunct Professorship at Queen's University, Canada. Trained as a medical anthropologist, he author of *Sport, Professionalism and Pain: Ethnographies of Injury and Risk* (Routledge, 2004) and *The Cultural Politics of the Paralympic Movement: Through the Anthropological Lens* (Routledge, 2008).

Shane Kerr is an independent Sports Strategy Consultant. In 2016, Shane completed his doctoral research at Loughborough University on the sociological critique of London 2012's Paralympic Legacy. His doctoral research examined disability legacy strategies from multiple stakeholder perspectives including the media, corporate partners, government, disability and disability sport organisations. Shane now works in sports strategy, analysing sports bid strategies, sports businesses, start-ups and charities. Most recently Shane led the strategy analysis of the Saudi Arabian government's review of elite sport as part of their 2020 National Transformation plan.

13

Social Legacies of Olympic and Paralympic Games in East London

Ian Brittain and Leonardo Jose Mataruna-Dos-Santos

Introduction

This chapter presents findings from a research project[1] which evaluates the social legacy of the London 2012 Olympic and Paralympic Games in the five London Host Boroughs of Greenwich, Hackney, Newham, Tower Hamlets and Waltham Forest.[2] The research commenced in September 2013 and lasted for two years. This chapter was written just as initial evaluation of collected data had taken place and is,

---

[1] The research project 'From the East End of London to the Favelas of Rio de Janeiro: The relevance and transferability of the social legacy programmes of London 2012' was carried out as part of a Marie Curie International Incoming Fellowship by Dr Leonardo Mataruna from Brazil and supported by Dr Ian Brittain as his Scientist in Charge.

[2] A sixth Host Borough (Barking and Dagenham) was added by the UK government and the organising committee much later in the planning process after the Games had been awarded (GOV.UK; https://www.gov.uk/government/news/east-village-big-winner-at-london-planning-awards), but was not included in this research.

I. Brittain (✉) · L.J. Mataruna-Dos-Santos
Coventry University, Coventry, UK
e-mail: aa8550@coventry.ac.uk; mataruna@gmail.com

© The Author(s) 2017   **357**
P. Cohen, P. Watt (eds.), *London 2012 and the Post-Olympics City*,
DOI 10.1057/978-1-137-48947-0_13

therefore, based only upon a selection of key initial findings that may contribute to the knowledge pool surrounding the use of sporting and other mega-events as tools to bring about social change. This involves analysing the nexus between the impact of sport and other mega-events and issues of human security to produce new data concerning the use of sport and other mega-events as tools for the promotion of peace and development. The use of sporting and other mega-events to bring about transformation of socially deprived areas of major cities is becoming an increasingly important part of the raison d'être for hosting such events, especially given the immense costs involved and the current economic climate. The tax-paying public increasingly have to be persuaded of the benefits, beyond the event itself, to spend the nation's resources in this way. The central thesis of this research was, therefore, the examination of the impact of selected social legacies of the London 2012 Olympic and Paralympic Games and their transferability to the Rio de Janeiro 2016 Games. This research raises issues regarding the effectiveness of using sport and other mega-events to transform the lives of people living in socially deprived areas and whether any positive impacts seen as a result of such events in one area are replicable using the same or similar programmes in another city in another part of the world where the culture and the issues may be very different.

As stated before, the London 2012 Games were largely located in five London Host Boroughs to the east of London. The British government decided to locate the Games in this area of East London because it is an area of high social deprivation and the hope was to use the Games to regenerate the area. In the lead up to the Games, of the 354 English Local Authorities all five of the Host Boroughs are ranked inside the top 27 according to the Index of Multiple Deprivation (IMD), which covers seven main topic areas – income, employment, health, education and skills, housing, crime and living environment. Three of the Host Boroughs – Hackney (2nd), Tower Hamlets (3rd) and Newham (6th) – were ranked in the top six most deprived areas according to the IMD (MacRury and Poynter, 2009). In 2008 Stephen Timms, Member of Parliament for East Ham, wrote 'unemployment in my constituency – East Ham – is 7%. In West Ham it is 8% and in Tower Hamlets it is 9%, compared with a 3% rate across the country as a whole'. The five Host

Boroughs also have rising populations, a high percentage of young people, higher-than-average crime figures and a lack of affordable housing (Timms, 2008). As a result of the regeneration programmes bought about by the London 2012 Games, MacRury and Poynter (2009: 132) claim the area 'has entered the 21st century at the centre of the largest urban renewal in Europe'. The Host boroughs are home to 1.25 million people, approximately a sixth of London's total population. Collectively, the boroughs have twice the population of Glasgow, three times the population of Manchester and half again the population of Birmingham (Host Boroughs Unit, 2009).

Greater London Authority (GLA) data highlights the extreme levels of diversity present within the five boroughs and some of the key issues such as the high levels of unemployment, especially amongst the youth ranging from 20.5 to 32.7 per cent (GLA Intelligence, 2014). The extremely high multi-cultural mix amongst the population is clearly evident with the percentage of residents born abroad ranging from 31.6 per cent in Greenwich to 49.6 per cent in Newham and the percentage of people aged three plus whose first language is not English ranging from 16.9 per cent in Greenwich to 41.4 per cent in Newham. Average house prices in each of the boroughs range from 8.1 times average annual salary in Newham to 11.6 times average salary in Hackney. It is perhaps not surprising then that the proportion of people living in rented accommodation (local authority, housing association or private landlord) ranges from 49.8 per cent in Greenwich to 69.7 per cent in Newham (GLA Intelligence, 2014). Overall the figures paint a picture of a culturally diverse and economically stretched population.

Data Collection

Data was collected two years after the London 2012 Olympic and Paralympic Games had ended from across the five East London boroughs over a period of three months via the application of a questionnaire using both face-to-face interviews and focus groups. Data was collected by a team of up to seven Brazilian researchers who were in the UK as part of a Marie Curie International Research Staff Exchange

Scheme project managed by Dr Brittain. Interestingly, the fact that all the researchers were Brazilian appears to have aided the data collection process as many respondents who took part in the face-to-face interviews in the field commented that they were only willing to take part due to the fact that they wished to assist the people of Brazil so that they might not suffer the same perceived injustices they felt had been born upon them in the hosting of the London 2012 Games.

The questionnaire consisted of some demographic details (age, gender, borough lived in, etc.) followed by 11 questions that were a mixture of open-ended and tick-box answers. A purposive sampling approach was taken with the two main criteria being that participants were 18 years of age or over and that they lived in one of the Host Boroughs and had done so in the lead up to the Games. In total 1,046 fully completed questionnaires were collected with roughly 200 collected in each of the five Host Boroughs. Of the completed questionnaires, 46.2 per cent were completed by women and 53.8 per cent by men. A breakdown of the sample by borough, gender and average age can be seen in Table 13.1, which clearly shows that a good range of opinions were collected in each borough across all age groups and both genders.

Initial Findings

What follows are some of the initial findings from the data collection regarding a selection of the questions that were posed to the respondents.

Perceived Impact of Hosting the London 2012 Games

A joint report by HM Government and Mayor of London (2013: 33) entitled *Inspired by 2012* reiterated the claim that the 'London 2012 Games would be a catalyst for the revitalisation of the Lower Lea Valley' and states that there has been £6.5 billion of transport investment with overall plans for the development of 11,000 homes on the Queen Elizabeth Olympic Park (QEOP) and the creation of 10,000 jobs, with the goal of accelerating urban regeneration across East London.

Table 13.1 Breakdown of sample by borough, gender and average age

Newham

Age range	Men No.	Men Average age	Women No.	Women Average age	Combined No.	Combined Average age
18–24	9	21.56	18	20.17	27	20.86
25–44	44	33.40	55	33.61	99	33.50
45–64	31	53.42	30	55.59	61	54.51
65+	23	73.09	27	71.94	50	72.52
All	107	45.37	130	45.33	237	45.35

Greenwich

Age range	Men No.	Men Average age	Women No.	Women Average age	Combined No.	Combined Average age
18–24	14	20.79	17	20.12	31	20.45
25–44	34	32.97	42	34.34	76	33.66
45–64	32	55.06	25	55.80	57	55.43
65+	16	73.19	20	72.65	36	72.92
All	96	45.50	104	45.73	200	45.62

Tower Hamlets

Age range	Men No.	Men Average age	Women No.	Women Average age	Combined No.	Combined Average age
18–24	15	21.07	17	20.41	32	20.74
25–44	56	34.11	45	32.50	101	33.57
45–64	27	54.92	22	54.92	49	54.92
65+	10	71.50	8	76.00	18	73.75
All	108	45.24	92	45.96	200	45.6

Waltham Forest

Age range	Men No.	Men Average age	Women No.	Women Average age	Combined No.	Combined Average age
18–24	21	20.32	10	19.13	31	19.72
25–44	53	34.74	34	33.88	87	34.31
45–64	34	53.15	20	52.30	54	52.72
65+	16	71.86	14	75.13	30	73.49
All	124	45.02	78	45.11	202	45.06

Hackney

Age range	Men No.	Men Average age	Women No.	Women Average age	Combined No.	Combined Average age
18–24	25	21.28	8	21.13	33	21.20
25–44	62	32.90	32	34.52	94	33.57
45–64	36	51.62	32	51.64	68	56.05
65+	5	77.75	7	68.00	12	72.88
All	128	45.89	79	43.82	207	44.86

Five Boroughs combined

Age range	Men No.	Men Average age	Women No.	Women Average age	Combined No.	Combined Average age
18–24	84	21.00	70	20.19	154	20.59
25–44	249	33.62	208	33.77	457	33.72
45–64	160	53.63	129	54.05	289	54.73
65+	70	73.48	76	72.74	146	73.11
All	563	45.43	483	45.19	1046	45.31

The first question, therefore, that respondents were asked was whether they felt that significant changes had occurred within their borough as a result of hosting the London 2012 Olympic and Paralympic Games. In all ages and both genders the majority of respondents stated that they felt there had been major changes with 61.5 per cent of men and 65.4 per cent of women answering yes. The respondents were then asked to name some of the changes, both positive and negative, that they felt had occurred as a result of hosting the Games. Participants were not given any kind of list to select from and so could say whatever came into their heads. Answers were then grouped under appropriate headings, examples of which can be seen later. The top three answers, based on the number of times each issue was mentioned, by borough and gender can be seen in Table 13.2. It would appear that some of the answers given appear to have a somewhat tenuous link at best to the hosting of the 2012 Olympic and Paralympic Games and it is likely that they were present long before the Games, for example, traffic jams, drugs and crime and the cost of parking, although it is possible that there may have been a perceived increase in these issues as a result of an increase in the number of people being attracted to the area as a result of the regeneration that has occurred, the improved transport links and the addition of Europe's largest shopping mall – the Westfield Centre.

On the whole the same positive themes recurred throughout the five boroughs irrespective of gender. Regeneration of the area, the building of new housing stock and new sports facilities and increased job opportunities all featured heavily amongst the top answers given. However, just as there was relative uniformity amongst the boroughs in highlighting positive issues the same can also be seen in the negative issues highlighted. Almost without failure the increasingly high cost of living in the five boroughs was the number one issue raised by the respondents. According to the *Convergence Framework and Action Plan 2011–2015* (Growth Boroughs Unit, 2011), one of the main purposes of the legacy plans for London 2012 was to increase the number of affordable homes and reduce overcrowding. However, according to Blunden (2012) staging an Olympic Games and the associated

Table 13.2 Positive and negative changes witnessed by respondents as a result of hosting London 2012, by borough and gender

	Positives			Negatives		
	1	2	3	1	2	3
Hackney						
Male	Sports facilities	Regeneration	Transport	Cost of living	Jobs not permanent	Drugs and crime
Female	Regeneration	Sports facilities	Job opportunities/ transport	Cost of living	Noise and pollution	Drugs and crime
Total	Sports facilities	Regeneration	Transport	Cost of living	Drugs and crime	Noise and pollution
Newham						
Male	Regeneration	Job opportunities	Transport/new housing	Cost of living	Overcrowding	Drugs and crime
Female	Job opportunities	Regeneration	New housing	Cost of living/ overcrowding	Cost of living	Traffic jams
Combined	Regeneration/ job opportunities	Regeneration	New housing	Cost of living	Overcrowding	Drugs and crime
Greenwich						
Male	Sports facilities/ regeneration		New housing	Cost of living/over-crowding/lack of change		
Female	Regeneration	New housing/ tourism		Overcrowding	Cost of living/traffic jams	
Combined	Regeneration	Sports facilities	New housing	Overcrowding	Cost of living	Lack of change/ traffic jams

(continued)

Table 13.2 (continued)

	Positives			Negatives		
	1	2	3	1	2	3
Hackney						
Waltham Forest						
Male	Regeneration	New housing	Sports facilities	Cost of living	Noise and pollution	Overcrowding
Female	New housing/regeneration		Shopping	Cost of living	Noise and pollution/overcrowding/traffic jams/cost of parking/jobs not permanent	
Combined	Regeneration	New housing	Sports facilities	Cost of living	Noise and pollution	Overcrowding
Tower hamlets						
Male	Regeneration	New housing	Sports facilities/job opportunities	Cost of living	Jobs not permanent/traffic jams	
Female	Regeneration	New housing	Sports facilities	Cost of living	Overcrowding	Lack of investment/cost of parking
Combined	Regeneration	New housing	Sports facilities	Cost of living	Overcrowding	Traffic jams

regeneration of the host region can actually escalate housing costs (rental and purchase prices), and this has indeed occurred in East London as Chapter 4 discusses. In relation to other costs, Kennelly and Watt (2012) highlight increased food costs including fast food outlets in the Stratford area of Newham. As discussed earlier, one of the negative issues raised was the increased cost of parking. This was put down to new buildings being put up as part of the regeneration process taking away parking spaces. The lack of parking spaces combined with the increase number of people (and with them their vehicles) being attracted to the area by the new housing and jobs meaning that parking spaces are at a premium and so prices go up.

The increased cost of living was closely followed by the issue of overcrowding, although what was meant by overcrowding actually depended upon which borough the respondent was from. In Newham it actually just referred to the sheer number of people visiting or working in the area on a daily basis, with the increased transport links and the building of the Westfield shopping centre bringing thousands of extra visitors a day to the area to either work or to shop. However, in Greenwich, Waltham Forest and Tower Hamlets the respondents referred to overcrowding in terms of housing, or rather a lack of available housing stock for the number of people wishing to live in these areas combined with a loss of green spaces to developers making the areas feel cramped. In Hackney the issue of overcrowding didn't even make it into the top three negative issues nor was new housing mentioned as a positive. These findings appear to fit with the comments of Poynter (2013: 511), who stated that 'Hackney and Newham have a higher proportion of local authority housing stock than the rest of London and England' and that Hackney has a higher percentage of Registered Social Landlords compared to the rest of London and England. This issue of overcrowding is inherently tied up with some of the other negative issues raised around noise, pollution and traffic jams. The respondents of Newham and Hackney also highlighted drugs and crime amongst their top three negative issues. Respondents in several boroughs also felt that the lack of permanency of many of the jobs provided as a result of hosting the Games was also a major negative issue.

Impact on Respondents' Lives and Communities

Respondents were asked whether they felt the Games had any impact on their own lives or the lives of their communities. In a straight yes-no choice the majority (63.3 per cent) claimed that they had witnessed significant positive changes; see Table 13.3. It should also be noted that females (65.4 per cent) were slightly more positive than males (61.5 per cent).

Perhaps unsurprisingly there was a vast range of answers to this question. We will now depict this range via a selection of quotes, both positive and negative, that depict the range of viewpoints put forward. One of the key issues highlighted in Table 13.2 was that of jobs and the fact that many of them were only temporary. One participant, who was fortunate enough to get a more permanent position before the Games, highlighted how things had turned out very differently for many of his friends.

> Yes, I have had a new job since before the Games started. But my friends worked only during the games and after they lost their jobs, because they were only contracted for a short time period. Temporary jobs may help some people but they do not change lives. (Hackney, M, 42)

With reference to previous Olympic Games, Malfas et al. (cited in Horne, 2007) claim that the majority of the jobs created were low paid and short term. Pillay and Bass (2008), writing ahead of the FIFA World Cup in South Africa in 2010, expected that the majority of job opportunities would be mainly short term, which would do little to help reduce unemployment rates. According to Carlsen and Taylor

Table 13.3 Participants witnessing significant changes in their lives or the lives of their communities as a result of hosting London 2012 (%)

	Yes	No
Male	61.5	38.5
Female	65.4	34.6
Combined	63.3	36.7

(2003), mega-events have often been cited as being a way forward for creating jobs; however, they claim this is more through the work experience, qualifications and skills gained leading to an improved CV, allowing for applications to more permanent positions. In fact, the majority of new permanent jobs in the area are more likely to be a result of other developments such as the Westfield shopping centre, which the Chairman of the Westfield Group predicted would bring 10,000 permanent new jobs to the area (Kennelly and Watt, 2012: 154), rather than from the event itself.

Although the upgraded transport system was seen as a great benefit and asset to the community, one female resident of Hackney felt that it has actually come at a great cost, with a loss of diversity in the products and facilities available, meaning that the cost of living for members of the local community had increased whilst the choices available to them had decreased. This highlights how the impacts of the Games can be perceived, at the same time, as both positive and negative.

> I believe that the community now has access to an efficient transport system. The problem in my view is the loss of our popular market. It destroyed people's lives. Sellers on the one hand lost the space to work and people have now lost cheap prices, diversity of products and facilities. (Hackney, F, 54)

As highlighted in the HM Government and Mayor of London (2013: 30) legacy report, 'sport and healthy living represent an investment in the long-term health of the nation. Efforts have been made to ensure a legacy which reaches beyond sport, to help drive change in the nation's health and the way people live'. They would certainly therefore be happy to hear the following quote from a woman in Waltham Forrest: 'now I do more exercise to improve my health motivated by the publicity to do sport' (Waltham Forest, F, 54).

The Paralympics had a profound effect on one elderly woman from Newham who after watching them on television was inspired never to complain again about the small things in life that tend to upset so many people. Although disability activists might decry the choice of wording used by the woman as being from the supercrip model (Silva and Howe,

2012; Braye et al., 2013), it is likely that the British government and the International Paralympic Committee would claim that this quote would highlight the possibility for the Paralympic Games to change attitudes towards people with disabilities, which is one of the Paralympic values (Equality) (IPC website, 2015).

> Absolutely! The Paralympics changed my perception of the world. Watching them on TV, I saw that I am a loser when I cry about little things in my life. Everybody can do something productive, can make a difference and be happy about others victories. They are Super-heroes and surprised me with their abilities and happiness. It's fantastic when people change your mind because they proved something unexpected. I will support the Paralympics forever and never complain about small things again. (Newham, F, 69)

Another woman from Newham highlighted the positive impact upon the local community of the infrastructure changes that had occurred as a result of the Games coming to London: 'the Olympics changed the community bringing a new shopping centre, an efficient transport system and a leisure centre' (Newham, F, 42).

However, whilst acknowledging the new construction projects and regeneration, a male participant from Tower Hamlets felt that these had come at the cost of greatly increased prices and that much of the new infrastructure (e.g. hotels) was of benefit more to visitors to the area than those who actually live there.

> To be honest, I have not seen any evidences of changes in my life. For my community they made new arrangements, constructions and regeneration (new schools, hospitals, houses) along with exorbitant prices and infra-structure for visitors. However, only a portion of the people that live here really felt any impact from the Games. (Tower Hamlets, M, 39)

The next three questions about whether respondents felt part of the Games, whether they watched the Games and whether they felt con-sulted and listened to during the lead up to the Games all appear to be interrelated and highlight the importance of carefully consulting and

Table 13.4 Participants who felt part of the Games before, during and after the Games took place (%)

	Before		During		After		
	Yes	No	Yes	No	Yes	No	Never
Male	22.6	77.4	52.6	47.4	21.5	78.5	41.6
Female	23.8	76.2	57.3	42.7	24.4	75.6	36.8
Combined	23.1	76.9	54.8	45.2	22.8	77.2	39.4

listening to the local community in the preparation for a Games if the aim is to truly get them to feel involved in and part of the Games experience.

Did Respondents Feel Involved in the Games?

All of the respondents were asked if they felt part of the Games before, during and after they occurred. Before and after the Games around 80 per cent of respondents stated that they did not feel part of the Games, whereas during the Games around 55 per cent said they did feel part of the Games, possibly drawn in by the party atmosphere that enveloped London during the Games period. However, overall 39 per cent of all respondents stated that they never felt part of the Games at any point in time. Interestingly the only borough that felt overall that they weren't part of the Games during Games time was Newham, where the QEOP is and where 58 per cent of males and 51.5 per cent overall did not feel part of the Games during Games time (see Table 13.4).

Did Respondents Watch the Games?

Asked whether or not they watched the Games in some form 25.9 per cent claimed to have attended live at some point. This figure ranged from 30 per cent in Hackney to only 22.8 per cent in Newham, which may be a further reason why the majority of respondents from Newham claimed not to have felt part of the Games during Games time as highlighted in the previous question. Overall, 88.1 per cent followed

Table 13.5 Whether participants actually watched the Games and in what format (%)

	Venue		Television		Internet		
	Yes	No	Yes	No	Yes	No	Not watched
Male	27.9	72.1	87.7	12.3	19.5	80.5	12.6
Female	23.6	76.4	88.6	11.4	15.5	84.5	9.3
Combined	25.9	74.1	88.1	11.9	17.7	82.3	11.1

the Games on television and 17.7 per cent had used the internet to follow proceedings. Only 11.1 per cent claimed to have not watched the Games at all; see Table 13.5. However, the number of participants who claimed not to have watched the Games at all did vary widely by borough with 16.5 per cent of respondents in Greenwich claiming to have not watched at all down to 3.5 per cent of respondents in Waltham Forest. The fact that only 25.9 per cent of the participants were able to watch the Games live at a venue, whether due to cost or availability of tickets, may partly explain why many of the participants did not feel part of the Games as highlighted in Table 13.4.

Did Respondents Feel Their Opinions Were Consulted or Listened to in the Lead Up to the Games?

Asked whether they felt that there were opportunities for them to express their opinions in the planning for and lead up to the Games, the great majority of respondents answered no (75.1 per cent); see Table 13.6. It should also be noted that more females (29.4 per cent) felt that their

Table 13.6 Did respondents feel their opinions were consulted or listened to in the lead up to the Games? (%)

	Yes	No
Male	21.0	79.0
Female	29.4	70.6
Combined	24.9	75.1

Table 13.7 Consultations carried out in the lead up to London 2012

Type of consultation	Number of consultations
Public drop-in sessions	44
Community meetings and events	38
Pubic information displays	44
Stakeholder meetings and events	95
Total	221

Source: MacRury (2013: 153)

opinions had actually been listened to than males (21.0 per cent). These responses may also partly further explain why many of the participants did not feel part of the Games as highlighted in Table 13.4.

According to MacRury (2013), the Olympic Games Impact (OGI) study that is required to be filled out by all host city organising committees requires them to document engagement and consultation with the local community as part of the OGI process. The pre-Games report identifies 221 consultation opportunities in London linked to the plans for the Games. These are broken down as follows in Table 13.7.

However, just because 'consultations' were held this does not automatically mean that the opinions garnered from such events were actually listened to or acted upon or that the format of the consultation was actually an effective way of engaging with the local community in question. When discussing why they felt their opinions had or had not been listened to a large range of reasons were given. We will now depict this range via a selection of quotes, both positive and negative, that depict the range of viewpoints put forward. One male from Greenwich felt that as all the major decisions were being taken by people who were not from the area and had no real understanding of the needs of the local community they, therefore, failed to recognise these needs when making decisions:

> Your opinion, my opinion, our opinion, doesn't change the world, doesn't move the economy. The people in charge of the event are coming from other regions to here, other cities, other countries and perhaps from another planet, because they did not recognise the real needs of this part of the city. (Greenwich, M, 46)

A female participant from Greenwich actually attended one of the Council meetings, but felt that all decisions had already been made before the meeting took place and that she and the others present were there simply to be told what was going to happen: 'I went in one of the preliminary Council meetings and they spoke unilaterally. We could just listen and make no comments' (Greenwich, F, 54).

Another man from Newham highlighted the issue of language and successful communication between the decision makers and the local community. He felt that his poor command of English prevented him from successfully understanding and getting his views across, although he also expressed a certain lack of trust of the promises made by politicians:

> Yes, but I can't express my expectations as I wished. English is my problem and also for most of the people here. The problem is the same in every place. The politician promises, the population trust but the results are still the same. (Newham, M, 43)

Another woman from Newham also highlighted the issue of successful communication, given the range of non-native English speakers living in the area and suggested that other forms of communication might be more successful in achieving mutual understanding. It also may partly explain why a majority of participants felt that their opinions were not consulted or listened to.

> In Newham is difficult to find people whose first language is English. We have more than 200 dialects used here and sometimes videos, images, and cartoons are more informative than words. This gap between informer and receptor causes a range of problems for understanding. (Newham, F, 28)

One deaf female participant from Tower Hamlets felt completely isolated from the decision-making process and described how she took to social media to make herself heard as this is a format she felt the deaf community could better communicate with and be heard. In many ways this is a similar communication issue to the one raised by the non-native English speakers earlier, especially as there are those in the deaf community that consider themselves as a linguistic minority rather than having a form of disability (Bramwell et al., 2000).

No I haven't. I used the social media to beat the Games and made my protest on the internet. In this way, more people could hear the deaf community and me. (Tower Hamlets, F [deaf], 26)

Overall the underlying experience of these respondents appears to be in line with Poynter's (2009: 147) claim that for local communities 'mega-events bring a form of urban regeneration that happens to them rather than being influenced by them; with tokenistic forms of community consultation being the predominant form of local participation'.

The next two questions about whether the respondents felt the Games had been essential for development and whether they were satisfied with the legacies left behind as a result of hosting the Games have almost identical positive responses and appear to indicate a certain amount of interrelatedness between the two issues.

Did Respondents Agree or Disagree That Hosting the London 2012 Games Was Essential for Development?

Asked whether they felt hosting the Games was essential for development of the area, 63 per cent of males and 66 per cent of females (64 per cent overall) felt that hosting the Games was indeed essential for development of the area; see Table 13.8. This result was roughly consistent for all five boroughs and both genders ranging from 52 per cent overall agreement in Tower Hamlets to 80 per cent agreement in Newham. This difference in overall satisfaction between the residents of Tower Hamlets and Newham is possibly a reflection of where the majority of the infrastructural developments related to the Games occurred.

Table 13.8 Was hosting the London 2012 Games essential for development? (%)

	Agree	Disagree	Neutral
Male	62.9	33.2	3.9
Female	65.6	30.6	3.8
Combined	64.1	32.0	3.9

Overall Were Respondents Satisfied or Dissatisfied with the Legacies or Heritage of London 2012?

Asked whether, overall, they were satisfied or dissatisfied with the legacies left behind by the London 2012 Olympic and Paralympic Games there appears to have been a strong feeling of satisfaction with 63.6 per cent of males and 67.7 per cent of females (giving an overall of 65.5 per cent) stating that they were satisfied with the legacies that they perceived from the hosting of the London 2012 Games. This result was roughly consistent for all five boroughs and both genders ranging from 53 per cent overall satisfaction in Tower Hamlets to 75 per cent satisfaction in Newham; see Table 13.9. This difference in overall satisfaction between the residents of Tower Hamlets and Newham is again possibly a reflection of where the majority of the infrastructural developments related to the Games occurred and, therefore, the overall tangible legacy perceived by local residents.

Overall it can be seen that the majority of respondents in all five boroughs felt that hosting the Games was essential for the development of the area and that almost exactly the same majority felt satisfied overall with legacies left behind as a result. We have been unable to find a similar survey of local residents with which to compare these answers, but it appears clear that in the view of these respondents at least hosting the Games in 2012 had been an overall positive experience bringing much needed regeneration, housing and jobs to the area. Even if these things did come at the price of an increased cost of living and overcrowding, for these respondents at least it appears to have been worth it.

Table 13.9 Were respondents satisfied or dissatisfied overall with the legacies or heritage of London 2012? (%)

	Satisfied	Dissatisfied	Neutral
Male	63.6	21.3	15.1
Female	67.7	20.3	12.0
Combined	65.5	20.8	13.7

What Advice Would Respondents Give Brazilian's Living in the Favelas Regarding the Hosting of the Olympic and Paralympic Games in 2016?

One of the aims of this piece of research was to try and ascertain whether the social legacy programmes had any relevance to the favelas of Rio de Janeiro – the host of the next summer Olympic and Paralympic Games in 2016. We, therefore, asked the respondents if they had any advice for the inhabitants of Rio's favelas in the lead up to 2016. Later we highlight a cross section of typical responses from participants.

One male participant from Greenwich encouraged the inhabitants of Rios favelas to take advantage of the commercial opportunities that the Games will bring to the city and seize the opportunity to make some money out of the Games. It is unclear whether his claim that the 'Olympics is for everybody' refers to the spectacle of the Games or the opportunity to make money!

> Sport is a business. However my message to the people is to make money with the Games. Push the informal commercialization into the favelas. Try to mix the favelas and city with the same atmosphere, sentiments and expectation. The Olympics is for everybody. (Greenwich, M, 49)

The next comment by another male participant in Greenwich encourages the inhabitants of Rio to use the opportunity of the Games to highlight the social problems in the city through protest, which they indeed have (see Chapter 14). The last sentence of their comment would appear to suggest that their own experience, or at least opinion, of the Games in London was not a happy one.

> I expect the Brazilians to make protests in the street against the government. Take to the streets to highlight your problems. Don't be quiet, because the Games will come, use you and then spit on you. (Greenwich, M, 33)

One male resident from Newham suggested that the inhabitants of Rio should do everything they can to learn about the legacy promises being made for the Games in Rio as early as they can, possibly to ensure that these promises can be monitored and those who made the promises held to account: 'Open your eyes for the promises. Ask about the legacies to be delivered before the start of the Games' (Newham, M, 52).

On a more positive note a male participant from Waltham Forest highlighted the importance of opportunities for people to get involved in sport, especially people with disabilities as they felt that the Paralympics in London had clearly demonstrated the positive impact of such opportunities.

> Make opportunities for people to be more involved in the actions and involved with sports and include people with disabilities. The Paralympics are a good example of successful practices. (Waltham Forest, M, 37)

This idea was reiterated by a female participant from Tower Hamlets who also highlighted the importance of a re-distribution of the sports equipment used at Rio 2016 to benefit people across the city as well as continued use of the Games facilities by the local community as a way of improving the health of all citizens.

> Use the facilities left from the Games as the people of Stratford have done. Exercise for health is important and every place in the host city should receive a part of the sports equipment and facilities to improve the health of all people. (Tower Hamlets, F, 39)

A male participant from Hackney raised the issue of social inequalities and the need for change, something that is equally relevant to both London and Rio: 'social changes are necessary to have a more equal society and offer job opportunities for youths' (Hackney, M, 27).

On a final positive note a woman from Hackney highlighted the unique experience and atmosphere of hosting the Games: 'I suggest the people [of Rio] leave their houses and go into the city to experience the emotion of the Games and the unique experience. This is a once in a lifetime thing' (Hackney, F, 57).

Discussion

Overall what these initial findings appear to highlight, in general and with limited exceptions, is the conformity of perceptions across the five boroughs irrespective of age or gender about the social impacts of the London 2012 Paralympic Games. Regeneration, new housing stock (despite the apparent increased costs of both rents and purchase prices witnessed in the region), sports facilities and job opportunities were all seen as positive outcomes and the increased cost of living, overcrowding, noise and pollution and traffic jams were all seen as negative impacts of the Games, which could all possibly be results of the regeneration attracting even more people to the area. Perhaps more interesting and possibly a little surprising is the number of people who felt that as individuals that they personally hadn't benefitted from the Games taking place, but at the same time agreed that the Games were both essential for the development of the area and were generally satisfied with the legacies or outcomes of the Games, despite the perceived negative impacts that came with it.

There also appears to be a general perception that although in some cases they felt able to put their opinions across in the lead up to the Games the majority appeared to believe that their opinions were not really listened to. Some even suggested that these opportunities were more PR exercises rather than a genuine attempt to listen to and include the opinions and needs of the local community, with the needs of big business taking precedence over all else. Amongst those who felt that they didn't feel able to put their opinions forward perhaps the most interesting issue raised was that of language. With English being a second language for nearly half of residents in Newham, where the QEOP was situated, understanding what is being suggested and then making your opinions understood proved very difficult, if not impossible, for a large proportion of the residents.

This perceived lack of inclusion in the planning process is clearly demonstrated in the number of people who did not feel part of the Games in either the lead up to or after the Games were over. However, the perceived party atmosphere of the Games and the opportunity to follow the Games and be surrounded by thousands of people from all over the world may well have given a large number of people a greater sense of being part of the Games whilst they were on. This does not, however, explain why the majority of residents of Newham didn't feel part of the Games whilst they were on. It is possible that as the QEOP is in Newham and so this is where the majority of spectators congregated that the overcrowding and difficulties in getting around may have made local residents feel somewhat trapped in their own homes.

The fact that so few residents attended any of the Games events in person (25.9 per cent) may possibly be due to a combination of the cost of the tickets and their availability combined with the overall poverty and cost of living within the five boroughs. This in turn may well be part of the reason why people claimed not to have felt part of the Games when they were on, particularly in Newham, as they could either not afford or simply were unsuccessful in obtaining tickets for an event taking place in their own backyard. In hindsight it would have been interesting to find out from those who did attend an event whether it was an Olympic or a Paralympic event, where the tickets were much cheaper, although almost as difficult to obtain at times. What did come through from the research, however, is the genuine surprise, pleasure and even inspiration drawn by many of the residents from witnessing the exploits of the Paralympians.

Conclusion

Overall, if claims for any genuine kind of social legacy are to be perceived by local residents, what the initial findings of this research appear to highlight are the importance of listening to the local people that live in areas impacted by the Games in order to best understand their long-term needs and their anxieties surrounding the hosting of such sport mega-events. This also needs to be communicated in languages and in formats that are easily accessible and understood within such a culturally and linguistically diverse community. The need for long-term job opportunities rather than temporary short-term jobs and the inclusion of the local culture and the local community in the planning of any social legacy programmes following on from the event can help overcome some of the feelings of marginalisation felt by local residents.

References

Blunden, H. (2012) 'The Olympic Games and housing', in H. Lenskyj and S. Wagg (eds.) The Palgrave Handbook of Olympic Studies. Palgrave MacMillan.

Bramwell, R., Harrington, F. and Harris, J. (2000) 'Deafness - disability or linguistic minority?' British Journal of Midwifery 8(4): 222–224.

Braye, S., Dixon, K. and Gibbons, T. (2013) '"A mockery of equality": An exploratory investigation into disabled activists' views of the Paralympic Games', Disability & Society, Vol. 28(7); 984–996.

Carlsen J. and Taylor, A. (2003) 'Mega-events and urban renewal: the case of the Manchester 2002 Commonwealth Games', Event Management 8(1): 15–22.

GLA Intelligence. (2014) ONS 2013 mid-year population estimates.

GOV.UK (2015) https://www.gov.uk/government/news/east-village-big-win ner-at-london-planning-awards

Growth Boroughs Unit. (2011) Convergence Framework and Action Plan 2011–2015. London: Growth Boroughs Unit.

HM Government and Mayor of London, 2013, Inspired by 2012: The legacy from the London 2012 Olympic and Paralympic Games. https://www.gov. uk/government/uploads/system/uploads/attachment_data/file/224148/ 2901179_OlympicLegacy_acc.pd)

Horne, J. (2007), The Four 'Knowns' of sports mega-events. Leisure Studies, Vol. 26 (1); 81–96.

Host Boroughs Unit. (2009) Strategic Regeneration Framework: An Olympic Legacy for the Host Boroughs. London: Host Boroughs Unit.

IPC. (2015) 'The IPC – who we are – about us – Paralympic values – equality', http://www.paralympic.org/the-ipc/about-us, accessed 25 August 2015.

Kennelly, J. and Watt, P. (2012) 'Seeing Olympic effects through the eyes of marginally housed youth: changing places and the gentrification of east London', Visual Studies 27(2): 151–160.

MacRury, I. (2013) 'Involving East London communities: the evocative Olympic Games and the emergence of a prospective "legacy"', in V. Girginov (eds.) Handbook of the London 2012 Olympic and Paralympic Games (Volume One). London: Routledge.

MacRury, I. and Poynter, G., (2009), London's Olympic Legacy: A "Thinkpiece" report prepared for the OECD and Department for Communities and Local Government.

Malfas, M., Theodoraki, E. and Houlihan, B. (2004) The Four 'Knowns' of sports mega-events. Leisure Studies, Vol. 26 (1); 81–96.

Pillay, U. and Bass, O. (2008) 'Mega-events as a response to poverty reduction: the 2010 FIFA World Cup and its urban development implications', Urban Forum 19: 329, http://link.springer.com/article/10.1007/s12132-008-9034-9

Poynter, G. (2009) 'The 2012 Olympic games and the reshaping of East London', in R. Imrie, L. Lees and M. Raco (eds.) Regenerating London. London: Routledge.

Poynter, G. (2013) 'The Olympics: East London's renewal and legacy', in H. Lenskyj and S. Wagg (eds.) The Palgrave Handbook of Olympic Studies. Basingstoke: Palgrave MacMillan.

Silva, C. F. and Howe, P. D. (2012) 'The (in)validity of Supercrip Representation of Paralympian athletes', Journal of Sport and Social Issues 36(2): 174–194.

Timms, S. (2008) 'The 2012 Olympic games and the communities of East London', 21st Century Society 3(3): 313–317.

Ian Brittain is a Research Fellow in the Centre for Business in Society at Coventry University. His research focuses upon historical, sociological and sports management aspects of disability and Paralympic sport. He is an experienced researcher who is Co-ordinator and Co-Principal Investigator on an €853k Marie Curie International Research Staff Exchange Scheme project around managing the impact of mega-events and acted as Scientist in Charge for two Marie Curie International Incoming Fellowships for Dr Leonardo Mataruna from Brazil and Prof. Jill Le Clair from Canada. His books include *The Paralympic Games Explained* (2nd Ed.) with Routledge, *From Stoke Mandeville to Sochi: A History of the Summer and Winter Paralympic Games* with Common Ground Publishing, *The Palgrave Handbook of Paralympic Studies* (Co-edited with Aaron Beacom) due out in 2017, and *Legacies of Mega-events: Fact or Fairy Tales?* (Co-edited with Jason Bocarro, Terri Byers & Kamila Swart) also due out in 2017 with Routledge.

Leonardo Jose Mataruna-Dos-Santos is Associate Research and Marie Curie Fellow in the Centre for Trust, Peace and Social Relation at Coventry University. He is also Visiting Lecturer at Anglia Ruskin University in the United Kingdom, Visiting Researcher at Federal University of Rio de Janeiro in Brazil, and Visiting Professor at Universidad de Occidente in Mexico. He is licensee 1st Lieutenant of the Brazilian Navy and is part of Brazilian Judo Confederation. He attended as part of the Judo team the Olympics of Sydney 2000, Athens 2004, Beijing 2008, London 2012 and Rio 2016; the Paralympic

Games of Athens 2004 as coach and, Beijing 2008, London 2012 and Rio 2016 as journalist (commentator of SPORTV Channel); and the Winter Olympics of Torino 2006, Vancouver 2010 and Sochi 2014, as scientist and observer. He is Member of the Brazilian Olympic Academy, member of the Brazilian Pierre de Coubertin Committee and Director of International Relation of International Federation of Physical Education - FIEP. His key research interests in the legacies of Olympic and Paralympic Games, Mega Events, Social Media, e-Sport, Sport for Peace, Innovation and new technologies for sport.

Part IV

From London 2012 to Rio 2016 and Tokyo 2020

14

The Rio Dossier: The Exclusion Games

Phil Cohen and Paul Watt

World Cup and Olympics Popular Committee of Rio de Janeiro
State and local authorities should refrain from forced evictions in the
preparation for mega-events. Where evictions are justified, they should
be undertaken in full compliance with the relevant provisions of
international human rights law. (United Nations Human Rights
Council, 2009)

Editors' Introduction[1]

What follows is an extract from the fourth report of the Popular
Committee on Mega Events and Human Rights, which was established

---

[1] This introduction draws on text from Ian Brittain and Leonardo Mataruna.

P. Cohen (✉)
University of East London, London, United Kingdom
e-mail: pcohen763@hotmail.co.uk

P. Watt
Department of Geography, Birkbeck,
University of London, London, United Kingdom
e-mail: p.watt@bbk.ac.uk

© The Author(s) 2017
P. Cohen, P. Watt (eds.), *London 2012 and the Post-Olympics City*,
DOI 10.1057/978-1-137-48947-0_14

in Rio de Janeiro in the run up to the 2014 World Cup and which has been at the forefront of coordinating popular education about and resistance to the 2016 Games. The Report, like the committee which produced it, draws on the work of a broad coalition of progressive forces in the city and brings together the methods of academics and activists in an exemplary fashion. The local importance of these reports has to be understood against the background of the lack of information, and even dis-information, about the impact of the Games on its host communities in the favelas, on the part of both the Brazilian government and the city authorities.

Jules Boykoff, one of the most sophisticated opponents of Olympic-led urban regeneration, recently compared Rio 2016 with London 2012, in terms of its displacement effect on working-class housing and jobs and accelerated gentrification. Yet his critique of what he calls 'celebration capitalism' and the cultures of resistance it has provoked (Boykoff, 2013, 2014) does not fully take into account the fact that the support for sport, and indeed for the Sporting Spectacle generated by mega-events, is concentrated amongst the most deprived and marginalised sections of the host communities precisely because it represents a principle of hope not otherwise available in their everyday lives. It may, of course, turn out to be a false hope and it is for that very reason that urban social movements which focus on the negative regeneration impacts can take root where and whenever popular frustration, disillusion and disap-pointment with the Olympic project wells up.

The report of the Popular Committee does not fall into the Olympophobic trap. Its opposition is not to the inspirational and even utopian principles of the Games and its Legacy Ideal, but to its dystopian practical outcome, the comprehensive failure of Brazil's political class and the Rio authorities in particular, to live up to egalitarian and internation-alist principles and to carry them over from the sporting arena to the city itself. As well as providing a devastating critique of the delivery authorities and a close documentation of the disastrous consequences of their policies for Rio's urban poor, the dossier also outlines a manifesto which seeks to use the Olympics as a platform for alternative planning initiatives based on democratic deliberation, transparency and the people's needs.

In comparison with London 2012, the governance and delivery of the Rio Games are mired in concealment and corruption. By the same token, the big difference in the response of the people of East London to the Olympics, compared to that of the favelistas of Rio, comes from the fact that the scale of displacement was far less and that, however cynical they may have been about the legacy promises, the failure to deliver on them would not have such a widespread or catastrophic effects (Cohen, 2013). In London protest was confined to a relatively small number of those whose lives and livelihoods were directly impacted (Boykoff, 2014). These included, for example, taxi drivers excluded from the exclusive Olympics lanes (Boykoff, 2014), the displaced residents from the Clays Lane housing estate (Cheyne, 2009; see Chapter 8) and residents from the threatened Carpenters housing estate (Watt, 2013; see Chapter 4). In addition, there was a dissenting intelligentsia of artists, writers and environmentalists, who tended to be concentrated in nearby Hackney Wick, on the edges of the Olympic Park (Powell and Marrero-Guillamón, 2012). In Rio, in contrast, the regeneration programme directly affects the whole favela population of the city, at a time when popular distrust of the country's corrupt political class has led to mass demonstrations (Jovchelovitch, 2015; Anderson, 2016).

The bid for the Rio Games was used by the government led by President Lula as a political instrument to implement an economic policy which aimed to combine payoffs to the business elite with dividends for the poor. In delivering this aim, the Worker's Party quickly became enmeshed in the culture of bribery and kickbacks which is endemic to the way politics as well as business is done in Brazil. While his party remained in hock to the big corporations and construction companies, for whom the advent of the mega-events was an unexpected windfall, Lula and the mayor of Rio launched a 'war against poverty' that quickly turned into a war against the poor.

Urban violence has been a serious problem in Brazil for the last half-century, and Rio de Janeiro has been no exception (Stahlberg, 2012). Homicides are the main cause of death for 15–44 year olds and Rio has one of the highest homicide rates in Brazil. Research carried out in the favelas by the London School of Economics and UNESCO concluded that security is a key issue and plays a major role in the way people who live in the favelas are socialised. There exist complex relationships between the residents of the favelas, the police and the drug traffickers. The researchers found that the centrality of drug trade is unequivocal and has been provider, legislator and organiser of everyday life in favelas over decades, offering a parallel system of rules for behaviour as well as a possible career choice for many. In contrast the police, as the main representative of the State in the favelas, are often seen by those living there as persecutory and aggressive, making no differentiation between the everyday inhabitants of the favelas and the drug dealers and other criminals.

In 2009 the Brazilian government made a public announcement on television and radio, possibly prompted by the award of the 2014 FIFA World Cup and the 2016 Olympic and Paralympic Games, that they would be instigating a new kind of police force, adopting foreign methods to combat social problems and occupy territories dominated by criminal organisations, that is, the favelas. They set up Police Pacification Units, whose purpose, is (i) to take back state control over communities currently under strong influence of ostensibly armed criminals; (ii) give back to the local population peace and public safety, which are necessary for the integral exercise and development of citizenship; and (iii) contribute to breaking with the logic of 'war' that currently exists in Rio de Janeiro. According to Rodrigues (2014) there are currently 37 Police Pacification Units operating in Rio, with 9,073 Military Police in 252 favelas and in the pacification process the local government has tried to contribute to the consolidation of the peace process and the promotion of local citizenship in pacified territories through the promotion of urban, social and economic development and by attempting to integrate these areas into the city as a whole (RIO+Social, 2015). That is the rhetoric of regeneration. The reality is that every single one of the favelas that have come under 'pacification' is on or around one of the four venue zones for the Rio 2016 Olympic and Paralympic Games, which raises the question of who the pacification process is really meant to benefit – those who live in the favelas or visitors to and people living in areas of the venue zones outside the favelas? This is the starting point for the work of the Popular Committee of Mega Events and Human Rights, excerpted below (Fig. 14.1).

Fig. 14.1   Rio and the Olympics

The Rio Context

The sporting mega-events in Rio de Janeiro marked the return of the most violent form of attack on housing rights in the city. A coalition of political forces, added to the interests of large building companies, accelerated the 'social cleansing' of prime locations in the city and its surrounding areas, converting them into new profitable construction sites for middle and upper-class housing developments. It is a policy of relocation of the city's poorest population in the service of real estate interests and business opportunities, accompanied by violent and illegal actions. Related developments include new sporting facilities, renovation of existing sporting equipment, infrastructure for urban mobility (modernisation and expansion of the Underground, construction of bus corridors and urban transportation systems, road works and renovations at the International Airport Tom Jobim) and urban restructuring projects.

This report focuses on the evicted communities and what happened to the areas they occupied. It presents the situation of communities which are threatened with removal, and who are facing uncertainties, lack of information and psychological terrorism promoted by City Hall. These are dramatic cases, in which City Hall tries to defeat residents through weariness, the spreading of lies and even denying the residents the right to defence.

The data collected in this report reveals a situation of severe violations of human rights. The lack of access to information and social data is also serious. The failure in presenting information by the public authorities may come from changes in the development plans after public hearings and public bidding processes, but it can also be interpreted as part of a strategy to increase psychological pressure to hinder resistance movements, or even as a mechanism to cover up potential illegalities in transactions.

The withholding of information and the absence of a democratic public debate reinforce these circumstances where the most vulnerable lose the little they have achieved in the daily struggle for access to the city. The governmental attitude is, in itself, a form of rights violation. It is clear that the need to attract inward investment, strongly advertised by state and municipal governments in relation to both the 2014 World Cup and the 2016 Olympic Games, has been as an important element in the expulsion of the poor from prime locations, such as Barra da Tijuca and Recreio districts, or from areas which are scheduled for public redevelopment, such as the districts of Vargem Grande, Jacarepaguá, Curicica, Centro and Maracanã. In these districts City Hall acts as a popular housing destruction machine opening up areas for real estate exploitation. The majority of evictions are focused on areas with the largest increases in house prices.

Public investments in transportation (BRTs) privileged these same areas, multiplying opportunities for other investment and for financial rewards in the construction of luxury housing for the middle and upper classes, and for commercial properties. As for the buildings destined for athletes and sporting facilities – the Athletes Village at Riocentro and the Olympic Park – these will be transformed into luxury residential developments after the games, to be traded by construction companies which are partners of municipal and state governments (Figure 14.2).

In the case of residential complexes built by the programme *Minha Casa, Minha Vida* (My House, My Life), which aims to house the displaced population, these were directed towards better off families

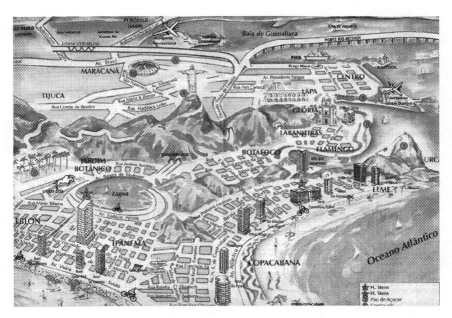

Fig. 14.2   Rio's favelas

with income three times the minimum wage and are mostly not located within the regeneration areas created by the World Cup and Olympics investments, but in the suburbs of the city, areas which have very poor public services and a precarious urban infrastructure. It is important to point out that, in some cases, the absence of public services is caused by the arrival of an enormous number of people without a corresponding expansion of services.

Four questions are brought to light by this Dossier, which contradict the official discourse of the International Olympic Committee, the federal and state governments and, mainly, Rio de Janeiro's City Hall, and deserve to be especially highlighted as reveal the direction of the ongoing transformations of the city.

Firstly, contrary to the discourse of City Hall, which tries to deny and conceal the cause of forced removals that are taking place, this report demonstrates that the removals connected to the Olympics go on affecting or threatening thousands of families, through coercion or institutional violence, gravely violating human rights, especially housing rights. Secondly, the absence of a sporting legacy that benefits the whole city of Rio de Janeiro, democratising the population's access to sporting equipment, is evident. On the contrary, justified by the Olympics' discourse, we can see a series of violations associated with the privatisation of public spaces, disrespect of environmental legislation and the closure of sporting facilities used by athletes and the population. Thirdly, it is possible to observe the growing militarisation of the city, within an aggressive and racist public safety policy, which affects mainly young black males living in slums and the suburbs, who are murdered daily by the police. However, everyone is affected by this fear-based policy through the creation of visible and invisible walls which promote the socio-spatial segregation of the city, and through the growing criminalisation of social movements. Finally, it is worth remarking on the right to information and to the transparency of public management. While concealing information, City Hall spreads the idea that public costs are smaller than private costs. Our report unmasks the fallacy of this claim and shows that the costs of the Olympics, besides being higher than those officially divulged, have a public impact way above the private contribution. Moreover, through public-private partnerships and the concentration of contracts with a few large building companies, the Olympics represents the transfer of public resources to the private sector, subordinating public interests to market logic.

Unfortunately, however, the impacts are not limited to these highlights, but comprise a mobility project, a forced transfer of population, subordinated to real estate interests, the repression of street vendors and prostitutes and the violation of the rights of children and adolescents. Since the moment in which the choice of Rio de Janeiro as the 2016 Olympics host was announced, the mainstream media, politicians and public commentators have been emphasising the opportunities from investment growth in the city, highlighting the possibilities in solving large problems such as those in urban mobility and the recovery of degraded spaces for housing, commerce and tourism, as in the case of the harbour area. The population of the city, however, has already realised that the project 'Rio Olympic City', which comprises the developments for the 2014 World Cup, and the 2016 Olympic and Paralympic Games, as well as large projects such as

Porto Maravilha, will not bring the promised benefits. Street protests that erupted during the Confederation Cup, in June 2013, questioned the priority inversion in the city, highlighting the lack of popular participation. While the city becomes more expensive, public services are privatised and get worse, and the poorer population loses the little they achieved throughout their lives, while seeing their basic rights disrespected. Forced removals are the tip of a project of deep transformation of the urban dynamics of the city comprising, on the one hand, new processes of gentrification and commercialisation and, on the other hand, new patterns of relationship between the State and economic and social agents, marked by the denial of democratic opportunities for decision-making and by authoritarian interventions. Rio has become a 'city of exception'. New legal and institutional frameworks openly violate the principles of impersonality, universality and public accountability of the Law and public administration. During the 2014 World Cup, the street economy population organised a series of protests for their rights and experienced at first hand an increase of police repression and the new ways of criminalising social movements.

Many of the criticisms developed in this report draw on these street protests and wider urban social movements. The Committee has sought to give both political articulation and a strong evidence base to the issues raised by these popular struggles, to create agendas and actions which give these demands greater social visibility. So far our achievements are limited and fragile in face of the scale of the regeneration projects imposed on the city. The violation of rights, especially those of the poorest population, did not start with the sporting mega-events, but, as our report shows, has intensified during this period. When looking at the city's preparations for the Olympics, it is possible to assert, disappointingly, that Rio 2016 Olympics is the exclusion games!

The Manifesto: Sixteen Demands

This Dossier is also an invitation to popular movements, unions, civil society organisations, human rights defenders and citizens committed to social and environmental justice, to join us in the struggle a different project for the city, a project derived from democratic debate, with the assurance of permanence of all popular communities and districts situated in intervention areas, a project which respects the right to work, so that workers are not punished for trading in public spaces; a project in which the environment is effectively preserved; and especially, one where the rights of citizens are put above the interests of large economic groups.

1. End of removals in all communities of Rio de Janeiro, such as Vila Autódromo, Vila União de Curicica, Indiana, Santa Marta, Horto and many others, with compensation to all those affected, in particular to children who lost schools, medical treatment and leisure activities, and the democratic construction of a Housing Policy focused on the needs of the large majority of the population, especially those historically forgotten by the State.

The sporting mega-events in Rio accentuated, in the most violent manner, the disregard towards housing rights in the city. According to official data, from 2009 to 2013, 20,299 families were evicted, representing around 67,000 people. To put it into perspective, this corresponds to the removal of more than ten houses a day for four years. These appalling numbers could be even higher since the access to information is another constantly violated right. It is an alarming picture of grave violations of housing rights in the 'Olympic City' associated with violent removal processes, as was seen in the first months of 2015. Families were removed as a result of illegal decrees, constant threats and coercion. The interruption of basic urban services as a psychological pressure tool, night-time demolitions and physical violence comprises the present housing policy of the city, guided by real estate market interest in clearing already consolidated central areas to open up new expansion fields for their enterprises. The end of all removals must happen without delay, as well as the creation of an ample, participative and democratic housing policy that ensures the right to adequate housing for all the population.

2. End of harassment of the Prefecture of Rio towards street vendors, with review and extension of licences issued under popular overview and participation. Removal of inspections powers from the Municipal Guard (GM).

In the context of mega-events, Rio's City Hall established the policy of Order Shock and set about militarising the GM to deal with street vendors and the homeless population. The Mayor Eduardo Paes presented a decree allowing for the use of more lethal weapons by the GM, leading to two Public Ministry Complaints, one demanding the suspension of use of such weapons by the GM, and the other for administrative misconduct by the Mayor and his former Secretary Rodrigo Bethlem, due to a breach in municipal norms and impairing human dignity when dealing with the homeless population. Perhaps it is worth noting that Mr Bethlem, former Congressman and former Secretary of the Special Secretariat of Public Order, is being accused on several accounts of embezzlement. During his term as head of the Secretariat, he was responsible for putting forward a disastrous registration process for street vendors and increasing their harassment by the police. In this atmosphere, it is paramount to demilitarise the GM and return them to their original constitutional role, viz. to protect public property.

3. Reconstruction and reopening of the Célio de Barros Athletics Stadium and the Júlio Delamare Water Park, under public management and for collective use.

The stadium and park suffered from the demolition and renovation of Maracanã Stadium for the 2014 World Cup, and the privatisation of the whole site which brings together sporting and cultural facilities. These historic public facilities would give way to shopping centres and parking lots in the original plan. Due to popular protests against this decision, the demolition of facilities was cancelled, but they were partially destroyed and closed until today, and shut off to training athletes. Until the inauguration of the Engenhão, it was at Célio de Barros that the main state and national athletics competitions took place. The Júlio Delamare Water Park, in its turn, has the only diving pool adequate to high-performance athletes in the State of Rio de Janeiro. It had 10,000 pupils in its swimming and diving pools, which are empty at present, therefore barring the access of its users to physical activities, including the elderly and handicapped who did physiotherapy exercises there. Besides hosting national competitions, both the Célio de Barros and the Julio Delamare catered to the city's population and could easily be used in the 2016 Olympics, even as a training facility for the event. These two facilities, however, are in no condition to be used at present and there are no set dates for their reconstruction. It is essential to have a modernisation plan for the two stadiums and to reopen these facilities to the population in the shortest time possible, ensuring their public management, with the participation of social and sporting associations and public overview, as a means of preserving their collective use.

4. *For a public and popular Maracanã.*

A symbol of sport and culture in the country and a listed heritage site, the stadium was practically demolished for the construction of an 'arena' in compliance with FIFA's standard requirements. The intervention was notable for its authoritarian nature and lack of popular participation, and was considered a 'crime' by the body responsible for its preservation. The demolition and reconstruction of Maracanã cost more than R$1,000 million, financed by the public coffers while benefiting construction companies such as Odebrecht, which is part of the consortium that won the bidding for the stadium's privatisation. The values and circumstances under which the contract was signed show losses for the government and raise suspicion of undue advantage, monopoly and corruption. Beyond complaints of irregularities and the loss of architectural characteristics, the 'New Maracanã' buried some of its main characteristics: it is not the 'world's largest' anymore, with its audience capacity greatly reduced; it is no longer the symbolic stage of Rio's Carnival, now limited or precluded by European standards of 'arenas'; and, as a symbol of the whole process, it is no longer the democratic stage of popular participation and gathering of the city, with its new VIP areas and ticket prices that prevent the attendance of the poorer sections of the population. This whole process also damaged football clubs, as they now have a high-maintenance stadium, as well as having to share the profits from games with the infamous Consortium. Due to these factors, we defend the implementation of a new management model, based on social overview and with direct participation of all users of the facilities from its immediate neighbourhood including local residents, school students, football supporters and students from the State University.

5. *Reforestation of the Environmental Protection Area (APA) of Marapendi, with immediate interruption of the Olympic Golf Course developments and the construction of luxury towers at the site.*

The APA of Marapendi was established in 1991. In 2012, a Complementary Law project, authored by the Executive Power, approved the exclusion of an area measuring 58,500 square meters from the APA, a local previously classified as a Wildlife Conservation Zone, which impeded developments there. The change, approved by the City Council, had the alleged objective of allowing for the construction of a golf course for the 2016 Olympics. However, the real intentions of the project involved manoeuvres to benefit real estate speculation in the region, as City Hall's permit to destroy the area included the permission to build 22 towers with 22 storeys each. It has been estimated that the profits from the towers would surpass R$1,000 million, while the construction of the golf course will cost less than R$60 million. The construction of a golf course in an environmental protection area is unsustainable. There is already a place which hosts international competitions – the Itanhangá Golf Club – which made itself available to make the necessary adaptations to host the Olympic event, nullifying the need to build a new golf course. We defend the immediate cessation of the Olympic golf course development and the construction of luxury towers at the site, with a review of the Complementary Law and the reforestation of the APA of Marapendi with native vegetation.

   6. For the right to protest without criminalisation and institutional violence, with the release and acquittal of all political prisoners.

   Several popular protests against human rights violations and the negligence of the government occurred during the preparations for the 2014 World Cup and were violently repressed by police, which used the law to criminalised protesters. In this process, several illegal strategies were observed, including counterfeit evidence, as well as institutional violence against citizens. In Rio there were 23 young people prosecuted with one of them incarcerated for over a year until May 2015. We demand the release of all political prisoners criminalised during the 2014 World Cup protests. Furthermore, it is paramount to guarantee freedom of speech and the right to public demonstrations as fundamental democratic rights.

   7. Demilitarisation of the city, with the end of Military Police and their occupation of shantytowns, justified as a supposed safety measure for mega-events. For the end of the removal and killing of the black population. Against police violence, especially that directed to children and adolescents residing in shantytowns and the suburbs of the city.

The State of Rio de Janeiro has acted to ensure the execution of market led developments needed for the mega-events as well as promoting gentrification of touristic areas by means of a public safety policy tied to the city's 'postcard' sites. The installation of CCTV in crucial areas created 'safety bubbles' but in fact these sites are turning into control traps for the poorer population. Securitisation grows visibly in all regions of the city and, with it, the removal and extermination of the young black population, the most common target of summary executions by police. Children and adolescents are particularly affected by police violence. The notion of 'public safety' increasingly fades out when the impact of securitisation are evident in the lives of people affected by those policies. The occupation of shantytowns transforms all their social dynamics, putting especially black women in situations of vulnerability, the same women who see their children murdered by the Military Police in the streets where they live, and who resist their presence daily reality. To demilitarise the city is to find another rationale of public safety, one that is not based on using violence to deal with social problems.

8. *Sports as education, health and leisure and not as business.*

The Brazilian Olympic Committee and its sponsors hope and expect that Brazil will end up as one of the ten countries with most Medals in the 2016, beating its own record in these competitions. However, the country has already lost the most valuable of all prizes, independently of the final ranking of the Games: the opportunity to use the Olympics for the advancement of sports as a public policy of education, to build and maintain health for the population, especially for the youngest and poorest. It is commonly said that there is no public sports policy, but there is one, albeit in the opposite direction to what is stated in the Brazilian Constitution, Article 217, Item II, which determines the priority of public spending on educational sports. In contrast all the incentives and investments go to elite performance sports to the detriment of sport as an educational tool.

Sponsorships by state and private enterprises are an example of this misdirection of the sporting legacy as millions are invested in high-performance athletes while giving little or nothing to sporting structures for state schools and popular sporting centres. This perverse policy ignores the fact that, many studies show that investments in participatory sports potentially reduce health costs and improves the quality of life for the population. It is vital to change this rationale of sports as business and to transform sport into a fundamental right of human wellbeing.

9. All surplus land from public developments must be used for the construction of affordable housing and common facilities for the population.

At the end of the Games, the city will 'inherit' large stretches of surplus land from Olympic uses. It is necessary to fight for this land so it does not end up in the hands of the private developers or on real estate market. It is paramount to ensure the social function of these plots of land, assigning them to the construction of social housing or facilities of collective use, such as plazas, parks, schools, cultural facilities and health clinics.

10. End of privatisation and gentrification of the Rowing Stadium at Lagoa and the Glória Docks.

Despite the existence of a Law currently in effect (905/57, of the old Federal District), which preserves the use of the area for the advancement of sport, the Rowing Stadium was privatised and transformed into a leisure centre for the elite, with film theatres, bars, luxury shops and restaurants. The space was relinquished without a bidding process to entrepreneurs from the wealthy Marinho family. At present, the Rowing Stadium at Lagoa is losing the character of a public sporting venue and as a major site for rowing in the city. In the case of the Glória Docks, IPHAN approved a project, without a Public Hearing or any other form of divulgation, that represents, in practice, an 'un-listing' of Flamengo Park. As sites of public access to the sea, the Glória Docks and Flamengo Park should be available to everyone who wants to engage in water sports and not just restricted to a wealthy elite who can pay high prices to keep their vessels in private marinas and clubs. With the privatisation of the Glória Docks, the new management of BR Marinas blocked public access to the sea, gentrifying even more the pursuit of sailing and other water sports. An alternative project should aim to provide activities of sport and leisure at low cost to all citizens. Small renovations to comply with Olympic standards for sailing competitions should also consider the area's future use for environmental education. For this purpose it is crucial to implement a public management model with social overview, and to guarantee public access to the sea at Glória Docks.

11. For the end of the public-private partnership (PPP) of Porto Maravilha and the Olympic Park. For a popular project at the Harbour area and the Olympic Park.

The Special Urbanistic Interest Area of the Harbour Region of Rio de Janeiro encompasses five million square meters and is situated right in the centre of the city. Concomitantly to this urban operation, the largest PPP of Brazil was created managed by a mixed-ownership company created by the Prefecture, and the consortium which won the public bidding process, Porto Novo A.S. (composed by the construction companies OAS Ltd, Norberto Odebrecht Brasil A.S. and Carioca Christiani-Nielsen Engineering A.S.). Porto Novo will manage, through an administrative concession scheme, the renovation and operation and maintenance of services for 15 years. This involves the modernisation of urban structure, environmental sanitation, IT and communication networks, aiming at improving commercial and residential enterprises. As part of this there were threats of eviction to residents of Morro da Providência and Pedra Lisa, situated within the range of the Porto Maravilha project. In the region of Barra da Tijuca, the Prefecture opened a public bidding process, in November 2011, for the concession of public land and the establishment of a PPP for the construction of the Olympic Park, which includes the Athletes Village.

After the Games, it is expected that 75 per cent of the area of 1,180 million square meters will be assigned to a high-standard housing development to be traded by a joint-venture company, which is already involved with the sale of luxury apartments of Ilha Pura condominium. In addition to the Olympic Park PPP and the construction of the BRTs Transcarioca and Transolímpica, there is an attempt to remove the community of Vila Autódromo, and a series of human rights violations during the demolition of part of the community's houses. In our view the advancement of urban renovation through a PPP represents the subordination off these urban spaces to market reasoning, as managing companies take decisions based on economic efficacy and profit maximisation. It is crucial to annul these PPP contracts and establish a managerial council composed by public bodies and civil society organisations, assuring housing rights to all residents of these areas, and especially the residents of Morro da Providência and Pedra Lisa (at Porto Maravilha) and Vila Autódromo (at Barra da Tijuca/Jacarepaguá). We need to advance a housing plan based on social interest which guarantees that new real estate enterprises are available to low-income residents.

12. Sports cannot be practiced in the sewer: for the depollution of Guanabara Bay, and the Rodrigo de Freitas and Jacarepaguá lagoons.

The legacy promise of 80 per cent depollution of Guanabara Bay has been abandoned by authorities, who today aim for an average of only 40 per cent. Athletes have to face pollution and foul smell to practice nautical sports not only in Guanabara Bay, but also in the Rodrigo de Freitas Lagoon and the lagoon complex of Jacarepaguá. In the lagoons at Barra, Marapendi and Jacarepaguá, buildings without proper sanitation result in algae proliferation, which may lead to the eutrophication of lagoons. In Rodrigo de Freitas, this is already a routine problem. Guanabara Bay is an ecosystem affected for years by the oil industry and organic pollution coming from raw sewage dumping. Within the Olympic context, there is the expansion of potentially polluting developments such as those coming from the Petrochemical Complex of Rio de Janeiro (Comperj) and harbour activities. These impacts are directly felt by artisanal fishermen, who have to live with the constant contraction of their fishing areas, and the surrounding communities, who are deprived of these areas as leisure spaces. Moreover, the whole area of the APA of Guapimirim is threatened by the quality of bay waters. The need to guarantee basic sanitation to all communities surrounding Guanabara Bay is urgent, as well as for the areas of Jacarepaguá Bay and Rodrigo de Freitas Lagoon.

13. Against privations of collective transportation services and the concentration of investments in areas of interest to the real estate market. Adequate public transportation free of charge for all.

The transportation revolution promised by the Prefecture means, in fact, the privatisation of services, fare increases and the concentration of investments in some areas, especially Barra da Tijuca (BRTs), Southern Zone (the Underground) and the central area (LRV), subordinating collective transport services to real estate (and touristic) market interests. Meanwhile, train and ferry services remain very precarious, there is no investment in metropolitan integration – remarkably between Rio de Janeiro, the metropolitan East and the Fluminense Lowlands – and bus services are very poor in many suburban districts of the city. So it is important to review the licences of Fetranspor (buses), Metrô Rio (Underground), Supervia (urban trains) and Barcas A.S. (ferries), in order to ensure adequate public transport, free of charge, guaranteeing the universal right to mobility.

14. Immediate reinstatement of street cleaners and teachers unjustly 'red for fighting for their rights and a fairer city'. Protesting is not a crime and striking is a right.

In the recent strikes by street cleaners and teachers of state schools, union leaders were unjustly fired for fighting for better work conditions and a fairer city. Once again, the State criminalised social and labour movements, hampering their legitimate protests and demands. This situation must be reversed, with the reinstatement of those dismissed and ensuring the right to strike for these occupational categories.

15. For the end of forced removal of street children and adolescents as a means of 'street cleansing'. For public policies that respect their rights.

Part of the preparations for the Olympics has taken the form of 'cleansing' the city of its street population, especially street children and adolescents, by compulsory internment in municipal shelters and/or in facilities run by General Department of Socio-Educational Actions even without any indication of criminal activities. This strategy was adopted as a way of keeping these 'dangerous classes' away from the main touristic points of the city during the event. After the end of the World Cup, many were gradually released and started to report abuses they suffered. It is necessary to respect the rights of children and adolescents, especially those who are in vulnerable situations, and to implement public policies for the advancement of social inclusion. It is known that compulsory internment was put forward in a violent manner by the Military Police, Civil Guard and the City Hall, especially just before sporting mega-events. This happened repeatedly both before and during the World Cup, resulting in countless violations of rights, including the disappearance of many children and adolescents, without any action of the State to investigate those cases.

16. For the end of the 'World Cup Law', which is also in effect for the Olympics. Against the project of the Olympic City of Rights Violations and Exclusions. For a fair and democratic city.

While the most recent scandal involving FIFA only confirmed what everybody already knew, the International Olympic Committee managed to create a different image. Nevertheless, just as FIFA, the IOC uses sports to achieve their main goal: profit. For example, the General World Cup and Olympics Law assures that FIFA, the IOC and their respective sponsors did not pay a single penny in taxes. IOC = FIFA. Sports are of and by the people, not a business. All projects connected to the Olympics are imposed and implemented without any participation of affected communities or society in general. Furthermore, there is no transparency about the public debt being contracted by the Prefecture and its impacts on the municipality's finances in future years. It is crucial to demanding a Post-Olympic City based on social justice and democratic participation. In this sense, it is necessary to strengthen democratic decision-taking processes concerning the governance of mega-events, ensuring stronger popular participation regarding decisions about investment priorities, and recognising the knowledge and experiences coming from the most vulnerable communities and groups.

Bibliography

Anderson, P. (2016) 'Crisis in Brazil', *London Review of Books* 38(8), 21 April.

Boykoff, J. (2013) *Celebration Capitalism and the Olympic Games.* London: Routledge.

Boykoff, J. (2014) *Activism and the Olympics: Dissent at the Games in Vancouver and London.* New Brunswick: Rutgers University Press.

Cheyne, J. (2009) 'Olympian masterplanning in London', *Planning Theory and Practice* 10(3): 404–408.

Cohen, P. (2013) *On the Wrong Side of the Track: East London and the Post Olympics.* London: Lawrence and Wishart.

Jovchelovitch, S. (2015) *Underground Sociabilities: A Study of Rio's Favelas.* London: Bloomsbury Academic.

Marrero-Guillamón, I. (2012) 'Olympic state of exception', in H. Powell and I. Marrero-Guillamón (eds.), *The Art of Dissent: Adventures in London's Olympic State.* London: Marshgate Press.

RIO+Social. (2015) RIO+Social 2015, Programme, http://www.riomaissocial. org/programa/, accessed 30 August 2015.

Rodrigues, R. (2014) 'The dilemmas of pacification: news of war and peace in the "Marvellous City"', *Stability: International Journal of Security and Development*, 3(1): 22.

Stahlberg, S. (2012) *Pacification of Favelas in Rio de Janeiro*, http://iis-db. stanford.edu/pubs/23471

Watt, P. (2013) '"It's not for us": Regeneration, the 2012 Olympics and the gentrification of East London', *City* 17(1): 99–118.

Phil Cohen is Professor Emeritus at the University of East London, and a Research Fellow at the Young Foundation. He is the founder/research director of the LivingMaps Network and the editor-in-chief of its online journal *LivingMaps Review*. His ethnographic fieldwork over the last 30 years has been based in East London and has dealt with issues of racism and multi-culturalism, public safety and danger, the role of the cultural economy in urban regeneration, and popular participation in planning. His research with young people has developed new methods of visual ethnography, social mapping and dialogic engagement with informants. Most recently he directed a multi-project initiative examining the Post Olympic Legacy in East 20. He is the author of *On the Wrong Side of the Track? East London and the Post Olympics* (Lawrence and Wishart, 2013). Other books include *Knuckle Sandwich: Growing up in the Working Class City* (with Dave Robins, 1978), *Rethinking the Youth Question* (1997), *New Ethnicities, Old Racisms* (2001), *London's Turning: the Making of Thames Gateway* (edited with Mike Rustin, 2008). He has also published a memoir *Reading Room Only: Memoir of a Radical Bibliophile* (Five Leaves, 2013) and a book of poetry and prose, *Graphologies* (Mica Press, 2014). A collection of his new research, *Material Dreams: Maps and Territories and the Un/making of Modernity* is forthcoming from Palgrave Macmillan. www.philco henworks.com

Paul Watt is Reader in Urban Studies at Birkbeck, University of London. He has published widely on topics including the London housing crisis, social rental housing, urban regeneration, suburbanization, and the 2012 Olympic Games. He is the co-author (with Tim Butler) of *Understanding Social*

Inequality (Sage, 2007), co-editor (with Peer Smets) of *Mobilities and Neighbourhood Belonging in Cities and Suburbs* (Palgrave Macmillan, 2014) and co-editor (with Peer Smets) of *Social Housing and Urban Renewal: A Cross-National Perspective* (Emerald, 2017). He sits on the Editorial Board of City (Taylor & Francis) and is Board Member of the Research Committee on Sociology of Urban and Regional Development (RC21), International Sociological Association.

15

From London 2012 to Tokyo 2020: Urban Spectacle, Nation Branding and Socio-Spatial Targeting in the Olympic City

Grace Gonzalez Basurto

Introduction

The hosting of the 2020 Olympic and Paralympic Games (the Olympics, henceforth) has been envisioned by Japanese politicians as a hope for Japan's renewal; a policy tool to boost the country's economic growth and renovate the nation brand after the 3/11 triple disaster – which refers to the tsunami and nuclear crises ensued by the Great Eastern Japan earthquake in 11 March 2011. The first time Tokyo hosted the Olympics in 1964, the city and the country underwent an accelerated physical and symbolic modernisation. The 1964 Olympics were the first held in Asia and the first to make use of satellite communications to broadcast live worldwide. They were also declared by the International Olympic Committee (IOC) the greatest Olympics ever, and at the time, the most expensive Games ever staged (Tagsold, 2010; Odeven, 2013). In this regard, the timing of both the 1964 and 2020 Olympics could

G. Gonzalez Basurto (✉)
Hosei University, Tokyo, Japan
Doshisha University, Kyoto, Japan
e-mail: grace.b.gonzalez.87@hosei.ac.jp

© The Author(s) 2017
P. Cohen, P. Watt (eds.), *London 2012 and the Post-Olympics City*,
DOI 10.1057/978-1-137-48947-0_15

407

be described as a watershed in the history of Japan, not only because of the nature of the task per se, but also because of its socio-economic significance. While the former were delivered in a context of postwar reconstruction, re-industrialisation, and rapid growth; the latter will be hosted in a context of a 20-year economic deflation and stagnation, lack of nuclear safety, a public-debt ratio above 226 per cent of Gross Domestic Product (GDP) (Organisation for Economic and Co-operation Development, 2015), and a super-ageing society.

Following the widely perceived 'success' of the London's event-led regeneration for the 2012 Olympics, the Tokyo Metropolitan Government (TMG) has set in motion an Olympic bid-inspired urban regeneration for Tokyo, which includes new and improved transport networks, disaster-resilient infrastructure, and greenery. Also emulating London, the TMG intends on capitalising on the Cultural Olympiad to brand Tokyo as the Asian metropolis of culture.

The chapter examines the employment of the Olympics as a vehicle and catalyst for urban branding, economic diversification and socio-cultural revitalisation in the host cities of London and Tokyo.[1] In doing so, it addresses the utilisation of mega-events as barometers and image builders of urban competitiveness through festivalisation, staged experiences and cultural tourism (Johansson and Kociatkiewicz, 2011). The chapter argues that the lack of transparency and accountability in the development of Olympic-related infrastructure will not only hinder the perceived outcome of Tokyo's event-led regeneration, but also taint its sought-after branding in areas related to Olympic legacy, financial and environmental sustainability, and socio-spatial innovation. The chapter identifies mega-event 'policy mobility/assemblage' as an inherent factor of intra-urban disjointedness and solipsism. Policy mobility and assemblage refers to the circulation and partial or complete transfer/assemblage of policy knowledge as 'best practices'. Under this approach, policy knowledge is implicitly taken as universally applicable (Dolowitz and Marsh, 2000; Ong and Collier, 2005; McCann, 2011).

---

[1] This work was supported by the Center for the Study of the Creative Economy, Doshisha University.

The chapter draws on semi-structured interviews conducted by the author with key stakeholders in London (March 2014) and Tokyo (November 2013–October 2014), in both private and government sectors. Informants include those directly involved in the planning and delivery of the London 2012 Olympics and the Tokyo 2020 Olympics, such as city officials, arts managers, Olympic legacy representatives, cultural and place-making consultants, and urban strategists. Focus group interviews with displaced residents from the Toei Kasumigaoka Danchi (apartment complex) and homeless/rough sleepers (or *nojukusha* in the Japanese context[2]) in areas adjacent to the National Olympic Stadium were also conducted by the author between December 2015 and March 2016. Additional data is comprised of first-hand accounts from stakeholders of the London 2012 Olympics collected at forums organised by the British Council and Tokyo Arts Council in February 2014 in Tokyo; field trips to the Queen Elizabeth Olympic Park (QEOP) in March 2014; several field trips to the new national stadium premises and the Tokyo 1964 Olympic venues (to be reused for the 2020 Olympics) from November 2014 to April 2016; and official documents and reports. While efforts were made to attain interviews with representatives of both the London Legacy Development Corporation (LLDC) and the Tokyo Vision 2020 Office, these were denied on the bases of either 'busy schedules' or 'large volume of requests'. A request to view and photograph the scale model of the then design of the new Olympic national stadium (unveiled to the press in March 2015) was also refused by the Japan Sports Council (JSC). The chapter uses discourse analysis to assess the socio-spatial and socio-cultural implications for the two capital cities as the result of hosting the Olympics.

The first part of the chapter reviews the London 2012 event-led regeneration through socio-economic and socio-spatial impacts. It also links these impacts with the making of the London/UK brand as both, business model and export. The second part addresses the scope and scale of Tokyo's long-term urban regeneration in tandem with the spatial and fiscal sustainability of the 2020 Olympic venues. Likewise,

---

[2] The literal meaning of *nojukusha* is 'camper' or 'those who live outdoors' and it is the term that interviewed homeless/rough sleepers use to describe themselves.

it examines the policy approaches and core elements behind the city and nation branding for the Tokyo 2020 Olympics. Lastly, the chapter draws links between London and Tokyo as host cities (through policy mobility/assemblage) and sketches Japan/Tokyo's Olympic prospects in terms of socio-economic and socio-spatial legacies.

London 2012: Event-Led Regeneration and Socio-Spatial Targeting

The Socio-Economic and Socio-Spatial Impacts of the London 2012 Olympics: A Road Map for Tokyo 2020?

The London 2012 Olympics have been deemed by the official narrative as the most successful Olympics in recent times, particularly with regard to economic and social legacies. However, the socio-economic impact analyses of mega-events do not tend to consider the displacement of other economic activities and the opportunity cost of public funds conversely used to finance other projects or to lower the financial burden on taxpayers (Oxford Economics, 2012: 6; DCMS, 2013). Upon close inspection, the socio-economic and socio-spatial impacts of the London 2012 Olympics, as well as the London success story, derive from an event-led regeneration. Event-led regeneration can be described as an urban policy that uses mega-events to regenerate (or redevelop) inner-city areas in the form of permanent new infrastructure (Smith, 2012). As such, the economic contribution of the 2012 Olympics to UK GDP mainly concentrated on the construction, tourism, labour market, and housing sectors. Of the estimated £16.5 billion (year 2012 prices) contribution to the UK GDP from 2005 to 2017, 82 per cent of this was expected to stem from the construction activity required to stage the Olympics and deliver their legacy, such as infrastructure, athletic venues and private sector development projects (Oxford Economics, 2012). Similarly, 78 per cent of the estimated employment was to be created in construction work, with the main contribution within the Olympic-related construction projects being indirect (that is, the employment generated in the construction industry's supply chain), particularly between 2008 and 2017 (Oxford Economics, 2012). Furthermore, the majority of the employment opportunities for Londoners from the six Host Boroughs during the preparation and staging of the Olympics were low-skilled and semi-skilled jobs such as site clearance, catering, retail and security (DCMS, 2013). The continuation of participation programmes and investment in infrastructure beyond 2015 will only be for Olympic venues (until 2016) and Sportivate (until 2017), a project for 11–25 year olds to discover sport through free or subsidised coaching (DCMS, 2013).

While the Olympics are generally a media spectacle for international audiences, the total number of domestic and international visitors during the Olympics decrease, and the tourism industry mainly benefits from domestic tourists' spending during the duration of the event (Oxford Economics, 2012; DCMS 2013). A major challenge was therefore the displacement of international and domestic tourists. In this sense, the tourism effect was generated in the aftermath of the Olympics with additional tourism of 48 per cent and the largest beneficiary is the hotels and restaurants' sector (Oxford Economics, 2012: 18–19). As one interviewee specialised in London's urban competitiveness pointed out, 'There is a real tension between on the one hand, managing expectations [from visitors] and on the other, managing patters of activity by locals, the latter being very important to a city's economy'.

The above conundrum is largely represented by the infrastructure-related bottlenecks in the Olympic host city, which for London's case meant congestion and unreliability of the transport network; mainly the bus and underground services. Consequently, organisers deliberately spread the message to locals to stay at home during the Olympics, creating an 'unwarranted mobility panic' (Giulianotti et al., 2015: 130) and simultaneously immobilising not only Londoners' everyday life tasks but also the local economy.

The socio-economic impact of the Olympics was deemed unclear by the majority of London interviewees, particularly in the long term. Furthermore, they expressed the view that the post-Olympic landscape was 'scary' in the post-Crash climate of economic 'austerity' (see, for instance, Mooney et al., 2015). Nonetheless, they invariably thought of London 2012 as a success story, particularly compared to Sochi 2014, which was labelled as an economic and political 'disaster of epic proportions' by many of them.

One of the main goals in hosting the 2012 Olympics was to reconnect communities across the UK through intergenerational and cultural links, simultaneously empowering young and disabled segments of the population. At the core of this social change was the transformation of East London – one of the most socio-economically deprived areas of London – in order to raise the quality of life in East London and ensuring its residents the same life chances as fellow Londoners by 2030 (see Introduction). All interviewees referred to the East London regeneration as positive, indicating an accelerated transformation of 'poor, derelict, post-industrial toxic' sites that would not have occurred without the 2012 Olympics. For example, in order to erect the Olympic Park, 2.3 million cubic meters of soil were excavated and cleansed of industrial pollutants (DCMS, 2012: 33). The QEOP encompasses 45 hectares of wildlife and plant habitats, landscaped parklands and green infrastructure, across the former industrial wasteland of Lea Valley (DCMS, 2012). However, event-led regeneration often creates mixed legacies. The new Olympic Park, replaced 'the loss of previously designated sites of natural conservation importance' (Shepherd, 2011: 1) and 'range of habitats including watercourses, wetland, woodland and brownfield land' (Shepherd, 2011: 3) in the area. Likewise, the 2012 Olympics brought the spotlight to East London through an 'extremely targeted investment' and 'forced' regeneration in the area, according to a couple of interviewees working on programmes (funded via the National Lottery and Arts Council England) related to children, youth, and the 2012 Olympic legacy. In current austerity-focused policies, the scenarios expressed by the majority of interviewees are either 'let things decline' or rely 'more and more' on private sector funding. Nonetheless, the public sector invested an extra £550 million to materialise the development of the Athletes Village and Westfield Stratford City's connecting roads (Hewison, 2014). Westfield Stratford City was opened in 2011 and is one of the largest urban shopping malls in Europe. According to commentators such as Minton (2012) and Giulianotti et al. (2015), this mega-mall embodies a citadel of high-end retail brought about by a 'corporate kettling' that strategically bypasses the socio-economic marginalisation of East London through physical infrastructure; this corporate kettling is, however, only made feasible by publicly funded infrastructure.

Furthermore, whereas unlocking copious investment in a short period of time is considered as an unparalleled opportunity, the overall rationale behind hosting a sporting mega-event propels a model of trickle-down economics. In other words, a basic stimulus wrapped in the form of mega-events to catalyse planned developments, boost trade, and attract inward investment, especially in periods of economic downturn (DCMS, 2013: 31). According to an interviewee who specialises on urban regeneration and culture, a knock-on 'regeneration' effect will be created by joining up 'big plates' such as Stratford, Canary Wharf and Hackney, provided that new commercial and residential developments in London continue at current pace. He further stated that this kind of urban renewal draws on place-making strategies by 'pulling out a mix of people, place, architecture, history and heritage'. For instance, a representative of the Greater London Authority emphasised that 'much effort' was being put into trying to link up the Millennium Dome with the Olympic Park through a new sculpture trail along the River Thames; as an ongoing sculpture commission, to make sure that 'bit' of East London is not forgotten post-Olympics. As a corollary, the LLDC is working towards the fruition of the 'Olympicopolis', a new culture and education quarter in partnership with the V&A, Sadler's Wells and University of Arts London by 2021 (see Chapter 2). Consequently, 'East London has become one of the most sought after places to live, work, visit and invest in the UK' (HM Government and Mayor of London, 2014: 37), largely because of the development of largely private, market-priced new housing around the QEOP (see Chapters 4–6), and the aforemen-tioned cultural and educational quarter. Nonetheless, the dangers to achieving convergence through *de facto* gentrification and resident mobility are imminent and have already been noted by government agencies (DCMS, 2013) and academics (Watt, 2013; Bernstock, 2014).

London's Branding and the 2012 Olympics

Even though the UK, and London in particular, is perceived as holding a worldwide strong brand,[3] the Olympics were utilised to not only

---

[3] As suggested for instance by their top ranks in the Anholt-GfK Roper (2013a) Nation Brand index and Anholt-GfK Roper (2013b) City Index and the Global Power City Index or Mori Index (Institute for Urban Strategies, 2013, 2014).

enhance – or rehabilitate[4] – the country's external image but also to provide local business with a potential global platform through the staging of mega-events as a means of public diplomacy (Zimbalist, 2010; Grix and Houlihan, 2014). Interviews revealed that the London 2012 Olympics helped to modernise the image of London as a comfortable, efficient and diverse place. London's rebranding focused therefore on the 'vibrancy' of the city reflected in the quality and diversity of social amenities such as restaurants and bars, accessibility and friendliness of people. According to interviewees, this assessment derived mainly from the media coverage during the London 2012 Olympics. It is worth pointing out that this narrative was controlled by stakeholders, who actively provided freelance or non-accredited journalists in London during the 2012 Olympics first-hand information – as the host city would otherwise be depicted in an unfavourable manner, 'telling audiences about London's underbelly'. Interestingly, other measures highlighted by interviewees consisted in 'thinking and fixing' the urban realm surrounding the Olympic Park. For instance, a policy consultant working on high profile and major infrastructure projects in London pointed out:

> There's not much point in having a beautiful, new regenerated 500-acre patch surrounded by urban devastation [East London]. So, one of the things which a lot of thought and some money went into in London was, dressing the streets where people [visitors] would go to, that were nowhere near Stratford but the sorts of places you would go in the evening. It made the whole city feel as it was part of the theme.

It is worth mentioning here that while East London is on the whole a deprived area, the above appraisal employs an exaggerated imagery of 'urban devastation' to hyperbolise the 'positive' effects of the scale and intent of the 2012 event-led regeneration.

Interviewed stakeholders in London also revealed that hosting the Olympics was employed as a catalyst to host continuous mega-events in the hope to attracting inward investment. This strategy has been

---

[4] Owing to UK's involvement in the 2003 invasion of Iraq.

translated into over 20 major events since the London 2012 Olympics and more than 30 events secured until 2019 in the UK; including the Tour de France Stage 3 in 2014, the 2015 Rugby Union World Cup, the 2017 the International Association of Athletics Federations and International Paralympic Committee World Athletics Championships and the 2018 Women's Hockey World Cup (HM Government and Mayor of London, 2014). Likewise, the enactment of the Host2Host Programme has provided UK businesses with high-value opportunities by targeting future hosts of major sporting events around the world, selling their expertise on successfully preparing and delivering these mega-events. As such, sports-focused trade missions have won contracts for the Brazil 2014 FIFA World Cup and the Rio 2016 Olympics, Socchi 2014 Winter Olympics and 2018 FIFA World Cup (UKTI, 2013). A Host2Host agreement was also signed by Japanese Prime Minister Shinzo Abe on early May 2014 to facilitate sports advisory services (for example, in master planning, management, communications and legacy) and trade connections (HM Government and Mayor of London, 2014; UKTI, 2015).

Without exception, interviewees in London referred to the 2012 Olympics as an institutional 'game changer' across sectors in the realms of public-private partnerships and intergovernmental collaborative work, for example, in terms of funding, venues, marketing and audience development. However, ensuring that collaborators do not route back into their 'pre-Olympic silos' was described as one of the challenges. Only a few interviewees expressed that, on the one hand, the 'massive' socio-economic inequality was not manifested or 'discussed' during the 2012 Olympics; and on the other, that the public had already forgotten about the 'Olympic feel' after only two years. Likewise, it is worth noting that only a handful of interviewees spoke about the pressure to sell simultaneously the Olympic and the local urban brands; the inability to talk and discuss mistakes made; and the risk of falling into a cycle and mindset of jumping straight 'onto the next project'. In this sense, it can be argued that this practice potentially deterriorialises and decontextualises the everyday life routines in cities (Johansson and Kociatkiewicz, 2011: 394) by prioritising urban themes or choreographed activities. Furthermore, such festivalisation could decouple cities from their complex narratives, effectively turning them into all-year-round theme parks with little genuine socio-cultural innovation.

To summarise, the London establishment favoured a strategy in which a 'distinctive' or 'renewed' profile was anchored to the 2012 Olympics in order to mobilise stagnant, niche or potential economic sectors in the long-term. As for the London 2012 Olympics-led business model, the discourse of success adeptly overrode the negative impacts of the event-led regeneration and its related urban socio-spatial restructuring in East London. This per se could be categorised as a breakthrough in contemporary urban governance for 'entrepreneurial cities' (Harvey, 1989). The case of Tokyo, a fellow entrepreneurial and Olympic host city, is now analysed in the following part of the chapter to cast light on the scope, scale and implications of London's policy transfer to Tokyo's event-led regeneration and branding.

Tokyo 2020 Olympics: Between Grand Projects and Gesture Politics

Beyond Tokyo 2020: Urban Regeneration and Branding

The Tokyo Vision 2020 was enacted in December 2011 as Tokyo's most comprehensive urban strategy yet. It aims at developing Tokyo as a sustainable, disaster-resilient and highly competitive city. Its key new urban features include (TMG, 2012a):

1. the creation of water and greenery corridors across the city and development of 433 hectares of urban parkland, inclusive of 170 hectares of metropolitan parks;
2. the promotion of a low-carbon lifestyle, with hydrogen as the next-generation renewable energy source;[5]

---

[5] The TMG has set up a ¥40 billion fund to promote hydrogen as the next energy source for the mega-city, including the provision of fuel cells for business and industrial uses, fuel cell buses and hydrogen stations. In this regard, the quantitative target is to build 35 hydrogen stations and have 6,000 fuel cell vehicles by the year 2020 (Masuzoe, 2014a). Fuel cell buses and electric vehicles will be used for transportation between the Olympic Village and the competition venues.

3. the development of sports clusters and revitalisation of communities through hosting a myriad of international sporting events, mainly, the 2020 Olympics;
4. The enhancement of Tokyo's profile in the areas of tourism and culture.

The Tokyo Vision 2020 and its predecessor, 'Tokyo's Big Change – The 10-year Plan 2006–2016' were largely drawn around the potential hosting of the 2016 or the 2020 Olympics; that is, event-led regeneration. The Olympics are above all envisaged by the TMG as a landmark event that brings 'dramatic change' to the culture and society of hosting cities (Masuzoe, 2014a). The Tokyo Vision 2020 has recently been supplemented by 'Creating the Future: The Long-term Vision for Tokyo (2014–2024)', encompassing 360 policy targets by focusing on welfare (for children, the elderly and the disabled), risk management (including natural disasters and terrorism), economy, city diplomacy and sporting mega-events (TMG, 2014a). Further emphasis on city diplomacy, urban competitiveness and cultural branding instilled in the Long-Term Vision is the result of Governor Masuzoe's touring to the Olympic cities of London, Sochi, Beijing, as well as Seoul and Berlin throughout the year 2014 (Masuzoe, 2014b). For instance, Governor Masuzoe's visit to the QEOP and remarks at Chatham House in October 2014 underlined a keen interest in following the example of London as an Olympic host city. This to not only improve Tokyo's international rankings, but 'Tokyo aims to take the opportunity presented by the 2020 Games to rise to the number-one spot' [city in the world] (Masuzoe, 2014c: 3) by delivering the best Olympics in history. The policy knowledge that has been mobilised, transferred and/or assembled from past Olympic host cities (particularly London) by the TMG is, firstly, the operationalisation of event-led regeneration (inclusive of resident displacement and eviction and homeless removal, see below) as Olympic legacy; secondly, the use of sporting mega-events as catalysts and barometers of urban competitiveness and cultural and urban (re)branding; and thirdly, event logistics such as security and crowd control (Masuzoe, 2015b).

For the TMG, cultural tourism represents a key aspect of global urban competitiveness. On the whole, the above strategy seems to aim at a more accessible country/capital for visitors through a twenty-first-century repackaging of contemporary culture and heritage. Interviewed stakeholders in Tokyo showcased a tangible anxiety to envision the direction that Japan, and Tokyo as its capital, should take in terms of cultural prowess. For instance, interviewees in Tokyo amply commented on the challenge of creating partnerships and networking between national and regional cultural organisations in order to deliver a successful Cultural Olympiad – as equally successful as that of the London 2012 Olympics. Similarly, the majority of interviewees referred to the challenge of thinking about and propelling the role, imagery and significance of Japanese arts and culture vis-à-vis the national ethos in the aftermath of 3/11. Interviewees from the Ministry of Economy in particular reasserted that although the Tokyo 2020 Olympics were 'not a business event', much effort was going to be devoted to presenting a 'clean, beautiful, safe, technologically advanced, and hospitable' country.

The Tokyo 2020 Olympics: The Glossy and the Opaque

Compactness and sustainability were promoted by Tokyo as key bidding and delivery aspects of the venues for the 2020 Olympics. Reusing 15 existing facilities as competition venues – three of which were built for the 1964 Olympics (see Figs. 15.1–15.4) – seemed a firm commitment towards a more sensible staging of this mega-event. That is, reducing the number of underused sports facilities and in so doing, lessening the related environmental impact and resident displacement. The Tokyo 2020 Olympics approach was especially appealing, as hosting the Olympics represents a colossal economic undertaking. Solely bidding to host the Olympics can cost up to $100 million to applicant cities (Zimbalist, 2010). Host cities undergo urban development or redevelopment requiring vast infrastructure and logistic-related investments as an implicit clause. As such, cost overruns have become an intrinsic element in the planning and delivery of the Olympics (through legally binding guarantee letters) with a consistent gross discrepancy between the projected (bidding phase) and the final costs. This places the Olympics as 'one of the most financially risky type of megaproject that exists' (Flyvbjerg and Stewart, 2012: 3). For instance, the average Olympics' cost overrun from 1960 to 2012 for both summer and winter is, in real terms, 179 per cent; with summer Olympics having an average cost overrun of 252 per cent (Flyvbjerg and Stewart, 2012). Yet, The Tokyo 2020 Candidature File states (TMG, 2012b: 66) states:

> The TOCOG [Tokyo Organising Committee of the Olympic and Paralympic Games] budget has been formulated fairly conservatively relative to previous Olympic and Paralympic Games, and other large scale sports events.

Figs. 15.1–15.4 (clockwise): Yoyogi National Stadium 2nd Gymnasium, Tokyo Metropolitan Gymnasium, Budokan, and Yoyogi National Stadium 1st Gymnasium

Source: Author

Given the data on Olympics' cost overruns, the above seems at best naïve and counter-intuitive and, at worst, deliberately deceptive and manipulative. Nonetheless, underestimating budgets and overestimating benefits is a common political tool to appeal to the general public and stakeholders (Zimbalist, 2010; Flyvbjerg, 2014). While a combination of biases, errors, misinformation and misrepresentation appears to be the preferred formula when drawing Olympic bid books, current socio-political climates in various applicant and host cities (from street protests in Brazil and Tokyo in July 2014 and January 2015, respectively, to withdrawals from Stockholm, Lviv, Oslo and Krakow from the 2022 Winter Olympics bid and Boston from the 2024 Summer Olympics bid) over the large-scale urban transformations and multi-billion dollar costs have forced the IOC to rethink the bidding process.

In order to address the above issues, the IOC enacted the Olympic Agenda 2020 in December 2014 to, amongst others, reduce the cost of the bidding process, promote the 'maximum' use of existing facilities and temporary venues, allow competitions to take place outside the host city or even outside the host country and provide explicit assessment on the opportunities and risks associated with the planning and staging of the Olympics (IOC, 2014a, 2014b). However, long-term structural changes in the governance of this mega-event, particularly vis-à-vis taxpayers' protection, remain elusive. And how might these reforms benefit Tokyo as a host city? The TMG was able to cancel the construction of three facilities; the Yumenoshima Plaza Arena A and B and the Wakasu Olympic Marina for which the competitions of 10 sports will be relocated to neighbouring prefectures such as Chiba, Kanagawa and Saitama. Likewise, the TMG has revised the plan for the Sea Forest Waterway and relocated the canoe slalom venue at Kasai Rinkai Park, the latter owing to environmental concerns voiced by not-for-profit organisations and members of the general public. Although this decision compromises the 'athletes first' goal of the Tokyo 2020 Olympic bid, reducing the percentage of the competition venues within an 8 km radius of the Olympic Village, this measure will result in approximately $1.7 billion in savings (IOC, 2015), fewer white elephants and the reduction of environmental impact of the Olympics for the Tokyo megalopolis.

The 2020 Olympic Venues and Related Urban Infrastructure

The new national stadium constitutes the main venue for both the 2020 Olympics and the 2019 Rugby World Cup. Categorised as 'Japan's greatest world-class stadium' by the JSC (2012), this stadium is set to convey the message of a 'new age' for Japanese society. According to the Tokyo 2020 Bid Book (2012c), the new stadium is to be built irrespective of the 2020 Olympics. Nonetheless, it would be highly implausible to justify such expenditure in the absence of a sporting mega-event. The Bank of Japan (2016: 15–16), for instance, has forthrightly underlined the difficulty in reaching consensus to enact large-scale urban regeneration projects – and in so doing, stimulate economic activity in the private sector – in the absence of mega-events such as the Olympics. Furthermore, the Bank of Japan cites East London as a 'successful' example of event-led regeneration in which hosting the Olympics served as catalyst to resolve a 'long-standing problem'.

London-based Zaha Hadid Architects were selected on 15 November 2012 as the winners of the new national stadium International Design Competition. Proposals were evaluated on the grounds of design originality, technical ambitiousness, ambience and construction feasibility by a committee headed by Pritzer Architecture Prize awardee Tadao Ando (JSC, 2012). However, building costs, operating costs and overall financial sustainability of the stadium seemed absent from these guidelines. The functional requirements focused on a stadium that could accommodate 'modern international sporting events' such as track and field, rugby and soccer as well as cultural events such as concerts, inclusive of seating arrangements for 80,000 spectators. The new stadium is to be built in Jingu Gaien, a district designated by the TMG for landscape preservation purposes.[6] Furthermore, Hadid's design meant building a stadium of a 'massive size fitted into a narrow site' and on a tight schedule (JSC, 2012). This scale-and-site conundrum could even be spotted by the untrained eye when visiting the premises (see Fig. 15.5). Notwithstanding the Minister of

---

[6] The percentage of Tokyo's public green space, that is, parks and gardens is only 3.4 per cent compared to 38.4 per cent of public green space in London (Mayor of London, 2012).

Fig. 15.5   New National Stadium site, 22 May 2015
Source: Author

Education, Culture, Sports, Science and Technology (MEXT), Hakubun Shimomura and former Tokyo Governor, Naoki Inose, anticipated in October 2013 that the new national stadium could cost between ¥185 billion and ¥300 billion (Kameda, 2013), the Candidature File (TMG, 2012c) states the cost of the stadium at approximately ¥130 billion, emphasising that all venues were 'fully aligned' with the socio-spatial sustainability of Tokyo under the Tokyo Vision 2020.[7] To draw a parallel, the cost of the 2012 Olympic Stadium in Stratford ballooned from £280 million (stated in the 2012 bid book) to £701 million, inclusive of the venue's conversion to make it suitable for football and athletics (Gibson, 2015). It is worth noting that in addition to bear the

---

[7] All budgeting calculations for the 2020 Olympic venues were based on US dollar 2012 values and exchange rates.

construction and 94.5 per cent of the conversion costs, taxpayers will also pay for the majority of the running costs (Roan, 2015).

The design, size and, above all, location of Hadid's stadium drew a myriad of critical viewpoints from renowned Japanese architects, including that of Pritzker Prize Laurates Fumihiko Maki and Toyo Ito, as well as Isozaki Arata (Wainwright, 2014; Osaki, 2014). Several architects and architect associations, the Japan Federation of Architects and the Japan Institute of Architects submitted petitions to governmental stakeholders to either refurbish the 1964 Olympic stadium, or scale down Hadid's design, or reconsider the plan altogether (Kameda, 2013; Wainwright, 2014). In tandem, various efforts to propose alternative visions of the stadium emerged from architectural firms such as Toyo Ito's and Timberize (the latter featuring all temporary venues built with sustainably sourced timber).

As the result of the growing criticism towards the new national stadium, Hadid Architects made design and size revisions in May 2014, substantially reducing the cost of the stadium from ¥300 billion ($3 billion) to ¥169 billion ($1.7 billion). An architect, activist and co-signatory of one of the petitions to refurbish the existing Olympic facilities (January and May 2014)[8] for the Tokyo 2020 Olympics commented on these revisions in the following manner:

> They reduced the size of the building by 20% and strangely, the budget was reduced by 50%. It doesn't make sense. I wouldn't be surprised if in reality it exceeds the ¥300 bn. yen. So, they'll just have to pour in taxpayers' money to build it.

Stating that the design of the new national stadium was better suited for the desert, the above interviewee referred to Hadid's design as an 'eyesore and tax burden'.

---

[8] Since November 2013, various citizens' groups self-appointed as 'The Custodians of the National Stadium, Tokyo' organised forums and submitted written petitions enquiring the JSC, the Governor of Tokyo and President of the Japanese Olympic Committee on the environmental impact and sustainability of the design of the new national stadium. The Custodians, renowned Japanese architects and academics have also written on these issues several times to the IOC President throughout 2014. See 2020-tokyo.sakura.ne.jp/

You are going to have a 70m-wall that's going to continue for hundreds of meters. All around. It will diminish the width of the pedestrian path but, most of all, it'll have an overwhelming, overbearing psychological impact. Moreover, the area is already built up and so its infrastructure, such as the capacity of the roads, is not going to respond to the new stadium. As a result, it would create lots of friction between drivers and pedestrians.

While the interviewee – along with other signatories of the above-referenced petition – had repeatedly requested information on the planning of the new national stadium to respective authorities 'throughout', they seldom received information. Furthermore, this interviewee personally contacted Minister Shimomura and the President of the Japanese Olympic Committee on this matter. The response he received, however, was that the decision had been made and it was 'too late' to overturn it.

Nonetheless, in early June 2014, the Tokyo Governor Yoichi Masuzoe announced the revision of the plans for the 2020 Olympic venues (see above) in view of rising costs for construction materials and labour derived from the consumption tax hike (from 5 to 8 per cent) of April 2014 and yen depreciation[9] (The Associated Press, 2014; Lies, 2014). Furthermore, disagreements between the National Government and the TMG over the payment of approximately ¥50 billion ($408 million) towards the total construction cost of the new stadium had a knock-on effect on widespread public scrutiny. Statements made by Japanese officials at the end of June 2015 noted an escalated cost of ¥250 billion ($2 billion) for the new national stadium – the most expensive ever built (Kyodo, 2015).

By mid-July, more than 70 per cent of voters opposed the construction of the new national stadium (Asahi Shimbun, 2015). In the midst of another national political controversy over security bills designed to

---

[9] The value of the Japanese yen has depreciated approximately 28 per cent since December 2012 (Afp-Jiji, Reuters, Bloomberg, 2015). This is the result of a monetary stimulus to help sustain export growth and potentially reach a 2 per cent annual inflation target under the so-called 'Abenomics'.

expand the role of Japan's armed forces overseas, Prime Minister Shinzo Abe decided to scrap the construction of the new national stadium. MEXT Minister Shimomura and his Deputy Minister Shinichi Yamanaka resigned as a result of the stadium controversy.

The failed construction of the new stadium cost the taxpayers ¥6 billion (approximately $48 million) in payments to design and construction companies (Aoki, 2015; Reuters, 2015). To put things in perspective, that represented nearly half of Tokyo's budget for the dissemination of arts and culture in the year 2013 (TMG, 2014b). Another ¥46.52 million worth of promotional items bearing the Tokyo 2020 Olympic logo were wasted as the logo was withdrawn amidst accusations of plagiarism (Jiji Press, 2015b). In addition, it has been publicly acknowledged that the JSC concealed initial estimates of ¥346.2 billion for the construction of the national stadium since July 2013 (Kyodo and Jiji, 2015); that is, before the selection of Tokyo as the host of the 2020 Olympics and the tax hike of April 2014. The new design guidelines included a total cost of ¥155 billion, 68,000 seat capacity and harmony with the surrounding milieu (Jiji Press, 2015a). Yokohama stadium is set to replace the new national stadium as the venue for the 2019 Rugby World Cup.

In terms of the redevelopment[10] of the Jingu Gaien district, the TMG, in partnership with the Meiji Shrine Corporation and JSC, aims at rebuilding the Jingu Stadium and the Prince Chichibu Memorial Rugby Ground – adjacent to the new national stadium – by the end of 2026 (Kameda, 2015; TMG, 2015). The proposed redevelopment covers a total of 17 hectares (see Fig. 15.6) and it is intended to attract consumers post-2020 Olympics by building an office and commercial complex in the area, as well as a new JSC headquarters.

---

[10] Redevelopment or regeneration in the context of Japanese cities (Tokyo being a prime example) refers to an urban restructuring fuelled/facilitated by the national and local governments in partnership with corporate developers in the form of mix-use clustered skyscrapers in central and inner-areas. These developments unfold with relaxed building regulations (that is, floor space and height of buildings) and tax incentive regimes (Waley, 2007). Since the early 2000s this urban policy approach has aligned with that of the global 'entrepreneurial city' (Harvey, 1989).

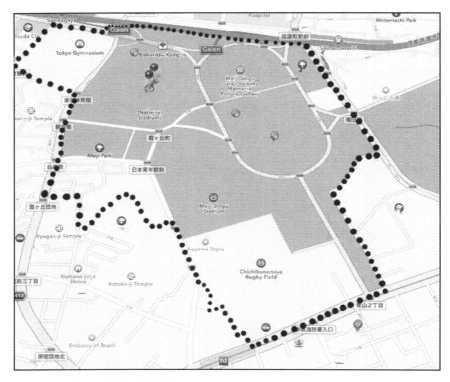

Fig. 15.6 Jingu Gaien District

Source: Elaborated with satellite and on-site maps and data from the Tokyo Metropolitan Government, 2015

Note: Dotted demarcation indicates the area targeted for redevelopment

The environmental impact of the redevelopment of the Jingu Gaien district seems particularly troublesome. The Science Council of Japan (SCJ, henceforth) published a report of seven recommendations and an inventory of the species of the Jingu forest in April 2015. Although the main recommendations highlighted the inadequacy of Hadid's design vis-à-vis the surrounding ecosystem and infrastructure, one of the most alarming issues pointed out by the report was the loss of trees in the area. Out of the 1,764 trees that existed in the premises of the 1964 Olympic Stadium, only 12.4 per cent (219) were to be replanted. Accordingly, 1,545 would be (or had already been) cut down.

Tokyo 2020 Olympic Infrastructure: The Socio-Spatial Paradox

In order to accommodate the new national stadium and advance the redevelopment of the area, the Toei Kasumigaoka Danchi, a 10-building public housing complex (see Fig. 15.7) standing across the premises of the new National Olympic Stadium, will be demolished. The Kasumioka Danchi was ironically built for evictees of the 1964 Olympics. A total of 300 households and small business owners – a third of whom are over 70 years old – faced eviction and the dislocation of their communities twice in their lifetime (Sato, 2013; Whiting, 2014). As the result of 'early relocation requests' the number of households in the Kasumigaoka Danchi was reduced to 140 (Kasumigaoka Residents Association, 2015).

Fig. 15.7   Toei Kasumigaoka Housing Complex
Source: Author

By early December 2015, only 10 households had yet to decide upon a housing site, as the options given by the TMG were deemed unsuitable in terms of apartment location and size/layout. These households were mainly comprised of senior citizens (aged from early 70s to mid-90s), living alone and with varying degrees of physical disabilities and diminished mobility (for instance, bed-stricken or amputated). As such, they needed hospitals (for surgeries and physical rehabilitation) and daycare services in close proximity, as well as space to accommodate walkers or wheelchairs, furniture, and other belongings accumulated in the course of decades.

The Kasumigaoka residents approached Governor Masuzoe through several letters sent in 2014 and 2015 (and the IOC President in September 2009) to no avail, as the TMG 'urged' residents to move out by January 2016 (Kasumigaoka Residents Association, 2015), that is, in the middle of the winter season. As amply commented by Kasumigaoka residents during focus group interviews, TMG representatives would exert 'much pressure and harassment' through letters, constant phone calls and visits, and ultimately, threats to cut lifeline services such as water and electricity to expedite their relocation. As of late March 2016, all buildings of Kasumigaoka Danchi but two, in which the remaining two households (three female senior citizens) still inhabit, have been closed off by the TMG (see Figs. 15.8–15.9).

Interviewees shared their memories of moving into the complex and unalloyed sentiments towards the breakdown of their community and way of life at the Kasumigaoka Danchi, their despair in view of their relocation, and contempt towards the TMG, as they felt they were 'handled as unwanted leftovers'. Furthermore, their vitality had been curtailed by stress and illness stemming from the pressure to relocate. An interviewee with severe physical disabilities even expressed 'losing the will to live' under the above-referenced circumstances. By and large, their accounts reflect narratives of socio-spatial inequality, and the multilayered dimensions of housing and urban socio-economic displacement in a mega-city like Tokyo, and the ways in which space is perceived and fought by communities standing in the way of event-led regeneration. It is worth pointing out that the only monetary compensation the Kasumigaoka residents received for relocation oscillated between ¥160,000 and ¥180,0000 for moving costs, per

Figs. 15.8–15.9 (L–R) Enclosure of Toei Kasumigaoka Buildings
Source: Author

household. No other form of compensation was devised by the TMG. Antithetically, the Tokyo 2020 Candidature File (TMG, 2012b: 52) states:

> Venues will be built according to strict building standards and guidelines. Also, because new venues will be built on vacant land within urban areas, they will have no adverse effect on local communities, natural or cultural resources.

While the mainstream Japanese media has seldom reported on the eviction of the Kasumigaoka residents as the result of the construction of the new National Stadium, Governor Masuzoe was inquired on the feasibility to spare 3–4 buildings for residents who wanted to remain on-site, at a press conference in early September 2015. Adamantly, Governor Masuzoe answered that nothing could be done as this was 'ageing' infrastructure and part of a larger regeneration project envisaged long before his term in office (Masuzoe, 2015a). Furthermore, Governor Masuzoe has yet to publicly acknowledge any negative impacts on Tokyoites as the result of this event-led regeneration. His policy speeches have veered towards highlighting the legacy of a world-class new stadium and its universal design in central Tokyo and the strengthening of the area's disaster resilience. Implicitly, the discordant, ageing Toei Kasumigaoka Danchi is giving way to a full-gentrification of the affluent district of Jingu Gaien, an area already fitted with upscale boutiques, galleries and restaurants.

The eviction of the Kasumigaoka residents echoes the decanting and displacement of longstanding communities in the Clays Lane Housing Cooperative and Carpenters council estate in the lead-up to the London 2012 Olympics (Watt, 2013; Bernstock, 2014; Giulianotti et al., 2015; see also Chapters 4 and 8). Social housing standing in the way of event-led regeneration is commonly described as derelict and dilapidated sites in urgent need of change (Bernstock, 2014: 31). However, these approaches often entail meagre compensation packages and lack of institutional support with regard to age-related medical disabilities, the disruption of community ties and associated psychological fragility (Bernstock, 2014).

Other groups affected by the construction of the new National Stadium are the homeless/rough sleepers (predominantly middle-aged males as observed during the author's field trips). These groups, comprised of dozens of *nojukusha* (semi-fixed) and 'nomads', as expressed by interviewees, have camped for at least the past 10 years on premises adjacent to the now demolished 1964 National Olympic Stadium; mainly along the Gaien Nishi 418 avenue (see Figs. 15.10–15.11) and within the Meiji Park (see Fig. 15.12). By and large, Tokyo is practicing the well-documented 'Olympic urban cleansing' (Davis, 2011; Kennelly and Watt, 2011; Kennelly, 2013) for which the homeless, the derelict and the 'uncool' get diligently hidden or swept away, as they are considered detrimental to the city's imagery.[11]

Interviewees emphatically remarked that authorities had been clearing homeless or relocating them within the park grounds as soon as the new stadium plans were unveiled. As of late December 2015, approximately four middle-aged males and one middle-aged female still had tents set up within the Meiji Park. However, on 27 January, the TMG transferred the management rights of the park to JSC. On the same date, JSC representatives and security guards forcefully removed homeless people and protesters from the park, as well as shutting down the public restroom facilities, which are vital for these *nojukusha*. This led to confrontation between *nojukusha* and security guards/police officers. Interviewees pointed out that JSC had previously agreed not to remove the *nojukusha* until construction of the new National Stadium started. The latest clash at the time of writing occurred on 16 April when policy officers and security guards had once again removed *nojukusha* from the grounds of the Meiji Park while confiscating their belongings. As observed by the author (as of early April 2016), the adjacent areas of the Stadium are fenced off and security guards obstruct access to the park throughout the day (see Figs. 15.12–15.13).

Interestingly, some of the interviewed *nojukusha* have formed the 'Anti-Olympics Group' (*Hangorinnokai*). These homeless activists (see Hasegawa, 2006) organise demonstrations in front of the JSC and TMG headquarters, distribute flyers in central areas Tokyo, provide updates on the local impacts of the planning of the Tokyo 2020

---

[11] Similarly, in the lead-up to the Tokyo 1964 Olympics, campaigns were enforced to improve to citizens' public etiquette (e.g. to cease honking or public urination), as well as clearing the streets of 'unpleasant-looking' mobsters, beggars, streetwalkers, vagrants and stray dogs (Whiting, 2014). On the occasion of the Vancouver 2010 Winter Olympics, the provincial government enacted a law empowering the policy to remove homeless/rough sleepers from highly visible tourist areas and forcibly place them into shelters (Hyslop, 2010).

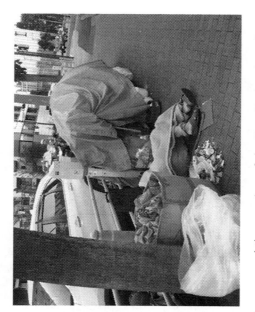

Figs. 15.10–15.11 (L–R) Rough sleepers and their belongings around the premises of the New National Stadium

Source: Author

Figs. 15.12–15.13 (L–R) Enclosure of the Meiji Park

Source: Author

Olympics on blogs and various social media platforms (for example, Twitter and Facebook) and post short videos on YouTube of events such as those on 27 January and 16 April. While the *Hangorinnokai* members assert that they are not against the concept of the Olympic Movement, they perceive the Olympics to bring the 'worst' of corporate money and government policies and measures, disrupting the daily life structure and dynamics of local populations, especially that of the urban poor; very similar comments were made by potential displacees in 2012 East London (Watt, 2013).

The statements posted by the *Hangorinnokai* on social media emphasised that the evictions of residents and homeless/rough sleepers from the surrounding areas of the National Stadium contravene the welfare measures of the 'Basic Policy to Support the Self-sufficiency of the Homeless' (2002), the International Covenant of Economic, Social and Cultural Rights (Article 11 and related General Comments) and the Olympic Movement's Agenda 21 (on human habitat and settlements). While the above-referenced recognise adequate housing as a fundamental human right (regardless of the local culture), protect populations from forced evictions, even in the context of mega-events, and are legally binding for both local and national governments (that is, the TMG and national agencies/bodies such as JSC), the Olympics foster a 'state of exception' (Boykoff, 2013; Gray and Porter, 2015) and a paradigm that curtails the economic rights, civil liberties and socio-political spaces of local populations in host cities. Likewise, this state of exception justifies draconian measures to fulfil related event-led regeneration (for instance, expedient evictions and property expropriation) in the name of the public good (physical legacies, investment, etc.) by circumventing or suspending local legal frameworks (Gray and Porter, 2015).

Overall, the lack of transparency and accountability to taxpayers with regard to Tokyo's event-led regeneration strips current socio-spatial strategies such as the long-term urban vision for Tokyo from its socio-political legitimacy and effective enactment. Not the least, because the TMG policy targets focused on the welfare of the elderly and the disabled (see above) seem to be disregarded in the case of forced relocation and eviction experienced by the very same elderly and disabled groups this

'vision' is purport to prioritise. In this vein, the 2020 Olympic legacy is rooted in social injustice and socio-spatial inequality; both, expressions of *de facto* neoliberal urban policies.

Conclusion

The making of urban branding through the hosting of sporting mega-events is increasingly becoming the ultimate conduit to outperform rival cities in international rankings. The primary sources of this study suggest that one of the most striking legacies of London 2012 was the ability to brand London and the UK as competitive hubs and models for sporting mega-events and economic revitalisation. Therefore, in a global context where perception is reality, London as an Olympic host city has carefully crafted and delivered a compelling official narrative of efficiency, successful urban regeneration, national unity and social empowerment. As such, mega-event policy transfer/know-how as a viable business model for governmental agencies and private enterprises – in the form of consulting services and trade – represents the current zeitgeist of global urban governance.

The above has resonated with other global cities like Tokyo, which are perceived to struggle to stay relevant and/or materialise an all-winning policy formula to reactivate their local economy. In this sense, the discourse of 'feel-good factor and diversion' in times of social, economic and political crises (for instance, the London terrorist bombings of July 2005, the London riots of August 2011, and the 3/11 triple disaster in Japan) is prevalent in both Olympic cities. Thus, the underlying message is to look forward to a progressive future or a nostalgic past (the nation) while escaping the troubled present (Smith, 2012). The overwhelming assertion by interviewed stakeholders both in London and Tokyo that the large sums of public money devoted to sporting mega-events are considered not only a worthy investment, but also a measure of last resort in order to breed 'success' is of particular concern.

As previously pointed out, there is an explicit intent from the TMG to follow the 'London model' in order to not only deliver a successful Olympics, but also to establish a new long-term brand for Tokyo and

Japan. However, it can be argued that the policy knowledge provided by the London 2012 Olympics seems to reflect a model of socio-economic inequality and socio-spatial displacement. Moreover, the Olympic-related environmental sustainability in both host cities seems to be reigned by ad hoc and replacement practices, in which urban greenery and/or natural habitats are lost and somehow recreated post-regeneration, being the QEOP and the Jingu Gaien district indicative of these practices. On the institutional front, collaboration and positive change observed by inter-viewees in London as the result of the London 2012 Olympics could face the most challenging scenarios for Tokyo 2020. Disagreements over the financial co-responsibility of the Olympic venues and competition between national and local branding, for instance, will potentially hinder the overall sense of partnership and collaboration amongst stakeholders. Furthermore, the Olympic stadium and logo design fiascos have tarnished Tokyo and Japan's branding efforts, thus eroding the opportunities to recreate the London 2012 'success story' and turning the hosting of the Olympics into a global business model.

The Tokyo 2020 Olympics are portrayed by the Japanese national government and the TMG as the springboard to overhaul Japan's brand in the twenty-first century. This branding entails positioning Japan as the world's bastion of a brighter and greener future. Tokyo, at the helm of this transformation, has kick-started a literal and metaphorical cleans-ing in which hydrogen is set to ultimately substitute nuclear energy, effacing Fukushima's disaster-stricken imagery throughout. Nonetheless, the path towards discovering and adhering to a better tomorrow – Tokyo's Olympic slogan – will be most visibly determined by the fate of the new Olympic infrastructure, especially that of the National Stadium and its related legacy of socio-spatial displacement.

Even though the Olympics may provide an unparalleled opportunity to revamp ageing infrastructure and transport systems in Tokyo, this event-led regeneration in its current form represents a twentieth-century monumentalism, unfit for the socio-economic and socio-spatial needs of twenty-first-century local populations. Lastly, while staging mega-events such as the Olympics should ignite renewed conversations about the present and future of Japanese society, the current tenor of government stakeholders suggests that the galvanisation of a positive socio-economic change will likely be traded for a painstakingly crafted, yet tangential social occurrence.

Acknowledgements I would like to express my sincere appreciation to all the interviewees in London and Tokyo who graciously agreed to participate in this study. In particular, I am grateful to the Kasumigaoka evictees and *nojukusha* who generously opened their homes and spaces and, candidly, shared their journey and views on the issues here covered.

Bibliography

Afp-Jiji, Reuters and Bloomberg. (2015) 'Japan's economy emerges from recession, but growth weaker than forecast', *The Japan Times*, 16 February 2015.

Anholt-GfK Roper. (2013a) 'Nation Brand Index 2013', http://www.gfk.com/news-and-events/press-room/press-releases/pages/nation-brand-index-2013-latest-findings.aspx

Anholt-GfK Roper. (2013b) 'City Index 2013', http://www.gfk.com/news-and-events/press-room/press-releases/Pages/London-and-Sydney-Knock-Paris-off-the-Best-City-Pedestal.aspx

Aoki, M. (2015) 'Abe says National Stadium responsibility falls on him, but promises "all-out effort" to complete project', *The Japan Times*, 7 August 2015.

Asahi Shimbun. (2015) 'Japan looking at other designs to slash cost of Olympic Stadium', http://ajw.asahi.com/article/behind_news/social_affairs/AJ201507160052, accessed 20 July 2015.

Bank of Japan. (2016) 'Economic impact of the Tokyo 2020 Olympic Games', https://www.boj.or.jp/en/research/brp/ron_2016/data/ron160121b.pdf, accessed 23 January 2016.

Bernstock P (2014) *Olympic Housing: A Critical Review of the 2012 Legacy*. Farnham: Ashgate.

Boykoff, J. (2013) *Celebration Capitalism and the Olympic Games*. London: Routledge.

Davis, L. K. (2011) 'International events and mass evictions: a longer view', *International Journal of Urban and Regional Research* 35(3): 582–599.

DCMS. (2012) *Beyond 2012: The London 2012 Legacy Story*. London: DCMS.

DCMS. (2013) *Report 5, Post-Games Evaluation: Meta Evaluation of the Impacts and Legacy of the London 2012 Olympic Games and Paralympic Games*. London: DCMS.

Dolowitz, D. and Marsh, D. (2000) 'Learning from abroad: the role of policy transfer in contemporary policy-making', *Governance: An International Journal of Policy and Administration* 13(1): 5–24.

Flyvbjerg, B. (2014) 'What you should know about megaprojects and why: an overview', *Project Management Journal* 45(2): 6–19.

Flyvbjerg, B. and Stewart, A. (2012) 'Olympic proportions: cost and cost overrun at the Olympics 1960–2012', *Saïd Business School Working Papers*, Saïd Business School: 1–23.

Gibson, O. (2015) 'Back in business: the £701m stadium', *The Observer*, 19 July 2015.

Giulianotti, R., Armstrong, G., Hales, G. and Hobbs, D. (2015) 'Global sport mega- events and the politics of mobility: the case of the London 2012 Olympics', *British Journal of Sociology* 66(1): 118–140.

Gray, N. and Porter, L. (2015) 'By any means necessary: urban regeneration and the "State of Exception" in Glasgow's Commonwealth Games 2014', *Antipode* 47(2): 380–400.

Grix, J. and Houlihan, B. (2014) 'Sports mega-events as part of a nation's soft power strategy: the Cases of Germany (2006) and the UK (2012)', *The British Journal of Politics and International Relations* 16(4): 572–596.

Harvey, D. (1989) 'From managerialism to entrepreneurialism: the transformation in urban governance in late capitalism', *Geografiska Annaler* 71(1): 3–17.

Hasegawa, M. (2006) *'We Are Not Garbage!' The Homeless Movement in Tokyo, 1994–2002.* New York & London: Routledge.

Hewison, R. (2014) *Cultural Capital. The Rise and Fall of Creative Britain.* London and New York: Verso.

HM Government and Mayor of London. (2014) *Inspired by 2012: The Legacy from the London 2012 Olympic and Paralympic Games* (Summer 2014). London: Cabinet Office.

Hyslop, L. (2010) 'Winter Olympics on slippery slope after Vancouver crackdown on homeless', *The Guardian*, 3 February 2010.

Institute for Urban Strategies. (2013) 'Global power City index', The Mori Memorial Foundation, http://www.mori-m-foundation.or.jp/gpci/pdf/GPCI2013_eng.pdf, accessed 4 November 2013.

Institute for Urban Strategies. (2014) 'Global power city index', The Mori Memorial Foundation, http://www.mori-m-oundation.or.jp/gpci/pdf/GPCI14_E_Web.pdf, accessed 17 November 2014.

IOC. (2014a) 'Olympic Agenda 2020: 20+20 Recommendations', http://www.olympic.org/Documents/Olympic_Agenda_2020/Olympic_Agenda_2020-20-20_Recommendations-ENG.pdf, accessed 20 November 2014.

IOC. (2014b) 'Olympic Agenda 2020: 127th IOC Session', http://www.olympic.org/documents/olympic_agenda_2020/olympic_agenda_2020_session_presentation.pdf, accessed 11 December 2014.

IOC. (2015) 'IOC Executive Board confirms Tokyo 2020 venue locations for eight more sports', http://www.olympic.org/news/ioc-executive-board-confirms-tokyo-2020-venue-locations-for-eight-more-sports/246260, accessed 6 June 2015.

Jiji Press. (2015a) 'Japan begins fresh search for new National Stadium design', *The Japan Times*, http://www.japantimes.co.jp/news/2015/09/02/national/japan-begins-fresh-search-for-new-national-stadium-design/#.VjureqJD-T8, accessed 10 September 2015.

Jiji Press. (2015b) 'Sponsor entities smarting, left sporting the failed Tokyo Olympics logo', *The Japan Times*, http://www.japantimes.co.jp/news/2015/09/02/business/sponsor-entities-smarting-left-sporting-failed-tokyo-olympics-logo/#.VkGeJ0WnBz8, accessed 12 September 2015.

Johansson, M. and Kociatkiewicz, J. (2011) 'City Festivals: creativity and control in staged urban experiences', *European Urban and Regional Studies* 18(4): 392–405.

JSC [Japan Sports Council]. (2012) 'New National Stadium Japan', http://www.jpnsport.go.jp/newstadium/Portals/0/NNSJ/en/NNSJ.html, accessed 16 December 2013.

Kameda, M. (2013) 'National Stadium plan hit as too grandiose', *The Japan Times*, 25 November 2013.

Kameda, M. (2015) '"Sacred" but aging Tokyo sports district faces major redevelopment', *The Japan Times*, 20 April 2015.

Kasumigaoka Residents Association. (2015) 'A letter to IOC', http://kasumigaoka2020.blogspot.jp/2015/09/letter-to-ioc.html#more, accessed 27 October 2015.

Kennelly, J. (2013) '"You're making our city look bad": Olympic security, neoliberal urbanization, and homeless youth', *Ethnography* 16(1): 1–22.

Kennelly, J. and Watt, P. (2011) 'Sanitizing public space in Olympic host cities: the spatial experiences of marginalized youth in 2010 Vancouver and 2012 London', *Sociology* 45(5): 765–781.

Kyodo. (2015) '¥252 billion price tag for National Stadium confirmed', *The Japan Times*, http://www.japantimes.co.jp/news/2015/06/29/national/price-tag-for-building-olympic-stadium-soars-to-%C2%A5252-billion/#.VjcmT0WnBz8, accessed 30 June 2015.

Kyodo & Jiji Press. (2015) 'Olympics stadium cost was projected at ¥346 billion in 2013', *The Japan Times*, http://www.japantimes.co.jp/news/2015/08/19/national/olympics-stadium-cost-projected-%C2%A5346-billion-2013/#.VkFPnkWnBz8, accessed 21 August 2015.

Lies, E. (2014) 'Olympics-Rising costs force review of Tokyo 2020 venue plans', *Reuters*, http://www.reuters.com/article/us-olympics-japan-idUSKBN0EM0QB20140611, accessed 12 June 2014.

Masuzoe, Y. (2014a) 'Policy Speech by the Governor of Tokyo', First Regular Session of the Tokyo Metropolitan Assembly, 26 February, 2014, http://www.metro.tokyo.jp/ENGLISH/GOVERNOR/SPEECH/2014/0318/index.htm

Masuzoe, Y. (2014b) 'Policy Speech by the Governor of Tokyo', Second Regular Session of the Tokyo Metropolitan Assembly, 10 June 2014, http://www.metro.tokyo.jp/ENGLISH/GOVERNOR/SPEECH/2014/0725/index.htm

Masuzoe, Y. (2014c) *Visions for Tokyo 2020 and Beyond.* London: Chatham House.

Masuzoe, Y. (2015a) 'Chiji Bōtō Hatsugen', http://www.metro.tokyo.jp/GOVERNOR/KAIKEN/TEXT/2015/150904.htm, accessed 13 September 2015.

Masuzoe, Y. (2015b) 'Policy Speech by the Governor of Tokyo', Fourth Regular Session of the Tokyo Metropolitan Assembly, http://www.metro.tokyo.jp/GOVERNOR/KAIKEN/TEXT/2015/150904.htm, accessed 15 October 2015.

Mayor of London. (2012) *World Cities Culture Report.* London: Greater London Authority.

McCann, E. (2011) 'Veritable inventions: cities, policies and assemblage', *Area* 43(2): 143–147.

Minton, A. (2012) *Ground Control. Fear and Happiness in the Twenty-First-Century City.* London: Penguin.

Mooney, G., McCall, V. and Paton, K. (2015) 'Exploring the use of large sporting events in the post-crash, post-welfare city: a "legacy" of increasing insecurity?', *Local Economy* 30(8): 910–924.

Odeven, E. (2013) 'A look back at when Tokyo was awarded 1964 Olympics', *The Japan Times*, 24 August 2013.

Ong A. and Collier, S. (2005) *Global Assemblages*. Malden, MA: Blackwell Publishing.

Organisation for Economic Cooperation and Development. (2015) *OECD Economic Surveys Japan*, OECD Publishing April 2015, http://www.oecd.org/eco/surveys/Japan-2015-overview.pdf

Osaki, T. (2014) 'Renowned architect condemns Olympic stadium design', *The Japan Times*, http://www.japantimes.co.jp/news/2014/11/06/national/renowned-architect-condemns-olympic-stadium-design/#.VJUtsCjDvA, accessed 8 November 2014.

Oxford Economics. (2012) *The Economic Impact of the London 2012 Olympic & Paralympic Games*. London: Oxford Economics.

Reuters. (2015) 'Japan backs guidelines for new National Stadium', *The Japan Times*, http://www.japantimes.co.jp/news/2015/08/15/national/japan-backs-guidelines-new-national-stadium/, accessed 16 August 2015.

Roan, D. (2015) 'West Ham: taxpayers to meet Olympic Stadium running costs', BBC Sport, http://www.bbc.com/sport/0/football/33780720, accessed 2 November 2015.

Sato, S. (2013) 'Two-time evictee bears Olympic-size grudge', *The Japan Times*, 15 September 2013.

Shepherd, P. (2011) *Learning Legacy: Lessons Learned from the London 2012 Games Construction Project*. London: ODA, http://learninglegacy.independent.gov.uk/documents/pdfs/design-and-engineering-innovation/307-bio-action-plan-dei.pdf

Smith, A. (2012) *Events and Urban Regeneration*. Abingdon: Routledge.

Tagsold, C. (2010) 'Modernity, space and national representation at the Tokyo Olympics 1964', *Urban History* 37(2): 289–300.

The Associated Press. (2014) 'Japan Olympics organizers review Tokyo 2020 plans', *The Asahi Shimbun*, http://ajw.asahi.com/article/behind_news/sports/AJ201406100079, accessed 12 June 2014.

TMG [Tokyo Metropolitan Government]. (2012a) *Principal Policies of the Tokyo Metropolitan Government*, http://www.metro.tokyo.jp/ENGLISH/PROFILE/IMG/2012_en_39-55.pdf, accessed 22 October 2013.

TMG. (2012b) 'Tokyo 2020: discover tomorrow', Candidature File, Vol. 1, http://www.tokyo2020.jp/en/plan/candida-ture/dl/tokyo2020_candidate_entire_1_enfr.pdf, accessed 12 December 2013.

TMG. (2012c) 'Tokyo 2020: discover tomorrow', Candidature File, Vol. 2, http://www.tokyo2020.jp/en/plan/candidature/dl/tokyo2020_candidate_entire_2_enfr.pdf, accessed 12 December 2013.

TMG. (2014a) 'Tōkyōto Chōki Bijon: Sekaiichi no Toshi Tōkyō', http://www.seisakukikaku.metro.tokyo.jp/tokyo_vision/vision_index/, accessed 10 January 2015.

TMG. (2014b) 'Yumetokibō o moteru toshi no (Hōdō happyō shiryōjitsugen)', http://www.metro.tokyo.jp/INET/KEIKAKU/2014/02/70o2i114.htm, accessed 2 August, 2015.

TMG. (2015) 'Jingū gaien chiku machitsukuri ni kakaru kihon oboegaki wo teiketsu', http://www.metro.tokyo.jp/INET/OSHIRASE/2015/04/DATA/20p41200.pdf, accessed 7 April 2015.

UKTI [United Kingdom Trade and Investment]. (2013) *London 2012: Delivering the Economic Legacy: Progress Report*, https://www.gov.uk/government/uploads/system/uploads/attachment_data/file/295088/London_2012_-_Delivering_the_Olympic_Legacy.pdf, accessed 20 March 2014.

UKTI. (2015) 'Opportunities to engage in Japan's major global sporting events', *News Article*, https://www.gov.uk/government/world-location-news/opportunities-to-engage-in-japans-major-global-sporting-events, accessed 20 January 2015.

Wainwright, O. (2014) 'Zaha Hadid's Tokyo Olympic stadium slammed as a 'monumental mistake' and a 'disgrace to future generations', *The Guardian*, http://www.theguardian.com/artanddesign/architecture-design-blog/2014/nov/06/zaha-hadids-tokyo-olympic-stadium-slammed-as-a-monumental-mistake-and-a-disgrace-to-future-generations, accessed 15 November 2014.

Waley, P. (2007) 'Tokyo-as-World city: reassessing the role of capital and the state in urban restructuring', *Urban Studies* 14(8): 1465–1490.

Watt, P. (2013) '"It's not for us": Regeneration, the 2012 Olympics and the gentrification of East London', *City* 17(1): 99–118.

Whiting, R. (2014) 'Dark Side of the Games', Whiting's World -Olympics Part 2, *The Journal*, https://journal.accj.or.jp/whitings-world-olympics-part-2/, accessed 2 August 2014.

Zimbalist, A. (2010) 'Is it worth it? Hosting the Olympic Games and other mega sporting events is an honor many countries aspire to – but why?' *Finance & Development* 47(1): 8–11.

Grace Gonzalez Basurto is lecturer in the the Department of Global and Interdisciplinary Studies, Hosei University (Japan) and Reseach Fellow at the Center for the Study of the Creative Economy, Doshisha University (Japan). She holds Ph.D. in International Political Economy from the University of Tsukuba. Grace specialises in contemporary issues of urban political economy, particularly those reconfiguring the form and function of the city in the context of the knowledge/creative economy. Her current research focuses on policy trends and frameworks of creative industries, urban branding and mega-events in London and Tokyo. Her publications include 'Muddling Through Internationalization in the University of Tsukuba: A Case Study' (in *The Impact of Internationalization on Japanese Higher Education*, Sense Publishers, 2016), and 'Asian and Global? Japan and Tokyo's Cultural Branding Beyond the 2020 Olympic and Paralympic Games' (in *Asian Cultural Flows: Creative Industries, Cultural Policies and Media Consumers*, Springer, forthcoming 2017).

16

Conclusion: New Directions in Olympic Legacy Research

Phil Cohen and Paul Watt

Moving on from Mega-Events

The contributions to this book have all referred directly or indirectly to the notion of 'Olympic legacy' and in many cases also to the 'Post-Olympic City'. It is clear however that these terms, which are so often taken for granted in the discourses elaborated around the Games, are portmanteau words; they mean lots of different things to different people, and by the same token they are extremely slippery as analytic constructs. Do they refer to short- or long-term impacts? To deep or surface structures of urban change? To 'soft' or 'hard' legacies?

P. Cohen (✉)
University of East London, London, England
e-mail: pcohen763@hotmail.co.uk

P. Watt
Department of Geography, Birkbeck, University of London, London, England
e-mail: p.watt@bbk.ac.uk

© The Author(s) 2017   **445**
P. Cohen, P. Watt (eds.), *London 2012 and the Post-Olympics City*,
DOI 10.1057/978-1-137-48947-0_16

In fact these terms gloss an extremely complicated set of negotiations between public bodies charged with delivering specific objectives, private interests that have a financial stake in the outcomes, the political representatives of the communities that are interpellated as beneficiaries and the disparate groups that form in opposition or support to the Games. Each host city convenes a unique configuration of these elements, which come together around the contested promise and process of regeneration and whose bargaining power can change considerably over time. The great weakness of 'mega-event' analysis is that it is purely conjunctural; it lacks a sense of historical transition, which is largely due to its overwhelmingly functionalist model of causal explanation.

The 'Post Olympic' is about the transition of the legacy narrative from the realm of the social imaginary to a putative and contested social fact. It is also about how the narrative legacy of a Games becomes embedded in an official memoryscape, through the intervention of the Olympic heritage and research industries, to establish its reputational position in a league table of past successes and failures.

So is that transition a matter of *transference* – the transference of assets and functions from one regime of envisagement to another and also a carryover of structures of feeling (hope or pessimism) associated with them? Or is it more a question of *translation* – in which something is both lost and gained through the shift in idiom or setting? Or perhaps it is more a case of *transformation* – a process of transvaluation which fundamentally reconfigures the meaning and weight of some elements of the Olympic compact, whilst conserving its underlying structure? Or finally is it a matter of simple *erasure* – the bulldozing of one set of principles and priorities and their replacement by another?

These different modes of transition have very different implications for how legacy and the post-Olympic are defined and evaluated. For example if legacy is defined in term of a moral economy of worth, that is, as the transmission of a gift, with or without strings, then the question become how far in the transition to the post-Olympic is that bequest honoured or traduced, for example, by being translated from the idiom of a moral economy into the very different priorities of a market economy, as a dividend or payback for a prior investment? In contrast if the legacy is measured in purely economistic terms, then cost/benefit analysis becomes the sole arbiter of value, and the notion of endowment which is central to the moral economy of worth is marginalised. On the other hand, if legacy is given an added symbolic value as an heirloom, something to be held in trust for future generations, then civic bodies representing host communities have a much larger stake and say in the outcome.

Secondly, if public debate about the value or otherwise of the Olympics to host cities is not just to be driven by short-term political and media agendas, then it will have to break with the principles of periodicity that the Games' time frame currently imposes and instead use the Olympics to raise wider issues about the direction of travel in which host cities and host societies are going.

For example, the graph of academic publications shows an exponential rise in the run up to a Games followed by an equally drastic fall away until the cycle starts up again with the advent of new Olympiad. In contrast the time frame applied to the evaluation of legacy is infinitely elastic- the Games are never over, they are continually being compared and re-evaluated; this process is inevitably confined to an interpretive community made up almost exclusively of those professionally involved in the Olympic movement and its academic and consultancy research arms. In neither case is the opportunity taken to create a public forum in which crucial issues of urban policy could be debated and decided by those host communities who find themselves in the front line of the changes being brought about.

Given the highly bureaucratic, opaque and sometimes corrupt nature of international sports administration, the command and control structure of Olympics delivery authorities and the fact that turbo-charged regeneration is driven by global economic forces that governments can at best partially mitigate, it is unlikely that this democratic deficit is going to be fully addressed any time soon (see Raco, 2014). But until it is, until those poorer communities in whose name the Olympics are increasingly pledged have a direct political voice and stake in its governance, the claim that the Olympics can tackle, rather than perpetuate and even strengthen social inequalities, will continue to have a hollow ring. The hollowness of the 'five rings' grandiose impact claims is indeed becoming increasingly transparent to both host cities and potential host cities as our chapters on Rio and Tokyo highlight. As Jules Boykoff (2016: 241) rightly says, 'Fewer and fewer cities are game for the Games. For too long host cities have worked in service of the Olympics. It's time for the Olympics to start working in service of host cities'.

Towards Post-Olympic Studies?

One issue to emerge from the past is how can we establish a conceptual and heuristic framework for the field of Post-Olympic Urban Studies which is not hidebound by the official governmental logics of IOC-determined indicators and mega-events' analysis. We think that several chapters in the book are moving in this direction, not least in the sense that, as we discuss in the Introduction, they are written by authors who have had a long-term engagement with the sub-region of 'East London', that over-signified realm of the urbanists' imagination (Cohen, 2013).

Furthermore, we think that there are considerable epistemological problems in relation to *who* is doing the evaluations and *what interests* they might have. This issue as to who is undertaking post-regeneration evaluation was raised in particularly stark terms by Chris Allen (2008) in his *Housing Market Renewal and Social Class*, an analysis of the Housing Market Renewal (HMR) programme, one of New Labour's flagship regeneration schemes. Through employing a combination of phenomenology and Bourdieusian sociology, Allen reveals the heavily interest-laden rationale of the consultants – some of whom went onto become academics – who were not only the architects of the HMR programme, but then subsequently became key players in its official evaluation. Being too close to state power and its most powerful lobbying agencies – especially under New Labour with its managerialist 'what works' policy mantra (Southern, 2001) – can clearly be intellectually debilitating. In illustrating the often-found tensions between regeneration managers and the communities who are supposed to be the beneficiaries of said-regeneration, Southern (2001: 266) highlights the shallow governmental and intellectual framework for regeneration in the UK: 'The current "fix" is output driven, does not capture many of the more qualitative aspects of regeneration, and is a philosophy more comfortable with the notion of "what matters is what works"'.

This 'can do – what works' philosophy is of course exaggerated when the poacher turns gamekeeper, as Allen (2008) so assiduously argues in the case of HMR. Such role-switching can also be identified in Olympic evaluations where these have been undertaken by the same people who were the architects and implementers of the Games' regeneration and rebranding strategy. In the case of London 2012, this can be seen in some of the vignettes contained in the back of the UEL (2015) report. Other examples include journal special issues purporting to 'explore' the nature of the 2012 regeneration initiatives, based on articles each of which 'has been written by a *professional closely linked with the delivery of the games*' (Tallon, 2012: 294; our emphasis), with seemingly no sense that this might be epistemologically problematic.

We have argued that an alternative way forward for Post-Olympics Studies is to embed itself within a framework of democratic debate, a framework which, as Raco (2014) argues, the 2012 Olympics itself contributed towards eroding. The question then arises as to how we can challenge the knowledge – power relations that currently prevail in both academic and operational research about the Olympics? One suggestion is to implement a methodology of participant action research that widens the interpretive community to include those who are other-wise mere 'informants' (Cohen, 2016). This implies a public sociology which is more than sociologists learning how to perform as public intellectuals, acting as the advocates of communities whose voices are not much otherwise heard; it implies a transfer of interpretive power so that tacit, locally situated informant knowledge is not simply valorised by being encoded or translated into a 'social scientific' idiom but transformed into an instrument of reflexive critique in the hands of citizens themselves. The East Village project reported in Chapters 5 and 6 begins this process.

Another approach is to embed academic research *within* an explicit ideological critique of the manifold gulf between Olympics legacy dreams and realities. Such a critique can clearly be identified in the case of the Rio 2016 Games, as Chapter 14 powerfully illustrates. There a dubious political regime, supported by an even more dodgy local Olygarchy, is using the Games as an opportunity to bulldoze the favelas, and under pretext of making the city safe from narcotic gangs and gun crime, it has set out to systematically destroy the social networks of mutual aid on which the urban poor rely. Under these conditions, a vigorous citizen social science has emerged to document the patterns of exclusion that have been set in motion and analyse their wider effects. The dossier produced by the World Cup and Olympics Popular Committee of Rio de Janeiro (2015), a group of scholar activists and community representatives, is a good example of how the official Olympic discourse can be challenged, and even turned against itself. Here the notion of 'mega-event' is used critically to demonstrate how the Games are destroying important aspects of Rio's popular culture, while the 'impact study' is returned to its origins (before it was adopted as an instrument of corporate social engineering), as a platform for providing evidence to support communities facing existential threat from major new developments. At the same time, the Rio Dossier advances a series of detailed policies for the regeneration of the city, aimed at prioritising the housing, educational, welfare and cultural needs of the poor. This is not about 'convergence' but a genuine redistribution of power and opportunity.

The London 2012 Games did not produce the same scale of political opposition as Rio 2016, although it was not insignificant either as Boykoff (2014, 2016) details. Again, although the Rio Games have probably produced a more visible academic oppositional voice, London-based academics have mounted considerable critical scrutiny of the 2012 Games, a scrutiny which several of the books' authors have contributed towards. In some cases, this has involved academics allying themselves with those bottom-up, East London-based campaigns which have attempted to demystify the official regeneration and legacy parameters around which the 2012 Games were framed notably that they were all about improving the lives of existing East Londoners. This can be seen in the case of anti-gentrification/regeneration protests (Watt, 2013) and the Focus E15 'social housing not social cleansing' campaign (Watt, 2016). Indeed, as Gillespie et al. (2016) argue, the latter campaign can be regarded as an unofficial 2012 legacy in relation to the ongoing struggles over London's seemingly intractable housing crisis,

If Post-Olympic Urban Studies is to develop a properly comparative frame, it surely has to learn from the one discipline in the human sciences that has taken the comparative study of cultures as its main task and developed a methodology fit for that purpose (Graeber, 2002). The extraordinary efflorescence of post-colonial anthropology is partly due to the way it has developed a highly nuanced understanding of the politics of its own research practice (Clifford, 2003); at the same time ethnography has been able to track global circuits of communication and commodification through their points of local intersection in a way that allows the research story to tell itself through the voices of protagonists *and* through the affordances of the things they make (Knowles, 2014). Nothing less is needed if we are to be able to move fluently between the Olympics bid as civic compact, Games Time as Sporting Spectacle, and Legacy as networked material and social infrastructure, considering each instance from both local and global, synchronic and diachronic points of view.

Does this mean that there is never any end to the story? On the contrary, it allows us to arrive at a principle of narrative closure. Whenever it becomes clear that no further iterations are possible, that the terms and conditions of the Compact are fixed, that the Spectacle is not subject to re-visioning and the Legacy, in whatever form, cannot be reconstructed, then we can draw a line under the event and move on. In the case of London 2012, that point has not yet been reached. This is not because there are milestones still ahead in the planned development of the Olympic Park and its environs, but because the sociological imagination of London as a Post-Olympic City is not yet exhausted, even if it has been largely hijacked by corporate 'imagineers'. How to reclaim and renew the imagination of a better world and embed it where it matters most, in the everyday lives of citizens, and at a time when the principles of hope which animate such a project are being undermined on every side, that is the challenge, at once political, conceptual and heuristic that we face.

Bibliography

Allen C. (2008) *Housing Market Renewal and Social Class*. Abingdon: Routledge.

Boykoff, J. (2014) *Activism and the Olympics: Dissent at the Games in Vancouver and London*. New Brunswick: Rutgers University Press.

Boykoff, J. (2016) *Power Games: A Political History of the Olympics*. London: Verso.

Clifford, J. (2003) *On the Edges of Anthropology*. London: Prickly Pears Press.

Cohen, P. (2013) *On the Wrong Side of the Track: East London and the Post Olympics*. London: Lawrence and Wishart.

Cohen, P. (2016) 'Our kind of town', *LivingMaps Review* 1(1), http://www.livingmaps.review/.

Gillespie, T., Hardy, K. and Watt, P. (2016) 'The beginning of the end of the housing crisis: defending and expanding the urban commons in East London', Paper presented at the RGS-IBG Annual International Conference, 2 September 2016.

Graeber, D. (2002) *Towards an Anthropology of Value*. Basingstoke: Palgrave Macmillan.

Knowles, C. (2014) *Flip Flop: A Journey Through Globalisation by Its Back Roads*. London: Pluto Press.

Raco, M. (2014) 'Delivering flagship projects in an era of regulatory capitalism: state-led privatization and the London Olympics 2012', *International Journal of Urban and Regional Research* 38(1): 176–197.

Southern, A. (2001) 'What matters is what works? The management of regeneration', *Local Economy* 16(4): 264–271.

Tallon, A. (2012) 'Editorial: regeneration and the London Olympics and Paralympics', *Journal of Urban Regeneration and Renewal* 5(4): 293–295.

UEL [University of East London]. (2015) *Olympic Games Impact Study – London 2012 Post-Games Report*. London: University of East London.

Watt, P. (2013) '"It's not for us": Regeneration, the 2012 Olympics and the gentrification of East London', *City* 17(1): 99–118.

Watt, P. (2016) 'A nomadic war machine in the metropolis: en/countering London's 21st century housing crisis with Focus E15', *City* 20(2): 297–320.

World Cup and Olympics Popular Committee of Rio de Janeiro. (2015) *Rio 2016 Olympics: The Exclusion Games*. Rio de Janeiro: World Cup and Olympics Popular Committee of Rio de Janeiro.

Phil Cohen is Professor Emeritus at the University of East London, and a Research Fellow at the Young Foundation. He is the founder/research director of the LivingMaps Network and the editor-in-chief of its online journal *LivingMaps Review*. His ethnographic fieldwork over the last 30 years has been based in East London and has dealt with issues of racism and multiculturalism, public safety and danger, the role of the cultural economy in urban regeneration and popular participation in planning. His research with young people has developed new methods of visual ethnography, social mapping and dialogic engagement with informants. Most recently he directed a multi-project initiative examining the Post Olympic Legacy in East 20. He is the author of *On the Wrong Side of the Track? East London and the Post Olympics* (Lawrence and Wishart, 2013). Other books include *Knuckle Sandwich: Growing up in the Working Class City* (with Dave Robins, 1978), *Rethinking the Youth Question* (1997), *New Ethnicities, Old Racisms* (2001) and *London's Turning: the Making of Thames Gateway* (edited with Mike Rustin, 2008). He has also published a memoir *Reading Room Only: Memoir of a Radical Bibliophile* (Five Leaves, 2013) and a book of poetry and prose, *Graphologies* (Mica Press, 2014). A collection of his new research, *Material Dreams: Maps and Territories and the Un/making of Modernity* is forthcoming from Palgrave Macmillan. www.philco henworks.com

Paul Watt is Reader in Urban Studies at Birkbeck, University of London. He has published widely on topics including the London housing crisis, social rental housing, urban regeneration, suburbanisation and the 2012 Olympic Games. He is co-author (with Tim Butler) of *Understanding Social Inequality* (Sage, 2007), co-editor (with Peer Smets) of *Mobilities and Neighbourhood Belonging in Cities and Suburbs* (Palgrave Macmillan, 2014) and co-editor (with Peer Smets) of *Social Housing and Urban Renewal: A Cross-National Perspective* (Emerald, 2017). He sits on the Editorial Board of *City* (Taylor & Francis) and is Board Member of the Research Committee on Sociology of Urban and Regional Development (RC21), International Sociological Association.

Index

© The Author(s) 2017
P. Cohen, P. Watt (eds.), *London 2012 and the Post-Olympics City*,
DOI 10.1057/978-1-137-48947-0